BARCELONA & BEYOND

CAROL MO

MY FAVORITE
EXPERIENCES

DISCOVER
BARCELONA & BEYOND

Standing bold and boisterous on the shores of the Mediterranean, Barcelona is a law unto itself. Always avant-garde, this beguiling city combines dreamlike architecture, colorful festivals, rich gastronomy, and perpetual nights with a creative energy that sends nerve endings into overdrive. Two thousand years of history unravel as the labyrinthine streets wind their way around the city's ancient heart, spilling out onto medieval squares, 19th-century boulevards, and a glamorous waterfront. A cosmopolitan metropolis bound only by its topographical limits, Barcelona is a hundred different cities rolled into one, and every experience of it is unique.

6

The show-stopping capital of Catalonia is the jewel in the region's crown. But while it's easily the star dish, it's on a tasting menu of epic proportions. Abounding with natural wonders, cultural riches, and traces of bygone civilizations, Catalonia packs a great deal of contrasts into a compact corner of Spain. Snow-capped peaks set a fairy-tale backdrop to medieval villages and dormant volcanoes, while crystalline coves stretch out onto golden shores. A distinct language and cultural identity set this self-declared nation apart from the rest of the country, with a proud, industrious population that has long since established Catalonia as an economic powerhouse. It's little wonder that this sunny slice of fertile land has long been a bone of contention.

Explore the four provinces of Catalonia and you'll start to connect the dots between the region and its capital. Notice how the soaring towers of Gaudí's Sagrada Família recall the crags of Montserrat, appreciate the ruins of Roman Barcino as part of the ancient Via Augusta, and unearth the roots of Catalan nationalism in rural towns of medieval splendor. Accompany this fiesta of cultural vitality with a glass of cava and some earthy Catalan cuisine along the way, and you'll get an authentic taste of this diverse region and the stories that have shaped it.

1 La Rambla

2 Mercat de la Boqueria

3 Tarragona

4 Pont de Besalú, La Garrotxa

5 Monument als Castellers, Tarragona

6 Camí de Ronda, Costa Brava

CONTENTS

1 Gazing up at **La Sagrada Família,** Gaudí's unfinished fantastical masterpiece, as its soaring towers glow in the golden afternoon light (page 73).

2 Partaking in *vermut* hour (weekends around midday), when locals gather to sip the traditional aperitif with a tasty tapa or two (page 132).

3 Contemplating the extraordinary geological outcrop of **Montserrat** from the Sant Jeroni viewing point (page 206).

4 **Scuba diving** the crystalline waters of the Costa Brava (page 282).

5 Hiking through the volcanic landscape of **Parc Natural de la Zona Volcànica de la Garrotxa** (page 318).

6 Watching *castellers* scramble to death-defying heights to construct a human tower up to 10 tiers high (page 230).

7 Traversing the rugged cliffs and picture-perfect *calas* of the Costa Brava along the **Camí de Ronda** (page 294).

<<<

8 Feeling your heart attune to the beat of the drums as the latest *festa major* kicks off in a riot of revelry (page 365).

9 Following in the footsteps of Roman gladiators in Tarragona's seaside **Amfiteatre Romà** (page 218).

ʌ
ʌ ʌ

10 Trekking through stunning mountain scenery in the **Aigüestortes i Estany de Sant Maurici National Park** (page 348).

11 Tucking into fresh **seafood paella** after a day at the beach (page 276).

<<<

EXPLORE
BARCELONA & BEYOND

Three days is enough to get a feel for Barcelona, though you may be already planning your next visit before they're up; such is the abundance and allure of the Catalan capital. Escaping the city—be it to the beach, the mountains, or both—offers the perfect antidote to its intense urban vitality, and there are numerous single and multi-day trips within easy reach.

Montserrat and **Sitges** are the nearest and most popular day trips, and are both easily accessed by train. **Girona** and **Tarragona,** too, are easily reached by train, and are of a manageable scale for a one-day exploration. Driving is the most convenient option for exploring more rural areas of Catalonia. Although technically accessible by bus, you will need a car to make the most of your time in **La Garrotxa, Vall de Boí,** and the **Costa Brava.**

Arc de Triomf

BEST OF BARCELONA & BEYOND

For a map and a more detailed version of this Barcelona itinerary, see Itinerary Ideas, page 48.

>DAY 1: THE CIUTAT VELLA

Dive into the old walled city, the Ciutat Vella, on your first day in town.

- Take a leisurely ramble down **La Rambla,** enjoying the sights and sounds of the city's most famous street.

- Feast your senses on the glorious produce of **Mercat de la Boqueria.**

- Unravel 2,000 years of history as you lose yourself in the **Barri Gòtic.**

- Trace the roots of a genius at the **Museu Picasso.**

- Peek inside the magnificent gothic basilica of **Santa Maria del Mar,** and marvel at its soaring, stripped-back interiors.

- Celebrate a day well spent with some Catalan bubbles and a plate of *jamón* at traditional bodega **El Xampanyet.**

>DAY 2: MODERNISME MASTERPIECES

Appreciate two of Gaudí's finest works on your second day.

- Marvel as the morning light dapples kaleidoscopic colors across the tree-like stone pillars of **La Sagrada Familia.**

- Enter into a topsy-turvy underwater world at **Casa Batlló,** one of Gaudí's most spectacular creations.

- Join the buzz at **Vinitus** and order up some fresh and tasty tapas.

- Finish the day on a high with a drink on one of the city's many hotel **rooftop terraces.**

>DAY 3: DAY TRIP TO MONTSERRAT

Head to Montserrat, a meeting point of heaven and earth. This full-day itinerary combines the best of the mountain's physical and metaphysical elements. (Alternately, experience Barcelona like a local by following the itinerary on page 51.)

- Arrive early and catch the **Aeri de Montserrat** cable car to the monastery. Spend the morning exploring the **Monestir de Santa Maria de Montserrat.**

- Enter the Basilica, the monastery's centerpiece, and pay your respects to the **Virgin of Montserrat.**

- Take a seat and let the angelic voices of the famous **Escolania Boys' Choir** lift you up. (No performances on Saturdays.)

- Take the **Funicular de Sant Joan** to the top of the mountain and prepare for another transcendent experience: hiking amid this surreal landscape.

WHERE TO GO FROM BARCELONA

If You Want...	Destination	Why Go?	How to Get There from Barcelona	How Long to Stay
Art	Figueres (page 302)	Dalí's hometown houses the Teatre-Museu Dalí, designed by the artist himself.	train (1 hour)	1 day
Roman Ruins	Tarragona (page 212)	This former Roman settlement boasts an ancient aqueduct, plus an impressive 12th-century cathedral.	train (1 hour)	1 day
	Tossa de Mar (page 270)	Relax on the beach after exploring the remains of a Roman villa.	car (1.5 hours)	1-2 days
Cuisine	Girona (page 240)	Dine at world-renowned El Celler de Can Roca (reservations necessary); explore a preserved Jewish Quarter and emblematic cathedral.	train (40 minutes)	1 day
Beaches	Sitges (page 174)	Revel in sunny beaches, gay nightlife, and holiday vibes.	train (35 minutes)	1-2 days
	Costa Brava (page 263)	Relax on gorgeous beaches or get active by diving or hiking along the coast.	car (1.5-2.5 hours, depending on your destination)	2-3 days
Monasteries	Montserrat (page 197)	Visit a Benedictine abbey, then hike amid jagged pinnacles in the surrounding natural park.	train to cable car or train to rack railway (both around 1.5 hours)	half a day; full day with hiking
Hiking	La Garrotxa (page 309)	Trek through volcanic landscapes and visit historic villages.	car (1 hour 40 minutes)	2-3 days
	Camí de Ronda (page 294)	Portions of this long-distance seaside trail on the Costa Brava are well suited for day hikes.	car (1.5-2.5 hours)	1 day
A Little of Everything	Vall de Boí (page 331)	Hike and ski amid mountain scenery; visit Romanesque churches.	car (3.5 hours)	2-3 days

IF YOU'RE LOOKING FOR . . .

· **Architecture:** Barcelona

· **Art:** Barcelona, Figueres, Vall de Boí

· **Roman ruins:** Tarragona, Barcelona, Tossa de Mar, Girona

· **Beaches:** Sitges, Costa Brava, Barcelona

· **Relaxation:** Vall de Boí, Costa Brava

· **Hiking:** Montserrat, La Garrotxa, Vall de Boí

· **Nightlife:** Sitges, Barcelona

· **Churches and monasteries:** Montserrat, Vall de Boí

· **Small villages:** La Garrotxa, Costa Brava, Vall de Boí

SITGES-TARRAGONA

Base yourself in Sitges for a few days and sample the town's upbeat holiday vibe at a laid-back pace. Tarragona is one hour by train from Sitges and makes an easy addition to the itinerary for a good dose of history and culture.

Sitges and Tarragona are easily accessed by train from Barcelona, making this itinerary possible without a car. Staying two nights (or longer) in Sitges is perfect for a relaxed beach break. On the third day, set off early for Tarragona, catching the last train back to Barcelona at 10:15pm or staying the night.

>DAY 1: SITGES

■ Step off the train and look up at Sitges's **railway station** on arrival—this is the first stop along the *Ruta dels Indians*. Spot marvelous mansions as you stroll toward **Plaça Cap de la Vila.**

■ Drop off your luggage, then spend the morning exploring the narrow streets of the old town. Emerge from the old town to face the sea in front of the **Església de Sant Bartomeu i Santa Tecla,** the town's most emblematic landmark.

■ Descend the stairs outside the church and tuck into fresh seafood lunch at **Fragata.**

■ In the evening, soak up the city's nightlife on **Carrer Primer de Maig.**

BEACHES OF CATALONIA

The Catalan coastline stretches from the French border in the north to the delta of the Ebro river in the south, and is home to some of the most beautiful beaches and coastal scenery in Spain. Barcelona itself boasts 5 kilometers (3 miles) of golden sands along the seafront, but the real treasures lie beyond the city. If you're itching for a beach getaway, consider the following destinations:

THE COSTA BRAVA
The Costa Brava lives up to the Mediterranean ideal, where sweeping pine forests and windswept rocky headlands conceal hidden coves with crystalline waters. If beach time is your priority, there are scores of beautiful bays to choose from dotted right along these jagged shores, and it's perfect for a relaxing summer stay.

Platja Port Pelegri

SITGES
Sitges mixes beach life with a little culture and fun, capturing the holiday vibe of the Costa Brava in a more urban setting. It's a good option if you want to enjoy the best of both worlds, as it is within easy reaching distance of Barcelona.

>DAY 2: SITGES

- Spend the morning contemplating the town's artistic spirit at **Museu del Cau Ferrat,** former studio and home of Modernista painter Santiago Rusiñol, and the adjacent **Museu de Maricel.**

- Walk right along the seafront to the Port d'Aiguadolç and sample some of the **best paella in town** at Can Laury Peix.

- Spend the afternoon soaking up the sun on **Platja de Sant Sebastià.** Then let afternoon drift into evening with a cocktail in hand on an outdoor terrace.

>DAY 3: TARRAGONA

- Set off early for Tarragona (by 9am). Join the locals for a mid-morning coffee and croissant inside the **Mercat Central** and peruse the colorful produce.

- Explore **Roman Tarraco,** starting at the Amfiteatre Romà, where gladiators once dueled.

- After lunch, follow the Carrer Major up to the **Catedral de Tarragona,** and spend an hour exploring inside.

- Take an early evening stroll beside the **Roman walls.** Then, head back downhill and soak up the buzz with a well-deserved glass of cava in **Plaça de la Font.**

GIRONA-COSTA BRAVA-FIGUERES

This four-day whistle-stop tour combines some of Catalonia's finest features: beach and city, cuisine and culture, and plenty of history.

The itinerary requires you to move to a new hotel each night, but it could easily be extended to a week, or even two-week, holiday for a more leisurely pace. Renting a car is required to make the most of it, as access to the Costa Brava by public transport is slow and limited. Reserve hotels and restaurants in advance, particularly during high season.

During winter, skip the Costa Brava (days 2 and 3) and focus solely on culture and cuisine. This alternate version is easily accessible by train, as there is a high-speed (AVE) connection between Figueres, Girona, and Barcelona. Before you depart, make dinner reservations for your first night in Girona at Bionbo, where reservations must be made in advance by phone.

>DAY 1: GIRONA

- After you pick up your rental car, drive northeast on the **AP-7** to reach Girona, exiting at junction 7 or 6B. The drive is 100 kilometers (62 miles) and takes around 1 hour and 15 minutes. There is plentiful free parking in Girona.

- Head straight for the colorful banks of the Onyar river, Girona's most emblematic picture-postcard scene, and cross Gustave Eiffel's **Pont de les Peixateries.**

- Learn about the medieval city's prosperous Jewish community at the **Museu d'Història dels Jueus,** then let history bring the streets to life as you lose yourself in atmospheric **El Call** (the Jewish Quarter).

- After lunch, explore the imposing **Catedral de Girona,** followed by the **Basílica de Sant Feliu,** the city's oldest church.

- Sample the city's famous culinary scene with dinner at **Bionbo** (reservations required), an informal gastrobar that fuses Catalan roots with global flavors.

- Spend the night at **Hotel Nord 1901** or, if it's not too late, make the 50-minute drive to Begur.

>DAY 2: BEGUR

- Leave Girona early to beat the crowds to the beach at **Platja d'Aiguablava** for a heavenly morning swim or an easy hike along the **Camí de Ronda** trail to Fornells and back.

- Drive the dizzying coast road, skirting by the picturesque bays of Tamariu and Llafranc, en route to the old fishing village of **Calella de Palafrugell.**

- Tuck in to fresh local fish at **Sa Jambina,** then walk off the lunchtime feast by following the seafront trail along Calella's rocky shoreline.

- Find a spot on **Platja Port Pelegrí** and spend the afternoon soaking up the sun (and the buzz) on the tiny Calella cove.

- Head back to Begur and follow the **Ruta dels Indians** walking tour through the vibrant village,

CATALAN CUISINE

Gastronomy is at the heart of Catalan culture. Traditional cuisine reflects the diversity of the region's landscapes and is characterized by the variety of seasonal ingredients cultivated across its various climates. *Mar i muntanya* ("sea and mountain") is the combination of seafood and meat, and is common in many Catalan dishes. This "surf and turf" tendency is found in dishes such as *mandonguilles amb sípia* (meatballs and cuttlefish) and *pollastre amb llagosta* (chicken and lobster). To accompany its cuisine, 11 wine regions across Catalonia produce exemplary vintages, the most famous of which has to be the exuberant cava from the Penedès region—Catalonia's answer to Champagne.

fideuas

The region is at the cutting edge of haute cuisine, with 24 Michelin-starred restaurants in Barcelona, and 55 in Catalonia overall. But it's not all about deconstructed, molecular gastronomy. A seemingly innate sensibility for all things edible is celebrated in even the most ordinary bars and restaurants, and the opportunity to make a delectable discovery lies on every street corner.

Although tapas are commonly associated with Spanish cuisine, and you can get tapas all around the region, tapa culture is not a Catalan tradition. To appreciate authentic Catalan specialties, try some of the following dishes.

SALADS AND VEGETARIAN DISHES

- *Calçots:* Baby leeks barbecued and served with romesco sauce (made from tomatoes, garlic, and almonds). Calçots are served at the beginning of spring at traditional parties known as *Calçotadas*. Don a bib and gloves, and get dipping: it's an experience like no other.

- *Escalivada:* Roasted peppers, eggplant, and onion, served as a side dish.

- *Esqueixada:* Salad of peppers, tomatoes, onions, red wine vinegar, and shredded *bacalao* (salted cod).

finishing up with a sundowner at **El Jardí de Can Marc.**

- Spend the night at **Hotel Aiguaclara,** a colonial-style mansion in the heart of the village.

>DAY 3: BEGUR TO CADAQUÉS

- Spend the morning exploring the medieval villages of Baix Empordà, starting with **Pals.**

- Move on to **Peratallada,** and delight in the enchanting cobbled

lanes and ancient architecture of this fairy-tale village. While you're here, surprise your senses with the weird and wonderful ice-cream flavors at **Gelat Artesà de Peratallada.**

- *Espinacs amb panses i pinyons:* Fresh spinach sautéed with olive oil, raisins, and pine nuts.

- *Castanyas i moniatos:* Roasted chestnuts and roasted sweet potatoes are available on street corners around La Castanyada, which is celebrated on and around All Saints' Day (November 1).

SEAFOOD

- *Fideuas:* Seafood and short noodle dish, reminiscent of a noodle paella.

- *Suquet de Peix:* "Catch of the day" seafood stew with potatoes, garlic, and tomato.

- *Arròs negre:* Paella flavored and colored with squid ink, sometimes served with homemade garlic mayonnaise (allioli).

STEWS

- *Escudellla:* Stew made with meat, beans, potatoes, cabbage, and sometimes pasta.

- *Faves a la Catalana:* Stew of broad beans, sausage, and pancetta.

MEAT AND PASTA

- *Xai Rostit Amb 12 Cabeçes d'All:* Lamb roasted with 12 heads of garlic.

- *Canelons:* Pasta rolls stuffed with stewed meat and béchamel sauce, traditionally eaten on December 26 with the leftovers from Christmas dinner.

- *Ànec amb peres:* Duck stewed slowly with pears.

- *Cargols a la llauna:* Roasted snails, abundant during the Festival of Cargols that takes place in May in Lleida, west of Barcelona.

- *Mongetes amb botifarra:* Dish of sausage and white beans.

DESSERTS

- *Crema Catalana:* Similar to crème brulée but more yellow in color, a bit sweeter, and made with cinnamon.

- *Mel I Mato:* Soft goat cheese served with honey and walnuts.

- *Panellets:* Small round sweets made with almonds, sugar, eggs, and pine nuts. Seen in bakeries throughout October and November.

- Drive north to Cadaqués (1 hour 20 minutes), in time for fine dining at **Compartir** (reservations required). Tip: Park in one of the car parks on the edge of town, as parking in central Cadaqués is nearly impossible.

- Relax after the feast with an afternoon of bliss on the beach at **Platja de Ses Oliveres.**

- Follow a windy road to the most easterly point on the Iberian Peninsula: the **Cap de Creus.** Stop at the lighthouse for a coffee and spectacular views of the cape's jagged silhouette as the sun goes down.

- Rest up at the **Tramuntana Hotel,** a boutique retreat buried in the old town.

>DAY 4: CADAQUÉS TO FIGUERES

- Hop over to **Portlligat** on foot—it's just one kilometer (0.6 miles) north of Cadaqués.

- Kick-start a day inside the surreal world of Salvador Dalí with a peek inside the artist's former home, **Casa Salvador Dalí.**

- Enjoy Mediterranean flavors of a different kind at **El Barroco,** a hidden Lebanese jewel and former haunt of the artist.

- After lunch, leave Cadaqués behind and drive 45 minutes west to Figueres, where you can continue your hallucinatory tour at the **Teatre-Museu Dalí.** Housing a collection of more than 1,500 works, the museum is the artist's greatest legacy.

- Head back to Barcelona.

BEFORE YOU GO

WHEN TO GO

Barcelona is Spain's most popular destination and one of the world's most-visited cities, and in the past 30 years the annual number of visitors to the city has increased almost six-fold. All parts of Catalonia are packed with tourists during the summer months, and many visitors now opt for **spring or fall** to get a better choice of accommodation and better prices.

Geographically, Catalonia is very varied, from the high peaks of the Pyrenees to the Mediterranean beaches that dot the scenic coastline. Climate and temperature do not vary much within the region, but the mountainous areas tend to be a little more comfortable during the hot summer period. The sea temperature is most suitable for swimming from late May until early October.

Like most of Spain, Catalonia has no shortages of festivals all year-round. Most of Barcelona's larger festivals take place between late spring and early fall.

SUMMER (JUNE-AUGUST)

Summer in Catalonia is June-August, with temperatures of **18-30°C** (64-86°F). It is also the **peak tourist season.** Late July and August are the most hot and humid, and residents of Barcelona traditionally take summer vacations away from the city in

Cap de Creus

Currency: Euro (€)
Conversion rate: €1=$1.13 USD; €1=£0.89 GBP
Entry Requirements: For visits of up to 90 days for tourist or business purposes, visas are not required for citizens of the EU, UK, US, Canada, Australia, or New Zealand. Visitors from South Africa are required to obtain a Schengen visa.
General emergency line: 112 (fire, police, ambulance)
Medical emergencies: 061
Time Zone: UTC+01:00
Electrical system: 230V, 50Hz; round, two-prong plugs

August, leaving it mainly to the tourists. **Many restaurants and shops in Catalonia also close in August,** thus limiting the choice for both dining and shopping.

SPRING AND FALL (MARCH-MAY AND SEPT.-NOV.)

Visiting Barcelona in late spring or early fall is more comfortable, with fewer crowds, mild temperatures, and lower humidity. Spring temperatures are around **9-23°C** (48-73°F); fall temperatures are around **11-27°C** (52-81°F). Accommodation prices are at mid-season levels during these periods.

Most of the rainfall occurs in April, but spectacular storms can occur at any time during the year.

WINTER (DEC.-FEB.)

Winter temperatures are approximately **7-15°C** (44-59°F). Days are crisp and usually sunny but can also be cold. The tramontana wind often blows from the Pyrenees along the Catalan coast, which can be cooling in summer but very cold in winter.

Winter is a more comfortable time for city sightseeing and shopping in Barcelona. Accommodation and airfare prices are generally more affordable, and visits to popular attractions like Sagrada Familia do not involve the long waits experienced during peak times. Christmas and New Year festivities attract an extra influx of visitors over the holidays.

GETTING THERE

Catalonia has three international airports (Barcelona-El Prat, Girona-Costa Brava, and Reus), though most international flights arrive in **Barcelona-El Prat Airport** (BCN, 90/240-4704, www.aena-aeropuertos.es), including direct flights from the UK and some flights from outside Europe, including North America. There are no direct flights from Australia, New Zealand, or South Africa.

You can also arrive in Catalonia by bus: International connections across mainland Europe are operated by **Eurolines** (90/240-5040, eurolines.es) and **Flixbus** (flixbus.com). Some travelers may arrive by train from London St Pancras (**Eurostar,** eurostar.com) via Paris (transferring in Paris from Gare du Nord to Gare du Lyon) and the **TGV** service to Barcelona. Ferries run from Italy, Morocco (both with

BUDGETING

Beer: €2 for a 200ml (7oz) *caña*
Glass of wine: €2-€4
Cocktail: €9-€15
Coffee: €1.20-€2
Lunch: €10-€15 (3-course lunch menu including a drink)
Dinner: €15-€25
Tapas: €2 (croquette or *montadito*); €18 ("racion" of jamón or grilled octopus)
Hotel: €30-50 (hostel); €70-100 (budget); €250+ (luxury)
Car rental: €16/day + extra mileage + gas
Gasoline: €1.28/liter (1/4 gallon) of regular unleaded gas
Parking: €19-€25/day, €6-€8/2 hours
Single metro/bus journey: €2.20
T10 ticket (10 public transport rides): €10.20
Taxi fare: €1.03/km (minimum pickup charge: €7.00)

Grimaldi, 90/253-1333, www.grimaldi-lines.com, and Grandi Navi Veloci, 93/443-7139, gnv.it), and Algeria (Algerie Ferries, algerieferries.dz).

GETTING AROUND
IN BARCELONA

Barcelona is best experienced on foot, and most sites are within walking distance of the center. The metro and bus lines are also extensive and easy to use, and information in English is available online at **tmb.cat.** Parking is difficult and renting a car is not necessary within the city.

OUTSIDE BARCELONA

The best way to travel between Barcelona and the rest of Catalonia is by bus, train, or car rental. Most buses arrive and depart from Estació de Nord (Carrer d'Alí Bei, 80; barcelonanord.cat). **Monbus** (90/229-2900, monbus. es) serves central and southern Catalonia, including Tarragona, Reus Airport, and Penedès; **Sarfa** (90/230-2025, moventis.es) covers the Costa Brava, including direct transfers from Barcelona-El Prat Airport; **Teisa** (93/215-3566, teisa-bus.com) covers the eastern Pyrenees and Girona; and **Sagalés** (90/213-0014, sagales.com) operates throughout the region.

The fastest way to travel between Catalan cities is by train. Most arrive and depart from **Barcelona Sants** (Plaça dels Països Catalans, 1-7; 93/495-6020; www.adif. es). **Renfe** (www.renfe.com) and its subsidiary, **Rodalies de Catalunya** (rodalies.gencat.cat), service the region, including Barcelona, Girona, Lleida, Tarragona, and Figueres. For a scenic drive, or to access more remote locations, car rental is the best way to explore the region. Rental companies are abundant at airports and in the city.

Many day trip destinations, including Sitges, Montserrat, Tarragona, Girona, and several towns on the Costa Brava, are easily navigated on foot after you arrive. A car enables you to explore deeper in the Costa Brava, La Garrotxa, and Vall de Boí.

DAILY REMINDERS

Nearly all shops and markets, as well as many bars and restaurants, are closed on **Sunday** across Catalonia.

IN BARCELONA

Museums and other attractions in Barcelona are mostly closed on **Monday,** except on public holidays. Many restaurants also close on Monday.

Attractions open on Monday include: Park Güell, Gran Teatre del Liceu, Cathedral, La Pedrera (Casa Milà), Sagrada Familia, Monument a Colom, Museu d'Art Contemporani de Barcelona (MACBA), Poble Espanyol, Aquàrium, Palau de la Musica Catalana, Palau Güell, and Camp Nou.

Admission to the Museu Nacional d'Art de Catalunya (MNAC) is free on **Saturday after 3pm**, and on the first Sunday of each month.

Admission to many museums and attractions is free on the **first Sunday of every month**, as well as some public holidays: February 12, April 23, May 18 (international museum night), September 11, and September 24.

On **Sunday,** many museums offer free entrance after 3pm, including: Picasso Museum, Centre de Cultura Contemporània de Barcelona (CCCB), Museu d'Història de Barcelona (MUHBA), Museu d'Història de Catalunya, Jardí Botànic, Museu Marítim.

BEYOND BARCELONA

Sights in Sitges are generally closed on **Monday,** as are many sights in Tarragona, and some sights in Girona outside of July and August. Catedral de Tarragona is closed on **Sunday** during certain times of the year. The Escolania Boys' Choir (Montserrat) performs every day except **Saturday.**

SIGHTSEEING PASSES
BARCELONA CARD

The Barcelona Card is a 3-in-1 transport card, museum pass and discount card that can be purchased at tourist information offices in Barcelona (full price) or online (discount) at barcelonacard.org. There are three available formats: 72-hour (€46 adults/€22 children 4-12 years), 96-hour (€56 adults/€28 children 4-12 years), and 120-hour (€61 adults/€33 children 4-12 years). Cardholders receive a free city guide, unlimited use of public transport, free entry to many sights, and discounted entry to others, including Gaudí's monuments and Camp Nou. It is activated on first use, so there is no harm in buying it in advance.

KEY RESERVATIONS

In high season, accommodation and restaurant reservations are recommended across the region, particularly in Barcelona and the Costa Brava

IN BARCELONA
Advance booking is recommended for **Park Güell**, the **Sagrada Familia**, and **Museu Picasso.** It's necessary to book ahead for the following restaurants: **Disfrutar, Tickets** (reservations released online exactly two months in advance), and **Pakta.**

BEYOND BARCELONA
Advance reservations are advised for the **Teatre-Museu Dalí** in Figueres and required for **Casa Salvador Dalí** in Portlligat (both on the Costa Brava). If you'd like to tour Tarragona's **Catedral de Tarragona,** reserve at least 48 hours in advance via email (info@catedraldetarragona.com) or telephone.

Restaurant reservations are required for Girona's **El Cellar de Can Roca** (reserve up to 11 months in advance!) and **Bionbo.** Reservations are also required for **Compartir** in Cadaqués, **Les Cols** and **Ca l'Enric** near Olot, and highly recommended for **Diferent** and **Can Climent Platillos** in Begur.

HOP ON HOP OFF BARCELONA BUS TOUR

The Hop-On, Hop-Off official Barcelona bus tour has three routes which take you past the city's famous most landmarks. Tickets include an audio guide, discounts to attractions, and access to the app. It is available in 1-day (€27 adults/€16 children 4-12 years/€22.50 for over 65s and people with disabilities) and 2-day (€36 adults/€21 children 4-12 years/€31.50 over 65s and people with disabilities) tickets and can be purchased at tourist offices in Barcelona, or online at hoponhopoffbarcelona.org with a 10% discount. The online voucher is valid for 90 days and can be exchanged for a ticket at tourist offices or directly on the bus.

BARCELONA

Spain's second city is a spellbind-

ing Mediterranean jewel. Bursting with a unique
creative energy, from the fantastical creations of
Gaudí to its rich urban landscape and gastronomic wizardry, Barcelona is blessed with a whole
host of favorable characteristics and cultural bril-
liance. Sun, sea, art, architecture, beaches, food,
football: The city has it all.

Yet it's the simple, everyday delights that make
Barcelona so special. From the moment the sun
rises, the early morning Mediterranean light lifts
the spirit. Stepping outside, life here is on your

HIGHLIGHTS

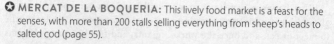

✪ MERCAT DE LA BOQUERIA: This lively food market is a feast for the senses, with more than 200 stalls selling everything from sheep's heads to salted cod (page 55).

✪ LA CATEDRAL DE LA SANTA CREU I SANTA EULÀLIA: Situated in the heart of the Barri Gòtic, Barcelona's eclectic cathedral is dedicated to the co-patron saint of the city, Santa Eulàlia; don't miss the magnificent Gothic cloister (page 59).

✪ SANTA MARÍA DEL MAR: Arguably Barelona's most beautiful church, Santa María del Mar is a a soaring symphony in stone and a magnificent example of Catalan Gothic architecture (page 66).

✪ MUSEU PICASSO: Focusing on Picasso's formative years spent in his adopted city, more than 4,000 works by the 20th-century master form the permanent collection in this extensive gallery (page 70).

✪ LA SAGRADA FAMÍLIA: More than 130 years in the making, the soaring towers of Gaudí's fantastical masterpiece became the emblem of the city long before its scheduled completion date (page 73).

✪ CASA BATLLÓ: This spectacular residence by Gaudí is a sculptural creation inside and out, culminating with a polychromatic tiled roof resembling a dragon's scaly back (page 78).

✪ LA PEDRERA: The undulating façade of Gaudí's audacious Modernista mansion generated waves of criticism at the time, but it remains one of the city's most iconic buildings, situated on its most elegant boulevard (page 80).

✪ PARK GÜELL: Filled with topsy-turvy porticos, labyrinthine walkways, and whimsical pavilions, this Gaudí-designed space feels like a fairy tale (page 84).

✪ CAMP NOU: Home of FC Barcelona, one of the world's most famous football clubs, the legendary Camp Nou is the biggest stadium in Europe and a place of pilgrimage for any football fan (page 100).

✪ BEACHES: Five kilometers (3 miles) of golden sands make Barcelona's beachfront the perfect backdrop for a sundrenched stroll (page 152).

doorstep. The dense cityscape is inherently walkable, creating a dynamic environment in which to live, work, and play.

As the day unfolds, a healthy obsession with food comes into focus. Whether browsing the local market for fresh fish or sitting down for an exceptionally long lunch, fulfilling the basic needs here is a source of sheer joy.

The late afternoon and early evening are made for wandering. As the frenetic city activity reaches its peak, neighborhoods burst into action, with young and old enjoying an outdoor life that is shared by all.

What happens next is anyone's guess. It's never too early or too late to meet or eat, and once the working day is done, the night is forever young. A sense of fun runs through the veins of this city, and there's always a chance you'll bump into some bizarre cultural traditions that will leave you bamboozled—nine-story human towers, papier-mâché giants, and fire-breathing dragons are just the start.

Barcelona captures the imagination and leaves you wanting more.

Orientation

Until the mid-19th century, Barcelona was a walled city covering the area known as the *Ciutat Vella* (old city). This district encompasses four neighborhoods—La Barceloneta, El Gòtic, El Raval, and La Ribera—and is immediately recognizable on the city map for its narrow streets and dense cityscape. The limits of the Ciutat Vella are an indication of where the medieval walls once stood. Beyond this, a gridded street pattern of L'Eixample stretches across the city, laid out in accordance with a visionary 19th-century masterplan.

Plaça de Catalunya, the city's central square, marks the meeting point of the old city and the 19th-century extension. From here, the main thoroughfare of Gran Via de les Corts Catalanes runs right across the middle of the city, parallel to the seafront, while the grand boulevard of Passeig de Gràcia connects the plaza with Avinguda Diagonal, another of the city's main arteries, which runs diagonally from the mountain to the sea.

Barcelona is bound to the east by the Mediterranean Sea, to the west by the Collserola mountain range, and to the north and south by the two rivers Besòs and Llobregat. It's difficult to comprehend cardinal directions in Barcelona, as nearly every map uses the city's distinctive physical geography as the key points of reference—with the Mediterranean running across the bottom and the Collserola Hills at the top—and that is the way the city is understood.

NEIGHBORHOODS
BARRI GÒTIC AND LA RAMBLA
For centuries the beating heart of city life, the tree-lined boulevard of La Rambla forms the backbone of Barcelona's old town. Branch off into the Barri Gòtic, which lies between Plaça de Catalunya, Passeig de Colom, Via Laietana, and La Rambla, and you'll enter a labyrinth of winding lanes, steeped in history whichever way you turn. The Roman settlement of Barcino was founded here in 15 BC, while Plaça del Rei was the heart of medieval Barcelona. Today, the Gothic Quarter remains the administrative nerve center of the city.

EL RAVAL
A cultural melting pot, this part of the Ciutat Vella is bound by La Rambla on one side and the neighborhood of Sant Antoni on the other. Once agricultural land, by the early 20th century

the overcrowded, impoverished neighborhood was known for its red-light nightlife. Today, Raval has cleaned up its act, with the MACBA (Barcelona's Museum of Contemporary Art), CCCB (the neighboring cultural center), and Rambla del Raval leading the way. The neighborhood retains a seedy undertone, but beneath its rough exterior, youthful subcultures, bohemian bars, and a lively arts scene exude a tangible zest for life.

LA RIBERA/EL BORN

This part of the Ciutat Vella lies between the Barri Gòtic and the Parc de la Ciutadella. A maze of narrow streets revolves around the Gothic Basilica of Santa Maria del Mar, while the medieval palaces along Carrer de Montcada—home to the Museu Picasso—are a reminder of the area's affluent past. The area between Carrer Princesa and Passeig de Colom, commonly known as El Born, is a hub of activity, particularly at night, with chic boutiques, artists' workshops, and lively tapas bars are dotted across the trendy neighborhood.

L'EIXAMPLE

The gridded streets of L'Eixample were constructed in the mid-19th century, after the medieval walls surrounding the Ciutat Vella were torn down. The district embodies the splendor of fin-de-siècle Barcelona, and is where most examples of Catalan Modernisme can be found, including La Sagrada Familia and the area around Passeig de Gràcia, known as the Quadrat d'Or, where the city's bourgeoisie built their palatial homes.

GRÀCIA, PARK GÜELL, AND BEYOND

Once an independent village, Gràcia's narrow streets and pleasant squares retain a unique identity that's somewhere between hippie and hipster, with a distinctly revolutionary streak. Somehow, the neighborhood balances an avant-garde art scene with gentrification, a Catalan separatist soul with a large foreign community, and a family-friendly vibe with a lively nightlife—resulting in a palpable energy. Slightly uphill from the old village, nature and architecture find their own harmony in Gaudí's fantastical Park Güell.

MONTJUÏC, POBLE-SEC, AND SANT ANTONI

Montjuïc is Barcelona's seaside mountain, situated south of the city center. Green and relatively uninhabited, its creases cradle many cultural institutions, including the Fundació Joan Miró, Mies Van de Rohe's Barcelona Pavilion, and the Museu Nacional d'Art de Catalunya. On its northern slopes, the 19th-century neighborhoods of Poble-sec and Sant Antoni lie on either side of Avinguda del Paral·lel. This is the city's most up-and-coming area, with hip cafés, haute cuisine, and vibrant streetlife.

WATERFRONT

Barcelona's proximity to the Mediterranean Sea is one of the city's defining characteristics. From south to north, the Waterfront area encompasses the city's old port (Port Vell), the fishermen's neighborhood of Barceloneta, the 1992 development of

Barcelona

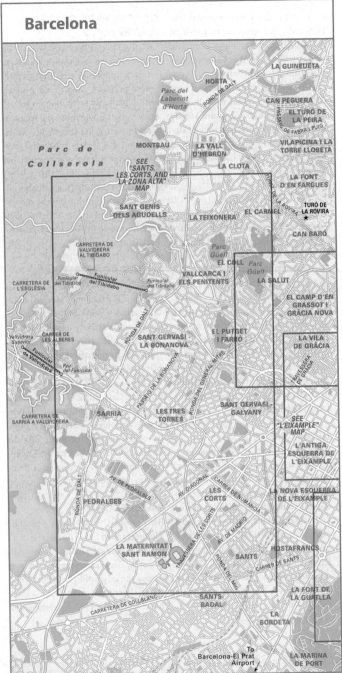

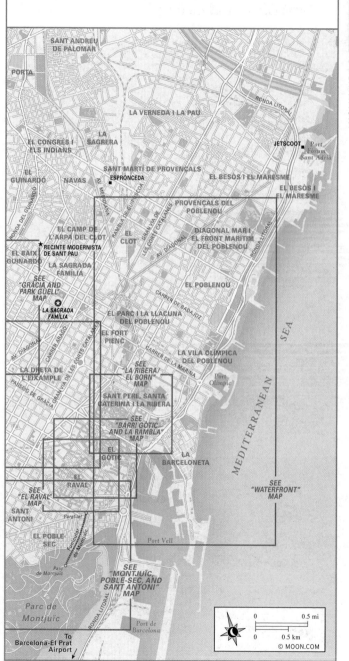

Barri Gòtic and La Rambla

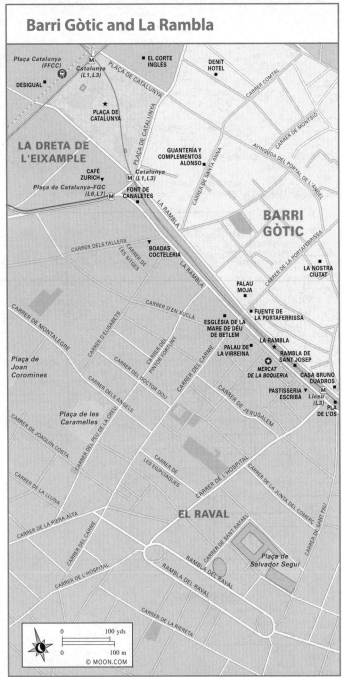

Plaça Catalunya
(FFCC)

Catalunya
(L1,L3)

DESIGUAL

PLAÇA DE CATALUNYA

EL CORTE INGLÉS

DENIT HOTEL

CARRER COMTAL

★ PLAÇA DE CATALUNYA

LA DRETA DE L'EIXAMPLE

PLAÇA DE CATALUNYA

CARRER DE MONTSIÓ

AVINGUDA DEL PORTAL DE L'ÀNGEL

GUANTERÍA Y COMPLEMENTOS ALONSO

CAFÉ ZURICH

Plaça de Catalunya-FGC
(L6,L7)

Catalunya
(L1,L3)

FONT DE CANALETES

CARRER DE SANTA ANNA

LA RAMBLA

BARRI GÒTIC

CARRER DELS TALLERS

BOADAS COCTELERIA

CARRER DE LES SITGES

LA RAMBLA

CARRER DE LA PORTAFERRISSA

LA NOSTRA CIUTAT

PALAU MOJA

CARRER D'EN XUCLA

FUENTE DE LA PORTAFERRISSA

ESGLÉSIA DE LA MARE DE DÉU DE BETLEM

PALAU DE LA VIRREINA

LA RAMBLA
★ **RAMBLA DE SANT JOSEP**

CARRER DE MONTALEGRE

CARRER D'ELISABETS

CARRER DEL PINTOR FORTUNY

CARRER DEL CARME

Plaça de Joan Coromines

CARRER DEL DOCTOR DOU

✪ **MERCAT DE LA BOQUERIA**

CASA BRUNO CUADROS

PASTISSERIA ESCRIBÀ

Liceu
(L3)

PLA DE L'OS

CARRER DELS ANGELS

Plaça de les Caramelles

CARRER DEL PEU DE LA CREU

CARRER DE JERUSALEM

CARRER DE JOAQUÍN COSTA

CARRER DE LES EGIPCIAQUES

CARRER DE L'HOSPITAL

CARRER DE LA JUNTA DEL COMERÇ

CARRER DE LA LLUNA

EL RAVAL

CARRER DE SANT PAU

CARRER DE LA RIERA ALTA

CARRER DE SANT RAFAEL

Plaça de Salvador Seguí

CARRER DEL CARME

RAMBLA DEL RAVAL

CARRER DE L'HOSPITAL

RAMBLA DEL RAVAL

CARRER DE LA RIERETA

| 0 | 100 yds |
| 0 | 100 m |

© MOON.COM

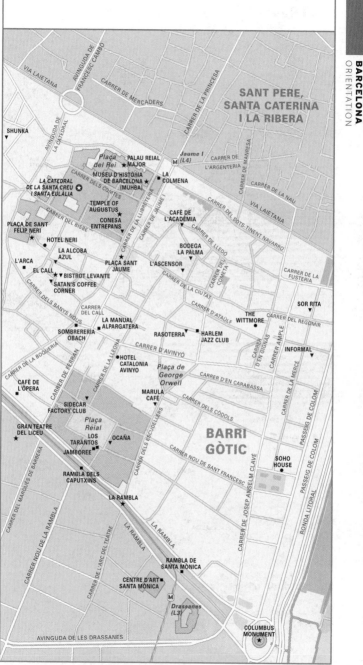

SHUNKA ▼

VIA LAIETANA
AVINGUDA DE FRANCESC CAMBÓ
CARRER DE MERCADERS
CARRER DE LA PRINCESA

**SANT PERE,
SANTA CATERINA
I LA RIBERA**

AVINGUDA DE LA CATEDRAL

*Plaça
del Rei* ★ **PALAU REIAL
MAJOR** ★

MUSEU D'HISTÒRIA
DE BARCELONA ★
[MUHBA]

Jaume I
Ⓜ (L4)

CARRER DE
L'ARGENTERIA

CARRER DE MANRESA

LA CATEDRAL
DE LA SANTA CREU
i SANTA EULÀLIA ✪

CARRER DELS COMTES

LA
COLMENA

CARRER DE JAUME I

CARRER DE LA NAU

VIA LAIETANA

TEMPLE OF
AUGUSTUS ★

CARRER DE LA LLIBRETERIA

CARRER DEL BISBE

CONESA
ENTREPANS ■

CAFÉ DE
L'ACADÈMIA ■

CARRER DELS SOTS-TINENT NAVARRO

PLAÇA DE SANT
FELIP NERI ★

HOTEL NERI ●

CARRER DE LLEÓ

BODEGA
LA PALMA ■

CARRER DE LA
FUSTERIA

LA ALCOBA
AZUL ★

PLAÇA SANT
JAUME ★

L'ASCENSOR
▼

CARRER DEL
COMETA

L'ARCA ■

EL CALL ■ ▼ BISTROT LEVANTE

SATAN'S COFFEE
CORNER ▼

CARRER DE LA CIUTAT

CARRER DELS BANYS NOUS

CARRER
DEL CALL

CARRER D'ATAÜLF

THE
WITTMORE ●

SOR RITA ■

CARRER DEL REGOMIR

LA MANUAL
ALPARGATERA ●

RASOTERRA ■

HARLEM
JAZZ CLUB ■

CARRER AMPLE

INFORMAL
▼

SOMBRERERIA
OBACH ■

CARRER D'AVINYÓ

CARRER DE LA LLEONA

CARRER D'EN GIGNÀS

CARRER DE LA MERCÈ

CARRER DE LA BOQUERIA

HOTEL
CATALONIA
AVINYÓ ●

*Plaça de
George
Orwell*

CARRER D'EN CARABASSA

PASSEIG DE COLOM

CAFÈ DE
L'ÒPERA ■

CARRER DE FERRAN

MARULA
CAFÉ ■

CARRER DELS CÒDOLS

**BARRI
GÒTIC**

SIDECAR
FACTORY CLUB ■

*Plaça
Reial*

OCAÑA ■

CARRER DELS ESCUDELLERS

SOHO
HOUSE

GRAN TEATRE
DEL LICEU ★

LOS
TARANTOS ■

JAMBOREE ■

CARRER DEL MARQUÈS DE BARBERÀ

RAMBLA DELS
CAPUTXINS

CARRER NOU DE SANT FRANCESC

CARRER DE JOSEP ANSELM CLAVÉ

PASSEIG DE COLOM

RONDA LITORAL

LA RAMBLA ★

LA RAMBLA

CARRER NOU DE LA RAMBLA

CARRER DE L'ARC DEL TEATRE

RAMBLA DE
SANTA MÒNICA ■

CENTRE D'ART
SANTA MÒNICA ■

Ⓜ
Drassanes
(L3)

COLUMBUS
MONUMENT ●

AVINGUDA DE LES DRASSANES

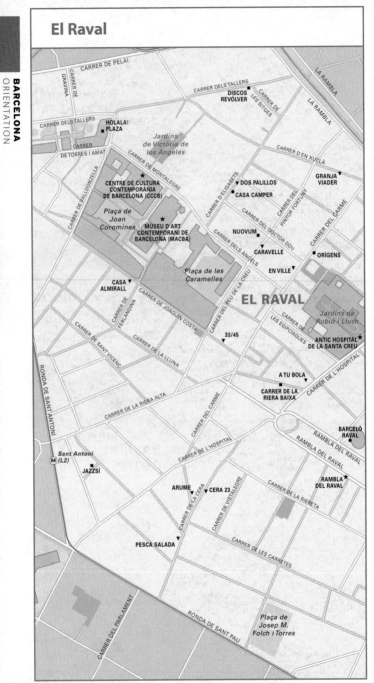

El Raval

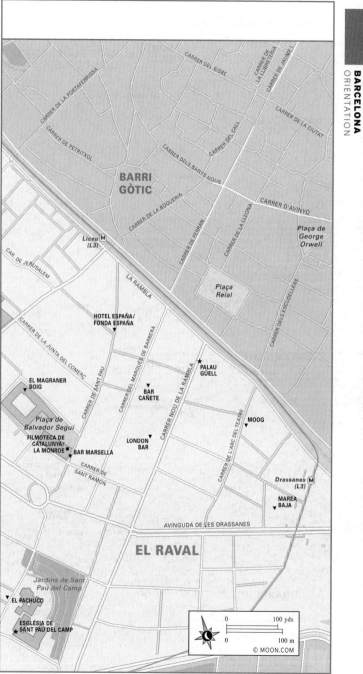

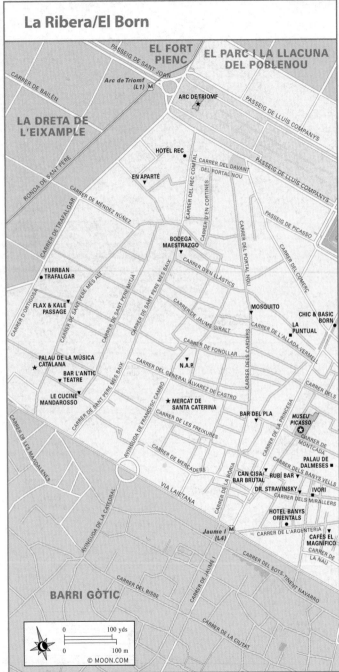

La Ribera/El Born

EL FORT PIENC

EL PARC I LA LLACUNA DEL POBLENOU

PASSEIG DE SANT JOAN

Arc de Triomf (L1) M

★ ARC DE TRIOMF

PASSEIG DE LLUIS COMPANYS

CARRER DE BAILÉN

LA DRETA DE L'EIXAMPLE

PASSEIG DE LLUIS COMPANYS

● HOTEL REC

CARRER DEL DAVANT DEL PORTAL NOU

RONDA DE SANT PERE

CARRER DEL REC COMTAL

▼ EN APARTÉ

PASSEIG DE PICASSO

CARRER DE TRAFALGAR

CARRER DE MENDEZ NÚÑEZ

CARRER D'EN CORTINES

CARRER DEL PORTAL NOU

CARRER DEL COMERÇ

BODEGA MAESTRAZGO ▼

CARRER D'EN LLASTICS

● YURRBAN TRAFALGAR

CARRER DE SANT PERE MÉS BAIX

CARRER DE SANT PERE MÉS ALT

CARRER D'ORTIGOSA

▼ FLAX & KALE PASSAGE

CARRER DE SANT PERE MITJA

MOSQUITO ▼

CARRER DE JAUME GIRALT

CHIC & BASIC BORN ●

CARRER DE L'ALLADA-VERMELL

LA PUNTUAL ▼

CARRER DE FONOLLAR

CARRER DELS CARDERS

★ PALAU DE LA MÚSICA CATALANA

▼ N.A.P.

CARRER DEL GENERAL ALVAREZ DE CASTRO

CARRER DELS

▼ BAR L'ANTIC TEATRE

CARRER DE SANT PERE MÉS BAIX

LE CUCINE MANDAROSSO ▼

★ MERCAT DE SANTA CATERINA

MUSEU PICASSO ★

CARRER DE MONTCADA

AVINGUDA DE FRANCESC CAMBÓ

CARRER DE LES FREIXURES

BAR DEL PLA ▼

CARRER DE LA PRINCESA

PALAU DE DALMESES ■

CARRER DE MERCADERS

CARRER DE LA BORIA

CARRER DELS BANYS VELLS

CARRER DE LES MAGDALENES

CAN CISA/ BAR BRUTAL ▼ RUBÍ BAR ▼

IVORI ▼

VIA LAIETANA

DR. STRAVINSKY ▼

CARRER DELS MIRALLERS

HOTEL BANYS ORIENTALS ●

AVINGUDA DE LA CATEDRAL

Jaume I (L4) M

CARRER DE L'ARGENTERIA

CAFÉS EL MAGNÍFICO ▼

CARRER DE JAUME

CARRER DE LA NAU

CARRER DEL SOTS-TINENT NAVARRO

BARRI GÒTIC

CARRER DEL BISBE

CARRER DE LA CIUTAT

0   100 yds
0   100 m

© MOON.COM

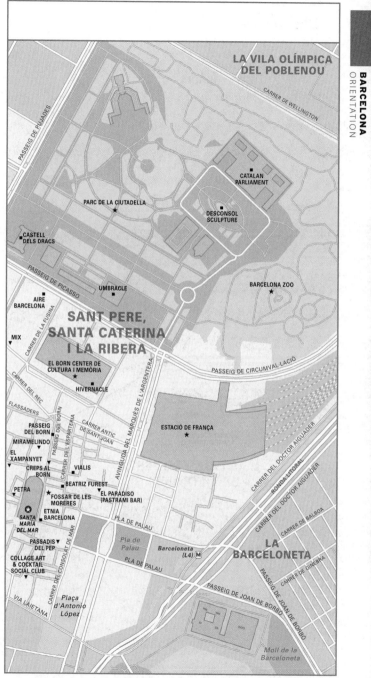

L'Eixample

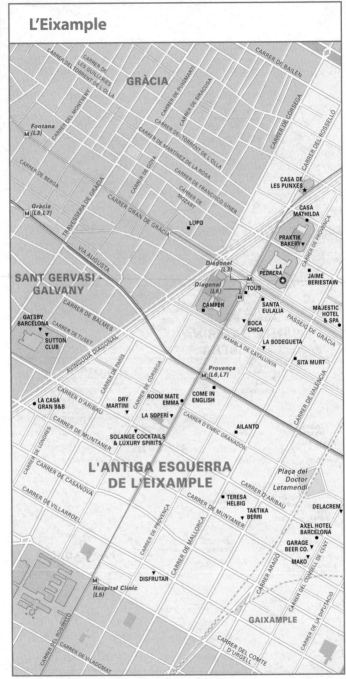

GRÀCIA

CARRER DE BAILÉN

CARRER DE LES GUILLERIES

CARRER DEL TORRENT DE L'OLLA

CARRER DE PUIGMARTÍ

CARRER DE SIRACUSA

CARRER DE CÒRSEGA

CARRER DEL ROSSELLÓ

Fontana
M (L3)

CARRER DEL MONTSENY

CARRER DE BERGA

CARRER DEL TORRANT DE L'OLLA

CARRER DE MARTÍNEZ DE LA ROSA

CARRER DE GOYA

CARRER DE FRANCISCO GINER

CARRER DE LA ROSA

CASA DE LES PUNXES ★

Gràcia
M (L6, L7)

TRAVESSERA DE GRÀCIA

CARRER GRAN DE GRÀCIA

CARRER DE MOZART

LUPO ■

CASA MATHILDA ■

CARRER DE PROVENÇA

PRAKTIK BAKERY ▼

VIA AUGUSTA

SANT GERVASI - GALVANY

CARRER DE BALMES

Diagonal (L3)

Diagonal (L6)

LA PEDRERA ✪

JAIME BERIESTAIN ■

M ▼ TOUS

GATSBY BARCELONA ▼

CARRER DE TUSET

CAMPER ■

M

SANTA EULALIA ■

MAJESTIC HOTEL & SPA ●

SUTTON CLUB

▼ BOCA CHICA

PASSEIG DE GRÀCIA

AVINGUDA DIAGONAL

CARRER DE PARÍS

CARRER DE CÒRSEGA

LA BODEGUETA ■

RAMBLA DE CATALUNYA

SITA MURT ■

CARRER DE VALÈNCIA

Provença
M (L6, L7)

LA CASA GRAN B&B ●

CARRER D'ARIBAU

DRY MARTINI ▼

ROOM MATE EMMA ■

COME IN ENGLISH ■

CARRER DE MUNTANER

LA SOPERÍ ▼

CARRER D'ENRIC GRANADOS

AILANTO ■

CARRER DE LONDRES

CARRER DE CASANOVA

SOLANGE COCKTAILS & LUXURY SPIRITS ▼

L'ANTIGA ESQUERRA DE L'EIXAMPLE

CARRER DE VILLARROEL

Plaça del Doctor Letamendí

CARRER D'ARIBAU

TERESA HELBIG ■

CARRER DE MUNTANER

DELACREM ▼

CARRER DE PROVENÇA

CARRER DE MALLORCA

TAKTIKA BERRI ▼

AXEL HOTEL BARCELONA ■

GARAGE BEER CO. ▼

MAKO ■

CARRER ARAGÓ

CARRER DEL CONSELL DE CENT

M
Hospital Clínic (L5)

DISFRUTAR ▼

GAIXAMPLE

CARRER DE LA DIPUTACIÓ

CARRER DEL ROSSELLÓ

CARRER DE VILADOMAT

CARRER DEL COMTE D'URGELL

To Sagrada Família,
Recinte Modernista
de Sant Pau

EL FORT PIENC

CARRER DE SARDENYA

CARRER DEL CONSELL DE CENT

CARRER DE SICILIA

CARRER DE NÀPOLS

Verdaguer (L4)

Verdaguer (L5)

CARRER DE MALLORCA

CARRER DE PROVENÇA

PASSEIG DE SANT JOAN

CARRER DE ROGER DE FLOR

GRAN VIA DE LES CORTS CATALANES

AVINGUDA DIAGONAL

CARRER DE MALLORCA

CARRER DE GIRONA

CARRER DE BAILÈN

CARRER DE LA DIPUTACIÓ

Jardins del Doctor Robert

Tetuan (L2)

CARRER DE VALÈNCIA

Girona (L4)

LA DRETA DE L'EIXAMPLE

CASA BONAY

FIREBUG

QUEVIURES MÚRRIA

CARRER D'ARAGÓ

CARRER DEL CONSELL DE CENT

CARRER DEL BRUC

GRAN VIA DE LES CORTS CATALANES

CARRER DE GIRONA

9 REINAS

CARRER DE ROGER DE LLÚRIA

CARRER DE CASP

CARRER D'AUSIÀS MARC

COTTON HOUSE HOTEL

QUADRAT D'OR

CARRER DE PAU CLARIS

Passeig de Gràcia (FFCC)

BIMBA Y LOLA

MARGOT HOUSE

Passeig de Gràcia (L3)

Urquinaona (L1)

CARRER DE TRAFALGAR

CASA BATLLÓ

CASA AMATLLER

ALMANAC

CARRER DE LA DIPUTACIÓ

Plaça d'Urquinaona

CASA LLEÓ MORERA

EL NACIONAL

THE5ROOMS

FUNDACIÓ ANTONI TÀPIES

Passeig de Gràcia (L4)

CARRER DE LES JONQUERES

Passeig de Gràcia (L2)

VINITUS

CARRER DE SANT PERE

Urquinaona (L4)

VIA LAIETANA

LATERAL

MUSEU DEL MODERNISME DE BARCELONA

MONVÍNIC

Plaça Catalunya (FFCC)

RONDA DE SANT PERE

CARRER DE BALMES

ARENA SALA MADRE

LLIBRERIA ALTAÏR

Catalunya (L1,L3)

Plaça de Catalunya

BARRI GÒTIC

GAIXAMPLE

BACOA

CAFÉ COSMO

HOTEL PULITZER

Catalunya (L1,L3)

LA ESQUINA

Plaça de Catalunya–FGC (L6,L7)

GRAN VIA DE LES CORTS CATALANES

Universitat (L1+L2)

CARRER DE PELAI

LA RAMBLA

Universitat

RONDA DE SANT ANTONI

TOC

0   200 yds
0   200 m

© MOON.COM

41

Gràcia and Park Güell

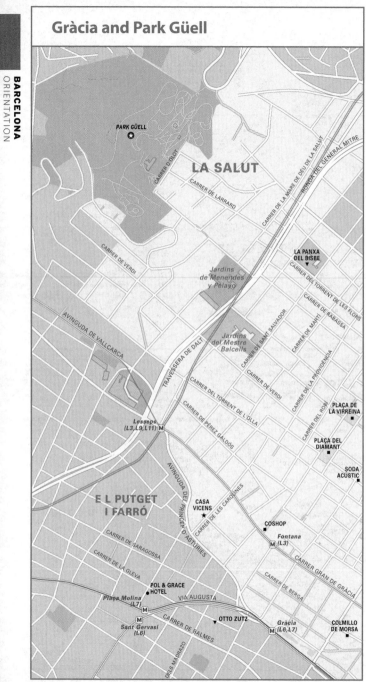

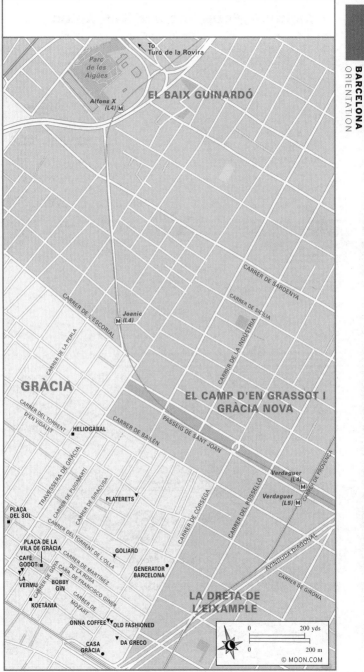

43

Montjuïc, Poble-sec, and Sant Antoni

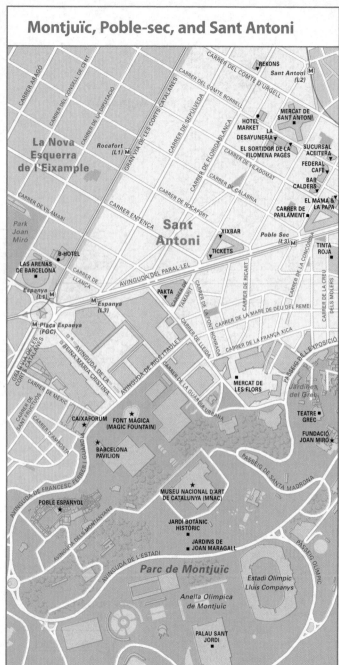

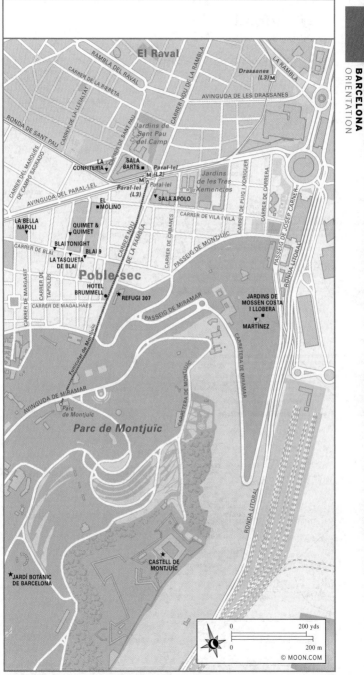

Waterfront

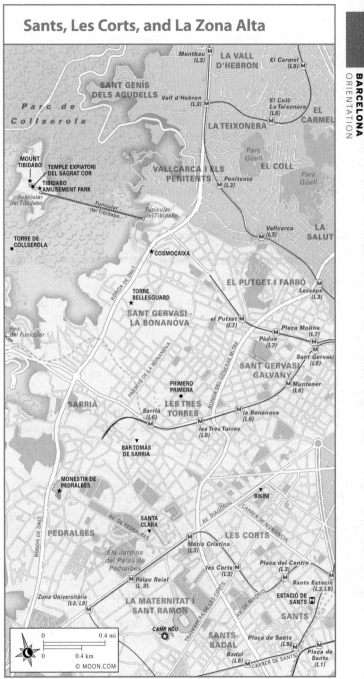

Sants, Les Corts, and La Zona Alta

Parc de Collserola

LA VALL D'HEBRON

Montbau (L3)

El Carmel (L5) M

SANT GENÍS DELS AGUDELLS

Vall d'Hebron (L3) M

El Coll/ La Teixonera (L5) M

EL CARMEL

LA TEIXONERA

MOUNT TIBIDABO

TEMPLE EXPIATORI DEL SAGRAT COR

TIBIDABO AMUSEMENT PARK

VALLCARCA I ELS PENITENTS

Parc Güell

EL COLL

Parc Güell

Funicular del Tibidabo

Funicular del Tibidabo

Funicular del Tibidabo

Penitents (L3)

TORRE DE COLLSEROLA

Vallcarca (L3) M

LA SALUT

COSMOCAIXA

EL PUTGET I FARRÓ

Lesseps (L3) M

RONDA DE DALT

TORRE BELLESGUARD

SANT GERVASI- LA BONANOVA

el Putxet (L7) M

Plaça Molina (L7)

Pàdua (L7) M

Peu del Funicular

Sant Gervasi (L6)

SANT GERVASI- GALVANY

PASSEIG DE LA BONANOVA

PRIMERO PRIMERA

Muntaner (L6) M

SARRIÀ

RONDA DEL GENERAL MITRE

LES TRES TORRES

Sarrià (L6) M

la Bonanova (L6) M

les Tres Torres (L6)

BAR TOMÁS DE SARRIÀ

MONESTIR DE PEDRALBES

BIKINI

AV. DIAGONAL

CARRER DE NUMÀNCIA

SANTA CLARA

AV. DE PEDRALBES

LES CORTS

PEDRALBES

Maria Cristina (L3) M

RONDA DE DALT

Els Jardins del Palau de Pedralbes

les Corts (L3) M

Plaça del Centre (L3) M

Palau Reial (L3) M

Sants Estació (L3, L5) M

Zona Universitària (L3, L9) M

LA MATERNITAT I SANT RAMON

AV. DE MADRID

ESTACIÓ DE SANTS M

TRAVESSERA DE LES CORTS

SANTS

CAMP NOU

SANTS- BADAL

Plaça de Sants (L5) M

Badal (L5)

CARRER DE SANTS

Plaça de Sants (L1) M

0   0.4 mi

0   0.4 km

© MOON.COM

Vila Olímpica, the former industrial area of Poblenou, the modern conurbation of El Fòrum, and 5 kilometers (3 miles) of golden sands.

SANTS, LES CORTS, AND LA ZONA ALTA

Inland and uptown, this extensive area stretches from the Estació de Sants, Barcelona's main railway station, to the Collserola hillside. Avinguda de Diagonal runs through its heart. The old village of Sants lies to the south, as well as the iconic Camp Nou stadium and the neighborhood of Les Corts. On the upper side of Diagonal, the exclusive residential enclaves of Pedralbes, Sarrià, and Sant Gervasi, known collectively as the Zona Alta, have an entirely different character from the dense downtown districts: lofty, leafy, and with more space to breathe. Greenery filters down from the nearby Parc de Collserola, and Modernista mansions sit beside contemporary condos.

Itinerary Ideas

BARCELONA ON DAY 1

Unravel 2,000 years of history as you delve into the old walled city, the Ciutat Vella.

1 Head straight for **Plaça de Catalunya,** where you can get your bearings while watching the morning buzz from the terrace of Café Zurich. Then set off on a leisurely ramble down La Rambla, taking in the sights and sounds of the city's most famous street.

2 Feast your senses on the glorious produce of the **Mercat de la Boqueria** food market, where anything from swordfish to pigs' trotters are snapped up by local chefs. Grab a stool at the legendary Bar Pinotxo and sample seasonal morsels, fresh from the stalls.

3 Back on **La Rambla,** continue until Joan Miró's Pla de l'Os mosaic appears beneath your feet. Turn left onto Carrer del Cardenal Casañas and lose yourself in the Barri Gòtic.

4 Pass through Plaça del Pi, and into the old Jewish quarter, known as El Call, pausing for thought in **Plaça de Sant Felip Neri.**

5 Emerge opposite the Catedral de la Santa Creu i Santa Eulàlia, then turn right along Carrer del Bisbe until you reach Plaça Sant Jaume, the city's administrative heart. Cross the square and head to the charming Plaça de Sant Just for a classic Catalan lunch at **Cafè de L'Acadèmia.** After lunch, cross Via Laietana to the Ribera district.

Itinerary Ideas

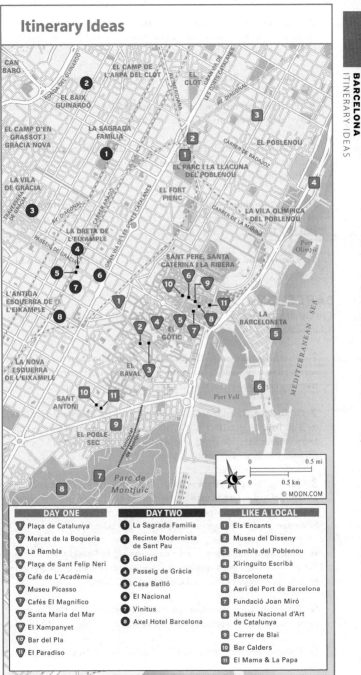

DAY ONE	DAY TWO	LIKE A LOCAL
1 Plaça de Catalunya	1 La Sagrada Família	1 Els Encants
2 Mercat de la Boqueria	2 Recinte Modernista de Sant Pau	2 Museu del Disseny
3 La Rambla	3 Goliard	3 Rambla del Poblenou
4 Plaça de Sant Felip Neri	4 Passeig de Gràcia	4 Xiringuito Escribà
5 Cafè de L'Acadèmia	5 Casa Batlló	5 Barceloneta
6 Museu Picasso	6 El Nacional	6 Aeri del Port de Barcelona
7 Cafés El Magnífico	7 Vinitus	7 Fundació Joan Miró
8 Santa Maria del Mar	8 Axel Hotel Barcelona	8 Museu Nacional d'Art de Catalunya
9 El Xampanyet		9 Carrer de Blai
10 Bar del Pla		10 Bar Calders
11 El Paradiso		11 El Mama & La Papa

6 Trace the roots of a genius at the **Museu Picasso,** the city's most-visited art gallery, where you can compare and contrast the artist's early representational drawings with his twilight works of abstraction.

7 Stop by **Cafés El Magnífico** for a quick pick-me-up *cortado.*

8 Enter the magnificent Gothic basilica of **Santa Maria del Mar** and marvel at its soaring, stripped-back interiors.

9 Celebrate a day well spent with some Catalan bubbles and a plate of jamón at **El Xampanyet,** a traditional bodega that has been serving cava to the locals since 1929.

10 Just a two-minute walk away, choose from a marvelous array of traditional and contemporary tapas in **Bar del Pla,** an old-school tapas den buried in El Born.

11 Finally, wind down with an original cocktail in **El Paradiso,** a hip speakeasy concealed behind a fridge door.

BARCELONA ON DAY 2
Two Gaudí masterpieces, La Sagrada Familia and Casa Batlló, are the highlights today.

1 Start bright and early at **La Sagrada Familia.** Look heavenward at the soaring towers of Gaudí's fantastical masterpiece before marveling as the morning light dapples the temple's interiors with kaleidoscopic colors.

2 Walk along Avinguda de Gaudí until you reach the **Recinte Modernista de Sant Pau,** designed by Lluís Domènech i Montaner, one of Gaudí's contemporaries and rivals. If you would rather skip the crowds of La Sagrada Familia, this is an excellent alternative.

3 Take the metro (L5) from Sant Pau | Dos de Maig to Verdaguer and head toward **Goliard** in Gràcia for a gourmet bistro lunch. En route, walk along Avinguda Diagonal and spot Casa de les Punxes (Avinguda Diagonal, 420) by another master of Modernisme, Josep Puig i Cadafalch.

4 Make your way along Carrer de Bonavista to **Passeig de Gràcia.** Wander down Barcelona's most elegant boulevard, a parade of fin-de-siècle wealth, bourgeoisie houses, and today, high-end shops.

5 Have a coffee or chocolate in Casa Amatller, then visit Gaudí's spectacular **Casa Batlló,** a lavish residence in the heart of Passeig de Gràcia.

6 Continue in style with an aperitif at the grandiose **El Nacional,** a former theater turned food court where you can pair your cava with an oyster or two, if it takes your fancy.

7 Take in some tapas at **Vinitus,** a buzzing bar near Passeig de Gràcia.

8 Finish the day on a high with a drink on one of the city's many hotel rooftop terraces, such as the Sky Bar at the **Axel Hotel Barcelona.**

BARCELONA LIKE A LOCAL

Bargain-hunting and beachfront paella, it's all in a day's work as a Barcelona local.

1 Begin your day with a little bargain-hunting at **Els Encants,** one of the oldest flea markets in Europe.

2 Take a short walk over to the **Museu del Disseny,** a massive arts institution that brings all things design together under one roof.

3 Ramble along the authentic **Rambla del Poblenou,** stopping off for some pre-lunch *patatas bravas* and a cold drink at El 58.

4 Continue to the beach and order up a fresh seafood paella at **Xiringuito Escribà** (reservation recommended).

5 After lunch, dip your toes in the Med and soak up the buzz with a leisurely stroll along the **Barceloneta** beachfront.

6 Jump into the **Aeri del Port de Barcelona** and enjoy unparalleled bird's-eye views over Port Vell as you glide toward Montjuïc.

7 Make a cultural stopoff to admire masterpieces of abstraction at the **Fundació Joan Miró,** dedicated to one of the city's most famous sons.

8 Continue round the mountain until you reach the **Museu Nacional d'Art de Catalunya** overlooking the Font Màgica. Pause to watch the fountains dance as dusk draws in, or witness one of modern architecture's most seminal moments at the Barcelona Pavilion.

9 Tapa-hop along **Carrer de Blai** in Poble-sec, making sure to stop at Quimet & Quimet.

10 Cross Avinguda del Paral·lel and explore Sant Antoni, one of the city's most up-and-coming areas. **Bar Calders** on Carrer de Parlament is a good option to continue eating or drinking.

11 End the day with a bang at **El Mama & La Papa,** where acrobats and drag queens swing from the rafters, and the dance floor fills up after midnight.

Sights

BARRI GÒTIC AND LA RAMBLA

PLAÇA DE CATALUNYA

Metro: Catalunya

This vast central square is where the *Ciutat Vella* (old town) meets the 19th-century gridded city. It's an interchange for all kinds of transport, and a crossroads that virtually all visitors traverse at some point.

Until the 19th century, this was rural land located in front of the city gates. After the medieval walls were demolished and the city was extended, it became a key connection point and a monumental plaza was built ahead of the 1929 International Exposition. At that time, it was a hub of cafés, theaters, and luxury hotels, most of which have since disappeared—with the exception of Café Zurich, a classic rendezvous point at the top of La Rambla.

Today, the square is bordered by chain stores, El Corte Inglés (Spain's primary department store), and a handful of hotels. Two of Barcelona's most prominent streets meet at Plaça de Catalunya—the upscale boulevard of Passeig de Gràcia begins at the northern corner, while the infamous La Rambla extends from the southern side.

On the northwest side of the plaza, two fountains overlook a large oval-shaped central area surrounded by six sculptures, including Josep Maria Subirachs's 1991 monument to the president of the Catalan government, Francesc Macià. Limited greenery and

the broad plaza of Plaça de Catalunya, full of people and pigeons

shaded benches offer a welcome refuge in an otherwise wide-open space, although the square is not somewhere to pause for thought and is largely overrun by pigeons.

Tip: For the best views of Plaça de Catalunya, head to the nith-floor café of El Corte Inglés for a bite to eat and excellent city panoramas.

LA RAMBLA

Metro: Catalunya, Liceu, or Drassanes

"The only street on Earth that I wish would never end"—that's how Spanish poet Federico García Lorca once described Barcelona's most famous street. For centuries the beating heart of city life, this tree-lined pedestrianized boulevard forms the backbone of Barcelona's old town and is buzzing day and night with market stalls, street performers, and throngs of passers-by.

Marking the boundary between the neighborhoods of El Raval and Barri Gòtic, La Rambla runs from Plaça de Catalunya to the Columbus Monument at Port Vell. The 1.2-kilometer (0.7-mile) promenade, flanked on either side by single-lane traffic, is actually a collection of short streets strung together—the Rambla de Canaletes, Rambla dels Estudis, Rambla de Sant Josep (or Rambla de Les Flors), Rambla dels Caputxins, and Rambla de Santa Mònica—which is why it is often referred to in the plural: *Las Ramblas*.

Built along the line of the 13th-century city walls, La Rambla was originally a dry riverbed that acted as a sewer and moat to the walled city, where heavy rainwater flowed down from the Collserola hills and market traders gathered to sell their wares outside the city gates. In the mid-18th century, the wall that ran along La Rambla was demolished, and plans for the infamous boulevard were laid out.

In a crowded city of narrow medieval lanes, the wide tree-lined avenue was an immediate hit. Citizens from every social class came here to breathe in the sights, sounds, and freedom of the vibrant open space. Market stalls thrived, selling anything from books and newspapers to caged birds and fresh flowers. Over the years, it has also seen its fair share of political activism and revolution, as well as fierce fighting during the Spanish Civil War, as described in George Orwell's *Homage to Catalonia* (1938).

The street continued as a focal point for locals well into the late 20th century, but it has changed significantly in the last 25 years. Today, La Rambla is still a hive of activity, although it caters more to tourists than locals. A victim of its own success, it is lined with a mixture of low-quality restaurants, souvenir shops, and high-street chains, and has become a notorious spot for pickpockets and peddlers pushing a whole host of illicit goods. The lively market stalls that once ran the length of the central promenade have been whittled down to a small number of flower sellers, and even the human statues are restricted to the bottom end of the street. Not a stranger to bloodshed in the past, La Rambla suffered its most tragic blow in recent history on August 17, 2017, when a devastating terrorist attack left 16 people dead and many more injured.

Nevertheless, no visit to Barcelona is complete without a ramble down La Rambla. Even if it isn't what it once was, La Rambla embodies a long and eventful history, and big plans are in the pipeline to help it flourish once more. In early 2017, an international

A RAMBLE DOWN LA RAMBLA

Starting at Plaça de Catalunya, spot the following sights as you saunter down La Rambla:

La Rambla

- First stop is the **Font de Canaletes,** a drinking fountain and ornate lamppost situated on the right-hand side of the Rambla de Canaletes, just beyond the entrance to the Catalunya metro station. Legend says that those who drink from the fountain will return to the city, although it is more famous for its association with fans of FC Barcelona, who come here to celebrate after every great victory.

- On the corner of Carrer del Carme stands the 17th-century **Església de la Mare de Déu de Betlem,** a rare example of Baroque religious architecture in the city. Every Christmas, an impressive exhibition of handmade nativity scenes (*pessebres* in Catalan) is held in the basement.

- Opposite the church, on the corner of Carrer de Portaferrissa, is the 18th-century Neoclassical **Palau Moja,** a former palace that now houses a Catalan heritage center, tourist information office, souvenir shop, and cafe. Exit Palau Moja onto Portaferrisa and spot the **Fuente de la Portaferrissa,** a colorful tiled plaque and fountain that pays homage to one of the gates to the medieval walled city, the Porta Ferrissa ("iron gate"), which stood at this point. The plaque depicts daily life at the gates of the walled city in the 18th century.

- Fresh flower stalls line the next section of the street, the **Rambla de Sant Josep,** where the ornate façade of the 17th-century **Palau de la Virreina** is located on the right. Beyond this, **La Boqueria** market is set slightly back on the right, while farther down on the left is the eclectic **Casa Bruno Cuadros.** The façade of this former umbrella shop is a colorful ode to Orientalism.

- Right in the middle of the promenade, halfway down La Rambla, the primary colors of Joan Miró's **Pla de l'Os** mosaic (1976) lie underfoot. Miró chose the spot where the Boqueria gate once stood.

- The next block on the right is the **Gran Teatre del Liceu,** the city's opera house and an important cultural landmark, which opened in 1847. Opposite the theater, the traditional **Café de l'Opera** has been popular with operagoers since 1929.

- A little farther along on the left, **Carrer de Ferran** cuts across the narrow streets of the Gothic Quarter, connecting La Rambla with **Plaça Sant Jaume,** the city's administrative heart, and the 19th-century **Plaça Reial,** filled with palm trees and a convivial atmosphere night and day.

- Back on La Rambla, pause to watch artists at work along the **Rambla dels Caputxins** (named after the Capuchin monastery that once stood on the site of Plaça Reial). Nearby, a statue of Spanish poet **Federico García Lorca** watches over what he once described as "the only street on Earth that I wish would never end, rich in sounds, abundant in breezes, beautiful encounters, ancient blood."

- As the street widens out, human statues and street performers animate the **Rambla de Santa Mònica.** On the right, the **Centre d'Art Santa Mònica** fills a former convent with contemporary art and cultural exhibitions. Finally, the street concludes with the **Columbus Monument** pointing out across the Mediterranean.

design competition was launched with the aim of regaining the avenue for local residents. Pedestrianization and a memorial to the victims of the 2017 attack are among the ideas under discussion, although the project is currently on hold.

✪ MERCAT DE LA BOQUERIA

La Rambla, 91; 93/318-2584;
www.boqueria.barcelona; Mon.-Sat.
8am-8:30pm; metro: Liceu

This bustling fresh food market is a carnival of color, smell, and flavor, with more than 200 stalls selling everything from sheep's heads to live lobster, along with a jaw-dropping array of fresh fish, meat, poultry, cheese, ham, nuts, and salted cod.

Market trading has taken place around this spot since the 13th century, when farmers came from surrounding villages to sell meat at the city gates. After centuries of ad hoc trading, the Mercat de Sant Josep de la Boqueria (its full name) became the first official neighborhood market in Barcelona when it opened in 1840. Initially a sea of temporary stalls assembled on the site of a former convent, the arrangement was gradually formalized with the addition of the iron roof and the stained-glass entrance arch in 1914. Keep an eye out for some of the more traditional stalls that still retain their decorative Modernista ironmongery.

Long a landmark on the Barcelona bucket list, tourists often outnumber local shoppers browsing the market's polychromatic stalls. Consequently, the very character of the market is changing, as ready-made products replace traditional produce in an attempt to cater to the streams of tourists. To support the vendors, make a point of buying an apple, olives, cheese, or jamón, all of which can be

Mercat de la Boqueria

vacuum-packed for the journey home. And if you're staying in an apartment, brave the mesmerising fish counters. That's when you'll really start to feel like a local.

Tip: The legendary **Bar Pinotxo** (93/317-1731; 6:30am-4pm) at the front of the market has been serving breakfast and lunch since 1940 and is a good spot for a traditional bite to eat, although it does get crowded.

GRAN TEATRE DEL LICEU

La Rambla, 51-59; 93/485-9900; www.liceubarcelona.cat; Mon.-Sat. 11am-5pm (times vary, check website for current schedule); standard guided tour €9/€7.50 students, over 65s, and people with disabilites; metro: Liceu

Barcelona's opera house stands proudly in the heart of La Rambla. A Baroque-style, horseshoe-shaped auditorium, decked out in plush red velvet and extravagant gilding, this is the spiritual home of Catalonia's most famous voices and an important cultural landmark in the city.

Built by and for the emerging bourgeoisie in 19th-century Barcelona, the theater opened on April 4, 1847. From the beginning, the building seemed cursed—struck down by fire, bombs, and civil war—yet it has always managed to rise again. The first fire in 1861 all but destroyed the original auditorium, which was subsequently rebuilt by architect Josep Oriol Mestres. Tragedy struck again in 1893, when a young anarchist, Santiago Salvador, threw two Orsini bombs into the stalls, killing 20 and injuring many more. At the time, Barcelona was embroiled in a workers' revolt—a war of the classes— and the Liceu and its patrons were a symbol of the middle class.

Later, parts of the building suffered as a result of heavy bombing during the Spanish Civil War; then, on January 31, 1994, a devastating fire ravaged the auditorium entirely. A huge reconstruction project followed. An exact replica of the auditorium was built (with the addition of modern technology), and the theater reopened in 1999.

Today, the original, eclectic-style lobby continues to welcome theatergoers into the prestigious world of opera. Neoclassical columns, Baroque gilding, and Rococo lights set the tone for the evening as the expectant audience glides up the grand marble staircase to the elegant mirrored ballroom. Tickets to the opera are still a coveted item, but it is undoubtedly the best way to experience the building. **Guided tours** are available between 11am and 4pm (except Sundays). Approximately once per month, the "Liceu Secret Tour" takes tourists backstage, while the "Prestige" tour (Mon.-Sat., 11am, noon) delves inside Spain's oldest private members' club, concealed behind the walls of the Mirror Hall. An integral part of the theater since its inception, the opulent Círculo del Liceo is spread across four floors and includes lounges, libraries, and a room full of priceless paintings by renowned artist Ramon Casas.

PLAÇA REIAL

Metro: Liceu

Although named in honor of the Spanish monarchy, there are no real regal connections to Plaça Reial, Barcelona's royal square. The 19th-century porticoed plaza certainly has an air of majesty, however, with symmetrical Neoclassical façades surrounding the central Font de les Tres Gràcies ("Fountain of Three Graces"), flanked by street lamps designed by a young Antoni Gaudí.

the neo-Gothic Pont del Bisbe (Bishop's Bridge) in the Barri Gòtic

Situated just off La Rambla, this palm tree-filled oasis is built on the site of a former Capuchin convent, its stately design in stark contrast to the narrow streets of the Gothic Quarter. Once choice real estate of the Catalan bourgeoisie, the square became known as a seedy nightlife spot in the second half of the 20th century.

Having reverted to respectability sometime in the early 2000s, today it is one of the city center's most vibrant (and most touristy) spots. Buzzing with busy café terraces, street entertainers, and plenty of people-watching potential during the day, the plaza really comes to life at night, when revelers gather and its rebellious nature surfaces once more. Give the mediocre restaurants a miss and return later on when the party gets started for a cocktail at Ocaña or live jazz at Jamboree.

EL CALL

Barcelona's ancient Jewish quarter, El Call, sits at the very heart of the Barri Gòtic. A tangle of narrow lanes and millennial stone buildings, these are some of the oldest streets in the city and maintain the same urban layout as Roman Barcino. The tiny gaps between the buildings filter out the hustle and bustle of the modern city center, and those who enter the Call feel as though they've slipped away to another century.

Occupied by Barcelona's Jewish population between the 11th and 15th centuries, this was a gated community, although its inhabitants didn't live in isolation. Jews ran market stalls and workshops in the city, farmed land on the Plain of Barcelona, and buried their dead on a nearby mountain, still known today as Montjuïc ("Jew's mountain"). Within the walls of the Call Major, several synagogues formed the center of the community. The Great Synagogue, or Sinagoga Major (Carrer de Sant Domènec, 9; 93/317-0790; www.sinagogamayor. com), was the principal place of worship and is thought to be one of the oldest in Europe. A second Jewish

57

quarter—known as the Call Menor—was built nearby in 1257, though little remains of that today.

Sadly, peaceful coexistence gradually deteriorated into conflict, and the Call was violently attacked in 1391, killing more than 300. One hundred years later, in 1492, the Jews were permanently expelled from Spain by the Catholic Monarchs.

The Call Major extends from Carrer de Call and Carrer dels Banys Nous to Carrer de Sant Honorat and Carrer de Sant Sever. A simple, self-led route through the Call is indicated by informative plaques on the walls. The Museu d'Història de Barcelona (MUHBA) has a small interpretation center, the **Centre d'Interpretació del Call** (Placeta de Manuel Ribé; 93/256-2122; museuhistoria@bcn.cat; Wed. 11am-2pm, Sat.-Sun. 11am-7pm; €2/€1.50 students under 29, over 65s), which showcases everyday objects from the 13th and 14th centuries and an exhibition about medieval Judaism in Barcelona. The center also runs walking tours and discussions.

PLAÇA DE SANT FELIP NERI
Metro: Jaume I

Get lost in the Gothic Quarter and you might just stumble upon Plaça de Sant Felip Neri, a quiet plaza that feels a million miles away from the surrounding city chaos. The baroque **Església de Sant Felip Neri** dominates one side of the square, with the luxurious Hotel Neri standing opposite, oriented around a central octagonal water fountain—an unexpected place to pause for a moment of peace, just a stone's throw from the busy Carrer de Bisbal, the Cathedral, and Plaça Nova.

Although beautifully quaint on the surface, the pockmarked church façade hints at a darker past. During the Spanish Civil War, two Fascist bombs killed 42 people, mostly children, in January 1938. A couple of plaques commemorate the atrocity. Other accounts allege that executions by firing squad also occurred here.

Today Plaça de Sant Felip Neri is the picture of tranquility, except during recess at the local school, when children's laughter fills the air. Carlos Ruiz Zafón fans take note: This is where Nuria Monfort lived, one of the characters from *The Shadow of the Wind*. Zafón describes it as a "small breathing space in the maze of streets that crisscross the Gothic Quarter."

PLAÇA SANT JAUME
Metro: Jaume I or Liceu

The administrative heart of Barcelona and Catalonia, two imposing powerhouses stand on opposite sides of Plaça Sant Jaume. On the northern side, the **Palau de la Generalitat** is the seat of the presidency and the Catalan government, while across the square, the **Casa de la Ciutat**, or City Hall, is the meeting place of the city council. Look for the four columns that surround the entrance to Palau de la Generalitat—they come from a Roman temple in Tarragona and date from the 2nd century. The site has long since been the city's political center. In Roman Barcino, the forum and the **Temple of Augustus** were located here, the remains of which can be visited nearby. The square's current layout dates from 1823.

The square itself is an important hub of city life. It often reflects the population's frame of mind, whether there's a celebratory parade of giant statues (*gegants*) or human castles (*castells*) during the annual Mercè and Santa Eulàlia festivals, or an impassioned political demonstration.

✪ LA CATEDRAL DE LA SANTA CREU I SANTA EULÀLIA

Pla de la Seu; 93/342-8262; www. catedralbcn.org; Mon.-Sat. 8am-7:30pm; entry €6 Mon.-Sat. 1pm-5pm, Sun. 2pm-5pm, free at all other times; metro: Jaume I

Barcelona's Cathedral is dedicated to the co-patron saint of the city, Santa Eulàlia, who was martyred during the persecution of Christians at the age of 13. The Cathedral of the Holy Cross and Saint Eulalia, also known as *La Seu*, overlooks Plaça Nova in the heart of the Barri Gòtic.

The site has long since been sacred ground. An early-Christian basilica was built here during the 4th century, replaced by a Visigothic chapel that al-Mansur's Moorish troops destroyed in 985. In the 11th century, a Romanesque church reestablished the site as a place of worship; the chapel of Santa Llúcia dates from that time. The present cathedral was constructed over the course of 150 years, between 1298 and 1448, although the principal neo-Gothic façade and bell tower were added in the late 19th century. Work was finally completed in 1913.

Though the intricate façade and mythical gargoyles recall the northern European Gothic, elsewhere the cathedral is grounded in the Catalan Gothic tradition, evident in its scant decoration and octagonal towers. An outer aisle flanks the entire perimeter, where 25 side chapels are dedicated to various religious figures. Spot the Holy Christ of Lepanto, a crucifix in the chapel of the Holy Sacrament, just to the right of the main entrance. Legend says that this cross was carried into the Battle of Lepanto in 1571, and that the Lord dodged a cannonball mid-battle, which explains his crooked stance.

Plaça Sant Jaume

Situated in the middle of the central nave, the beautiful wooden choir stalls of the Knights of the Golden Fleece are a must-see; the order met here before Emperor Charles V in 1519. Downstairs, the tomb of Santa Eulàlia is housed in the crypt; note the reliefs on the alabaster sarcophagus, which depict some of her tortures. Finally, don't miss the 14th-century cloister (Mon.-Sat. 8:30am-12:30pm, 5:15pm-7pm, Sun. 8:30am-1pm, 5:15pm-7pm)—a magnificent Gothic space filled with palm trees and a delightful fountain, where 13 geese roam free, one for each year of Santa Eulàlia's life.

Outside, Plaça Nova lies before the Cathedral's principal façade. Once the site of the city's hay market, one of the gates to the Roman city stood here, flanked by two circular towers and the ancient city walls. Some of this composition can still be spotted in the walls of the Casa de l'Ardiaca (Archdeacon's House; Carrer de Santa Llúcia, 1). A replica of a section of Roman aqueduct also emerges from the side of the house. On the opposite side of the square, a 1960s tower block houses the Col·legi de Arquitectes de Catalunya (the Catalan institute of architects). The giant, child-like scribbles on the frieze around its façade are the work of Picasso.

MUSEU D'HISTÒRIA DE BARCELONA (MUHBA)

Plaça del Rei; 93/256-2100;
www.museuhistoria.bcn.cat; Tues.-Sat.
10am-7pm, Sun. 10am-8pm; €7/€5 students
under 29 and over 65s/free under 16;
entrance free to all on the first Sunday of
the month; all other Sundays free after 3pm;
metro: Jaume I

The Museu d'Història de Barcelona (MUHBA) is a citywide group of museums, made up of 14 independent heritage spaces. Plaça del Rei is the museum's first site and headquarters, and traces the evolution of the city from its Iberian origins through to the Middle Ages. Visitors roll back the clock 2,000 years as they descend beneath the medieval square and emerge onto the streets of Roman Barcino, founded by the Emperor Augustus in AD 10. Four thousand square meters (43,000 square feet) of archaeological remains, dating from the 1st to the 7th century AD, were uncovered here in 1931. Visitors can follow the still-intact street layout through a district of factories and workshops, including a 2nd-century laundry and fabric-dyeing workshop, a 3rd-century factory for salting fish (*cetaria*), and a winemaking facility.

Leaving the Roman era behind, the count's palace houses a permanent exhibition on Barcelona in the Middle Ages (8th-13th centuries). Upstairs, the visit concludes with the Palau Reial Major.

Other MUHBA spaces across the city include El Call, Santa Catarina, Refugi 307, Park Güell, and Turó de la Rovira, among others. The entrance ticket to the Plaça del Rei museum grants access to all MUHBA sites for one year, with the exception of Park Güell (a 21 percent discount is applied there instead).

PALAU REIAL MAJOR

Plaça del Rei; €7; metro: Jaume I

The medieval Palau Reial Major, former residence of the Counts of Barcelona and monarchs of Aragón, dominates two sides of Plaça del Rei. A grand staircase leads up to the Gothic palace in the corner of the square, and is said to be the spot where a triumphant Columbus relayed his discoveries to King Ferdinand II of Aragon and Queen Isabel I of Castile upon returning from his maiden voyage to the New World.

The palace comprises a complex of medieval buildings, including the Saló del Tinell, a grand banqueting hall on the left-hand side of the staircase, above which the 16th-century watchtower of King Martí presides over events. On the other side of the staircase, the 14th-century Chapel of Santa Àgata is built on top of the Roman wall.

The royal complex forms part of the MUHBA, accessed via the 16th-century Casa Padellás, which sits on the eastern side of the square and was moved here, stone by stone, from Carrer Mercaders in 1931. Opposite the chapel, the 16th-century Palau del Lloctinent (Lieutenant's Palace) was built as a residence for the viceroy of Catalonia and later became a convent. It has housed the Archive of the Crown of Aragon since the 19th century and also runs temporary cultural exhibitions. Make sure you wander through its peaceful Renaissance-style patio. Look up above the main staircase to catch a glimpse of an intricate carved wooden ceiling.

TEMPLE OF AUGUSTUS

Carrer Paradís, 10; 93/256-2122;
Mon. 10am-2pm, Tues.-Sat. 10am-7pm, Sun.
10am-8pm; free; metro: Jaume I

The unassuming and wonderfully named Carrer del Paradís (Paradise Street), a narrow passage in the Barri Gòtic, takes you into a small medieval courtyard that is home to one of Barcelona's most surprising hidden gems—the remains of the Roman Temple of Augustus. At over 2,000 years old, the remains are around the same age as Barcelona itself.

The four gigantic stone columns

(now made all the more colossal by lying within this small courtyard, surrounded by buildings) are all that remain of the temple, built in the early 1st century BC as part of the forum in the Roman city of Barcino. The columns are 9 meters (30 feet) high and would have once surrounded the entire building. The remains of the temple were discovered in the 19th century and today are part of the Barcelona City History Museum (MUHBA).

Columbus Monument

COLUMBUS MONUMENT

Plaça del Portal de la Pau; 93/285-3832;
info@barcelonaturisme.com;
8:30am-7:30pm daily; €6; metro: Drassanes

The Columbus Monument is an iconic landmark on the Barcelona skyline. Standing atop a 60-meter (200-foot) Corinthian column at the bottom of La Rambla, a bronze statue of Christopher Columbus points purposefully out to sea. Contrary to local folklore, he is pointing neither in the direction of America nor his hometown of Genoa, but more in a southeasterly direction.

Designed by architect Gaietà Buïgas

for the 1888 Universal Exposition, the monument honors the explorer's life and expeditions: Barcelona, after all, was the intrepid Italian's first port of call upon returning from his maiden voyage to the Americas. Some *Barceloneses* are not so keen to celebrate the city's colonial connections, however. In 2017, a radical left-wing political party proposed the removal of the Columbus Monument. The proposal has, so far, been rejected by the city council, although some imperialist monuments have been removed in recent years.

A lift inside the column takes visitors to a viewing gallery inside the crown, just below Columbus, offering impressive 360-degree views of La Rambla, the city, and the port. At the sculptural base of the monument are reliefs that tell the story of Columbus's discoveries. Spot the decorative line of cannabis leaves on the upper part of the column—an ode to the plant's role in maritime history. Hemp was used for making ropes and sails, oil was extracted to keep lamps alight, and seeds were stored as a food reserve. A little "sea-weed" may also have helped Columbus to keep calm amid high seas.

EL RAVAL

PALAU GÜELL

Carrer Nou de la Rambla, 3-5; 93/472-5771; palauguell.cat; Apr.-Oct. Tues.-Sun. 10am-8pm, Nov.-Mar. Tues.-Sun. 10am-5:30pm; €12/€9 students and EU citizens over 65; metro: Drassanes

Palau Güell marked the beginning of a long and fruitful relationship between Eusebi Güell and Antoni Gaudí. Güell, a pioneering industrialist and politician, sought out the young architect after seeing a cabinet designed by Gaudí at the Paris World Fair, and

commissioned him to create this extraordinary residence on an unassuming street just off La Rambla. Güell went on to be Gaudí's greatest client and one of his closest friends.

This was one of Gaudí's first major commissions as a recent graduate, though it contains the essence of his prodigious architectural talent. The magnificent six-story mansion was built between 1886 and 1890 and, like many of his early works, reveals Moorish influences. An austere, symmetrical façade gives way to an innovative interior, where lavish materials and a seemingly limitless budget were used to create a flowing sequence of spaces.

trencadís tiling on Palau Güell's rooftop terrace

At ground level, two parabolic gates open into a grand, marble-lined vestibule and coach house, from which horses were led down a ramp to the stables in the brick-vaulted basement. Look for the quirky tethering rings and mushroom-shaped columns that support the entire structure above. Back on the ground floor, a central staircase ascends to the main floor, where the palace's showpiece central hall is located. Concerts and religious ceremonies were held in this three-story space crowned by a parabolic dome, which formed the social hub of the palace. The upper floors are oriented around the hall and contain bedrooms once occupied by Güell, his wife Isabel Lòpez, and their 10 children.

exterior of the ancient Antic Hospital

Though more straight lines are employed here than in Gaudí's later work, the architectural genius tested many imaginative solutions in Palau Güell that later became part of his emblematic style. The parabolic arch, a geometric shape that has a consistent presence in Gaudí's oeuvre, is used extensively throughout the mansion, from the wrought-iron gates to the central hall. Gaudí's high regard for the crafts and his close working relationship with artisans is also evident in the highly original decorative details formed in wrought iron, glass, stone, ceramics, and wood; don't miss the intricate coffered ceilings on the main floor and the masterful ironmongery throughout. But probably the most recognizable Gaudí moment comes on the rooftop, where he used his trademark *trencadís* tiling for the first time—a method of mosaic made from broken tiles—to adorn the many

chimney stacks, in a precursor of the celebrated terrace of La Pedrera.

The illustrious Güell Lòpez family lived here until they moved to Park Güell in 1907. In 1945, it was given to the provincial council by the family and was declared a UNESCO World Heritage Site in 1984. A major restoration project was completed between 2004 and 2011, during which time the building was closed to the public. Today, visitors can access all floors and an informative audio guide is included with the entrance ticket.

ANTIC HOSPITAL DE LA SANTA CREU

Carrer de l'Hospital, 56; metro: Liceu

The 15th-century Antic Hospital de la Santa Creu is one of the finest examples of Catalan civil-Gothic architecture. Built in 1401, this complex of buildings was the city's main hospital for over five centuries before it relocated to Hospital Sant Pau in 1926. One of its last patients was Antoni Gaudí, who died here after being hit by a tram.

Enter from Carrer de l'Hospital into a quiet courtyard, with a Baroque cross at its center and the pretty orange tree-lined garden, Jardins de Rubió i Lluch, at the far end. The first floor of the surrounding buildings is home to the Biblioteca de Catalunya, the national library (access restricted). Across from the library's entrance, El Jardí café (93/681-9234; 10am-midnight daily) is a hidden oasis—stop for a coffee or a quick bite.

Continue through the gardens in the direction of Carrer del Carme to reach the Reial Acadèmia de Medicina de Catalunya (Royal Academy of Medicine). Inside the 18th-century Neoclassical building is one of the best-preserved anatomical amphitheaters in Europe, complete with marble dissecting table. A guided tour (in Catalan) takes place on Wednesdays and Saturdays at 10.30am, 11.30am and 12.30pm. An English audio guide is available.

As you exit the complex onto Carrer del Carme, look for a peculiar array of signs and symbols inscribed around the stone archway—some of the oldest examples of graffiti in Barcelona. Back on Carrer de l'Hospital, the 15th-century hospital chapel is now a contemporary art space, **La Capella** (93/256-2044; lacapella.bcn.cat; Tues.-Sat. noon-8pm, Sun. 11am-2pm), which provides a platform for up-and-coming artists.

MUSEU D'ART CONTEMPORANI DE BARCELONA (MACBA)

Plaça dels Àngels, 1; 93/481-3368; www. macba.cat; Mon., Wed.-Fri., 11am-7:30pm, Sat. 10am-8pm, Sun. 10am-3pm; €10/€5 students and over 65s; free Sat. 4pm-8pm; metro: Catalunya or Universitat

There's something almost supernatural about the blinding white planes and prisms of Barcelona's Contemporary Art Museum (MACBA), which seems to levitate amid the densely populated streets of Raval. A bold architectural and urban design statement, the MACBA was a central element in the city's regeneration plan for the neighborhood and acted as a key catalyst for change when it opened in 1995.

The museum's collection traces the evolution of contemporary art since

Museu d'Art Contemporani de Barcelona (MACBA)

the mid-20th century and includes approximately 5,000 works by Spanish, Catalan, and international artists—from Miró and Tàpies to Hockney, Hamilton, and today's foremost artists. There is no permanent exhibition; works from the collection are curated into temporary exhibitions that change periodically, each one presenting a new discourse or vision of contemporary art. A complimentary tour in English takes place on Mondays at 4pm.

Richard Meier's assemblage of interlocking volumes is not just a container for art, but a sculptural work of art in and of itself. Light seeps into the atrium through open galleries and skylights, highlighting the geometric Corbusier-inspired composition. Outside, an international crew of skateboarders animates the public realm day and night. Don't miss Keith Haring's red linear mural, *Todos juntos podemos parar el sida* (Together we can stop AIDS), located on a concrete wall around the left side of the building. This is a reconstruction of a 1989 mural that Haring painted in nearby Plaça de Salvador Seguí.

On the other side of Plaça del Àngels, the 16th-century Convent dels Àngels holds additional exhibition space. The Gothic nave and adjoining Peu de la Creu chapel (La Capella) are imposing, solemn spaces, contrasting the modern character of the main building.

CENTRE DE CULTURA CONTEMPORÀNIA DE BARCELONA (CCCB)

Carrer de Montalegre, 5; 93/306-4100; www.cccb.org; Tues.-Sun. 11am-8pm; €6/€4 under 25s and over 65s; free Sundays after 3pm; metro: Catalunya or Universitat

The challenges of 21st-century society. The advent of new social and political models. The intersection of art, science, humanities, and technology. These are just some of the thematic lines explored at the CCCB, Barcelona's center for contemporary culture. A space for creation, research, exhibition, and debate, the diverse, interdisciplinary program includes some of the city's most thought-provoking temporary exhibitions, covering all kinds of subject matter, from climate change and philosophy to the annual World Press Photo show. Complementary activities run alongside the exhibitions, as well as regular debate and performing-arts series. It is well worth checking out what's on when you're in town.

Situated alongside the MACBA (Barcelona's Museum of Contemporary Art), the CCCB is housed within the Casa de Caritat buildings, a former almshouse for the city's poor, which operated from 1802 until 1957. From the main gate, visitors proceed through to the Pati de les Dones, a pleasant outdoor square enclosed on three sides by the original building, with a clever stark, mirrored façade on the final side. Entry into the building itself is via a ramp that descends underneath the plaza. On the far side of the complex there's a larger, more open square—Plaça de Joan Coromines—with a café terrace and a theater space connected to the center.

Occasional concerts take place in the Pati de les Dones, as well as an outdoor film festival, known as *Gandules*, throughout August. On select Sundays throughout the year, there is free access to the Sala Mirador on the fifth floor, which offers magnificent city views (check the website for dates). Finally, pop your head in next door at the Pati Manning, a 17th-century cloister with semicircular arches and *sgraffito* on the walls; it's a historic space that juxtaposes the modern cultural complex.

RAMBLA DEL RAVAL
Metro: Liceu or Paral·lel

Lined by palm trees and café terraces, Rambla del Raval brings some much-needed breathing space to its densely populated surroundings. A number of streets and dilapidated buildings were cleared in 2000 to make way for this leafy boulevard running from Carrer de Sant Pau to Carrer de l'Hospital, where the local residents sit and watch the world go by, and markets and cultural events pop up sporadically. The introduction of this central artery acted as a catalyst for gentrification in the surrounding area, though Raval is still distinctly edgy. The highlight here is Fernando Botero's fat cat sculpture, which has become a symbol of the area. (This is one of two rotund creatures by the Colombian artist in the city; the other is a horse and lives in Terminal 2 at Barcelona-El Prat Airport.)

ESGLÉSIA DE SANT PAU DEL CAMP
Carrer de Sant Pau, 101; 93/441-0001;
www.santpaudelcamp.info; Mon.-Fri.
9:30am-12:30pm, 3:30pm-6:30pm, Sat.
9:30am-12:30pm; €3; metro: Paral·lel

Hemmed in by the densely populated streets of Raval, it's hard to imagine that the church of Sant Pau del Camp, meaning "St. Paul in the Fields," was once located beyond the city walls, surrounded by agricultural land. Built in the 10th century as part of a Benedictine monastery, this is the oldest surviving church in Barcelona and one of the best-preserved examples of the Catalan Romanesque.

Over the course of its long and eventful history, it has been a place of worship, a safe haven, a school, a hospital, and an inspiration to many, including a young Pablo Picasso, who produced sketches and paintings of the cloister. These thick stone walls have suffered as a consequence of various historic moments, from the onslaught of Al Mansur's troops in 985 to the arson attacks of Catalonia's tragic week in 1909 and the Spanish Civil War in 1936, and have been reconstructed many times. A medley of elements representing different styles and time periods, including Visigothic marble capitals on the main façade, can be spotted amid the Romanesque structure.

An austere yet intimate space, the medieval church has a simple cross-shaped floor plan and an impressive acoustic. The real gem here, however, is the tiny, 12th-century cloister, shrouded in symbolism. A combination of Romanesque and Moorish styles, the 48 capitals that support the arches are decorated with geometrical and plant-like motifs. Look out for Adam and Eve standing next to the tree with the serpent, and a woman being tormented by two toads.

Tip: Classical music recitals are regularly held in the church and are a lovely alternative way to experience the space. Ask for details.

LA RIBERA/EL BORN
✪ SANTA MARÍA DEL MAR
Plaça de Santa Maria, 1; 93/310-2390;
www.santamariadelmarbarcelona.org;
Mon.-Sat. 9am-8:30pm, Sun. 10am-8pm;
cultural visits Mon.-Sat. 1pm-5pm, Sun.
2pm-5pm; €10 during visiting hours, free at
other times; Sunday mass at noon, daily at
7:30pm; metro: Jaume I or Barceloneta

Santa Maria del Mar may not be

Barcelona's most famous church, but it is arguably its most beautiful. Built in just 54 years (1329-1383)—record timing for a medieval church of this stature—Santa Maria del Mar is one of the finest examples of Catalan Gothic architecture, exemplifying an unusually unified style thanks to its speedy build time. Its bulky, austere shell belies a light and spacious interior, where exacting proportions and svelte octagonal columns combine to create a soaring symphony in stone.

Santa Maria del Mar

A place of worship is thought to have existed on this site since the 7th century, or even earlier. In the 14th century, the basilica of Santa Maria del Mar ("Our Lady of the Sea") was conceived in the context of a flourishing neighborhood, known for its shipbuilding, mercantile trading, and artisan workshops. The construction of the church was a joint effort by the people of La Ribera, the guilds, and, above all, the *bastaixos* (porters) and fishermen who transported the stone, block by block, from nearby Montjuïc:

Look for the relief dedicated to them above the door.

The main entrance opens onto Plaça de Santa Maria and is dominated by a great rose window, which was destroyed during an earthquake in 1428 and rebuilt soon after. The imposing interior is composed of three aisles, defined by two rows of columns set 13 meters (43 feet) apart—the largest span in any existing medieval building. The side aisles are half the span of the central nave, and the overall width is exactly the same as the height—proportions based on *ad quadratum* geometry—resulting in a dramatic sense of space and verticality.

Small chapels dedicated to various saints line the nave and apse, though the stone walls and rib-vaulted ceiling are noticeably devoid of religious iconography. This is partly due to a devastating arson attack in July 1936, when the church burned for 11 days. Miraculously, the structure and upper-level stained glass windows survived.

Between 1pm and 5pm, visitors pay to enter and can access the church, museum, galleries, and crypt (€10). There is also a guided tour of the towers and rooftop available (€8). Church services are open to the public; check if there are any concerts scheduled to experience the building's excellent acoustics. If that leaves you feeling inspired, the bestselling historical novel *La Catedral del Mar* (*Cathedral of the Sea*) by Ildefonso Falcones is based on the construction of the basilica, and was adapted by Netflix in 2018.

ESTACIÓ DE FRANÇA

Avinguda del Marquès de l'Argentera;
90/232-0320; www.renfe.es;
5am-midnight daily; metro: Barceloneta

Arriving by train to the Estació de

El Born Center de Cultura i Memòria

França is something special. A fine example of wrought-iron architecture, it's a shame that this isn't the city's main railway station. Opened in 1848 and rebuilt for the 1929 International Exposition, the station served as the main terminus for trains arriving from the Costa Brava and France, as the name suggests. Passengers enter into an ornate lobby embellished with marble and bronze before proceeding through to the platforms, enclosed by a curved metal and glass canopy that floods the space with natural light. Few trains run from the station today, but it's worth taking a peek inside this elegant, 20th-century edifice—a monument to the golden age of rail travel.

EL BORN CENTER DE CULTURA I MEMÒRIA

Plaça Comercial, 12; 93/256-6851; elbornculturaimemoria.barcelona.cat; Tues.-Sun. 10am-8pm; free/€4.40 for exhibitions; metro: Barceloneta

This cultural center located in the former Mercat del Born opens a window to the past—more specifically, to the War of Succession and its impact on the city. Following the siege and fall of Barcelona in 1714, a large portion of La Ribera was destroyed to make way for Philip V's nearby Ciutadella fortress (most of which no longer stands). Mercat del Born, a neighborhood market, was constructed over the destroyed area in the 19th century. Inaugurated in 1876, the Mercat del Born served the city for 95 years, until 1971. In 2002, work began to convert it into a library. When the site was excavated, however, archaeologists uncovered the medieval remains of entire streets, houses, and a treasure trove of artifacts that, together, paint a vivid scene of city life in the early 1700s, as well as the consequences of the 1714 siege.

The cultural center opened its doors on September 11, 2013. Access is free to the large central area, which overlooks the ruins and is lined with excellent explanatory panels about both the market building and the War of Succession. Visitors can also roam the ruins below street level as part of a guided tour (Tues.-Sun. 4:30pm, €6). The Sala Villarroel (€4.40) contains a collection of archaeologists' findings from the site, including porcelain vases, Oriental textiles, cooking implements, and legal documents.

PARC DE LA CIUTADELLA

Passeig de Picasso, 21;
www.bcn.cat/parcsijardins; 10am-10:30pm
daily; metro: Ciutadella Vila Olímpica or Arc
de Triomf; bus H14, H16

As well as lush grassy areas and plentiful palm trees, this 70-acre park is home to the Palau del Parlament de Catalunya (the Catalan parliament building), a monumental fountain, a lake, several museum buildings, and the city zoo.

The park takes its name from the military citadel that once stood here, a gargantuan fortress constructed by Philip V following the city's defeat in the 1714 Siege of Barcelona. Catalans hated the citadel, regarding it as a symbol of oppression. When it was torn down in 1869, the area was converted into a park, and later became the focal point of activity during the International Exposition of 1888. The park's layout and many of its structures date from that time.

Josep Fontserè, with the help of a young Antoni Gaudí, designed the ornate fountain situated in the northern corner of the park between 1875 and 1881. Loosely modeled on Rome's Trevi Fountain, a series of pools, rocks, and winged dragons surround Venus emerging from a shell. Climb the stairs on either side of the fountain to catch an aerial view of the park. Nearby, there's a bandstand, which comes alive with swing dancing on Sunday evenings (first and third Sunday of the month, 6pm-8:30pm; free) for an

Parc de la Ciutadella

informal, outdoor meetup, and a small boating lake.

Across the lake are the remaining buildings of the citadel, where today, ironically, the Catalan Parliament meets inside the former arsenal building. In front of the parliament, Josep Llimona's 1907 sculpture of a distressed female figure, Desconsol, is the focal point in the formal garden of Plaça d'Armes.

On the Passeig de Picasso side of the park is a series of buildings that were built for the International Exposition. The Modernista Castell dels Dracs ("Castle of the Three Dragons") is the most impressive and greets visitors at the main entrance gate. Designed by Domènech i Montaner, this fanciful faux-castle initially served as a café during the 1888 event, and then housed the Museum of Zoology until that was relocated to the Edifici Fòrum in 2010. As of 2019, the building is undergoing renovations. Next up, the defunct Hivernacle (greenhouse) sits just inside the park's side entrance, followed by the former Museum of Geology, a Neoclassical structure designed by Antoni Rovira i Trias in 1882. Finally, the Umbracle—the only Exposition building that continues to function—is a steel-and-brick structure with a slatted roof that houses tropical plants (93/402-7000; Mon.-Fri. 10am-3pm). The city zoo occupies the rest of the park.

A leisurely stroll to take in the park's main highlights is doable in half an hour. Bring a blanket and picnic for some time out here during the week. On weekends, every man and his dog are here—from jugglers and drummers, to yogis and young families—and there's generally a carnival atmosphere. Look up and spot the lime-green parakeets, an unlikely, noisy settler from lands afar.

✪ MUSEU PICASSO

Carrer Montcada, 15-23; 93/256-3000; www.bcn.cat/museupicasso; Mon. 10am-5pm, Tues.-Sun. 9am-8:30pm (Thurs. until 9:30pm); €12/€7 18-25-year-olds and over 65s; free Thurs. 6pm-9:30pm and first Sunday of the month; metro: Jaume I

Pablo Ruíz Picasso moved to Barcelona in 1895, aged 13, marking the beginning of a powerful connection with the city that would last a lifetime. The Museu Picasso is a celebration of that relationship, and with over 4,250 works by the Malaga-born master, it is one of the most extensive collections of his work anywhere. Founded in 1963 by Picasso's longtime friend and secretary Jaume Sabartés, this was the first museum dedicated to the artist and the only one to open during his lifetime. The collection focuses on his formative years, so don't expect to find his most famous paintings here. It does, however, give a comprehensive insight into the development of a genius and the foundations of his illustrious career.

The visit starts with sketches and oil paintings dating from 1890-1895, including several portraits that demonstrate tremendous talent even for a teenager. Next, Picasso opens a window to fin-de-siècle Barcelona with atmospheric sketches and paintings from around the city. His early days in Paris follow, with the Blue Period (1901-1904) and Rose Period (1904-1906), before jumping back to Barcelona with works that recall the artist's extended stay here in 1917. A small number of paintings fill the gap between this and the 1957 "Las Meninas" series—Picasso's deconstructed interpretation of the

Mercat de Santa Caterina

Velazquez masterpiece, displayed here in its entirety. The collection concludes with creations from the Cubist master's twilight years, including his dove paintings, engravings, and ceramics.

The museum is located in five adjoining medieval palaces along Carrer de Montcada in El Born. The pretty courtyards, arcades, coffered ceilings, and grand staircases of the stone-built Gothic residences, dating from the 13th and 14th centuries, make a unique setting worth a visit in itself.

Book online—this is the city's most-visited art gallery and it has a limited capacity. Guided tours in English give an excellent synopsis of both the collection and its historic setting (Wed. 3pm, Thurs. 7pm, Sun. 11am; €6).

MERCAT DE SANTA CATERINA

Avinguda de Francesc Cambó, 16;
93/319-5740; Mon., Wed., and Sat.
7:30am-3:30pm, Tues., Thurs., and Fri.
7:30am-8:30pm; metro: Jaume I

The theatrical roof of the Mercat de Santa Caterina is the work of one of the city's modern-day masters, Enric Miralles (1955-2000), and his wife Benedetta Tagliabue, who together formed the EMBT architecture studio. An undulating magic carpet of color, the roof's glazed ceramic surface—made up of 325,000 hexagonal tiles in 67 colors—is a modern take on Gaudí's trademark *trencadís* tiling and derives its palette from the myriad hues of the fruit and vegetable market stalls within.

Originally the site of a 13th-century convent—the remains of which can be viewed at the back of the market in a space managed by the MUHBA (93/256-2122; Mon.-Sat. 8:30am-3:30pm; free)—the neoclassical food market was built in the mid-19th century and was renovated by EMBT between 1997 and 2005. Inside, tree-like steel columns support a rolling timber ceiling, beneath which a wondrous variety of fresh produce tempts the senses. Sample it at the ever-popular

Cuines Santa Caterina on the corner of the market, or try the low-key, locals' favorite, Bar Joan, situated inside, next to the ruins.

PALAU DE LA MÚSICA CATALANA

Carrer Palau de la Música, 4-6;
93/295-7200; www.palaumusica.cat;
10am-3pm daily; €20; metro: Urquinaona

The Palau de la Música Catalana was built between 1905 and 1908 by Lluís Domènech i Montaner, master of Catalan Modernisme. No expense was spared in the creation of this steel-framed music box, funded by local industrialists and music aficionados, and it soon became a symbol of Catalan identity and a focal point for the cultural movement of the time.

The lavish concert hall is richly adorned inside and out with decorative art created by local artisans and craftsmen. The exquisite façade fuses Catalan and Arabic motifs, articulated through brick, ironwork, nature-inspired mosaics, colorful stained glass, glazed ceramic tiling, and sculptures of a whole host of heroes, from local musicians to Catalan patron Sant Jordi (St. George).

Inside, a grand foyer and staircase leads visitors up to the 2,146-seat concert hall, a temple of light, color, and sound. The pièce de résistance is, undoubtedly, the inverted stained-glass dome, which represents a radiant sun and illuminates the concert hall with natural light. As with all Modernisme or Art Nouveau creations, nature is never far away and organic forms and natural motifs, including the rose of Sant Jordi, are embedded into the intricate decor.

Guided tours in English take place every day on the hour from 10am until 3pm, and include a short video in the rehearsal room followed by a visit to the concert hall and a brief recital on the 3,000-pipe German organ. The best way to see this musical masterpiece, however, is to experience it as a member of the audience. With more than 300 performances per year, ranging from symphonic and chamber music to jazz and flamenco, there are plenty to choose from.

ARC DE TRIOMF

Passeig de Lluís Companys;
metro: Arc de Triomf

Unlike many triumphal arches across Europe, Barcelona's Arc de Triomf is a civil, rather than military, monument. The 30-meter-high (98-foot) arch doesn't honor any specific victory, and was actually designed by Catalan architect Josep Vilaseca as the main entrance for the Universal Exposition of 1888, which took place in the nearby Parc de la Ciutadella.

The red-brick landmark stands prominently at the top of Passeig de Lluís Companys. The abundant sculptural and decorative finishes teem with symbolism pertaining to agriculture, science, arts, industry, and commerce. On the façade facing Passeig de Sant Joan, a frieze depicts Barcelona welcoming the nations to the Expo, while the frieze facing the park shows medals being presented to participants. Around the top of the arch, the shields of the 49 Spanish provinces are presided over by a larger Barcelona coat of arms.

From here, it's a pleasant stroll to the Parc de la Ciutadella along the palm tree-lined Passeig de Lluís Companys, which is popular with cyclists, skaters, and street artists. At the park end of the promenade, there's a map of the medieval old town (pre-1714) painted on the floor.

FOSSAR DE LES MORERES

Plaça del Fossar de les Moreres; metro:
Jaume I or Barceloneta

An eternal flame burns over the Fossar de les Moreres ("Cemetery of the Mulberry Trees") in honor of those who lost their lives during the year-long Siege of Barcelona. This poignant memorial square was originally a cemetery serving the adjacent basilica of Santa Maria del Mar, before it became a mass grave during the siege.

In 1989, the buildings that had been constructed here in the intervening period were demolished to create a symbolic space of remembrance: a sunken square, paved in red brick, that slopes gently down toward the steel torch sculpture, which was added in 2001. A low, red granite wall runs along the west side of the square, inscribed with the words of Catalan poet Frederic Soler: "In the graveyard of the mulberry trees no traitor shall be buried; even if our flags are lost, it will be the urn of honor." The poem refers to the story of a gravedigger who refused to bury his son here after he defected to the opposition.

The city fell on September 11, 1714, and every year on Catalonia's national day, which commemorates the defeat, thousands flock to the square to pay homage to the victims.

BARCELONA ZOO

Parc de la Ciutadella; 93/706-5656;
www.zoobarcelona.cat; Oct. 26-Mar. 29
10am-5pm daily, Mar. 30-May 15 and Sept.
16-Oct. 25 10am-6pm, May 16-Sept. 15
10am-7pm; €22/€13 children aged 3-12 /€11
over 65/€6 people with disabilities/free for
children under 3; metro: Ciutadella Vila
Olímpica

Made famous by Snowflake the albino gorilla, who lived here from 1966 until 2003, Barcelona Zoo opened in 1892 and occupies a large portion of the Parc de la Ciutadella. More than 7,000 animals from 400 species call the zoo home, from African elephants to sea lions and tropical birds. It's an ideal place for a family day out; spot the elusive Komodo dragon, mingle with amphibians in the impressive reptile house, or get hands-on at the petting zoo. The popular dolphin show was outlawed in 2015, and the zoo's collection is set to change quite dramatically over the next decade as it shifts its focus toward Mediterranean animals and endangered species. Discounts available online.

L'EIXAMPLE

TOP EXPERIENCE

✪ LA SAGRADA FAMÍLIA

Carrer de Mallorca, 401; tel. 93/208-0414;
www.sagradafamilia.org; Nov.-Feb.
9am-6pm daily, Mar. 9am-7pm, Apr.-Sept.
9am-8pm, Oct. 9am-7pm; basic ticket €15,
audioguided visit €22, guided experience
€24, top views €29; metro: Sagrada Familia

Barcelona's most famous monument is the Basilica and Expiatory Church of the Holy Family, widely known as La Sagrada Família. Now 70 percent complete, the construction of Antoni Gaudí's ambitious design began in 1882 and is projected to be completed in 2026, on the centenary of Gaudí's death. Pope Benedict XVI consecrated the basilica in 2010, and led the first mass in its 128-year history.

The world's longest-running modern-day architectural project is a firm fixture on the Barcelona skyline, its soaring spires and yellow cranes a sign of the work still to be done on the famously unfinished church. When he was asked, as he often was, when the church would be finished, Gaudí

Antoni Gaudí's masterpiece, La Sagrada Familia, is still being built today.

would reply, "Don't worry, my client is in no hurry. God has all the time in the world."

Gaudí designed the church to be the tallest building in Barcelona, its spires rising so high that they would unite heaven and earth. He aimed to depict the history of Catholicism in the façade of the church, a mammoth task that the architect knew would take more than one lifetime to complete. The design of Gaudí's masterpiece came to obsess and dominate his later life, to such an extent that he would often sleep in his onsite workshop.

Ticket Options

Tickets can be purchased online ahead of time; it's worth it to avoid queuing, and the disappointment of finding them all sold out. The 45-minute audioguide costs €7 extra, but allows visitors to explore at their own pace. You can also book a guided experience in English (€24, 50 minutes), with a qualified guide who will let you in on secrets and hidden details in Gaudí's work.

At least an hour is recommended to really appreciate the building. Getting there first thing is a good idea to beat the crowds. Attending mass (Sundays, 9am) is a special experience. There is an international mass open to members of the public in several different languages. There is no charge, but space is limited. Enter from the

sculpture by Josep Maria Subirachs on the Passion Façade

Nativity Façade (Carrer de la Marina) between 8:30am and 9am.

History

The Sagrada Família was commissioned by bookseller Josep Maria Bocabella, founder of the religious society the Spiritual Association of Devotees of St. Joseph, as a church that would atone for the sins of all the inhabitants of Barcelona.

Architect Franscico de Paula del Villar began work on the project, which he envisioned as a neo-Gothic church, in 1882. It was when Gaudí took over the project in 1883, after the original architect resigned, that it transformed from a straightforward, classical design into something radically different. Gaudí's new design was for a cathedral-sized church with 18 spires, representing the twelve apostles as well as the Virgin Mary, four Evangelists, and—the pinnacle and largest spire—Jesus Christ himself.

He left detailed models of how the church should be completed. Unfortunately, these models were destroyed during the Spanish Civil War, leaving subsequent architects scratching their heads at how to tackle the ambitious scale and detail with no plans. They painstakingly pieced together some of Gaudí's destroyed models and plans; more recently, they have employed the most up-to-date aeronautical engineering software to help them figure out the complex design, which at the time was unlike anything ever conceived.

While the Sagrada Família attracts millions of visitors every year and is one of Spain's biggest tourist attractions, it has not been without its critics. George Orwell called it "one of the most hideous buildings in the world." Whether or not today's work

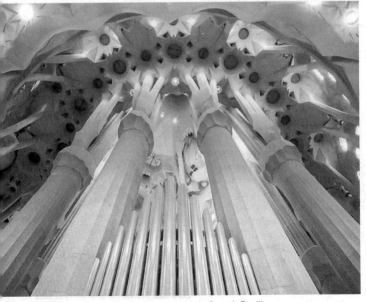

a symphony of light, shape, and color inside La Sagrada Familia

reflects Gaudí's vision, and whether the great architect would like what he saw if he were to return to 21st-century Barcelona, is up for debate. Some critics say the church can never truly resemble Gaudí's ideal, whereas others applaud the architects and engineers who have overcome huge obstacles to follow the original design as faithfully as possible.

Nativity Façade

The only façade to be completed during Gaudí's lifetime, the Nativity Façade—facing eastward onto Carrer de la Marina—was designed between 1894 and 1930. It is split into three porticos representing Hope, Faith, and Charity and is highly decorative, with motifs from nature visible throughout; notice the tortoises and turtles— to represent the land and the sea—at the base of the columns separating the porticos.

The birth of Christ is represented above the Charity portico, with the holy family surrounded by the shepherds, the three wise men, angels, and animals. Gaudí used plaster casts of locals to create many of the figures, even casting chickens and stillborn babies in his quest for a lifelike depiction.

Inside the Church

Stepping inside, you are immediately struck by the lofty, tree-like columns that soar toward a celestial canopy above. Taking his cues from nature, as ever, Gaudí felt that it was in the forest that man was closest to God, and so created a forest of stone. He used different types of stone, which adds depth to the space, and chose red porphyry from Iran, one of the world's strongest stones, for the columns bearing the heaviest load.

A warm glow streams into this sacred forest through the polychromatic stained-glass windows, which are more than two stories high. They filter in more light at the top and are darker at the bottom, with illustrations and texts. This helps draw the eye upward toward the heavens and toward the architectural details high up in the church, illuminated by the colored light. The streaming light, filtered by the stained glass, lends the white walls a bejeweled look.

Passion Façade and Glory Façade

The angular design of the Passion Façade, which faces Carrer de Sardenya, provides a stark contrast to the busy, intricate detail of the Nativity Façade. The façade depicts the suffering and crucifixion of Jesus and was completed between 1954 and 2018. Designed by famous local sculptor Josep Maria Subirachs, who, like Gaudí, took up residence inside the Temple, its simple geometrical shapes and sharp lines bring to mind the bones of a skeleton, the antithesis of the Nativity Façade. This radically different style was not well-received

interior of La Sagrada Familia

Casa Amatller (left) and Casa Batlló (right)

The Quadrat d'Or, or Golden Quarter, is a central area of L'Eixample where the city's bourgeoisie built their lavish, Modernista homes in the late 19th and early 20th centuries. It became something of an aesthetic competition, each patron striving to outdo their contemporaries with the most extravagant façade and decorative interiors. The result is an incredible architectural legacy that reveals the best of Modernisme. The area stretches from Carrer d'Aribau to Passeig de Sant Joan, centred around **Passeig de Gràcia,** and includes a multitude of magnificent masterpieces. Keep your eyes peeled for intricate floral embellishments, neo-Gothic details, and elaborate stained-glass windows as you wander this outdoor museum.

At the heart of the Quadrat d'Or is the **Manzana de la Discòrdia** (Block of Discord), where three of the most dazzling residences—**Casa Batlló, Casa Amatller,** and **Casa Lleó Morera** (Passeig de Gràcia, 35; closed to the public), by Gaudí, Puig i Cadafalch, and Domènech i Montaner respectively—sit alongside each other in distinctly contrasting styles.

To delve further into the history of Modernisme, consider following the **Barcelona Modernisme Route** (www.rutadelmodernisme.com), indicated via small red paving stones set into the pavement. A guidebook (€12) dedicated to the 120 works of Modernisme on the route is available at most bookshops, within many of the buildings themselves, or at the **Museu del Modernisme de Barcelona** (Carrer de Balmes, 48; 93/272-2896; www.mmbcn.cat; Mon.-Fri. 10:30am-2pm, 4pm-7pm; €10).

by critics at the time, though it was Gaudí's original intention for this façade to strike fear into the onlooker (which is why he began with the more accessible Nativity Façade).

In 2002, construction began on the Glory Façade, on the southeast side of the building, which will be the church's largest and most striking façade, depicting the Glorious Ascension of Jesus Christ and representing man's road to God. Death, Final Judgement, and Glory will be the main themes here. It will also reference purgatory, hell, the seven deadly sins, and the seven heavenly virtues. In order to complete the grand entrance to the basilica from the Glory Façade, some of the surrounding buildings may be demolished.

Towers

Of the 18 planned towers, four have been built over the Nativity Façade and four over the Passion Façade, representing eight of the apostles. The central spire, representing Jesus, will be topped with a gigantic cross—its height (170 meters or 558 feet) will be one meter lower than Montjuïc hill, as expressly designed by Gaudí, who believed man's creations should never surpass those of God. The completed spires will make the Sagrada Familia the tallest church in the world.

A tower-visit ticket (€29) includes access to one of the 65-meter (213-foot) towers, on either the Nativity Façade or the Passion Façade. At the top of the towers, visitors can appreciate Gaudí's use of mosaics, color, and quirky detailing. You can ascend the towers via an elevator, but the descent involves a rather claustrophobic staircase; people with mobility, cardiac, or pulmonary issues should not climb the towers.

✪ CASA BATLLÓ

Passeig de Gràcia, 43; 93/216-0306; www.casabatllo.es; 9am-9pm daily; €24.50; metro: Passeig de Gràcia

Casa Batlló is one of Gaudí's most spectacular creations. A lavish residence in the heart of Passeig de Gràcia, the building dates from 1877 but was remodeled by Gaudí between 1904 and 1906 to suit the whims of Josep Batlló y Casanovas, a textile tycoon, who purchased the building in 1903.

Casanovas wanted a statement building that would stand out on the city's most elegant boulevard, and statement is what he got. The exuberant marine-themed façade is a sculptural masterpiece divided into three distinct parts. The lower floors are clad in smooth stone and slender, skeletal columns, which give the house its colloquial name, the *Casa dels Ossos* (House of Bones). Next, a scintillating explosion of aquatic colors composed of glass and ceramic fragments creeps up the façade, punctuated by masklike cast-iron balconies. The pièce de résistance is the polychromatic tiled roof that is thought to represent a scaly dragon, alluding to the legend of St. George, Catalonia's patron saint. Following that theory, the tower, which culminates with a four-armed cross, represents the sword of St. George buried in the dragon's back.

Inside, Gaudí carries the marine concept through to the finest details. At ground level, turtle-shell lamps, fish-scale walls, and a sinuous, spine-like staircase simulate the underbelly of some mythical sea creature. Upstairs, on the first floor (or "noble" floor, where the Batlló family lived), a whirlpool twists the fluid ceiling of the main living room. As always, Gaudí worked closely with artisans to achieve unique, intricate craftsmanship throughout the building, from ergonomic handrails and gill-like air vents to organic-shaped oak doors and mollusc-themed stained glass. Visitors proceed through the living spaces, which conclude with a courtyard at the rear. As the building

The spectacular living room of Casa Batlló overlooks Passeig de Gràcia.

rooftop of Casa Batlló

is still privately owned and occupied, the visit jumps from the first floor to the attic and roof terrace. Climb the staircase en route and find yourself submerged in an entire spectrum of blues in the central light well, which cleverly distributes air and light entering from the skylight above.

Gaudí's emblematic catenary arches are implemented in the attic, formerly a service area for the building's tenants, to create a unique space that evokes an immense thorax—perhaps that of the dragon, whose colorful skin can be examined up close as one finally emerges onto the rooftop.

Casa Batlló was declared a UNESCO World Heritage Site in 2005 and has been open for cultural visits since 2002. Entrance tickets include an imaginative virtual-reality audio guide that brings the spaces to life.

Tip: From May to November, the "Magic Nights" series (€39) invites visitors to explore the house by night, followed by live music and a drink on the terrace.

CASA AMATLLER

Passeig de Gràcia, 41; 93/461-7460;
amatller.org; 10am-6pm daily; €19/€17.10
students and over 65s/€9.50 children aged
7-10/free for children under 7;
metro: Passeig de Gràcia

The stepped façade of Casa Amatller might seem a little staid compared to flamboyant Casa Batlló, located right next door, but this neo-Gothic urban mansion is anything but conventional, and is a Modernista gem in its own right. Originally constructed in 1875, the building was purchased by chocolatier Antoni Amatller in 1898; he commissioned Josep Puig i Cadafalch to remodel it as his home.

What the architect came up with is a curious ode to the Gothic style, combined with an extravagant Dutch-style gable that recalls the townhouses of Amsterdam. The ochre-and-white sgraffito façade is crowned with a border of red and gold Valencian tiles, while typical medieval details emerge around the window and door openings. Look for the Eusebi Arnau stone sculpture of Saint George and the dragon by the entrance, and the fantastical creatures that surround the first-floor windows.

Behind the façade, the foyer opens onto a central courtyard, where light filters through a spectacular stained-glass skylight and an elegant stone staircase leads to the main (or "noble") floor, where the Amatller family lived. Much of the original decor and furniture still adorns the first-floor apartment, which opened as a museum in 2015. Guided tours in English are offered daily at 11am (€24/€21.60/€12). At the back of the ground floor, the Faborit café specialises in chocolate-based products and drinks, in keeping with the building's original owner.

FUNDACIÓ ANTONI TÀPIES

Carrer d'Aragó, 255; 93/487-0315;
fundaciotapies.org; Tues.-Thurs. and Sat.
10am-7pm, Fri. 10am-9pm, Sun. 10am-3pm;
€7/€5 students and over 65s;
metro: Passeig de Gràcia

A metallic cloud-like sculpture, *Núvol i cadira* ("Cloud and Chair") by distinguished local artist Antoni Tàpies, hovers above the Fundació Antoni Tàpies, hinting at the abstract artworks that lie within. The center owns one of the most complete collections of work by Tàpies—the most famous Spanish artist to emerge during the second half of the 20th century—mostly donated by the artist and his wife.

Influenced by Miró and Klee, Tàpies started out as a Surrealist but soon moved toward Art Informel—the European equivalent to Abstract Expressionism—producing mixed-media assemblages that elevated everyday objects to the realm of art. Intriguing temporary exhibitions tend to highlight a specific aspect or period of the artist's oeuvre. Shows by contemporary artists are also featured.

Although only steps from Passeig de Gràcia, the Foundation, located in a former publishing house designed by Modernisme master Lluís Domènech i Montaner, is generally skipped over by the masses. Many of the building's original Modernista details have been preserved, and though the collection can be a little perplexing to the uninitiated, the museum's calming top-lit interiors offer a hiatus from the well-trodden tourist trail.

Don't miss the *Mitjó* (1991), a sculpture depicting a large sock, on the museum's terrace. This is a model of a giant sculpture originally commissioned by the Museu Nacional d'Art de Catalunya (MNAC), who controversially rejected the final proposal.

✪ LA PEDRERA

Carrer de Provença, 261-265;
www.lapedrera.com; 9am-8:30pm daily;
€22/€16.50 students, over 65s, and people
with disabilities/€11 children aged 7-12/free
for children under 7; audio guide included
(these are online prices; note that the ticket
office charges €3 extra per person);
metro: Diagonal

The curvaceous shell of La Pedrera defies the norms of civic architecture, smack bang in the middle of Barcelona's most elegant boulevard.

The building's official name, Casa Milà, honors its patrons, Pere Milà and Roser Segimon, who commissioned Antoni Gaudí in 1906 to design one of the most audacious residential buildings of the time. Things got off to a rocky start. Not only was the Modernista building heavily criticized for its unorthodox aesthetics—it was dubbed La Pedrera, meaning "stone quarry," by those who disapproved of it—but the attic and rooftop also exceeded the permitted size set out in the strict planning laws, and it became the focus of several legal and financial disputes. Nevertheless, Gaudí's rhythmic work of art and architecture was soon recognized for its creative genius, and it went on to become one of the city's most iconic buildings.

As ever, Gaudí drew his inspiration from Mother Nature. The sculpted limestone waves of the exterior simulate the moving sea, interspersed with twisted wrought-iron balconies that recall clumps of floating seaweed. Sinuous, organic shapes continue inside La Pedrera, with an irregular geometry oriented around two interior courtyards, providing plentiful ventilation and light to the building's 16 apartments. The first floor was occupied by the Milà-Segimon family, while the rest of the building was rented out. Gaudí applied his concepts with rigor, down to the finest detail, evident here in the ergonomic furniture, doorknobs, and even the hexagonal-tiled footpath outside.

Two hundred and seventy brick arches create a remarkably poetic space in the attic, originally used as a communal laundry area. Today it contains the Espai Gaudí, a unique display devoted to the architect and his work, and includes numerous intricate models. Finally, one emerges onto the rolling rooftop terrace, where chimneys rise up like warriors marching into battle while ventilation towers and stairwells become sculptural objects in their own right.

La Pedrera was declared a UNESCO World Heritage Site in 1984. It is owned by the Fundació Catalunya-La Pedrera, whose headquarters are based in the building. The attic, rooftop, and a period-style apartment on the fourth floor are open to the public, as well as a temporary exhibition space on the

La Pedrera

first floor. Day and nighttime guided tours are available in English. The rest of the building is privately occupied. In summer, live jazz concerts take place on the terrace (Jun.-Sept., €35); the cover charge includes a visit to the Espai Gaudí, the concert, and a drink.

CASA DE LES PUNXES

Avinguda Diagonal, 420; 93/018-5242; casadelespunxes.com; 9am-8pm daily; €13.50/€10 children aged 8-18, students, over 65s, and people with disabilities/free for children under 8; metro: Verdaguer or Diagonal

Six dramatic spires crown the rooftop of this Modernista treasure, giving the building its moniker, Casa de les Punxes ("House of the Spikes"). Its official name is *Casa Terradas*, after the bourgeois family who commissioned it. Built between 1903 and 1905 for the three daughters of textile industrialist Bartomeu Terradas i Mont—Àngela, Josefa, and Rosa—this palatial building was designed by Josep Puig i Cadafalch, a family friend and one of the great architects of Catalan Modernisme.

Puig i Cadafalch's work typically married the technological advancements and creative thinking of the time with a solid grounding in Catalan history and culture, as well as a nod to Northern European and Gothic influences. All of these characteristics are evident in Casa de les Punxes. The architect envisioned three separate houses integrated into one unified, six-sided block evocative of a medieval castle. He drew imagery from Catalan tradition and from the Wagner-inspired Neuschwanstein Castle, and combined Romanesque, Gothic, and Modernisme motifs with intricate craftsmanship and symbolism.

The sisters lived on the main floor of their respective houses. The ground floor was originally used for storage; the upper floors were rented out and the servants' quarters were situated on the rooftop. Each house has its own entrance and emblems that reference the relevant owner. Look for the ceramic panels on the upper part of the façade: Àngela's house bears the image of an angel, while roses are depicted on Rosa's façade.

Casa de les Punxes

The building is now privately owned and is occupied primarily with commercial and residential use, but visitors can wander the main floor of Àngela's house and experience an audio-visual production based on the legend of St. George. Original hydraulic tiles and restored painted ceilings are present throughout, though no original furniture is intact, and the interior decor is relatively restrained in comparison with the exterior. The visit continues on the rooftop, where a detailed exhibition about Puig i Cadafalch is housed inside the distinctive spires. Tours in English are available on request (€20).

A complimentary audio guide is included with entrance.

RECINTE MODERNISTA DE SANT PAU

Carrer de Sant Antoni Maria Claret, 167;
93/553-7801; www.santpaubarcelona.
org; Apr.-Oct. Mon.-Sat. 9:30am-6:30pm,
Sun. and public holidays 9:30am-2:30pm,
Nov.-Mar. Mon.-Sat. 9:30am-4:30pm,
Sun. and public holidays 9:30am-2:30pm;
€14/€9.80 under 29s and over 65s/free
for under 12s; metro: Hospital de Sant
Pau-Guinardó or Sant Pau-Dos de Maig;
bus: 19, 47, 192, H6, H8

This stunning complex of ornate pavilions was home to the Hospital de la Santa Creu i Sant Pau from 1916 until 2009, but there's nothing sterile or institutionalized about this former hospital. Located at the opposite end of Avinguda Gaudí from the Sagrada Família, the Recinte Modernista de Sant Pau is one of the jewels of Catalan Modernisme.

The building was designed by Lluís Domènech i Montaner and built between 1902 and 1930. Above ground, aromatic plants and fruit trees flourish in the therapeutic gardens, while underground the various elements of the complex are connected by more than a kilometer of tunnels (about a mile). The intricate detailing and plentiful use of natural light and color throughout the hospital were intended to will patients back to health. The lofty pavilion ceilings are tiled in mint green, a color Domènech associated with hope, while floral designs dance across the walls. In a time when hygienism was just evolving, the architect worked closely with doctors to create exemplary healthcare design. White ceramic tiles lined the tunnels to ensure cleanliness, while sharp corners,

Gaudí's stone porticoes in Parc Güell blur the boundary between architecture and nature.

where germs might linger, were eliminated in favor of rounded finishes.

The first patients were admitted in 1916, although the hospital was not officially opened until January 16, 1930. The 15th-century Hospital de la Santa Creu in El Raval relocated here in 1926 and treatment was free; the hospital was run by the church and depended on charitable donations to survive.

The original buildings were carefully restored and opened to the public in 2014. Guided tours in English (€19/€13.30) take place every day at 10:30am and audio guides are also available (€17).

Tip: Spot the letters "P" and "G" dotted excessively over the façades of all the buildings, both in stone and tilework, in homage to the hospital's main benefactor, Pau Gil i Serra—a Catalan banker who bequeathed more than three million pesetas for the construction of a hospital in Barcelona, to be dedicated to Saint Paul.

GRÀCIA, PARK GÜELL, AND BEYOND

✪ PARK GÜELL

Carrer d'Olot; 93/409-1831; www.parkguell. cat; Oct. 28-Mar. 24 8:30am-6:15pm daily, Mar. 25-Apr. 29 and Aug. 27-Oct. 27 8am-8:30pm, Apr. 30-Aug. 26 8am-9:30pm daily; €7.50/€5.25 children aged 7-12, over 65s, and people with disabilities; €14.50/€12.25 with guided tour; metro: Vallcarca; bus: 24, 116, V19

One of the most extravagant housing estates ever imagined, Gaudí's original plan for Park Güell didn't quite come to fruition. But what was left after the project fell through is an enchanting space, filled with topsy-turvy porticoes, labyrinthine walkways, and whimsical pavilions—a scene lifted straight from a fairy tale.

In 1900, Antoni Gaudí was commissioned by his long-time patron and friend Eusebi Güell to develop plans for a bourgeois residential estate, inspired by the English garden-city movement (hence the English spelling of "park"). There were to be 60 plots in the spacious development, which boasted an unbeatable mountainside location with city and sea views.

Gaudí began by creating a complex network of paths traversing the tricky topography and native vegetation. Here, he worked closely with his greatest influencer: nature. Snaking paths supported by arcades and viaducts of natural stone harmoniously merge with the landscape, making it difficult to detect where Gaudí's work ends and nature begins.

The impressive entrance sequence came next. The two gingerbread gatehouses were completed by 1903, as was the central staircase, where the iconic tiled dragon can be found. The Hypostyle Room, designed as a covered marketplace for residents, was completed shortly afterward, the roof of which became a grand square, lined by a wavy bench

Park Güell's dragon, known as "El Drac," is one of the symbols of the city.

embellished with Gaudí's trademark *trencadís* tiling. Only two houses were ever built, however. Despite a spate of early interest, the development was not commercially viable and works were abandoned in 1914. Thereafter, it became a private garden and event space before the land was sold to the city council in 1922, following Güell's death. It opened as a public park in 1926 and became a UNESCO World Heritage Site in 1984.

one of the gatehouses at Park Güell

The easiest way to get to Park Güell is by bus (24) from Plaça de Catalunya. By metro, take the L3 to Vallcarca—from there it is a 15-minute walk up-hill—or alight at Lesseps and take the 116 bus. Most of the park can be visited free of charge, but a ticket is required to visit the "Monumental Core" area, which includes the entrance sequence described above. Advance booking is recommended as ticket numbers are limited and organized by time slot. Discounts are available online.

The park is also home to the Casa Museu Gaudí (93/208-0414; https://sagradafamilia.org/casa-museu-gaudi; Oct.-Mar. 10am-6pm daily, Apr.-Sept. 9am-8pm daily; €5.50), dedicated to the life and work of the architect. It is housed in one of the two show homes that were built, where Gaudí lived from 1906 until 1925.

CASA VICENS

Carrer de les Carolines, 20; 93/547-5980; casavicens.org; Mon.-Sun. 10am-8pm; €16/€14; metro: Fontana; FGC: Gràcia; bus: 24

Casa Vicens was the first house designed by Antoni Gaudí, at the age of 31, and it is considered one of the early masterpieces of Modernisme. Located in Gràcia, then a village on the outskirts of the city, it was commissioned by Manel Vicens i Montaner as a summer residence for his family and was constructed between 1883 and 1885.

At this early point in his career, Gaudí was yet to abandon straight lines in favor of more organic forms, but the seeds of his future style are evident in this eclectic, four-story mansion, awash with Moorish and Oriental influences. The extravagant, multi-colored façade bursts with the frenetic energy of a genius in the making and represented a dramatic departure from the style of the time.

Now hemmed in by its densely populated urban surroundings, the building was originally set among extensive gardens, which played a key role in Gaudí's design. Natural elements are integrated across the entire complex, from the cast-iron fan palms of the entrance gates to the French marigolds of the tiled façade. Gaudí explored every opportunity to blur the boundary between indoor and outdoor, most notably in the ground-floor gallery, a semi-enclosed terrace, which acted as a connection point between the house and gardens.

SQUARES OF GRÀCIA

Life in Gràcia (metro: Fontana) revolves around a series of squares, linked together via a network of narrow lanes. Fifteen plazas are dotted across the neighborhood—delightful spaces that break out from the otherwise tightly knit urban fabric. This is where the locals come to meet, chat, and live out their daily lives. Tracing a path from one light, open space to the next is an excellent way to sample neighborhood life.

clock tower in Vila de Gràcia

PLAÇA DE LA VILA DE GRÀCIA

Plaça de la Vila de Gràcia is the heart and soul of the *barri* and a logical starting point from which to explore. A 33-meter-high (108-foot) bell tower, built between 1862 and 1864, dominates the square. The sky-blue façade on the southern side belongs to the former town hall, designed by Gaudí's trusted assistant Francesc Berenguer in 1904. It now houses the district council offices; look for the wrought-iron coat of arms.

The square has been the epicenter of many historical moments, most notably the Conscripts' Revolt in 1870, when residents refused to enroll their sons in the army. The bell rang out for six days straight to keep the revolutionary spirit alive. Today it is a hive of activity, with cafés and bars spilling onto the square, children playing, and locals chatting.

PLAÇA DEL SOL

A couple of blocks north, Plaça del Sol has a distinctly youthful character that is at once rowdy and relaxed. At its peak on long, hazy summer evenings, the plentiful terraces and bars fill with students and crowds of young people until the early hours. From here, walk along Carrer de Ramon y Cajal toward **Plaça de la Revolució,** a long narrow square dotted with trees. Cross the square and wander up **Carrer de Verdi,** one of Gràcia's liveliest streets, lined with offbeat shops, quirky bars, and restaurants.

PLAÇA DEL DIAMANT

At Carrer de l'Or, turn left into Plaça del Diamant, one of the oldest and most emblematic squares. In this former jewellers' neighborhood, many of the surrounding streets are named after precious stones. A large air-raid shelter built by the locals during the Spanish Civil War is buried beneath the square and can be visited by appointment (email tallerhistoriagracia@gmail.com). The square gives its name to Mercè Rodoreda's 1962 novel, one of Catalonia's most important works of contemporary fiction (*The Time of the Doves* in English).

PLAÇA DE LA VIRREINA

Head back along Carrer de l'Or to Plaça de la Virreina. This pretty village square surrounds the church of Sant Joan, which has been destroyed and rebuilt twice—in 1909 and 1936. Inside, look for the Modernista-style Santíssim chapel, also designed by Berenguer. Round off the tour with a coffee or cold beer, relaxing on the low-key, leafy terraces outside.

Casa Vicens

This little-known Gaudí gem opened to the public for the first time in 2017. Guided tours are available in English (€19) at 10am and 3:30pm daily, although the friendly, knowledgeable staff on each level are on hand to offer useful insights throughout the visit. After wandering through the gardens and the ground and first floors, it is well worth spending some time browsing the permanent exhibition in the attic, where the building's evolution is explained through models, drawings, and audiovisuals.

TURÓ DE LA ROVIRA

Carrer de Marià Labèrnia; bus: 24, V17

Rising 262 meters (860 feet) above sea level, Turó de la Rovira offers one of the finest views of Barcelona. Situated just beyond Park Güell, which is located on Turó del Carmel, this *turó* (Catalan for "hill") is a world apart from the Modernista architecture and throngs of tourists found there. The 360-degree panoramas captivate all those who make the convoluted ascent

to the top, although the history that lies beneath the surface of this natural mound is just as fascinating.

Since its first Iberian settlement, the hill has been recognized as a natural vantage point. During the Spanish Civil War, Barcelona was subject to massive air raids, and Turó de la Rovira was considered an ideal location for anti-aircraft artillery. Four cannons were installed, as well as bunkers for accommodation, and the battery came into operation in March 1938. In the postwar years, the abandoned military structures were used to form the foundations of a new, makeshift neighborhood, housing immigrants from across Spain. Known as *Els Canons*, at its peak there were 600 inhabitants and 110 shanties. It was finally demolished on November 7, 1990, bringing an end to shantytowns in Barcelona.

Today the area is an official historic site managed by the Museu d'Història de Barcelona (MUHBA). Known locally as the **Bunkers del Carmel,** the remote beauty of this spot still flies relatively under the radar. The MUHBA has installed an informative exhibition inside the former command post that is well worth a look. Wander the site and reflect on the toil and trouble of its previous occupants, or simply pause and take in the views, particularly atmospheric at sunrise and sunset.

The easiest way to get there is by local bus. Take the V17 from Maremagnum (45 minutes), which passes through Gràcia and terminates just a few minutes walk from the bunkers, or the 24 from Plaça de Catalunya (40 minutes), which stops eight minutes away.

MONTJUÏC, POBLE-SEC, AND SANT ANTONI

MUSEU NACIONAL D'ART DE CATALUNYA (MNAC)

Palau Nacional, Parc de Montjuïc; 93/622-0376; www.museunacional.cat; Oct.-Apr. Tues.-Sat. 10am-6pm, May-Sept. Tues.-Sat. 10am-8pm, year-round Sun. and public holidays 10am-3pm; €12; metro: Espanya

Housed in the Palau Nacional, the Museu Nacional d'Art de Catalunya showcases a thousand years of Catalan art. The monumental Neoclassical palace, constructed for Barcelona's 1929 International Exposition, sits majestically on the slopes of Montjuïc—the grand finale of the fountain-filled Avinguda de la Reina Maria Cristina. Inside, visitors can journey from the Middle Ages right through to the modern day, taking in Romanesque, Gothic, Renaissance, Baroque, and modern artworks along the way.

Start with the collection of medieval Romanesque art. Dating from the 11th to 13th centuries, this is the museum's highlight, and is considered to be the best of its kind in the world. The collection includes an exceptional set of 21 murals and panel paintings, many of which were taken from Pyrenean churches in the early 20th century and reinstated here. Don't miss the Apse of Sant Climent de Taüll, a 12th-century polychromatic representation of the Christ in Majesty, and one of the masterpieces of the European Romanesque. It was relocated here from Vall de Boí between 1919 and 1923.

Moving on, the Gothic era in Catalonia (13th-15th centuries) is represented by a collection of wooden altarpieces, sculpture, parchment, and decorative works depicting naturalistic figures and scenes. Keep an eye out for the work of Bernat Martorell, Catalonia's most revered Gothic painter, and the exquisitely gilded "Consecration of Saint Augustine" by Jaume Huguet, a 15th-century altarpiece from the church of Sant Agustí Vell in Barcelona.

The Renaissance and Baroque collection (16th-18th centuries) comes next, with several masterpieces from the Spanish Golden Age, including Velázquez's "Saint Paul." Other prominent European artists displayed here include Rubens, Goya, El Greco, Zurbarán, and Titian, many of which form part of the Cambó Bequest or the Thyssen-Bornemisza Collection.

Rounding off the chronological journey, the museum's collection of modern art covers a range of styles from the 19th and 20th centuries, all beautifully presented in the recently renovated first-floor gallery. The multi-disciplinary collection is divided into four thematic sections, two of which focus on major Catalan movements of the time, Noucentisme and Modernisme, and includes works by Gaudí, Casas, Picasso, Dalí, Miró, and more. The museum's collection concludes in the 1950s with the Dau al Set avant-garde movement founded in Barcelona. More recent Catalan art is housed in the Museu d'Art Contemporani de Barcelona (MACBA).

There's a lot to take in under the domed roof of Catalonia's national gallery. Besides the encyclopedic collection of Catalan creativity, there is also a rich agenda of temporary exhibitions worth checking. Prioritize the Romanesque, dip in and out of the rest, and make sure you pause to take in the views from the rooftop (€2) or sit on the steps outside, particularly around sunset. The museum is a 10-minute walk from Plaça Espanya.

Tip: Book online to take advantage of the combined ticket (general admission and audio guide) for €14.

Fundació Joan Miró

FUNDACIÓ JOAN MIRÓ

Parc de Montjuïc; 93/443-9470; www.fmirobcn.org; Nov.-Mar. Tues.-Sat. 10am-6pm, Sun. 10am-3pm, Apr.-Oct.: Tues.-Sat. 10am-8pm, Sun. 10am-6pm; €13; bus: 55, 150

Joan Miró (1893-1983) had a clear vision of his legacy when he bestowed this extraordinary capsule of creative genius upon his hometown. He set up the Fundació Joan Miró—initially with works from his private collection, but with the idea of developing an international center for contemporary art—and commissioned his close friend, avant-garde architect Josep Lluís Sert, to design a suitably singular setting to house his masterpieces of abstraction.

Sert's creation, a Corbusier-inspired composition in a leafy Montjuïc setting, articulates a special dialogue between art and architecture. Level changes, lofty top-lit galleries, and a series of outdoor spaces emphasize movement through the building and allow Miró's works to be admired from multiple angles.

Opened in 1975, the foundation is packed with seminal works by one of the city's most famous sons, which give a comprehensive overview of his life and career. Among the 217 paintings, 178 sculptures, and more than 8,000 drawings, note the early Surrealist work that hints at the development of his signature style, and the 1939-44 "Barcelona Series" of lithographs, Miró's emotive reaction to the Spanish Civil War. Farther along, the large-scale canvases Miró produced in his twilight years are filled with color, free forms, and playfulness.

CAIXAFORUM

Avinguda de Francesc Ferrer i Guàrdia, 6-8; 93/476-8600; caixaforum.es/Barcelona; 10am-8pm daily; €4; metro: Espanya

Housed in a former textile factory at the foot of Montjuïc, CaixaForum is a lively cultural center, owned and managed by the charitable arm of La Caixa bank. Exhibitions and activities span all eras and disciplines, many of which are organized in collaboration with prominent international institutions, including the Louvre and the British Museum, as well as seven other CaixaForum centers across Spain. In recent years, the Barcelona center has presented many big-name exhibitions—Warhol, Dalí, and Goya, among others—so it is well worth checking what's on. Complementary events run in tandem with the exhibitions, as well as regular cinema cycles, family events, dance performances, live music, and conferences.

The building merits a visit in its own right. Built between 1909 and

1912, the intricate brick construction was designed by Josep Puig i Cadafalch, one of the masters of Catalan Modernisme. Its life as a factory was short-lived. After it closed in 1920, Fábrica Casaramona was used as a warehouse, and then as police stables from 1940 until 1992. A massive restoration project followed, resulting in a stunning juxtaposition of old and new, and it finally opened to the public in 2002.

Visitors enter beneath a pair of oversized steel trees, designed by Japanese architect Arata Isozaki, and descend into a subterranean patio of clean lines and luminous stone—an inverted homage to the adjacent Barcelona Pavilion. From there, a vast hall stretches under the original building, leading back up to ground level, where the three main exhibition spaces are housed in the old factory buildings (two are used for temporary shows and one is dedicated to contemporary art). Outside the middle exhibition hall, there is a permanent exhibition about the building, accompanied by a model. An audio guide tour of the building is available (€12) and guided tours can be arranged.

Tip: Visit the undulating roof terrace for an aerial view, and spot Puig i Cadafalch's not-so-subtle tribute to rival architect Antoni Gaudí: a colorful ceramic embellishment at the top of the southern tower.

FONT MÀGICA (MAGIC FOUNTAIN)

Plaça de Carles Buïgas, 1;
www.barcelona.cat; free; metro: Espanya

The Font Màgica is the climax of a series of fountains, cascades, and pools running the length of Avinguda de la Maria Cristina, from Plaça d'Espanya to the majestic Palau Nacional on Montjuïc. It was designed by Carles

CaixaForum

Buigas for the 1929 International Exposition. With 2,600 liters flowing through the fountain's three concentric pools per second, the fountain can produce an astonishing seven billion combinations of light and water, which come together in complex sequences choreographed to music. The spellbinding vision of the fountains dancing against the Barcelona skyline has become an icon of the city.

Throughout history, the fountain has played an important role in many of the city's biggest events. Perhaps its most memorable moment came on October 8, 1988, when Freddie Mercury and Montserrat Caballé performed their emotive duet, "Barcelona," in front of the fountain at the open-air La Nit festival. The song was chosen as one of two official themes for the 1992 Olympic Games, although Mercury passed away before the event. Their heart-stopping performance was to be Mercury's last live appearance, and still sends a shiver down the spine of anyone who has ever loved this city. Now that's a kind of magic.

Show times vary with the seasons. From June until September, shows take place Wednesday to Sunday at 9:30pm and 10pm; April, May, and October, Thursday to Saturday at 9pm and 9:30pm; November, December, early January, and March, Thursday to Saturday at 8pm and 8:30pm. The fountain is closed for maintenance from January 7 until February 28. During the city's annual festival, La Mercè, and on New Year's Eve, the fountains join forces with a spectacular fireworks display, attracting huge crowds that cram the wide boulevard.

BARCELONA PAVILION
Av. de Francesc Ferrer i Guàrdia, 7;
93/215-1011; miesbcn.com; Mar.-Oct.

10am-8pm daily, Nov.-Feb. 10am-6pm daily;
€4; metro: Espanya

Set back from the magic fountain, the Barcelona Pavilion reserves an irrefutable spot in the history of architecture. Designed by pioneering German architect Ludwig Mies van der Rohe as the German pavilion for the 1929 Barcelona International Exposition, this sleek, minimalist structure is an icon of Modernist architecture and, indeed, 20th-century design.

Raised up on a travertine plinth, intersecting planes of marble, onyx, glass, and water come together in a simple yet measured composition, rigorously planned on a grid-based geometry. A low, floating roof projects out over the exterior elements, creating a sense of weightlessness, while lavish materials run seamlessly inside and out to create an illusion of continuous space. Mies, who famously coined the Modernist dictum "less is more," experimented here with his hallmark technique of separating the load-bearing structure from the enclosing walls. This enabled a free-flowing open-plan interior, which he furnished sparsely with the emblematic Barcelona chair, designed specifically for the pavilion.

After the Expo, the pavilion was disassembled, only to be reconstructed more than 50 years later and opened to the public in 1986. A walk through the pavilion is one of modern architecture's most revered moments. Follow Mies's carefully curated sequence through this lyrical play of volumes, and keep an eye out for the curvaceous bronze sculpture by Georg Kolbe, which stands in the internal reflecting pool and contrasts the building's sharp lines. To a 21st-century visitor, the composition may feel familiar, but in 1929 the pavilion represented a revolutionary spatial concept. The very fact that it feels so familiar is testament to the impact that Mies and his contemporaries had on the world of architecture.

POBLE ESPANYOL

Av Francesc Ferrer i Guardia, 13; 93/508-6300; www.poble-espanyol.com; Mon. 9am-8pm, Tues.-Thurs. and Sun. 9am-midnight, Fri. 9am-3am, Sat. 9am-4am; €14; metro: Espanya; bus: 13, 23, 150

If you don't have time to venture beyond Barcelona during your stay, fear not: Poble Espanyol brings the best of the Iberian Peninsula together in an open-air architectural museum. Built for the 1929 International Exposition, scale reproductions of buildings, squares, and streets from across the country come together in a slightly twee celebration of all things Spanish. This staged village promises to take visitors on "a walk through the Spanish soul" and reflects on the diverse cultural riches of the nation.

Enter through the medieval city gate of Ávila and wander by foot from Córdoba to Cáceres via Mallorca and Madrid, and that's just before lunch. En route, you'll witness a snapshot of the peninsula's architectural styles, from Romanesque to Mudéjar, and learn some tricks of the trade from traditional artisans. Recent additions to the museum include "Feeling Spain"—an audiovisual journey through some of Spain's most emblematic landscapes and experiences—and "Fiesta," a multimedia space dedicated to the nation's weird and wonderful festivals.

All this is arranged in a pleasant setting at the foot of Montjuïc, said to have inspired the Disney theme parks, and is particularly popular with families. A huge range of events takes place within the park, from all-night music festivals to family craft workshops. Don't miss the Fundació Fran Daurel (93/423-4172; www.fundaciofrandaurel.com; admission included in Poble Espanyol entrance fee), which has an impressive collection of contemporary art, including pieces by Picasso, Dalí, Miró, Tàpies, and Barceló.

REFUGI 307

Nou de la Rambla, 175; 93/256-2100; museuhistoria.bcn.cat; Sun. 10am-2pm; €3.50; metro: Paral-lel

Carved into the Montjuïc mountainside, Refugi 307 is one of nearly 1,400 air raid shelters constructed in Barcelona during the Spanish Civil War. From early 1937 until January 1939, Barcelona was subject to massive and repeated air raids. It was one of the first cities to experience this terrifying warfare, a sinister precursor of what was to come across Europe throughout World War II.

The shelter was constructed by, and offered shelter to, the inhabitants of Poble-sec during the air raids. Accessed from Nou de la Rambla, it comprises nearly 400 meters (1,300 feet) of dark tunnels, a haunting reminder of the local community's struggle for survival. You can still see the remains of a toilet, water fountain, infirmary, children's area, and fireplace inside the tunnels, which measure 2.1 meters high by 1.5-2 meters wide (7 by 4-5 feet). Guided tours take place on Sundays, with an hour-long English tour starting at 10:30am (11:30am in Spanish, 12:30pm in Catalan). Reservations required.

CASTELL DE MONTJUÏC

Carretera de Montjuïc, 66; 93/256-4440; ajuntament.barcelona.cat/castelldemontjuic; Mar.-Oct. 10am-8pm daily, Nov.-Feb. 10am-6pm daily; €5/€3 for under 30s and

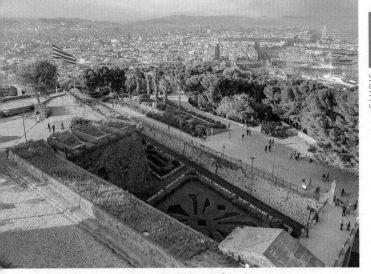

Castell de Montjuïc commands a panoramic view of the city.

over 65s/free for under 16s, free on Sundays
after 3pm; bus: 150 or Telefèric de Montjuïc

The Castell de Montjuïc casts a long shadow over Barcelona. Built to protect the city, the castle ultimately became its oppressor. Cannons have been fired, prisoners have been tortured, and politicians have been executed there over the course of its sinister history.

Strategically located at the top of Montjuïc, a lookout tower is thought to have existed on the castle's site since the 11th century. In 1640, following the onset of the Catalan Revolt (1640-1652), a defensive fortress was rapidly constructed around the tower. During the War of Succession (1701-1714), the fortress became the focus of military conflict due to its strategic position, and was occupied by Bourbon troops when the city fell on September 11, 1714.

Between 1751 and 1779 the castle was extensively remodeled by military architect Juan Martín Cermeños. His redesign remains intact today and involved the demolition of part of the old castle and the construction of new structures (entrance bridge, façade, four bastions, moat, and covered perimeter walkway) in an irregular trapezoidal layout adapted to the topography. The new castle was equipped with 120 cannons, which were used to bombard the city and its people during the 19th century in response to insurgent movements, on one occasion causing 335 deaths. Around the turn of the century, it became a prison for anarchists, trade unionists, and revolutionaries, many of whom were tried and executed there.

But perhaps the castle's most infamous period came during and after the Spanish Civil War (1936-1939). Nearly 1,500 people from both sides of the conflict were imprisoned there, and around 250 prisoners were executed. After the war, the Franco regime occupied the castle and it became a military prison for members of the Republican side, most notably Catalan president Lluís Companys, who was shot by firing squad in October 1940.

The castle continued to serve as a prison until 1960, when it was partly converted into a military museum. In 2007, it was returned to the city council. Today, visitors can wander the castle complex following multi-lingual information plaques, learn about its history at the Montjuïc Castle Interpretation Center, and contemplate unparalleled 360-degree views of the city, port, and Montjuïc. To delve a little deeper, the excellent guided tour grants access to restricted areas, including the castle dungeons and watchtower (€4, 11am daily and also at 4pm on weekends).

Take bus number 150 from Plaça d'Espanya (20 minutes) or from outside the Funicular de Montjuïc station (which connects with Paral·lel metro stop, L2 and L3). Alternatively, a cable car runs from Avinguda Miramar to the castle (€8.40 one way, €12.70 return). On foot, it's a steep but pleasant walk to the castle, and takes approximately 25 minutes from the funicular station.

Tip: Every summer, an outdoor cinema festival, Sala Montjuïc (www.sala-montjuic.org), is held on the western flanks of the fortress during July and August, screening classic and contemporary films in their original language. Pack a picnic and get there early to catch the live music performance beforehand.

JARDÍ BOTÀNIC DE BARCELONA

Carrer Doctor i Font Quer, 2; 93/256-4160; museuciencies.cat; Jun.-Aug. 10am-8pm, Nov.-Mar. 10am-6pm, Apr.-May and Sept.-Oct. 10am-7pm; €3.50/€1.70; bus: 13, 150, 55

Uphill from the Olympic Stadium, the Jardí Botànic de Barcelona zigzags its way toward the crest of Montjuïc. The 14-hectare park presents species from six regions around the world—the Mediterranean Basin, North Africa, California, Chile, South Africa, and Australia—all of which have similar climatic conditions.

Entering via a contemporary pavilion, visitors follow a gently inclined network of paths carved into the hillside. Landscapes are organized by region, from the hanging roots of the Port Jackson Fig (Australia) and the fiery flowers of the Cape Aloe (South Africa) to a pair of 300-year-old olive trees from the Balearic Islands.

The express route (45 minutes), detailed in the free map, gives a good overview, but if you have a little more time, pause to take in spectacular panoramas at the Plaça dels Voluntaris and other viewing points along the way; each offers a rare moment of peace in the city. Visit in late April/early May to see the gardens in full bloom. Guided tours are given every Saturday and Sunday morning by volunteers. Don't miss the permanent bonsai exhibition, open weekends and holidays. Bus numbers 150, 13, or 55 all stop within a 10-minute walk of the gardens. The Funicular de Montjuïc station is a 15-minute walk away.

Also on Montjuïc, situated in the hollows of two disused quarry pits just behind the Museu Nacional d'Art de Catalunya (MNAC), is the Jardí Botànic Històric (Av. dels Montanyans 26, free admission), which dates back to 1920. One of Montjuïc's best-kept secrets, the north-facing garden is enclosed by steep slopes and has a microclimate that favors the growth of Euro-Siberian plant species. Both gardens form part of Barcelona's Natural History museum, the Museu de Ciències Naturals de Barcelona.

WATERFRONT
PORT VELL
Metro: Drassanes or Barceloneta

Port Vell, meaning "old harbor," is the epicenter of Barcelona's maritime heritage, and is surrounded by a host of imposing buildings connected to port life. No longer the city's commercial port, the area had a huge makeover in the early 1990s, transforming it into a focal point for leisure and tourism.

The Columbus Monument stands at the southern extreme of Port Vell, beside the neoclassical customs house and the Museu Marítim de Barcelona (Av. de les Drassanes; 93/342-9920; mmb.cat; 10am-8pm daily; €10). The latter is housed in the beautiful Drassanes Reials, a 14th-century shipyard, and houses a major collection of exhibits that illustrate

Catalan seafaring culture. On the waterfront side of the monument, known as Portal de la Pau, a wooden walkway (Rambla de Mar) connects the quays to the Maremagnum retail complex and the Barcelona Aquarium.

Following the Moll de la Fusta quay to the north, a 1918 schooner, the Santa Eulàlia (93/342-9920; www.mmb.cat; Nov.-Mar. Tues.-Fri. and Sun. 10am-5:30pm, Sat. 2pm-5:30pm, Apr.-Oct. Tues.-Fri. and Sun. 10am-8:30pm, Sat. 2pm-8:30pm; €3 or free with entrance ticket to the Museu Marítim de Barcelona) is moored and can be visited. Small hobby boats populate this part of the harbor. Further along, there are a couple of notable public artworks: Gambrinus, a giant, friendly lobster by Javier Mariscal, and El Cap de Barcelona by Roy Lichtenstein.

On the Barceloneta side of the harbor, the former fishing docks now

Port Vell

host a completely different fleet: super yachts. Some of the world's most luxurious sailing crafts can be spotted here regularly.

The red-brick Palau de Mar, a former warehouse overlooking this side of the port, provides an anchor to the area's mercantile past and houses the Museu d'Història de Catalunya. From here, the Passeig de Joan Borbó leads to the Barceloneta seafront. On the quayside, the broad pedestrian zone is a hub of activity, often lined with immigrants selling counterfeit products (known as *manteros*). Illegal trading has spiraled out of control in recent years—a social issue that clashes awkwardly with the ostentatious armada of yachts parked alongside.

Tip: There are some great birds-eye views of Port Vell to be enjoyed from the surrounding buildings (and the cable car). Try the rooftop terrace of the Museu d'Història de Catalunya.

BARCELONA AQUARIUM

Moll d'Espanya del Port Vell; 93/221-7474; www.aquariumbcn.com; Mon.-Fri. 10am-8pm, Sat.-Sun. 10am-8:30pm; €20 11+/€15 children aged 5-10/€7 children aged 3-4; metro: Drassanes or Barceloneta

Barcelona's aquarium sits on a man-made protrusion of land in the middle of the harbor. It's one of the city's most-visited attractions: 11,000 fish and sea creatures, representing 450 different species, inhabit the Mediterranean and tropical tanks. The highlight is the spectacular Oceanarium, a microcosm of the Mediterranean Sea. Visitors can walk underwater through an 80-meter-long (260-foot) tunnel, spotting gilt heads, moray eels, ocean sunfish, rays, and two types of shark—sand tiger and sandbar. Feeding time is a particularly thrilling time to pass

through (times vary according to species). Adrenaline junkies can go one step further with the cage-diving experience inside the Oceanarium (€150), or ditch the cage and swim right alongside the sharks (€300).

TRANSBORDADOR AERI DEL PORT (PORT CABLE CAR)

Avinguda Miramar/Passeig de Joan de Borbó, 88; 93/430-4716; www. telefericodebarcelona.com; Oct. 30-Feb. 28 11am-5:30pm, Mar. 1-Oct. 29 10:30am-7pm (until 8pm Jun.-Sept.); €11 one way, €16.50 round-trip; metro: Barceloneta

A quick yet scenic route between Montjuïc and Barceloneta, the Aeri del Port de Barcelona travels 1,300 meters (4,265 feet) in approximately 10 minutes, and offers unparalleled views of the city's waterfront. The cable car was conceived nearly 100 years ago, ahead of the 1929 Barcelona International Exposition, although it wasn't completed until 1931. During the Spanish Civil War, the cable car was closed, the cables were removed, and the towers were used as strategic lookout points for the defense of the port. It came back into use in 1963 and the towers were restored in 1995.

The red and white cabins can accommodate 20 people (standing) and cross the port every 10-15 minutes at a height of between 70 and 90 meters (230 to 300 feet). Halfway through the journey, the cabins pass through a central tower, the Torre de Jaume I; it can be a little bumpy. The free-standing lattice Torre de Sant Sebastià, located at the portside terminus, also houses the Torre d'Alta Mar restaurant (torredealtamar.com; 93/221-0007), which offers fine dining with a view, but comes with a hefty price tag.

For the port terminus, take bus 39, 45, 59, D20, or V15 to Passeig Joan de

BARCELONETA'S STORIED PAST

Every day is a holiday in the waterfront neighborhood of Barceloneta—or so it seems. A triangular piece of land that juts out into the Mediterranean, Barceloneta is flanked by Port Vell on one side and golden beaches on the other; a never-ending tide of tourists floods its effervescent waterfront. Sea-view restaurants, *xiringuitos* (beach bars), and a constant stream of traders and entertainers line the promenade, stretching from the sail-shaped W Hotel up to Frank Gehry's *Peix* ("fish") sculpture.

Step back from the sand, though, and you'll find some clues to the neighborhood's former lives. Barceloneta was built on a reclaimed strip of land in the 18th century to accommodate the inhabitants of La Ribera who were displaced due to the construction of Philip V's Ciutadella fortress. Given its location

Barceloneta Beach

by the port, it naturally became a fisherman's village. Following industrialization, factories sprung up here and in the adjacent Poblenou area, and workers settled nearby. By the mid-20th century, living conditions in the overcrowded, working-class neighborhood were abysmal, with thousands of shanties populating the beachfront. Today, a memorial plaque to the residents of the famous Somorrostro shantytown, which was cleared in 1966, can be found on the beach of the same name.

Since the 1980s, Barceloneta has undergone a dramatic transformation, largely prompted by the 1992 Olympic Games. Vast quantities of sand were imported to create golden beaches along the polluted seafront, transforming the entire coastline. Mass tourism followed, and the rest, as they say, is history.

Longtime residents of the neighborhood, however, are not all convinced about Barceloneta's newfound glamor. With rental prices soaring, many struggle to recognize the modern waterfront playground as their own, and there's a certain nostalgia for the old community spirit. This general discontent has led to a number of public incidents, including neighborhood action against drunken tourists and illegal Airbnb rentals. Nevertheless, Barceloneta retains its fishing-quarter charm, with family-run restaurants, old-timers playing dominoes by the sea, and the blue and yellow neighborhood flag proudly hanging from balconies.

Points of interest include the **Carmen Amaya Fountain** on Plaça de Brugada, dedicated to the famous flamenco dancer, who was born in the Somorrostro shantytown. The **Casa de la Barceloneta** (Carrer de Sant Carles 6; 93/624-2666; https://ajuntament.barcelona.cat/casadelabarceloneta1761; Tues.-Fri. 10am-1pm, 4pm-8pm, Sat. 10am-2pm) museum is housed in a building dating from 1761 and provides a window into the neighborhood's culture, past and present. The Baroque **Església de Sant Miquel del Port** (Carrer de Sant Miquel, 39; Sunday mass 1pm) was the first building to be completed in the neighborhood and was famously built low enough for Ciutadella cannons to be fired over the top of it. Finally, the **Mercat de la Barceloneta,** situated in the central Plaça del Poeta Boscà, is an extraordinary reinterpretation of the original 1884 market structure, with an undulating roof designed by MiAS Arquitectes in 2007. Along the seafront, look for Rebecca Horn's **L'Estel Ferit** sculpture of four steel cubes stacked in a 10-meter (33-foot) tower.

Barceloneta is within easy walking distance of the Gothic Quarter and El Born, and can also be reached by **bus** (39, 45, 59, V15, D20), **metro** (L4, Barceloneta), and **cable car** (from Montjuic).

Borbó / Plaça del Mar, or the metro to Barceloneta (L4). The Montjuïc terminus is situated in front of the Hotel Miramar. Take the 150 bus from Plaça Espanya to Av Miramar-Pl Carlos Ibáñez, or plan to end up here after a wander around Montjuïc by foot.

MUSEU D'HISTÒRIA DE CATALUNYA

Palau de Mar, Plaça de Pau Vila, 3; 93/225-4700; www.mhcat.cat; Tues.-Sat. 10am-7pm (8pm Wed.), Sun. 10am-2:30pm; €4.50/€3.50 under 25s and over 65s; metro: Barceloneta

Housed in a 19th-century warehouse overlooking Port Vell, the Museu d'Història de Catalunya catalogs the complete history of Catalonia, from prehistoric times up to the present day. Starting with the Paleolithic period on the second floor, visitors are whisked through a chronological journey right up to the 18th century, covering Moorish invasions, Romanesque art, maritime power, and the Spanish War of Succession along the way. The permanent exhibition continues on the third floor, with the industrial revolution, civil war, and dictatorship, and concludes with a portrait of contemporary Catalonia. The first floor is reserved for temporary exhibitions. Explanatory panels are presented in Catalan, Castilian, and English, and an audio guide is available via mobile. The rooftop terrace bar is well worth a visit, offering fabulous panoramic views across the port.

MUSEU DEL DISSENY

Plaça de les Glòries Catalanes, 37-38; 93/256-6800; www.museudisseny.cat; Tues.-Sun. 10am-8pm; €6; metro: Glòries

An imposing, anvil-shaped building, Museu del Disseny presides over the evolving heart of the Glòries neighborhood. Opened in 2014, this massive

Museu Nacional d'Art de Catalunya

POBLENOU COMES TO LIFE

Dubbed in its 19th-century heyday as the "Catalan Manchester," the neighborhood of Poblenou (metro: Poblenou) was the epicenter of Catalan industrialization until industry declined, and the area lay derelict for many years. Today, Poblenou is home to a different kind of industry thanks to the 22@ Barcelona project, which has established the area as a technological and innovative district. Remnants of the area's past can be spotted here and there—brick chimneys, converted factories, and warehouse lofts—but there's a distinctly forward-thinking, creative outlook among those who gather in the studios, coworking spaces, and tech schools that have replaced their industrial predecessors.

a little beer spot on the Rambla de Poblenou

BARCELONA'S MOST AUTHENTIC RAMBLA

The leafy **Rambla del Poblenou** (two blocks from the Poblenou metro station) is the beating heart of the neighborhood, running from Avinguda Diagonal all the way to the seafront. This pedestrianized boulevard is full of lively terraces, ideal for a café con leche, tapas, or a cold beer, accompanied by a healthy dose of people-watching, and it's far enough from the center to maintain a distinctly local flavor. It is probably the city's most authentic *rambla*.

CAFÉS, SHOPS, AND GALLERIES

An arty edge runs throughout the neighborhood's revolution from hip furniture stores (**BD**, Carrer de Ramon Turró, 126; and **Noak Room,** Carrer de Roc Boronat, 69) and trendy brunch cafes (**Can Dendê,** Carrer de la Ciutat de Granada, 44) to third-wave coffee (**Nomad Roasters,** Carrer de Pujades, 95) and cultural institutions. Check out the **Museu Can Framis** (Carrer de Roc Boronat, 116-126), a former factory-turned-gallery with more than 300 contemporary Catalan paintings on display, or the many micro galleries dotted across the barrio: **La Plataforma** (Carrer de Pujades, 99; laplataformabcn.com), **La Escocesa** (Carrer de Pere IV, 345; laescocesa.org), and **Espronceda** (Carrer d'Espronceda, 326; www.espronceda.net).

UNDERGROUND ACTIVITIES

As is often the way, many of the cooler cultural activities in Poblenou are happening under the radar. To get a taste of the action, keep an eye out for the **Palo Alto Market** (paloaltomarket.com), a monthly hipster market with local design, food trucks, and live music; **Open Studios** (Tallers Oberts, www.tallerspoblenou.org) in mid-September; **Barcelona Design Week** (www.barcelonadesignweek.com) in early June; **La Fira del Poblenou** craft beer festival in July (www.lafiradelpoblenou.com); and the traditional **neighborhood festival** in early September (www.festamajorpoblenou.org). If tech is your thing, it doesn't take much probing to tap into the local scene—www.barcinno.com is a good place to start.

arts institution brings together all things design, from 4th-century textiles to modern products—a fitting homage to the integral role design plays in the city's cultural heritage.

The Museu del Disseny de Barcelona occupies four floors and combines exhibits from the former Museu de les Arts Decoratives (decorative arts), Museu de Ceràmica (ceramics), Museu Tèxtil i d'Indumentària (textiles and clothing), and the

Gabinet de les Arts Gràfiques (graphic arts). The result is an eclectic collection of more than 70,000 objects, a selection of which is presented in four semi-permanent exhibitions.

On the first floor, "From the World to the Museum. Product Design, Cultural Heritage" presents 238 hallmark products, from pioneering designs to everyday objects. The second floor accommodates "Extraordinary! Collections of Decorative and Author-Centred Art (3rd-20th Century)," a collection of 1,100 ceramics, textiles, furniture, glassware, clocks, wallpaper, and more, and includes some works by Picasso. "Dressing the Body. Silhouettes and Fashion (1550-2015)," on the third floor, explores the changing shape of the body as expressed through fashion—a fascinating journey through the history of culture, explained through 170 dresses and frames. Finally, on the fourth floor, "Do You Work or Design? New Visual Communication. 1980-2003" examines the role of graphic design in a changing political and social context, following Spain's transition to democracy.

Elsewhere, three exhibition spaces host a diverse range of temporary, multi-disciplinary shows, from David Bowie to Adolf Loos. The building also accommodates a library, café, auditorium, and the headquarters of design institutions BCD (Barcelona Centre de Disseny) and FAD (Foment de les Arts i del Disseny).

Tip: After dark, kids (and big kids) can enjoy hours of fun at the interactive sound and light installation, "BuumRuum!" by David Torrents y artec3 Studio, which forms part of the urban landscaping.

SANTS, LES CORTS, AND LA ZONA ALTA

✪ CAMP NOU

Carrer d'Aristides Maillol, 12; 90/218-9900; www.fcbarcelona.com; mid-Apr.-mid-Oct. and Christmas holidays 9:30am-7pm daily, mid-Oct.-mid.-Apr. Mon.-Sat. 10am-6:30pm, Sun. 10am-2:30pm; €25 guided tour and museum; metro: Palau Reial or Collblanc; bus: D20, 54, H8, H10

Home of FC Barcelona, the legendary Camp Nou is the biggest stadium in Europe and a place of pilgrimage for any football aficionado. Built in 1957, this magnificent curved structure seats nearly 100,000 spectators, and has been extended twice since it first opened. In 2016, plans by Nikken Sekkei + Pascual i Ausió Arquitectes were approved to remodel the stadium. The facility will be modernized, a roof will be added, and the stadium's capacity will increase to 105,000. Work is due to start in 2020.

Founded in 1899, FC Barcelona (known as Barça) is one of the world's most famous, and richest, football clubs. Although founded by a group of foreigners—led by Swiss footballer Joan Gamper—the club has long been considered a symbol of Catalan culture and identity, hence the motto *més que un club* ("more than a club"). The club's history is deeply rooted in Catalan nationalism, and at times has been inextricably linked to political turbulence in the region, most notably when the club's president, Josep Sunyol, was murdered by Franco's soldiers at the start of the Spanish Civil War.

Nevertheless, Barça's fame comes first and foremost from its spectacular success on the pitch, having won 26 La Liga titles, 30 Copa del Rey tournaments, and the UEFA Champions League five times. The team is admired the world over, and over the years, many of the game's greatest talents have donned the *blaugrana* (blue and burgundy) striped shirt, from Diego Maradona and Johan Cruyff to today's superstar striker Lionel Messi, who is widely regarded as one of the greatest players of all time.

Naturally, the best way to experience the emotion of Camp Nou is as a spectator—ideally at an El Clásico match against fierce rivals Real Madrid—though tickets are hard to come by. Tickets for lower-key games are available for general sale. For those who want to get behind the sidelines, the guided tour and museum, known as the **Camp Nou Experience**, is one of Catalonia's most-visited attractions and includes a walk down the tunnel and access to the dugout, the away side's changing room, the press room, and the commentary boxes. Numerous trophies and memorabilia are displayed in the museum, as well as multimedia installations that cover almost 120 years of club history and a dedicated "Messi Space."

MONESTIR DE PEDRALBES

Baixada del Monestir, 9; 93/256-3434;monestirpedralbes.bcn.cat; Apr.-Sept. Tues.-Fri. 10am-5pm, Sat. 10am-7pm, Sun. 10am-8pm, Oct.-Mar. Tues.-Fri. 10am-2pm, Sat.-Sun. 10am-5pm; €5/€3.50 under 30s and over 65s/free for under 16s; free first Sunday of the month and Sundays after 3pm; FGC: Reina Elisenda; bus: 63, 68, 78

Founded by Queen Elisenda de Montcada in 1327, the Monestir de Pedralbes is a religious enclave at the foot of the Collserola hills and a prime example of Catalan Gothic architecture. After her husband, King James II, died, the queen spent the rest of her

Camp Nou, home of FC Barcelona

days here, living alongside the Poor Clares (the Franciscan Clarist Order of nuns), many of whom were widows or unmarried women from privileged backgrounds.

A functioning convent until 1983, the well-preserved complex paints a vivid picture of monastic life. The convent and church are oriented around one of the world's largest cloisters, a magnificent three-story structure that surrounds a lush, harmonious garden. Around the garden, the cloister galleries provide access to the dormitory, refectory, kitchen, infirmary, chapter house, and abbey room, as well as the day cells, where the nuns withdrew for solitary reflection.

Inside the church of Santa Maria de Pedralbes (accessed from the square outside), keep an eye out for Queen Elisenda's double-sided sepulchre: one side faces into the church, where she is dressed in royal attire, the other into the cloister, where she is shown as a penitent widow. The contrasting images represent the two phases of her life.

The monastery's rich collection of religious art and artifacts is testament to the convent's wealthy inhabitants. In the lofty dormitory space, the "Monastery Treasures" exhibition displays an outstanding selection of art, furniture, and liturgical objects, much of which was donated by the nuns' families throughout the monastery's 700-year history. Don't miss the 14th-century St. Michael's Chapel, situated just off the cloister. Its magnificent floor-to-ceiling murals by Ferrer Bassa have been painstakingly restored in recent years.

Blissfully beyond the tourist trail, the monastery remains as secluded and tranquil today as it was in its heyday. An audio guide (€0.60) is available in English. The simplest way to get there is on bus 63 from Plaça de la Universitat (30 minutes approx.). Alight at Av d'Esplugues-Av Pearson, and walk north for five minutes. Alternatively, take the FGC train from Catalunya to Sarrià (L6), then the L12 from Sarrià to Reina Elisenda (15 minutes approx.)—from there it's a 10-minute walk.

TORRE BELLESGUARD

Carrer de Bellesguard, 20; 93/250-4093; bellesguardgaudi.com; Tues.-Sun. 10am-3pm; €9/€7.20 under 18s and over 65s/free for children under 8; FGC: Av. Tibidabo; bus V13, then 196

Set in the leafy heights of the Les Tres Torres neighborhood, Torre Bellesguard is one of Gaudí's lesser-known yet most unusual works. Commissioned by the Figueras family as a second residence and constructed between 1900 and 1909, this Modernista mansion represents a significant departure from Gaudí's signature organic style. Here, a rectilinear aesthetic prevails, something rarely found in Gaudí's work.

This, of course, was no accident.

Monestir de Pedralbes

Torre Bellesguard

The house stands on the site of the medieval castle of Martin the Humane, King of Aragón and the last monarch of the House of Barcelona, who died in 1410. Gaudí was fascinated by the site's history and designed Torre Bellesguard as a Neo-Gothic homage to its former residents. Pointed elements and straight lines express a sense of verticality across the theatrical façade, culminating with a soaring tower that rises dramatically over the entrance to the slate-clad house. Ruins of the 15th-century medieval castle form part of the gardens, while colorful mosaic benches on either side of the front door are imbued with historical symbolism.

Inside, the building's straight-edged exterior melts away into soft-edged, light-filled spaces, more typical of the architectural master. A spectacular, three-story entrance and staircase sits at the corner of the building's square plan, filled with vivid blue tiling and wrought-iron embellishes that hint at Moorish influences. This acts as a circulation space to the apartments on the ground and first floor, bypassing

a service floor and instead rising to the impressive attic space.

The visit concludes on the intricate roof terrace, where one instantly understands why this privileged spot was christened *Bellesguard*, meaning beautiful views. On the southern corner of the terrace, look up and spot Gaudí's dragon, an illusion created by four windows (two eyes, two nostrils) and the tower as its tail.

As the house is still inhabited, the tour of the interior is restricted to the entrance hall, attic, and terrace. An audio guide is included in the entrance fee and English guided tours (€16) take place at 11am on Saturday and Sunday. This "forgotten masterpiece" is well off the tourist trail. Take bus V13 or the FGC train (L7) to Av. Tibidabo; from there, the house is a 17-minute walk. Alternatively, catch bus number 196 from Plaça Kennedy nearby (bus 123 on the return leg).

COSMOCAIXA

Carrer d'Isaac Newton, 26; 93/212-6050; obrasociallacaixa.org; Tues.-Sun. 10am-8pm; €4; FGC: Av. Tibidabo; bus: 196, V13, V15

Barcelona's science museum, the CosmoCaixa, encompasses a world of intriguing and interactive exhibits. Albert Einstein welcomes visitors in the entrance hall of this elaborate red-brick Modernista building, a former asylum for the blind. Like CaixaForum, it is owned and managed by the social arm of La Caixa bank.

Visitors make their way to the fifth floor basement via a ramp that winds around a suspended Acariquara tree, and are greeted by a Foucault pendulum upon entering the main exhibition area. The highlight is undoubtedly the *Bosc Inundat* ("flooded forest"), a real-life slice of the Amazon rainforest complete with endemic flora and fauna and periodic downpours; wander through the woods and spot leaf-cutter ants and anacondas, and watch out for the capybara and alligator below the waterline.

With a bargain entrance fee, this is a classic rainy-day destination for locals, and is well beyond the tourist trail—although it is worth the detour, particularly for family vacationers. To get there, take the FGC train to Av. Tibidabo, from there it is a 15-minute walk. Alternately, the V13 and V15 buses terminate nearby.

Tip: Don't miss the views and sound telescope outside on Plaça de la Ciència—entertaining for all ages.

MOUNT TIBIDABO

Tibibus T2A from Pl. Catalunya; FGC: Av. Tibidabo, bus 196, and Tibidabo Funicular

Casting an ever-present watchful eye over the city, Mount Tibidabo is Barcelona's highest point, rising 512 meters (1,680 feet) above sea level. Part of the Serra de Collserola, which runs along the western limit of the city, Tibidabo's summit is populated with some prominent landmarks. The crowning glory is the Temple Expiatori del Sagrat Cor, a neo-Gothic church completed in 1961, topped by an enormous bronze statue of the Sacred Heart, looking down at the city *à la* Christ the Redeemer. Lit up by night, the church can be spotted from across the city.

To the south lies Norman Foster's Torre de Collserola (93/211-7942; Mar.-Dec. Sat.-Sun. noon-2pm), a futuristic telecommunications tower built for the 1992 Olympic Games. *El Mirador*, on the 10th floor, is an enclosed viewing point accessed via a glass elevator. At 560 meters (1,840 feet) above sea level, it is the highest

accessible place in Barcelona and provides unbeatable panoramic views across the metropolitan area and beyond. On clear days, visitors can see as far as Montserrat and the Cadí-Moixeró mountain range.

To reach Tibidabo, take the FGC train (L7) or bus numbers H4, V13, or V15 to Avinguda Tibidabo, switch to the 196 bus, and then the Tibidabo Funicular (€7.70 or €4.10 when purchased with a ticket to Tibidabo Amusement Park).

TIBIDABO AMUSEMENT PARK

Plaça del Tibidabo; 93/211-7942; www.tibidabo.cat; Dec. Sat.-Sun. and holidays 11am-6pm, Mar. until 7pm, Apr. and Nov. until 8pm, May-Jun. and Sept.-Oct. until 9pm, Jul. Wed.-Sun. 11am-10pm, Aug. 11am-11pm daily; general entrance €28.50/€10.30 children under 1.2 meters (4 feet) tall/€9 over 60s/free for children under 90cm (3 feet) tall; Panoramic Area €12.70/€7.80 children under 1.2 meters (4 feet) tall/free for children under 90cm (3 feet) tall; Tibibus T2A from Pl. Catalunya; FGC: Av. Tibidabo, bus 196, and Tibidabo Funicular

Perched upon Barcelona's highest point is a magical place close to the hearts of anyone raised in this city. Opened in 1905, the Tibidabo Amusement Park is one of the world's oldest amusement parks, still running after more than 100 years. There are 30 rides and attractions for all ages, including old classics like the Avió airplane ride (as seen in Woody Allen's *Vicky Cristina Barcelona*) as well as newer additions, like the 4D cinema Dididado, street theater, and picnic areas. It's no Universal Studios, but the unique backdrop of the city at your feet makes the loop-the-loop all the more thrilling. There are two types of entrance ticket: access all areas or access to the "Panoramic Area" only, home to some of the park's oldest attractions. A shuttle bus (T2A) to the park departs every 20 minutes from outside Desigual on Plaça de Catalunya (€3). Alternately, take the FGC train (L7) to Av. Tibidabo, change to the 196 bus, and then take the Tibidabo Funicular.

Food

Catalonia is at the cutting edge of haute cuisine, with 24 Michelin-starred restaurants in Barcelona and 55 in Catalonia overall. But it's not all about deconstructed molecular gastronomy. A seemingly innate sensibility for all things edible is celebrated in even the most ordinary bars and restaurants, and the opportunity to make a delectable discovery lies on every street corner.

BARRI GÒTIC AND LA RAMBLA
SPANISH AND CATALAN
Café de l'Acadèmia

Carrer dels Lledó, 1; 93/319-8253; Mon.-Fri. 1:30pm-4pm, 8:30pm-11:30pm; €10-€25, set lunch menu (weekdays) €15.75

Tucked away behind Plaça Sant Jaume, Café de L'Acadèmia offers refined Catalan cuisine in an authentic setting, surrounded by wooden beams, exposed stone walls, and dimly lit interiors. The space fills with crowds of animated government workers at lunchtime. The menu features modern classics—like the black pudding lasagne and the succulent cod served with a tomato, garlic, and saffron mousseline—and is best accompanied by wine from the proprietor's vineyard. The restaurant's terrace on Plaça Sant Just makes a beautiful al fresco option.

TAPAS
✪ Bodega La Palma

Carrer de la Palma de Sant Just, 7; 93/315-0656; www.bodegalapalma.com; Mon.-Fri. 9am-midnight, Sat. noon-midnight; €13-€25, set lunch menu (weekdays) €13

Bodega La Palma is a traditional tapas tavern dating from 1935. Keep it simple here and you can't go wrong: The *bravas* are outstanding, the pea and mint *croquetas* a revelation, and local wines are served straight from the barrel. Buried deep in the Barri Gòtic, this unassuming bodega may be hard to find but it's brimming with authentic, old-fashioned charm. Leave room for dessert.

INTERNATIONAL
Shunka

Carrer Sagristans, 5; 93/412-4991; www.koyshunka.com; Tues.-Sun. 1:30pm-3:30pm, 8:30pm-11:30pm; €17-€25

Shunka has become a stalwart of Japanese food in the city, along with its Michelin-starred sister restaurant, **Koy Shunka** (Carrer d'en Copons, 7; 93/412-7939). The understated entrance is easy to miss, but inside an expert army of chefs awaits in the spotless open kitchen. Ask for a seat at the bar and let their meticulous knifework impress as they prepare sushi, sashimi, makis, nigiris, and

TAPAS

Unlike in areas of Andalusia, Basque Country, and Galicia, where a bite may be served with every drink, tapa culture is not a Catalan tradition, save for the occasional bowl of olives, chips, or nuts. There are, however, many traditional cuisines that can be ordered tapa-style. Terms to be aware of are:

pinchos

- **Tapas:** Small dishes to be shared, such as patatas bravas (potatoes with spiced sauce and aioli).

- *Raciones:* Larger versions of sharing dishes, often for servings of cured meats.

- **Pinchos:** Bite-sized tapas served on top of pieces of bread. A Basque tradition.

- *Platos combinados:* This can refer to a personal plate of a meat and vegetable dish, or a larger spread of the tapas on offer.

Typical Catalan tapas include:

- *Pa amb tomaquet (pan con tomate):* Bread rubbed with fresh tomatoes and drizzled with oil and salt (vegetarian).

- *Butifarra negra:* An uncured spiced sausage, Catalonia's blood pudding.

- *Botifarra blanca:* White pork sausage.

- *Botifarra d'ou:* White pork sausage with egg.

- *Fuet:* A long thin sausage of dried, cured pork meat.

- *Embutidos:* Platter of cured meats including fuet and jamón.

more. Make sure you try the creamy tuna belly (*toro*).

Bistrot Levante

Placeta de Manuel Ribe, 1; 93/858-2679; bistrotlevante.com; Wed.-Fri. 11am-midnight, Sat.-Sun. 11am-1am; €6-€16

A warm glow emanates from the dining room of Bistrot Levante onto the narrow lanes of the ancient Jewish quarter. Inside, creative Mediterranean dishes with a Middle Eastern twist—such as spicy shakshuka with baked eggs, pulled lamb shoulder kubaneh, and a mouthwatering selection of meze plates—make up the popular brunch (11am-4pm), lunch, and dinner (8pm-11pm, 11:30pm Sat.-Sun.) menus. A cozy space with a simple aesthetic entices diners to linger with a glass of natural wine or a Turkish coffee with cardamom. The hummus is simply delicious.

VEGAN, VEGETARIAN, AND GLUTEN-FREE
Rasoterra

*Carrer del Palau, 5; 93/318-6926; www.
rasoterra.cat; Wed.-Sun., 1pm-4pm,
7pm-11pm; €8-€14, set lunch menu €15.50,
seasonal tasting menu €32*

This casual bistro near Plaça Sant Jaume presents innovative vegetarian cuisine that channels a gastronomic flair often reserved for fish and meat eaters. Faithful to the slow-food movement, the health-conscious kitchen uses local, seasonal ingredients in a lineup of interesting creations, such as codium seaweed and asparagus risotto. Add natural wines, friendly staff, and an unpretentious atmosphere, and the scene is set for a clean, green meal that satisfies mind, body, and soul. Gluten-free and vegan options are plentiful.

QUICK BITES
✪ Conesa Entrepans

*Carrer de la Llibreteria, 1; 93/310-1394;
www.conesaentrepans.com; 8:15am-10:15pm
Mon.-Sat., €3-€5*

Probably the best sandwich in Barcelona, Conesa Entrepans has been feeding the masses since 1951. This family-run establishment is a firm locals' favorite, situated on the corner of Plaça Sant Jaume. Offering a long menu of primarily pork-based fillings, including plenty of gluten-free options, many of Conesa's tasty *bocadillos* contain a variety of Catalan sausages sandwiched between a griddle-toasted baguette. The friendly, hard-working staff can cater for the lunchtime queues in no time, so it's worth sticking around.

FINE DINING
Informal

*Carrer de la Plata, 4; 93/169-1869;
8am-11:30am, 1:30pm-4pm, 7:30-10:30pm
daily (Fri.-Sat. until 11:30pm);
€18.50-€31.50, weekday set lunch menu €35*

A bright, contemporary dining room on the ground floor of the swanky Serras hotel, Informal's haute cuisine and attentive service reflect the five-star setting. Local, seasonal produce is the basis for Chef Marc Gascon's ultramodern take on traditional Catalan and Mediterranean recipes. The tempting menu changes regularly, and features indulgent dishes such as grilled lobster, roasted monkfish with autumn mushrooms, seared scallops, and the classic Chateaubriand. Although not quite as casual as the name suggests, this is certainly laid-back luxury. Enjoy a pre- or post-dinner drink with incredible port views at the El Sueño rooftop bar.

COFFEE
Satan's Coffee Corner

*Carrer de l'Arc de Sant Ramon del Call, 11;
66/622-2599; satanscoffee.com; Mon.-Sat.
9am-6pm, Sun. 10am-6pm; €3-€14*

"Roasts to make the devil proud"—that's the slogan at Satan's Coffee Corner, Barcelona's original specialty coffee shop. A short, all-day menu of simple snacks and Japanese-influenced street food accompany the quality coffee, sourced from local roasters Right Side. Coffee aficionados and creatives hang out at this secluded corner of the Barrí Gòtic, hypothesizing over a flat white or busting a hangover with a Japanese breakfast. Ideal for a clandestine caffeine fix just steps from Barcelona Cathedral.

Café Zurich

Plaça de Catalunya, 1-4; 93/317-9153;
Mon.-Fri. 8am-11pm, Sat. 9am-midnight,
Sun. 9am-11pm

A Barcelona institution since 1862, Café Zurich sits at the crossroads of La Rambla and Plaça de Catalunya—a hub of activity. This historical establishment has served as a classic meeting point for more than a century, both observing the constantly changing city and changing with it (its current reincarnation dates from 1999). Today it is something of a tourist trap, but the terrace is undoubtedly one of the best people-watching spots in town.

DESSERTS
Pastisseria Escribà

La Rambla, 83; 93/301-6027;
www.escriba.es; 9am-9:30pm daily

Pastisseria Escribà is a delight for the senses. A family-run bakery since 1906, the cakes and bakes that fill the antique window display are as beautiful and intricate as the building's mosaiced façade. The master pastry chefs at Escribà take sugarcraft to a whole new level, and are known for their edible murals, chocolate sculptures, and fantastical cake decorating. Housed in the Antigua Casa Figueras on La Rambla since 1986, the original flagship store is located on Gran Via, number 546. Stop here to satiate your sweet tooth.

EL RAVAL
SPANISH AND CATALAN
✪ Cera 23

Carrer de la Cera, 23; 93/442-0808;
www.cera23.com; Thurs.-Mon. 1pm-4pm,
7pm-11pm, Tues.-Wed. 7pm-11pm;
€11.50-€17.90

Cera 23 is a diamond in the rough; you know you're onto something when the crowds are flocking to an unsavory

backstreet. Opened by three Galician friends in 2010, reservations are essential at this tiny Raval nook, which offers Galician fare with a creative twist in a relaxed, jovial ambiance. Try the "volcano" of black rice with seafood "rocks" and saffron-flavored "lava," and don't miss the sensational blackberry mojitos.

Arume

Carrer d'En Botella, 11-13; 93/315-4872;
www.arumerestaurant.com; Mon.-Thurs
7pm-11:30pm, Fri.-Sun. 1pm-3:30pm,
7pm-11:30pm; €15.50-€19.50

Galician fare triumphs at Arume, just steps away from its sister restaurant, Cera 23. Former home of writer Manuel Vazquez Montalban, a small street front conceals a labyrinth of intimate, eclectically decorated dining rooms, where modern interpretations of classic dishes, such as *pulpo a la Gallega*, are served up by the friendly waiting staff. Reservations advised.

Fonda España

Carrer de Sant Pau, 9-11; 93/550-0010;
www.hotelespanya.com; 1pm-4pm daily,
and Mon.-Sat. 8pm-11pm; €18-€26

With its lofty ceilings, beautiful mosaic tiling, and crisp, white tablecloths, Fonda España exudes old-school class with a gourmet menu to match. Designed by Modernisme master Domènech i Montaner, this exquisite dining room is part of the four-star Hotel España, located just behind the Gran Teatre del Liceu. Attentive waiting staff serve beautifully presented traditional dishes, such as cod fritters with *all i olí* and baked hake with ganxet bean broth, and the set menus are excellent value (weekday lunch €28; evening €40). The *Viaje Modernista* tasting menu (€79/€114 with wine pairing) takes diners on a rich, 14-course journey through Catalan cuisine.

VEGAN, VEGETARIAN, AND GLUTEN-FREE
En Ville

Carrer del Doctor Dou, 14; 93/302-8467; www.envillebarcelona.es; Mon.-Sat. 1pm-4pm, 7:30pm-11:30pm; €13.20-€19.80, set lunch menu €13.90

Located on one of Raval's more refined streets, this elegant bistro serves a creative combination of Catalan and French cuisine. Everything on the varied menu is gluten-free (though non-celiacs will barely notice). Filet steak in a foie gras sauce, honey-glazed salmon on a bed of sauteed vegetables; chocolate fondant and *crema catalana*—it's all gloriously rich, and there are vegetarian options too. The weekday set lunch menu (1pm-4pm, €13.90) is popular; the marble-topped tables start filling up around 1:30pm.

TAPAS
✪ Bar Cañete

Carrer de la Unió, 17; 93/270-3458; www.barcanete.com; Mon.-Sat. 1pm-midnight; €5.20-€24.90

Traditional tapas get the gourmet treatment at Bar Cañete. Part bar, part restaurant, this lively locale offers you either a table in the upscale table-clothed bistro, or a bar stool from which you can watch the kitchen buzz as dinner is served. The superb lineup of tapas leads diners on a taste tour of classic Spanish highlights, from the Cordoba-style eggplant (aubergine) in sugar cane honey or the Galician razor clams to the Palamós prawns and *pimientos de Padrón* (mini green peppers). Seasoned locals and young foodies gather here to enjoy some of the city's more revered tapas, impeccably served by white-jacketed waiters.

La Monroe

Plaça de Salvador Seguí, 1-9; 93/441-9461; lamonroe.es; Tues.-Thurs. and Sun. noon-1am, Fri.-Sat. noon-2am; mains €8.90-€14.50, tapas €1.50-€10.90

A youthful eatery on Plaça de Salvador Seguí, La Monroe is a lively meeting place day or night. Situated on the ground floor of the **Filmoteca de Catalunya,** cobblestone floors and glazed walls make the whole place feel like an extension of the plaza. Noisy groups of friends gather round long benches, feasting on nachos, grilled prawns, and *papitas* (La Monroe's take on bravas), while cinemagoers grab a pre-show *bikini* (ham and cheese melt) and local hipsters lap up the vermouth. You can absorb the artsy neighborhood vibes at this social hub.

INTERNATIONAL
El Pachuco

Carrer de Sant Pau, 110; 1:30pm-2:30am daily; €7.50-€11.80

Squeeze into the excellent-value El Pachuco on the edge of the Raval to experience one of the city's most authentic Mexican eateries. Generous portions of tacos, homemade nachos, and fried green bananas are served up in a lively atmosphere, washed down with a refreshing michelada, margarita, or one of 30 types of mezcal. Arrive early, as this tiny dive bar soon fills up.

✪ El Magraner Boig

Carrer d'En Robador, 22; 93/011-8605; www.elmagranerboig.com; Tues.-Fri. 8pm-1am, Sat.-Sun. 1pm-1am; €9.20-€11.80

El Magraner Boig could easily be a casual neighborhood café in Athens or Thessaloniki. Here, fresh Greek flavors offer a lighter alternative to traditional tapas, with sharing plates of tempting classics—from tzatziki and moussaka to *kolokithokeftedes* (courgette fritters). Try as many as you can, washed down with a fruity Cretan rosé or an ouzo digestif. It's a lofty, simple space with tile-topped wooden tables and a lively, welcoming vibe; don't let the less-than-salubrious street outside put you off. Reserve online.

FINE DINING
⊙ Dos Palillos

Carrer d'Elisabets, 9; 93/304-0513;
www.dospalillos.com; Tues.-Wed.
7:30pm-11:30pm, Thurs.-Sat.
1:30pm-3:30pm, 7:30pm-11:30pm; tasting
menus €90/€110

Mind-blowing, Michelin-starred Japanese tapas surprise and delight at Dos Palillos. Head chef Albert Raurich—Ferran Adrià's right-hand man at elBulli—fuses Oriental techniques with Spanish ingredients to create delicate morsels that stretch the imagination, like the Iberian-Cantonese pork jowl, chicken sashimi, and king crab shumai dumplings. From the outside, it looks like just another bar, but inside, diners enter into an intimate secret lair where they can indulge the senses with one of two tasting menus (€90/€110, reservations required). Nearby **Dos Pebrots** (Carrer del Dr. Dou, 19; 93/853-9598) Raurich's second restaurant, is a little easier on the pocket.

QUICK BITES
A Tu Bola

Carrer de l'Hospital, 78; 93/315-3244;
www.atubolarest.com; Sun., Mon., and Thurs.
1pm-midnight, Wed. 1pm-11pm,
Sat.-Sun. 1pm-1am; €3-€11

"We shape great food into balls": that's the mantra at A Tu Bola, and that's exactly what they do. Asian chicken, Mexican pork, Indian lentils, Israeli falafel, French quinoa, and Moroccan

beef—all bound up in great balls of tasty goodness. A scattering of stools surround the open kitchen in this casual street-food café, where the Israeli owner and chef speedily grates cucumbers while churning out the next order. The pita and homemade lemonade special (€6.50) makes the perfect pit stop to refuel.

Caravelle café

CAFÉS AND BRUNCH
Caravelle

Carrer del Pintor Fortuny, 31; 93/317-9892;
www.caravelle.es; Mon. 9:30am-5:30pm,
Tues.-Fri. 9:30am-1am, Sat. 10am-1am,
Sun. 10am-5:30pm; €8-€12.50

At Caravelle, they brew their own beer, make their own pickles, smoke and cure their own meats, and have rightfully earned a reputation as a reference in the locally sourced and house-made field. Brunch, featuring an ever-changing menu of international flavors (think Moroccan-style baked eggs and coconut French toast), is the star attraction at this hip café. Lunch and dinner are just as varied—try the steak tostada with marrow beans, guacamole and green tomato pico de gallo, or the roast pumpkin salad. Arrive before 12:30pm to avoid queues.

COFFEE
✪ Granja Viader

Carrer d'en Xuclà, 4; 93/318-3486;
www.granjaviader.cat; Mon.-Sat.
9am-1:15pm, 5pm-9:15pm

The viscose *xocolata calenta* at Granja Viader is the stuff of legends. This traditional café and former urban dairy was opened by the Viader family in 1870, and specializes in chocolate beverages, *crema catalana*, and homemade cheeses (try the mató), made using recipes passed down through the generations. One hundred and fifty years on, the olde-worlde charm remains, as well as the marble tables around which Picasso and friends are said to have gathered, just a stone's throw from La Rambla.

LA RIBERA/EL BORN
SPANISH AND CATALAN
Passadis del Pep

Pla de Palau, 2; 93/310-1021; passadis.com;
Mon.-Sat. 1:30pm-3:30pm, 8:15pm-11:30pm;
tasting menus €60-€85

Follow a narrow passageway just off Pla de Palau and you'll find yourself in the foodie sanctuary of Passadis del Pep. With an emphasis on seafood, traditional Catalan cuisine of the highest caliber is served up in the classic, vaulted dining room. There's no menu—fresh market ingredients are the chef's daily inspiration—so open your mind and let them lead you on an authentic culinary expedition, from sea snails to wild rabbit. Meals are customized to suit taste and budget, but be prepared to lighten your wallet.

✪ Petra

Carrer dels Sombrerers, 13; 93/319-9999;
www.restaurantpetra.com; Mon.-Thurs.
1:15pm-4pm, 8:30pm-11pm, Fri.-Sat.
1:15pm-4pm, 8:30pm-midnight; €7-12,
weekday set lunch menu €12.50

A tiny hidden gem next door to the Basilica of Santa Maria del Mar, Petra offers a short but interesting menu of seasonal Mediterranean dishes at very reasonable prices. Full of quirks, from the stained-glass windows and cutlery chandeliers to the wine bottle menu, Petra is a unique locals' favorite in a largely touristy area. Make your reservation in advance.

TAPAS
Bar del Pla

Carrer de Montcada, 2; 93/268-3003;
www.bardelpla.cat; Mon.-Thurs. noon-11pm,
Fri.-Sat. noon-midnight; €4-€16.10

Hanging hams and a large wooden cask welcome diners into this old-school tapas den buried in El Born. Bar del Pla offers a marvelous array of traditional and contemporary tapas, exquisitely presented: try the mushrooms with wasabi and the squid-ink croquettes. With more than 100 bottles available, including biodynamic and natural, the in-house sommeliers take their wine seriously, so don't be shy to ask for a pairing. Reservations recommended.

Can Cisa / Bar Brutal

Carrer de la Princesa, 14; 93/295-4797;
www.cancisa.cat; Mon. 7pm-1:30am,
Tues.-Thurs. 1pm-4pm, 7pm-1:30am,
Fri.-Sat. 1pm-1:30am; €7.50-€17

Natural wine is the raison d'être at Bar Brutal, closely followed by the eclectic selection of original, innovative dishes. A wine bar (Can Cisa) and restaurant (Bar Brutal), this firm foodie favorite stocks 300 varieties of organic, biodynamic, and natural wines from around the world, perfect for an early evening aperitif or alongside a veritable feast. A seasonal menu of Mediterranean morsels, such as duck egg with cauliflower foam or smoked swordfish with grapefruit, awaits you here, tucked inside the nooks and crannies of this inviting tavern.

INTERNATIONAL
✪ N.A.P.

Avinguda de Francesc Cambó, 30; 68/619-2690; Mon.-Fri. 1:30pm-4:30pm, 8pm-midnight, Sat.-Sun. 1:30pm-midnight; €5.50-€9.90; no reservations

This no-frills, no-nonsense eatery serves up some of the city's best pizza, at the best prices. Produced in the Neapolitan tradition, light pizzas with a thin base, soft enough to fold, are churned out continuously from the wood-fired oven. For anyone who has ever been to the home of pizza, a bite of the classic Margherita or Marinara will, for a moment, take you back there. A second branch, with the same opening hours, is located in Barceloneta (Carrer del Baluard 69; 93/007-3639).

✪ Le Cucine Mandarosso

Carrer de Verdaguer i Callís, 4; 93/269-0780; www.lecucinemandarosso.com; Tues.-Sat. 1:30pm-4:30pm, 9pm-midnight; Sun. 1:30pm-4:30pm, 9pm-midnight; €13-€17, set lunch menu €12

This authentic Italian mamma's kitchen specializes in delicious homemade pasta and to-die-for desserts; think golden apple crostata or the creamiest white chocolate cheesecake. The tiled interiors of this quirky trattoria are lined with pantry shelving piled high with sundries and souvenirs, tucked away on a tiny street near the Palau de la Música. Get there early to sample the great value lunch menu (Tues.-Sat.)—there's usually a queue outside before it opens—or reserve for dinner.

En Aparté

Carrer de Lluís el Piadós, 2; 93/269-1335; www.enaparte.es; Mon.-Thurs. 10am-1am, Fri.-Sat. 10am-2am, Sun. 10am-12:30am; €8.50-€13

En Aparté is a French café for any hour of the day: a morning croissant and café au lait, lunch on the charming terrace (€12.50, Mon.-Fri., 12:30pm-4pm), or a charcuterie board and an intense Bordeaux to take you into the evening. Filled with natural light and vintage style, this little corner of France has a laid-back, welcoming vibe, close to the Arc de Triomf. Crusty baguettes, intensely creamy cheese, and rich pork rillettes are just some of the many indulgences on offer. Don't miss the homemade desserts.

Mosquito

Carrer dels Carders, 46; 93/268-7569; www.mosquitotapas.com; Mon. 7:30pm-1am, Tues.-Sun. 1pm-1am; €1.75-€7.95; no reservations

Itching for some dim sum? Mosquito is the place to alleviate your cravings. This popular Asian tapas bar fuses flavors from across the continent in a crowded tavern with a kitschy vibe. The focus is on dumplings—boiled, steamed, or fried, with tasty traditional fillings—although the steamy kitchen also turns out soups, noodles, and vegetable or meat dishes, all at reasonable prices. Wash it down with one of 40 craft beers. Reservations are not accepted, so arrive early before the queue builds up.

VEGETARIAN, VEGAN, AND ALLERGY-FRIENDLY
Flax & Kale Passage

Carrer de Sant Pere Més Alt, 31-33; 93/524-0052; www.teresacarles.com; Mon.-Fri. 9am-11:30pm, Sat.-Sun. 9:30am-11:30pm; €13-€26

Popular with coeliacs, veggies, and health-conscious hipsters, Flax & Kale Passage is a living lab of clean, green eating. The mainly plant-based menu stretches the imagination. Gluten-free wood-fired pizzas, topped with almond and cashew cheese, are surprisingly close to the real deal, while jackfruit imitates pulled pork and sauteed ackee fruit mimics scrambled egg. The industrial-chic interiors are nearly as eclectic as the mind-boggling menu. More alchemy awaits in the kombucha laboratory at the back.

COFFEE
✪ Cafés El Magnífico

Carrer de l'Argenteria, 64; 93/319-3975; www.cafeselmagnifico.com; Mon.-Sat. 10am-8pm

For a coffee on the run, El Magnífico is the best in town. At first glance, this 100-year-old coffee shop appears no different from the hundreds of others in the city. However, the current owner of this family-run roaster can be credited with introducing third-wave coffee to the city and, together with a knowledgeable staff, is happy to help patrons choose from a global selection of specialty brews. It's standing room only at the original branch, but if you'd like to take your time, visit the nearby sister store, El Mag (Carrer de Grunyí, 10; 93/488-5786; Fri.-Sat. 10am-6pm, Sun. 11am-6pm).

L'EIXAMPLE
SPANISH AND CATALAN
El Nacional

Passeig de Gràcia, 24 Bis; 93/518-5053; www.elnacionalbcn.com; Mon.-Sun. noon-1am

El Nacional brings the best of the Iberian peninsula together under one roof. Take your pick from four different bars—specializing in cocktails, beer, wine, and cava—and four restaurants: La Llotja (fish), La Taperia (tapas and paella), La Paradeta (delicatessen), and La Braseria (meat). Galician oysters, salt-crusted sea bream, and the famous aged beef from El Capricho in Leon are among the culinary delights that await in this grandiose food court, located just off Passeig de Gràcia. Built as a theater in 1889, this lofty space has assumed many guises—fabric-dye factory, car showroom, parking garage—and was restored to its former Modernista glory in 2014.

TAPAS
✪ La Bodegueta

Rambla de Catalunya, 100; 93/215-4894; www.labodegueta.cat; Mon.-Fri. 7am-1:45am, Sat. 8am-1:45am, Sun. 6:30pm-1:45am; €3.50-€20

Step down off the elegant Rambla de Catalunya into La Bodegueta and step back in time. Wine bottles and barrels line the walls of this family-run, classic tavern that serves no-nonsense tapas in the center of town, just steps from Gaudí's Casa Milà. Tuck into the traditional *huevos rotos* (fried potatoes with eggs) or some fine *jamón ibérico*, and follow their advice when it comes to wine—they've been doing this since 1942. A newer bodega run by the same people, at Carrer de Provença, 233 (93/215-1725), is also a good option without the old-style charm.

Taktika Berri

Carrer de València, 169; 93/453-4759; Mon.-Fri. 1pm-4pm, 8:30pm-11pm, Sat. 1pm-4pm; tapas from €1.50

It's all about *pintxos* at Taktika Berri: tasty bites mounted on bread, originating in the Basque Country. Twenty-five hot and cold varieties—don't miss the *tortilla de bacalao* (cod omelette)—are served up to an excitable local crowd at the bar. Get ready to grab a fresh one as they emerge from the kitchen, or sit down to sample the city's best Basque cuisine (reservations essential). Hang on to the cocktail sticks in each *pintxo*—that's how they work out the bill. Arrive early if you want to bag a spot at the bar.

Lateral

Carrer del Consell de Cent, 329; 93/348-7994; www.lateral.com; Sun.-Wed. noon-1am, Thurs.-Sat. noon-midnight; €2.80-€13.60

The Barcelona branch of a Madrid-based chain, this bistro-style restaurant offers a large variety of tapas that combine seasonal ingredients in classic and contemporary recipes, from grilled octopus and fried artichokes to tuna tartare with tobiko, wasabi, and black sesame. High ceilings, plush velvet sofas, and black-and-white checkered floors create an elegant setting with a warm, welcoming atmosphere.

Vinitus

Carrer del Consell de Cent, 333; 93/363-2127; 11:30am-1pm daily; €4-€13

A buzzing tapas bar close to Passeig de Gràcia, there's often a queue outside Vinitus, with patrons perched on every available surface. What draws the crowds? Tasty, reasonably priced tapas—all the usual classics and an impressive seafood selection, freshly prepared in an open kitchen. The *huevos cabreados* (fried eggs, potatoes, brava sauce, and aioli) are a decadent treat. Grab a seat at the bustling bar and make sure you check out the daily specials. To skip the queue, arrive ahead of the local rush hour (before 2pm at lunch and before 8pm in the evening).

INTERNATIONAL

9 Reinas

Carrer de València, 267; 93/272-4766; www.nuevereinas.com; Sun.-Thurs. 1pm-3:30pm, 7:30pm-11pm, Fri.-Sat. 1pm-3:30pm, 7:30pm-11:30pm; €16.50-€72.95

The succulent chunks of Argentinian steak served up at 9 Reinas are enough to delight any carnivore. A white-tableclothed locale with professional waiting staff sets a fancy scene in which to indulge in your meat fix, with prices to match. It doesn't get more authentic than the grilled *bife de chorizo* with a side of *chimichurri*. Check the menu's diagram to get up to speed on traditional South American cuts. A glass of Malbec rounds things off nicely.

✪ Mako

Carrer del Consell de Cent, 255; 93/269-6207; 1:30pm-4pm, 8:30pm-11:30pm daily; €9-€32

The lineup of oriental treats at Mako will tempt you away from tapas. Spicy tuna uramaki with crispy prawns, gyozas stuffed with pork jowl and mushrooms, and the spectacular soft shell crab bun bao are just some of the delicately prepared bites at this tiny Japanese tavern. A dark but trendy space with friendly, passionate staff makes an intimate ambience. Check the specials for surprising combinations that delight the senses.

CAFÉS AND BRUNCH

La Esquina

Carrer de Bergara, 2; 93/768-7242; laesquinabarcelona.com; 8:30am-6:30pm daily; €5-€12.50, set lunch menu €16 (1pm-4pm)

This cozy corner café serves hearty seasonal fare with international influences. Warm lighting, feel-good music, and Instagrammable decor

barbecued Catalan sweet onions, called *calçots*, with romesco sauce

invite passersby to start the day slowly with an exceptional cup of Marzocco-brewed coffee, just one block from Plaça de Catalunya. Although known for its weekend brunch menu—from poached eggs with avocado, goat's cheese, and dill to fresh fruit with pancakes—the weekday set lunch is refreshingly different from the standard Spanish offering. Three healthy courses—a soup or salad, a protein, and a pasta or grain dish—are served with soft rustic bread and a choice of homemade desserts or coffee to finish.

Café Cosmo
Carrer d'Enric Granados, 3; 93/105-7992; galeriacosmo.com; 10am-10pm daily; €5.50-€8
Breakfast, brunch, and lunch—that's when Cosmo is at its best, and, like most early risers, it's healthy, bright, and cheerful. Ingredients are largely sourced within a 100-kilometer (62-mile) radius and follow the seasons, coming together in a cosmopolitan menu of toasted sandwiches, salads,

fresh juices, locally roasted coffee, and delicious homemade cakes. Long timber benches and colourful artwork lend a laid-back air to the high-ceilinged café, which doubles as a gallery space, while the relaxed terrace on elegant Carrer d'Enric Granados is hard to beat.

Firebug
Passeig de Sant Joan, 23; 93/244-0209; firebugbarcelona.es; Mon.-Fri. 10am-2am, Sat.-Sun. 9am-2am; €4.50-10.95
A cozy corner café that spills out onto the pleasant boulevard of Passeig de Sant Joan, brunch is the headline here—eggs, pancakes, bagels, salads (until 4:30pm)—although a diverse selection of sharing dishes can be ordered after 7pm. The "drunken prawns," sauteed in butter, garlic, and white wine, and the "bang bang" chicken satay are seriously scrumptious, not to mention the jam-jar cocktails. The Irish owners also run Milk (Carrer d'en Gignàs, 21; 93/268-0922; milkbarcelona.com) in Barrí Gòtic

and Marmalade (Carrer de la Riera Alta, 4-6; 93/442-3966; www.marmaladebarcelona.com) in El Raval—each with a similar menu but distinct vibe. Be prepared to queue for weekend brunch.

La Soperí

Carrer del Rosselló, 197; 93/157-6288; www.lasoperi.com; Tues.-Thurs. 1pm-3:30pm, 7pm-1:30am, Fri.-Sat. 1pm-3:30pm, 7pm-2:30am, Sun. noon-7pm; €11-€22, set lunch €14.50

Opened in 2018, La Soperí is another new addition to the "local, seasonal market cuisine" category, but brings some truly surprising flavor combinations to the table, such as the broccoli and wasabi guacamole or the zucchini and orange-marinated salmon sashimi. The short but varied sharing menu is made with organic ingredients, all of which can be enjoyed in a cozy, unpretentious café ambience, where the decor is as delicate as the food preparation.

QUICK BITES
✪ Bacoa

Ronda Universitat, 31; 93/250-7290; www.bacoaburger.com; noon-1am daily; €5.90-€8.50

Leaving traditional fast-food joints in the dust, everything at this new-generation burger bar is homemade or locally sourced, from the roasted tomato ketchup to the hand-cut fries. Try the *Japonesa* with teriyaki glaze, the *Suiza* with potato rösti and Emmental, or the good old-fashioned *Clasica*—the burger upon which Bacoa was built. Founded by a Spanish-Australian couple, there are five trendy outlets across town; for the perfect meat-based pit stop, just select your meat, bread, and toppings.

FINE DINING
✪ Disfrutar

Carrer de Villarroel, 163; 93/348-6896; www.disfrutarbarcelona.com; entry times Mon.-Fri. 1pm-2:30pm, 8pm-9:30pm, experience lasts approx. 3.5 hours; four tasting menus to choose from, priced €150-€190, drinks not included

Taking Catalan cuisine to the extreme, Mateu Casañas, Oriol Castro, and Eduard Xatruch practiced molecular gastronomy at Ferran Adrià's elBulli and perfected it here, earning themselves two Michelin stars. The mind-blowing "Classic" tasting menu delivers a sensory feast of daring, delicate creations, but still manages to be fun, with beetroot meringues that "appear" from the earth, the infamous spherical olive, and a translucent pasta carbonara, to name but a few. Served in a bright, contemporary dining room with full view of the masters at work, this is a gastronomic experience like no other. Reservations essential.

DESSERTS
DelaCrem

Carrer d'Enric Granados, 15; 93/004-1093; www.delacrem.cat; Sun.-Thurs. 9:30am-9:30pm, Fri.-Sat. 9:30am-12:30am; €2.50-€4.50

Ice cream aficionados regularly wait in line for the copious cones of homemade Italian gelato dished up at DelaCrem. The tempting lineup of artisan flavors is entirely gluten-free and changes daily; the dulce de leche and pistachio are especially delish. They also do a mean chocolate brownie that, paired with the excellent Lavazza coffee, rounds off the sweet selection at this tiny corner café.

GRÀCIA, PARK GÜELL, AND BEYOND

SPANISH AND CATALAN

Goliard

Carrer del Progrés, 6; 93/207-3175; goliard.cat; Mon.-Sat. 1:30pm-4:30pm, 8:45pm-1:30am; €14.15-€18.75, set lunch €13.90, tasting menu €25.90

Goliard looks and feels gourmet but is easier on the pocket. An intimate backstreet bistro in the heart of Gràcia, the excellent-value menu is filled with modern riffs on traditional Catalan cuisine, from the confit duck croquette and pan-fried calamari to the smoked sardines with figs and mascarpone. Sample a little bit of everything with the 11-dish tasting menu—a steal at €25.90—or arrive early to beat the lunchtime rush.

Platerets

Carrer de Milà i Fontanals, 29; 93/463-6585; www.platerets.com; Tues.-Thurs. 1pm-4pm, 8pm-11pm, Fri.-Sat. 1pm-4pm, 8pm-11:30pm; €7.80-€12.80

Everything is designed to share at Platerets. Plate after plate of creative market cuisine is artfully presented to a trendy local crowd, who quickly fill the simple but inviting dining space. The menu is fresh and flavorsome, focusing on local products with an occasional Asian twist. Braised Ral d'Avinyo pork ribs with a honey and soy sauce glaze melt in the mouth, while updated Iberian classics, like the *butifarra* (Catalan sausage) omelette or the asparagus risotto, emphasize the earthy Catalan roots of this modern Mediterranean fare. Weekend brunch and vermouth (noon-3pm) is sometimes accompanied by a live DJ.

✪ La Panxa del Bisbe

Carrer del Torrent de les Flors, 158; 93/213-7049; Tues.-Sat. 1:30pm-3:30pm, 8pm-11:30pm (midnight Fri.-Sat.); €9-€14, €30/€38 tasting menus aimed at groups

The "Bishop's Belly" is an unfussy, brick-walled space where chef Xavier Codina reinterprets the humble tapa with dynamic energy and imagination. The lineup changes seasonally, with dishes such as courgette flowers with sea urchins and prawns, slow-roasted lamb and mint couscous, and oxtail cannelloni in a truffle and black garlic sauce. Tucked away at the top end of Gràcia, La Panxa del Bisbe makes a calming lunch spot pre- or post-Park Güell (a 10-minute walk away), or an off-the-beaten-track dinner among local foodies.

INTERNATIONAL

✪ Da Greco

Carrer de Santa Teresa, 10; 93/218-6550; Mon.-Sat. 1pm-4pm, 8:30pm-11:30pm; €12-€18, weekday set lunch menu €18

As soon as you lift the hand-shaped door knocker at Da Greco, you'll know you're on to something special. This clandestine Italian classic is housed in a small palace with lavish, Baroque-inspired interiors and spotless white tablecloths. Italian-born Tony Greco and his son John lead the kitchen, and pasta is the speciality. The tasting menu is exceptionally good value, but make sure you're hungry. Don't miss the risotto, prepared inside a huge Parmesan wheel.

CAFÉS AND BRUNCH

Café Godot

Carrer de Sant Domènec, 19; 93/368-2036; cafegodot.com; Mon.-Fri. 10am-1pm, Sat.-Sun. 11am-2am; Set lunch €13.50, Mon.-Fri. 1pm-4pm; €7.50-€14.10

Café Godot ticks all the boxes: delectable food at reasonable prices in a relaxed and friendly atmosphere. The diverse fusion menu has something for everyone, from calamari with wasabi mayonnaise to green curry scallops and homemade duck confit, as well as plenty of veggie and gluten-free options. A dimly lit, cavernous dining room welcomes all ages at all hours, whether it's young families gathered in the "Mini Godot" space or groups of friends chatting over weekend brunch (Sat.-Sun. noon-7pm). You may be tempted to visit more than once.

COFFEE
Onna Coffee
Carrer de Santa Teresa, 1; 93/269-4870; onnacoffee.com; Mon., Wed.-Fri. 8am-7pm, Sat.-Sun. 9am-7pm

One of a growing number of third-wave coffee shops in the city, Onna is committed to sustainably sourced specialty coffee. A small but welcoming space, this cute café is perfect for a caffeine boost morning, noon, or night.

The simple, clean interior design keeps the focus on the beans, which come from Costa Rica—just like the owner, Anahí Paez, who sources them direct from her homeland. Team it up with a healthy sandwich, cake, or pastry and you've got an excellent breakfast option (€3.90).

MONTJUÏC, POBLE-SEC, AND SANT ANTONI
SPANISH AND CATALAN
✪ Sucursal Aceitera
Carrer del Comte Borrell, 36; 93/342-7300; www.restaurantsucursal.com; €8-19

A former olive-oil warehouse, Sucursal Aceitera serves tapas with a gourmet twist. For a quick bite, pair a juicy slice of tortilla with a cool glass of cava, or book a table for a delicately executed dinner of grilled octopus, monkfish ceviche, or oxtail cannelloni. Look

Mercat de Sant Antoni

for the glazed peepholes in the floor, where you can catch a glimpse of the original oil cellar downstairs.

El Sortidor de la Filomena Pagès
Carrer del Comte Borrell, 65; 93/328-4408; grupfilomena.com/el-sortidor; 1pm-11pm daily; €4-€18, weekday set lunch menu €10.90

Spilling out onto Plaça del Sortidor in the heart of Poble-sec, El Sortidor de la Filomena Pagès oozes historical charm. Founded in 1908, the interiors reflect the splendor of Modernisme, while the menu brings a contemporary twist to traditional Catalan cuisine. Try the confit of cod with tomato and spring garlic or the locally inspired *seitotxo* (anchovies, beans, sausage, and caramelized onions), all served in modest but imaginatively presented portions. Inside, look for the old turquoise-tiled refrigerator—this once provided ice to the local area.

Martínez
Carretera de Miramar, 38; 93/106-6052; martinezbarcelona.com; 1pm-1:30am daily; €15.50-€56; set lunch menu €45

Dine with a view at Martínez, perched on the slopes of Montjuïc. This upmarket hillside haven boasts panoramic city and sea views and a charming outdoor terrace that dazzles by night. Paella is the specialty on the Mediterranean menu, which also features tapas, shellfish, chargrilled seafood, and meat. Going à la carte quickly adds up, but the set lunch menu, served 1pm-4pm, includes vermouth, tapas, salad, paella, dessert, and wine for €45. Request a window table to make the most of the vistas.

TAPAS
✪ Quimet & Quimet
Carrer del Poeta Cabanyes, 25; 93/442-3142; Mon.-Fri. noon-4pm, 7pm-10pm, Sat. noon-4pm; €2.50-€10

Serving up mouth-watering morsels since 1914, Quimet & Quimet is the quintessential bodega. Large wooden doors reveal a tiny, bottle-lined den crammed with customers. Fourth-generation owner Joaquim Pérez mans the bar, where dozens of tasty treats are concocted, based primarily on high-quality canned products. Frequented by locals and tourists, this standing-room-only bar retains its traditional charm and is perfect for a pre-dinner appetizer; the smoked salmon, yogurt, and truffled honey *montadito* (canapé on toast) is to die for.

Tickets
Avinguda del Parallel, 164; 93/292-4252; www.ticketsbar.es; Tues.-Fri. 7pm-10:30pm, Sat. 1pm-3pm, 7pm-10:30pm; €4.20-€38

The first venture in the Adrià brothers' el Barri project, Tickets has been serving seriously imaginative tapas to a full house since 2011, and was the first venture in the Adrià brothers' el Barri project (a series of concept restaurants all situated in the neighborhood, el-barri.com). Inspired by its location in Barcelona's traditional theater district, everything about this culinary playground is dramatic, from the whimsical decor to the deconstructed tapas; think Manchego foam, liquid olives, and oyster kimchi. Reservations are released online exactly two months in advance, at midnight, and are snapped up immediately.

TAPAS IN POBLE-SEC

The pedestrianized **Carrer de Blai** (metro: Poble Sec) at the heart of Poble-sec is the place to go for a Basque-inspired pintxos crawl. With bite-sized snacks starting at €1, diners roam from bar to bar, devouring a tapa or two at each stop en route: a mind-boggling selection fills the countertops in each establishment. This social dining procession attracts a lively, young crowd that spills out onto the outdoor terraces, and is at its busiest between 8pm and 9:30pm. The ever-busy **La Tasqueta de Blai** (Carrer de Blai, 17; 93/173-0561; grupotasqueta.com) is a good place to start, followed by **Blai 9** (Carrer de Blai, 9; 93/329-7365; blai9.com) or **Blai Tonight** (Carrer de Blai, 23; 63/938-4206), who kick-started the trend over 10 years ago. Wherever you go, keep an eye out for fresh trays of tapas emerging from the kitchen; microwaved reheats just aren't the same.

INTERNATIONAL
La Bella Napoli

Carrer de Margarit, 12-14; 93/442-5056;
www.labellanapoli.es; 1:30-4pm,
8:30pm-midnight daily; €6-€27

La Bella Napoli embodies an authentic slice of Naples. From the wood-fired pizzas and homemade tiramisu to the animated waiting staff and images of Vesuvius, Naples-born owner Rafaelle Iannone has perfected the classic Italian trattoria and the commotion that comes with it. The extensive pizza menu sees the humble Margherita appearing alongside more substantial toppings at slightly above average prices. Pasta is fresh, but don't expect it to arrive at the same time as the pizza. Reservations advised.

QUICK BITES
✪ Bar Calders

Carrer del Parlament, 25; 93/329-9349;
Mon.-Thurs. 5pm-1am, Fri. 5pm-2am,
Sat. 11am-2am, Sun. 11am-midnight;
€2.40-€10.80

If there's one establishment that sums up the spirit of Carrer del Parlament, it's Bar Calders. With a diverse menu of Mexican and Mediterranean bites, and several vermouths to choose from, this informal spot is popular with locals, who keep the side street terrace buzzing day and night. There's often a queue so arrive early, or join the waiting list and pop across the street for a drink while you wait. The kitchen is open 7pm-11pm every day, as well as noon-4pm on weekends.

✪ Rekons

Carrer Comte d'Urgell, 32; 93/424-6383;
empanadasrekons.com; Wed.-Mon.
10am-midnight, Tues. 6:30pm-11:30pm;
€2.30-€9.50

Homemade Argentinean empanadas are the star of the show at Rekons. These light and tasty pastry bites are served all day, although for extra indulgence, try the exceedingly cheesy potatoes, accompanied by a glass of homemade vermouth. Friendly staff and a lively corner terrace make this a popular neighborhood haunt for a cheap bite and beverage day or night.

CAFÉS AND BRUNCH
Federal Café

Carrer del Parlament, 39; 93/187-3607;
www.federalcafe.es; Mon.-Thurs. 8am-11pm,
Fri. 8am-1am, Sat. 9am-1am, Sun.
9am-5:30pm; €7-€13

Opened by an Australian duo in 2010, Federal is where the hipsterfication of Sant Antoni began. Inside this laid-back, street-corner café, a polished concrete staircase leads to a leafy rooftop terrace. Although known for its hearty breakfast and brunch, the kitchen is open all day and the menu also includes burgers, salads, cocktails, and more. Tuck into a ploughman's sharing platter at the wooden kitchen table, sip a *cortado* while people-watching from the window seats, or cool off up top with a green health shake.

La Desayunería
Carrer del Comte Borrell, 75; 60/834-1601;
www.ladesayuneria.com; Mon. 8am-3pm,
Tues.-Thurs. 8am-8:30pm, Fri. 8am-11:30pm,
9am-11:30pm, 9am-8:30pm; €4.50-€9.50,
weekday set lunch menu €10.50

Spain is not big on breakfast, but if you are, satisfy your morning munchies at this friendly café opposite the Mercat de Sant Antoni. Eggs, bacon, pancakes, and pastries—La Desayunería brings together the best of breakfast from around the world in an unpretentious, laid-back atmosphere. Whether it's a full English or a slice of avocado toast, the portions are big, the prices are low, and it's served all day.

FINE DINING
Pakta
Carrer de Lleida, 5; 93/624-0177;
pakta.es; Tues.-Thurs. 7pm-10:30pm;
Fri. 6:30-10:30pm; Sat. 1pm-2:30pm,
7:30pm-10:30pm; €2-€36, tasting menus
€120/€150

Sea anemone tempura, sea urchin nigiris, and meagre fish ceviche—these are the kinds of oceanic surprises that await at Pakta. Another member of the Adrià family, this relaxed Michelin-starred restaurant presents innovative Nikkei cuisine, best experienced with the 24-dish tasting menu. Like the food, Pakta's striking interior unites two cultures, referencing both the simplicity of Japanese design and the colorful exuberance of Peru. Reservations essential.

WATERFRONT
SPANISH AND CATALAN
✪ Xiringuito Escribà
Avinguda del Litoral, 62; 93/221-0729;
xiringuitoescriba.com; 1pm-10:30pm daily;
€15-€34

Nothing quite beats a good paella at lunchtime by the sea—make sure you try it at least once during your stay. Owned by the same family as the famous Escribà patisserie, Xiringuito Escribà serves several tasty riffs on the classic Valencian rice dish, prepared in an open kitchen; try the *mar y montaña* (surf and turf) with chicken, ribs, crayfish, mussels, cuttlefish, and mushrooms. Naturally, the desserts are also pretty special. This bustling beachfront restaurant overlooks Platja de Bogatel; reservations essential on weekends.

✪ Gallito
Passeig del Mare Nostrum, 19-21;
93/312-3585; www.encompaniadelobos.
com; Mon.-Thurs. noon-4pm, 8pm-11:30pm,
Fri.-Sat. noon-5pm, 8pm-midnight; Sun.
noon-5pm, 8pm-11:30pm; €13-€24

Situated at the foot of the W Hotel, Gallito radiates good vibrations with its laid-back surf-shack aesthetic. Rustic furniture, brightly colored pillows, and chillout beats set a relaxed scene for a lazy lunch looking out to sea. Tuck into globally-inspired Mediterranean eats beneath the vine-shaded terrace—from sea bass ceviche to shrimp, squid, and artichoke *paella*.

Can Majó
Carrer de l'Almirall Aixada, 23; 93/221-5455;
www.canmajo.es; Tues.-Sun. 1pm-4pm,
Tues.-Sat. 8pm-11:30pm; €16-€40

A solid option on the seafront, Can Majó has been serving up traditional rice and fresh fish to the people of

Barceloneta for half a century. The *caldero de arroz con bogavante* (lobster rice stew) is the house special, though a full range of paella and all the typical Spanish starters feature on the menu—kick-start the feast with the *chipirones a la andaluza* (Andalusian-style baby cuttlefish) or the seafood soup. Complete with terrace and Mediterranean views, this family-run haunt is a notch above its beachfront equivalents.

TAPAS
✪ Cervecería Vaso de Oro

Carrer de Balboa, 6; 93/3193-098; www.vasodeoro.com; Mon.-Sun. 11am-midnight; €12-18

For over 50 years, cheerful white-jacketed waiters have served up some of the city's best tapas in Barceloneta's Cervecería el Vaso de Oro. Diners squeeze in along the extremely narrow bar, rubbing shoulders with strangers as mouthwatering plates of *solomillo* (filet steak), *pimientos de padrón,* and succulent fresh tuna are prepared *a la plancha*. It's loud and lively with an authentic buzz; you'll need to shout to have your order heard. Wash it down with a house-brewed beer, served in a tall flauta glass.

La Bombeta

Carrer de la Maquinista, 3; 93/319-9445; Thurs.-Tues. 10am-midnight; €4-8, cash only, average spend €15-25; no reservations

The *bomba* is the star of the show here. Invented in nearby bar La Cova Fumada and adopted by La Bombeta, these meat and potato balls draw the crowds to this noisy Barceloneta institution, where you'll find yourself elbow-to-elbow with locals and travelers alike. Besides the bombas, there

is a whole range of good old-fashioned tapas at reasonable prices. Service is quick but curt, and the ambience authentic.

La Cova Fumada

Carrer del Baluard, 56; 93/221-4061; Mon.-Fri. 9am-3:15pm, Thurs.-Fri. 6pm-8:15pm, Sat. 9am-1pm; €2-12; no reservations

This no-frills tapas tavern remains largely unchanged since it opened in 1944, when every fisherman and factory worker in the working-class neighborhood stopped by for some finger-licking fried fish. The famous Barceloneta *bomba*—a breaded ball of meat and mashed potatoes served with aioli or a spicy sauce—was invented here by the current owner's grandmother, Maria Pla; it would be rude not to try. There's no sign over the door, so keep your eyes peeled for the heavy wooden doors that open onto Plaça del Poeta Bosca.

El 58

Rambla del Poblenou, 58; 65/631-1676; Tues.-Sat. 1:30pm-11pm, Sun. 1:30pm-4pm; €1.75-€14; no reservations

Right in the heart of the tree-lined Rambla de Poblenou, El 58 is a lively tapas bar popular with locals. The reasonably priced dishes combine traditional and international flavors, such as the langoustine and sweet chilli brochette or the popular salmon tartare. A casual, laid-back feel runs throughout the three distinct spaces within this former bodega, with exposed brick walls and a bright indoor courtyard at the back. The patatas bravas, made with Italian sun-dried tomato, fried onion, and plenty of paprika, are some of the best in the city.

INTERNATIONAL
✪ Madrelievito

Carrer de la Llacuna, 1; 93/667-8271; llacuna.madrelievito.com; Mon.-Thurs. 8pm-midnight, Fri.-Sun. 1pm-midnight; €5-€9.90

When a native Neopolitan tells you where to go for pizza, listen up. Madrelievito is a little off the beaten track, but churns out some of the city's best and most authentic pizza. The secret is in the fluffy sourdough base, made using Italian ingredients. Pizzas are quick, simple, and cheap; the classic margherita and marinara start at €5. The casual setting feels like a street scene from Naples itself, with Italian waiters buzzing about and a mock clothesline strung between window frames overhead. Save room for the Nutella pizza dessert.

CAFÉS AND BRUNCH
Café Menssana

Carrer de Sardenya, 48; 93/624-3505; cafemenssana.com; 9:30am-11:30pm daily; €6.50-€8.90

Eat Good. Do Good. Feel Good: That's the motto at Café Menssana, and the menu is just as aspirational. This healthy haven is well positioned opposite the Ciutadella campus of the Pompeu Fabra University (UPF). There is a great range of seasonal food with international appeal, and plenty of options for vegans, vegetarians, and meat eaters alike—from the earthy roasted eggplant (aubergine) salad to the fish tacos or BBQ pulled pork. Natural light floods the welcoming interiors, inviting the mainly student clientele to feed their creativity in a cozy wooden booth, lovingly handcrafted by the German-Ukrainian owners.

SANTS, LES CORTS, AND LA ZONA ALTA

SPANISH AND CATALAN
Santa Clara

Carrer Jiménez i Iglesias, 11; 93/203-8408; www.santaclararestaurante. com; Mon.-Fri. 7am-1am, Sat.-Sun. 8am-1am (kitchen open 1pm-3:30pm and 8pm-11pm); €10-€29

The spacious terrace garden at Santa Clara is a mellow oasis for relaxed outdoor eating, with refined Hamptons-style decor to match the upscale neighborhood. The menu features a mix of contemporary and classic Mediterranean dishes, from tartar and tataki to grilled meat and paella. An in-house branch of a renowned local bakery, Baluard, supplies the restaurant with tasty, rustic bread. An ideal lunch spot if you're sightseeing up this end of town. Leave room for dessert.

TAPAS
Bar Tomàs de Sarrià

Carrer Major de Sarrià, 49; 93/203-1077; www.eltomasdesarria.com; Mon.-Sat. noon-4pm, 6pm-10pm; €1.90-€9.10

The *patatas bravas* at Bar Tomàs are legendary. Locals flock from across the city to sample the star dish, paired with an ice-cold San Miguel on the main street of this uptown neighborhood. Don't be underwhelmed by the somewhat dated decor—this authentic bar sticks to its roots, and though the spuds are the speciality, the vermouth and tapas are not far behind. While you're here, take the time to wander the charming streets of Sarrià, once a rural village that was swallowed up by the city in 1921.

Bars and Nightlife

Barcelona has a huge array of entertainment on offer, from live music and dance shows to clandestine cocktail bars and swanky all-night clubs. There's something for everybody, every day of the week, whether it's sipping homemade vermouth (*vermut* in Catalan) on a Sunday lunchtime or dancing until dawn at a beachfront club.

Expect to pay €2.50-€3 for a beer (33cl/11oz). A smaller measure, known as a *caña* (20cl/7oz), costs between €1.50 and €2. The average price for a cocktail is around €10-12, though specialty cocktail bars may charge more. A spirit and mixer is known as a *cubata*—gin-and-tonics, known locally as simply "gintonic," are particularly popular, and rum and Coke is known as a *Cuba Libre*. Clubs generally charge a cover fee, which usually includes one drink (sometimes two). Be aware that spirits are served in large measures.

NIGHTLIFE DISTRICTS

BARRI GÒTIC

Plaça Reial is the epicenter of nighttime activity in the Barri Gòtic, and attracts many foreigners and some locals. Nearby Carrer de Ferran is tourist central, with a string of rowdy Irish bars, while the narrow streets that branch off from Carrer dels Escudellers harbor a plethora of eccentric dive bars.

EL RAVAL

El Raval combines a youthful, alternative vibe with some old-time haunts that date back to its heyday as an infamous red light district—a scene that's alive and well along some of the less salubrious streets. Elsewhere, students and twentysomethings fill the bars, particularly around Carrer de Joaquin Costa.

LA RIBERA

On the other side of the Ciutat Vella in La Ribera, Passeig del Born is at the heart of the action. Popular with tourists and locals alike, the bars here are cool and quirky, and concoct some fine cocktails. Branch off into the narrow lanes and you'll find the best of them buried on the back streets.

L'EIXAMPLE

Uptown L'Eixample is where the local glitterati go to get their groove on. The bars and clubs in this part of town are larger and more spacious than their old-town counterparts, just like the urban environment. Carrer de Tuset is a hotspot for slick clubs, while nearby Carrer d'Aribau and Carrer d'Enric Granados have a concentration of cocktail bars. Closer to Plaça Universitat, the "Gaixample" district—a rectangular area bordered by Carrer Balmes, the Gran Via, Carrer Urgell, and Carrer Aragó—is known for its lively LGBTQ+-focused scene.

GRÀCIA

There's a more local scene in Gràcia, where there is a bar for every taste concentrated around the neighborhood's lively squares. Plaça del Sol is especially popular with students and young crowds, while signature cocktails are mixed just meters away in hip bars hidden along quiet lanes.

WATERFRONT

Along the waterfront, the beachfront strip beside **Port Olímpic** is a cosmopolitan playground in summer, particularly popular with tourists. Ibiza-style clubs open straight onto the beach, with Balinese daybeds and ostentatious decor to complete the look.

POBLE-SEC AND SANT ANTONI

A recent renaissance in Sant Antoni has put **Carrer de Parlament** on the map as one of the hippest streets in town as evening draws in. It's casual, with a neighborhood buzz, and the laid-back hipster vibe is spreading to the surrounding streets and over to **Carrer de Blai** in Poble Sec.

BARRI GÒTIC AND LA RAMBLA

BARS

Ocaña

Plaça Reial, 13-15; 93/676-4814; www.ocana.cat; Mon.-Wed. 5pm-2am, Thurs. and Sun. noon-2am, Fri.-Sat. noon-2:30am

Café, terrace, restaurant, club: Ocaña is a little bit of everything. Easily the best spot on Plaça Reial, this multipurpose space morphs from day to night. By day, it's the perfect people-watching spot, and as night draws in, sip jam-jar cocktails in vintage armchairs or join the late-night buzz in the underground club. Named after José Pérez Ocaña (1947-1983), a cross-dressing performer and activist during the radical post-Franco years, drag hostesses encourage all to revel and rebel in his honor.

L'Ascensor

Carrer de Bellafila, 3; 93/318-5347; Sun.-Thurs. 6:30pm-2am, Fri.-Sat. 6:30pm-3am

This backstreet bar gets its name from the old elevator door through which you enter. L'Ascensor is a cozy, dimly lit cocktail bar that's been around for decades and counts many locals among its clientele. Perch on one of the well-worn pews and soak up the old-time ambience with a margarita in hand.

La Alcoba Azul

Carrer de Sant Domènec del Call, 14; 93/302-8141; Mon.-Thurs. noon-1:30am, Fri.-Sat. noon-2:30am, Sun. 6pm-1:30am (kitchen open until midnight)

Tucked away amid the city's oldest streets, this tiny bar oozes old-fashioned charm, embodied in its ancient stone walls, rickety timber tables, and decades of cascading candle wax. Squeeze in along the narrow bar or settle into a booth at the back. Drinks generally come with a complimentary bite, but there's also a tempting selection of tapas—try one of the *tostas* (toasted sandwiches). Outside, the bar has a terrace in the minuscule Placeta de Manuel Ribe.

Boadas Cocteleria

Carrer dels Tallers, 1; 93/318-9592; boadascocktails.com; Mon.-Thurs. noon-2am, Fri.-Sat. noon-3am

The oldest cocktail bar in the city, Boadas has been serving up authentic Cuban cocktails since 1933. The historic walls of this tiny, triangular tavern are plastered with nostalgic images from its heyday, when every prominent local personality stopped by for a daiquiri. The Cuban-born Catalan founder, Miguel Boadas Parera, learned his trade in Havana's famous *El Floridita* and brought the vibrant Caribbean flavors back to Barcelona. Still family owned, the dark brown interiors and tuxedoed bartenders keep the tradition alive.

Sor Rita

Carrer de la Mercè, 27; 93/176-6266; www.sorritabar.es; Sun.-Thurs. 7pm-2:30am, Fri.-Sat. 7pm-3am

This tiny, retro-kitsch bar is like the set of a Pedro Almodóvar movie, with mannequin heads lining the shelves while Barbie swings from the chandeliers. Pop culture and religious icons are plastered across the walls and renegade high heels march across the ceiling. With a musical repertoire that is just as eclectic—from '60s hits to '80s Spanish cheese—it's all about having fun here, and the cheap and cheerful lineup of classic cocktails makes it easy. Check out the tarot reading on Monday night if you dare.

LIVE MUSIC

Jamboree

Plaça Reial, 17; 93/304-1210; www.masimas. com/jamboree; live music at 8pm and 10pm; from €4; club from 12:30am, shows €5-€20

Jamboree is an institution on Barcelona's jazz scene. With two performances a day, 365 days a year, and a dance floor that keeps on jumping until the early hours, this basement jazz and dance club in Plaça Reial is a nonstop hub of live music and revelry. Founded in the early 1960s as a jazz cellar, it has hosted numerous legendary musicians over the years, but also welcomes up-and-coming artists. Don't miss the popular WTF Jam Sessions on Monday nights. After the show, hip-hop, R&B, and soul beats take over the cavern-like club.

Harlem Jazz Club

Carrer de la Comtessa de Sobradiel, 8; 93/310-0755; www.harlemjazzclub.es; Tues.-Sat. from 10:30pm; shows €8-€15

A legendary locale in the Gothic Quarter, Harlem Jazz Club offers an eclectic live music program of jazz, blues, funk, Cuban, salsa, tango, soul, and swing nearly every night. Known for its relaxed, welcoming atmosphere, this cozy concert hall fills up quickly, so arrive early. Argentinian singer and composer Hernán "El Chino" Senra leads a blues jam session every Tuesday, which is particularly popular. Night owls can stick around after the show's over for late-night DJ sets.

CLUBS

Sidecar Factory Club

Plaça Reial, 7; 93/302-1586; www.sidecar. es; Thurs. 7pm-5am, Fri.-Sat. 7pm-6am; €6-10 cover

Underground both physically and philosophically, Sidecar is a basement club dedicated to alternative music. Situated diagonally opposite Jamboree in Plaça Reial, this red-lit, low-ceilinged cavern attracts a young, casual crowd and pumps out cacophonous indie, punk, and garage rock until dawn. The club regularly hosts concerts and DJ sets (from €5), with live shows starting at 9pm. The lineup normally features local bands, with occasional big names performing intimate gigs here—Pete Doherty made an appearance in 2016.

Marula Café

Carrer dels Escudellers, 49; 93/318-7690; www.marulacafe.com/bcn; Wed.-Thurs. and Sun. 11pm-5am, Fri.-Sat. 11pm-6am; €12 cover, no cover before 2am

Slip through the thick velvet curtains into Marula Café for a night of funk, soul, and Latin beats. This intimate club has an upbeat vibe and an eclectic crowd that is up for a good dance. Located close to Plaça Reial, it attracts a mix of locals and tourists, as well as DJs from both home and abroad. Sunday's "We Funk!" jam session is a fun way to round off the weekend.

EL RAVAL

BARS

London Bar

Carrer Nou de la Rambla, 34; 93/808-2187; 1pm-3am daily

A classic Modernista watering hole, the bohemian London Bar has recently reopened under new ownership, but maintains its early-20th-century charm. Inside it feels like an authentic time capsule from the days of Dalí, Picasso, and Hemingway, with a traditional wooden shop front and colorful ceramic floor tiles.

Bar Marsella

Carrer de Sant Pau, 65; 93/442-7263; Sun.-Thurs. 10pm-2:30am, Fri.-Sat. 10pm-3am

Serving up potent glasses of absinthe since 1820, time stands still in Bar Marsella. Peeling paint and dusty cobwebs only add to the charm of this historic establishment—once frequented by Hemingway and Picasso—which you might recognize from a scene in Woody Allen's *Vicky Cristina Barcelona* (2008). The anise-flavored spirit is served with a sugar lump: slowly dissolve it over your drink until it turns cloudy. The crowd is an eclectic mix of bohemians, tourists, old-timers, and exchange students.

Pesca Salada

Carrer de la Cera, 32; 68/626-5309; Wed.-Sat. 8:30pm-3am

This tiny bar on the edge of El Raval recalls its former life as a fishmonger's with every inch of its interior decor. Handcrafted "scales" cover the ceiling and bar, while octopus lights illuminate aquarium-style tables. With 43 gins on offer, patrons are bound to find one that will float their boat; the elderflower-and-grape-juice gin fizz is a crowd pleaser.

33/45

Carrer de Joaquín Costa, 4; 93/187-4138; Mon. 5pm-2am, Tues.-Thurs. 1pm-2am, Fri.-Sat, 1pm-2:30am, Sun. 1pm-1:30am

Café by day, lounge bar by night, 33/45 has a laid-back vibe, popular with students and twentysomething hipsters. Pared-back interiors and chill electronic sounds set the scene for long lazy evenings gazing out of full-height windows onto the lively Carrer de Joaquín Costa. The bar hosts regular art exhibitions, occasional gigs, and pop-up markets, and the drinks are very reasonably priced. Order a tangerine gin-and-tonic, sink into a vintage armchair, and kick back.

Casa Almirall

Carrer de Joaquín Costa, 33; 93/318-9917; www.casaalmirall.com; Mon. 5:30pm-1:30am, Tues.-Wed. 5:30pm-2am, Thurs. noon-2:30am, Fri.-Sat. noon-3am, Sun. noon-12:30am

Founded in 1860, Casa Almirall is one of the oldest bars in Barcelona, situated deep in the Raval. Marble tabletops, dark wood furniture, and antique Modernista decor preserve a bohemian, 19th-century ambience, undisturbed by mass tourism and the modern city. Order a traditional Oliveta vermouth and a tapa or two, and party like it's 1888.

Marea Baja

Avinguda de les Drassanes, 6-8; 93/631-3590; mareaaltamareabaja.com; midnight-2:30am daily

Spectacularly located on the 23rd floor of the Edifici Colón, this marine-themed sky bar (whose name means "low tide") boasts incredible 360-degree views, with relaxed seating indoors and out. More than 12 varieties of sangria, the quintessential Spanish drink, are accompanied by oysters, jamón, and seafood tapas. It's a little pricey (sangrias start at €6.50), though worth it to catch the sun setting behind the Collserola mountains as the city lights begin to twinkle. Ideal for a special pre-dinner drink. Upstairs, the even pricier sister restaurant, Marea Alta, specializes in chargrilled fish and smoked dishes.

CLUBS
Moog
Carrer de l'Arc del Teatre, 3;
93/319-1789; www.masimas.com/en/
moog; Mon.-Thurs. midnight-5am, Fri.-Sat.
midnight-6am; €5-10 cover Mon.-Thurs.

Delve into the depths of Barcelona's underground techno and house scene at Moog, located on a narrow street just off La Rambla. This one-time concert café reopened as a club devoted to electronic music in 1996. The progressive programming at Moog attracts the latest techno talents and tends to be one step ahead; major international stars generally appear on Wednesdays. More mainstream electro-pop is played in the upstairs room.

LA RIBERA/EL BORN
BARS
Bar l'Antic Teatre
Carrer de Verdaguer i Callís, 12;
93/315-2354; www.anticteatre.com;
Mon.-Thurs. 10am-11:30pm, Fri.
10am-midnight, Sat. 5pm-midnight,
Sun. 5pm-11:30pm

Situated in a dilapidated Neoclassical palace built in 1650, this clandestine classic in El Born forms part of an independent social and cultural institution that hosts a program of live performances throughout the week. Students, artists, and travelers swap stories under the shady branches of a giant fig tree in the bohemian hidden garden, which has a chill, alternative vibe and is particularly pretty at night.

Rubí Bar
Carrer dels Banys Vells, 6;
67/144-1888; Sun.-Thurs. 7:30pm-2:30am,
Fri.-Sat. 7:30pm-3am

Tucked away among the winding medieval streets of El Born, an inviting red glow radiates from inside Rubí Bar. Another port of call for gin lovers, Rubí brew their own and infuse it with curious flavors, from strawberry and mint to chocolate orange. Cozy, casual, and reasonably priced, this tiny spot fills up quick, so get there before 10:30pm.

Miramelindo
Passeig del Born, 15; 93/310-3727;
www.barmiramelindobcn.com;
Mon.-Sat. 8pm-2:30am, Sun. 7pm-2:30am

Hidden behind the large wooden shop front of a Gothic building, Miramelindo is easy to miss. It is worth keeping an eye out, however, for the little camouflaged door that opens into this classic cocktail bar along Passeig del Born. Brimming with atmosphere, the colonial-style lounge fills up for after dinner drinks. Grab a wicker chair on the mezzanine and soak it up.

Creps al Born
Passeig del Born, 12; 93/269-0325;
www.crepsalbornbcn.com; Mon.-Thurs.
6:30pm-2:30am, Fri. 6:30pm-3am, Sat.
noon-3am, Sun. noon-2:30am
(kitchen closes at 11pm)

Despite the name, Creps al Born is better known for its creative cocktails than its French pancakes, although it does serve a good selection of the latter, both sweet and savory. The young, lively clientele at this bustling locale sing along to classic tunes while crowd-pleasing bartenders fuel the party atmosphere. Try the Zombie: four types of rum, pineapple, and passion fruit, set alight when served.

MIX

Carrer del Comerç, 21; 93/319-4696;
mixbcn.com; Tues. 9pm-3:30am,
Wed.-Sat. 10pm-3:30am; no cover

The party kicks off earlier at MIX, for those who want to get on the dance floor but still get up in the morning. A cocktail lounge with a club vibe, the resident DJs spin mainly deep house and electronic DJ tracks, although the music genre varies throughout the evening. Leather sofas, copper lamps, and lavish wall coverings add a touch of glam to this chic late-night bar.

Collage Art & Cocktail Social Club

Carrer dels Consellers, 4; 93/179-3785;
www.collagecocktailbar.com;
7:30pm-3am daily

Drinks are a work of art at the Collage Art & Cocktail Social Club. An experimental menu of over 30 classic and original cocktails are skillfully concocted and delicately presented in this tiny but trendy cocktail bar. Deep tones and vintage decor generate an intimate, private members' club vibe, with retro postcards and work by local artists adorning the exposed stone walls.

Dr. Stravinsky

Carrer dels Mirallers, 5; 93/157-1233; www.
drstravinsky.cat; Mon.-Sun. 7pm-2:30am

This quirky cocktail bar is lined with flasks and herb-filled jars. Weird and wonderful concoctions are dreamed up in this sophisticated drinks laboratory, such as the refreshing Camp Nou, which blends dill syrup, thyme, coriander, house-distilled gin, lime,

and chamomile. There are no artificial mixers; tonic water, shrub, kombucha, and kefir are all made in house and flavored with natural ingredients.

El Paradiso (Pastrami Bar)

Carrer de Rera Palau, 4; 93/360-7222;
www.paradiso.cat; 7pm-2:30am daily

A hip speakeasy concealed behind a fridge door, El Paradiso creates some of the city's most innovative cocktails. Re-distilled whiskey and the "Mediterranean Treasure" (served in a sea shell) are among some of the surprising signature combinations served up in this whimsical, jungle-themed cavern, alongside a selection of finger food. Rooftop Smokehouse's Pastrami Bar is the shopfront of the clandestine bar, and does a mean pastrami sandwich that will satisfy any late-night munchies.

WINE AND CAVA BARS

Bodega Maestrazgo

Carrer de Sant Pere Més Baix, 90;
60/231-0265; www.bodegamaestrazgo.com;
Mon.-Sat. 10:30am-3pm, 5pm-10pm

A traditional cellar, open since 1952, where you can try before you buy. Barrels and bottles are piled high around the shop, which offers a seemingly endless choice of exceptional wines. José Moliner, grandson of the founder, has an encyclopedic knowledge that he is willing to share, so head to the rustic bar at the back and experience vintages from across Catalonia and Spain, paired with a plate of jamón iberico or olives. Private tasting sessions are available (from €35).

El Xampanyet

Carrer de Montcada, 22; 93/319-7003;
Tues.-Sat. 11am-midnight

This classic bodega specializes in cava. Founded in 1929, the bar clings to its authentic charm despite its popularity as a tourist haunt, decorated with blue-and-white tiles, antique artifacts, and marble tables. It's always heaving, so perch where you can and order up a bottle of Catalonia's finest—and a plate of *jamón* for good measure.

L'EIXAMPLE

BARS

Solange Cocktails & Luxury Spirits

Carrer d'Aribau, 143; 93/164-3625;
www.solangecocktail.com; Mon.-Thurs.
7pm-2:30am, Fri. 7pm-3am, Sat.
7:30pm-3am, Sun. 7:30pm-2am

This sleek cocktail bar is named after *Casino Royale* Bond girl Solange Dimitrios. Lavish, golden interiors, velvet sofas, and dark wooden finishes set the tone inside this James Bond-themed bar, where heroes and villains could quite seamlessly mingle among the well-to-do clientele. The fruity cocktail list is based on titles from the 007 series—a little cheesy but skillfully shaken, not stirred.

Dry Martini

Carrer d'Aribau, 162; 93/217-5072;
www.drymartiniorg.com; Mon.-Thurs.
1pm-2:30am, Fri. 1pm-3am, Sat.
6:30pm-3am, Sun. 6:30pm-2am

Every detail of this English-style lounge bar exudes old-school class, from the wood, brass, and leather finishes to the formally dressed staff. Expert bartenders take pride in their creations and, having served more than a million of the bar's signature drink since it opened in 1978, experience is on their side. Stop by for a pre-dinner aperitif; there's a clandestine restaurant concealed behind the bar where you can continue the evening in similar style.

Boca Chica

Passatge de la Concepció, 12; 93/467-5149;
www.bocagrande.cat/en/boca-chica;
5pm-1:30am daily (Fri.-Sat. until 3am)

Boca Chica embraces old-world eclecticism with every luxurious detail. Dark woods, Persian carpets, cowhide stools, and elephant tusks create an extravagance only matched by its privileged location, just off Passeig de Gràcia. Situated above its sister restaurant, Boca Grande (1pm-midnight daily), this glamorous bar attracts an equally sophisticated clientele, there to enjoy the inventive (and expensive) cocktails. Make sure you visit the surreal bathroom.

WINE AND CAVA BARS

Monvínic

Carrer de la Diputació, 249; 93/272-6187;
www.monvinic.com; Tues.-Fri. 1:30pm-11pm,
Mon. and Sat. 7pm-11pm

A one-stop shop for any inquisitive oenophile, Monvínic offers 30 wines available by the glass, both Spanish and international, which change daily and can be browsed by region, grape, or producer on the tablet menu. Knowledgeable sommeliers are on hand to guide you; there's also an extensive library of wine-based literature and a lab-like cellar with over 3,000 bottles. The dark, contemporary space opens onto a vertical garden at the back. Pair your wine with a selection of sophisticated tapas or the set lunch menu (€19.50; kitchen open 1:30pm-3:30pm, 8pm-10:30pm).

CRAFT BEER

Garage Beer Co.

Carrer del Consell de Cent, 261;
93/528-5989; www.garagebeer.co;
noon-midnight daily

Garage Beer Co. is a micro-brewery and bar that makes and serves its own craft beer, as well as a few guest amber brews. Garage by name and by nature, the brewery sits at the back of a high-ceilinged industrial space, filled with retro furniture and fittings which lend a vintage vibe to this beer-lover's dream. Try the smooth *Riba* pale ale—the first of four original beers to flow through the taps—accompanied by *patatas bravas* or a tasty sandwich.

LGBTQ+
Arena Sala Madre

Carrer de Balmes, 32; 93/487-4342; grupoarena.com; 12:30am-5am daily, 6am on weekends; €10-12 cover

Arena Sala Madre is a classic gay club on the edge of the "Gaixample" district. Open 365 days a year, the club is the biggest of the Arena group's five venues in the city, and plays mainly electronic, house, and dance music. There are regular themed party nights, like striptease Mondays, drag queen shows, and foam parties in summer. Right next door, the relaxed sister club Arena Sala Classic (Carrer de la Diputació, 233; Thurs. 11pm-3am, Fri.-Sat. 11pm-6am) opens on the weekend, with a lesbian party from 11pm until 2am, followed by classic pop hits and commercial floor-fillers until 6am.

CLUBS
Sutton Club

Carrer de Tuset, 13; 66/743-2759; www.thesuttonclub.com; Wed.-Thurs. 11:30am-5:30am, Fri.-Sat. midnight-6am; cover €20

Party with the glitterati at Sutton Club, playground of the city's elite. House music and commercial floor-fillers, and the occasional superstar DJ, get this glitzy club jumping, while the more exclusive clientele—among them

FC Barcelona players—live it up in the plush VIP areas. Bring ID and dress to impress if you want to get in: glam and heels for girls, and dress shoes and collared shirt for boys. Minimum age is 23 at the weekend. Sign up for the guest list via the website for free entrance before 2:30am.

GRÀCIA, PARK GÜELL, AND BEYOND
BARS
Bobby Gin

Carrer de Francisco Giner, 47; 93/368-1892; www.bobbygin.com; 4pm-2am daily (Fri.-Sat. until 3am)

The city's gin craze continues at Bobby Gin. With more than 80 varieties on offer, the award-winning barman, Alberto Pizarro, happily guides patrons through the world of gin. A long wooden bar leads to a small lounge at the back, where dark timber floors contrast whitewashed stone walls. A patchwork collage of salvaged cupboard doors and drawers add a splash of retro fun to this quirky Gràcia watering hole. Accompany with a quick bite from the limited but delicious food menu.

La Vermu

Carrer de Sant Domènec, 15; 69/592-5012; Mon.-Thurs 6:30pm-midnight, Fri.-Sun. 12:30pm-4:30pm, 7:30pm-12:30am (midnight on Sunday)

Daytime drinking is the done thing at La Vermu, where locals flock to observe a time-honored weekend tradition: *la hora del vermut* (vermouth hour). The proprietors at this welcoming bar are passionate about the herb-infused fortified wine and produce their own, as well as offering several other artisanal varieties from across Catalonia. Get here

VERMUT

Vermouth, a fortified white wine flavored with botanicals, has always been a popular drink in Spain, but while it was long relegated to a drink beloved by grandmas, it has experienced something of a renaissance in recent years.

Traditionally vermouth was meant to stimulate the appetite and aid digestion, and in Spain it is usually enjoyed before lunch from around noon, a time known as *la hora de vermut* (vermouth hour). Spaniards typically drink sweet, red vermouth with a tapa—be it olives or potato chips, or something a little more elaborate.

enjoying vermouth with tapas

Many of the city's old taverns serve the drink from the barrel, with an olive and an orange slice garnish. Order the vermouth with soda water if you want to dilute it.

WHERE TO TASTE IN BARCELONA

- **La Vermu:** House-made vermouth, plus artisanal varieties from across Catalonia (page 131).

- **Balius:** Vermouth cocktails in a former ironmongers' in Poblenou (page 134).

- **Casa Almirall:** One of the oldest bars in Barcelona—founded in 1860—where you can enjoy your vermouth with a heavy side of ambience (page 127).

around midday and team it up with some olives, homemade chips, and anchovies to complete the ritual. *¡Salud y vermut!*

Old Fashioned

Carrer de Santa Teresa, 1; 93/368-5277; cocktailsbarcelona.oldfashionedbcn. com; Sun.-Mon. 5pm-2am, Tues.-Wed. noon-midnight, Thurs.-Fri. noon-3am, Sat. 5pm-3am

Mixology is a thing of beauty at Old Fashioned. Swing music, classic decor, and suspender-clad staff lend an air of 1920s nostalgia to this tiny watering hole, though there's nothing

antiquated about their cutting-edge cocktails, blended to perfection. Besides the bar's namesake drink, the world-class bartenders offer a multitude of artisan gin-and-tonics, Bloody Marys, signature creations, and innovative interpretations of the classics. Slip into an intimate, quilted booth, order a Fashionista (a 21st-century Old Fashioned) or an Al Capone, and let the show begin.

LIVE MUSIC
Soda Acústic

Carrer de les Guilleries, 6; 93/016-5590; www.soda.cat; Wed.-Thurs. and Sun.

8pm-2:30am, Fri.-Sat. 8pm-3am;
shows from €3

Conceived as an intimate meeting point for musical curiosity, Soda Acústic is an experimental live-music space with jazz roots. Performances range from gypsy jazz and Latin sounds to Afrobeat and Bossa Nova. Every Thursday at 8:30pm, there's a jazz jam session featuring upcoming local artists, while things get a bit old school at the weekend, with rock 'n' roll, soul, and funk taking over. Sunday evening is all about Brazilian beats.

Heliogàbal

Carrer Ramón y Cajal, 80; 93/676-3132;
www.heliogabal.com; Thurs.-Sat. 10pm-3am;
shows from €5

An institution among local musicians, Heliogàbal was founded as a platform for arts and culture and is one of the best spots for live music in Gràcia. The backstreet-bar ambience at this micro-venue makes a relaxed setting for musical performances and poetry readings. Each year, the venue organizes *Festigàbal*, a two-day festival on the nearby Plaça Rovira i Trias, to coincide with the neighborhood festival.

CLUBS
Otto Zutz

Carrer de Lincoln, 15; 93/238-0722; www.
ottozutz.com; Wed.-Thurs. midnight-5am,
Fri.-Sat. midnight-6am; cover €12-20

Otto Zutz is a refreshing alternative to the many electro-focused clubs in the city, with an industrial aesthetic that recalls its former life as a textile factory. Four rooms spread across three floors offer plenty of music choice. The main room plays hip hop and R&B; '80s, '90s, rock, and pop hits fill the "commercial" room, while the "hot" room jumps to Latino dance beats. Mainstream floor fillers are played on

the VIP-only third floor, "Los Altos," which is accessed separately. Clientele and prices match the uptown location.

MONTJUÏC, POBLE-SEC, AND SANT ANTONI
BARS
La Confiteria

Carrer de Sant Pau, 128; 93/140-5435;
www.grupconfiteria.cat; Mon.-Thurs.
7pm-2am, Fri.-Sat. 6pm-3am, Sun. 5pm-2am

Get a sweet taste of yesteryear at La Confiteria, where signature cocktails are served up in unconventional vessels. Vintage bottles and antique fittings line the walls of this former patisserie, which dates from 1912 and retains the original shop front. A warm glow from inside invites drinkers to slip back to the 20th century with a soundtrack to match.

Xixbar

Carrer de Rocafort, 19; 93/423-4314;
www.xixbar.com; Mon. 6:30pm-2:30am,
Tues.-Wed. 6pm-2:30am, Thurs.
5pm-2:30am, Fri.-Sat. 5pm-3am

The pioneering bar that kick-started the citywide gin-and-tonic craze in 2005, Xixbar serves up generous lashings of *ginebra* in the classic Copa glass. The Scottish owner travels the globe to source high-quality varieties of his favorite spirit, offered alongside a range of unconventional infusions and carefully crafted gin-based cocktails. Housed in a former dairy, quirky decor, sporadic live jazz, and late-night hours make this a popular haunt of Barcelona's gin aficionados.

El Mama & La Papa

Pg. de Pere Calders, 2; 93/441-7662;
www.elmama.barcelona; Wed.-Thurs.
7pm-2:30am, Fri.-Sat. 7pm-3am

A restaurant, bar, and cabaret show in

one, the highly entertaining El Mama & La Papa introduced a whole new dimension to the Sant Antoni scene when it opened in 2016. Acrobats and drag queens swing from the rafters of this former anchovy factory, while diners tuck into a menu of international flavors or sip creative cocktails at one of two bars. There's no entrance fee, but drinks are expensive. After midnight, the stage becomes a dance floor.

CLUBS
Sala Apolo
Carrer Nou de la Rambla, 113; 93/441-4001; www.sala-apolo.com; check website for hours; cover approx. €20

Sala Apolo is one of Barcelona's principal clubs and live music venues. A former ballroom dating from 1941, it attracts a young, frenetic crowd and is divided into two spaces: Sala Apolo, the old-time dance hall, and

La [2] downstairs. Music genre varies by night, ranging from rock 'n' roll (Mondays) and indie (Tuesdays) to reggae and soul (Wednesdays), pop (Thursdays), and electronic (Friday, Saturday, Sunday). As a concert hall, Apolo regularly attracts big-name bands and DJs—Stereophonics, Goo Goo Dolls, and Enter Shikari have all played in recent years—and with a capacity of 1,600, it is an intimate experience.

WATERFRONT
BARS
Balius
Carrer de Pujades, 196; 93/315-8650; www.baliusbar.com; Mon.-Wed. 5pm-1am, Thurs. 5pm-2am, Fri.-Sat. 4pm-3am, Sun. 4pm-1:30am

Run by the same folk as the gin-centric Xixbar in Sant Antoni, at Balius the focus is on vermouth, where they've built up an intriguing cocktail list

Sala Apolo

based on the fortified wine. Labeled a *gastro-cocteleria*, the slow tapas are organic and seasonal, and include a cod and potato dish mentioned in Cervantes's *Don Quixote*. All of this can be enjoyed in a former ironmongers' in Poblenou, with a laid-back, retro feel that's popular with hipsters but doesn't take itself too seriously. There's live jazz on Sundays at 8pm.

Eclipse

Hotel W, Plaça de la Rosa dels Vents, 1; 93/295-2800; www.eclipse-barcelona.com; Mon. and Wed. 6pm-2am, Tues., Thurs. and Sun. 6pm-2:30am, Fri.-Sat. 6pm-3am

Start the evening with a natural high on the 26th floor of the exclusive W Hotel. Magnificent Mediterranean views are the pièce de résistance in this slick sky bar, popular with the rich and jet set. DJ beats, creative cocktails, and sushi fusion cuisine pump up the VIP vibe every evening—make sure you dress for the occasion. Pricey and pretentious (cocktails from €14), but worth it for the views.

WINE AND CAVA BARS
Can Paixano

Carrer de la Reina Cristina, 7; 93/310-0839; www.canpaixano.com; Mon.-Sat. 9am-12:30am

Legs of *jamón* hang from the rafters and merry patrons spill onto the street outside Can Paixano, a classic cava bar that captures the convivial essence of the old Barceloneta. Better known as *La Xampanyeria*, the Catalan bubbles are available by the glass, though at €8 a pop, most tend to share a bottle (or two) between friends—beware, things can escalate quickly here. Accompany with a plate of cold meats or a yummy grilled sandwich. The bar is always jam-packed, but there's a shop counter at the back where you can pick up

a bottle of the Rosat Can Paixano to take home.

CRAFT BEER
La Cervecita Nuestra de Cada Día

Carrer de Llull, 184; 93/486-9271; Mon.-Tues. 5:30pm-11pm, Wed.-Sat. 11:30am-2pm, 5:30pm-11pm, Sun. 5:30pm-9:30pm

Craft beer takes center stage at La Cervecita in Poblenou. This down-to-earth bar and shop stocks a huge variety of bottled and draught beers, both local and international. The bar's founders are also behind La Fira del Poblenou, an annual craft beer festival that transforms the neighborhood's streets for one weekend in July. It's heaven for those looking for an original brew.

CLUBS
Razzmatazz

Carrer dels Almogàvers, 122; 93/320-8200; www.salarazzmatazz.com; Wed.-Thurs. midnight-5am, Fri.-Sat. 1am-6pm; €16 cover

A former industrial warehouse with five distinct spaces, Razzmatazz is Barcelona's biggest nightclub. Situated in the up-and-coming Poblenou district, there are sounds to match all tastes here—rock, indie, techno, house, and pop—although it is particularly popular with young hipsters and students. The club doubles as a live-music venue earlier in the evening, regularly hosting intimate concerts and DJ sets by internationally renowned artists, from Arctic Monkeys and the Gipsy Kings to Coldplay and Kanye West.

CDLC

Passeig Marítim de la Barceloneta, 32; 93/224-0470; www.cdlcbarcelona.com; midnight-5/6am daily; €20 cover

The Carpe Diem Lounge Club is one of a string of flashy beach clubs that bring the Ibiza party lifestyle to Barceloneta. The over-the-top boudoir decor channels an oriental vibe, with Moroccan-style tables, Balinese day beds, and plentiful Buddha statues meditating over the hedonistic highjinks. By day, Asian fusion cuisine is served up on the beachfront terrace, which becomes part of the club at night. Music is electronic, drinks are expensive, and the stylish, international crowd is here to be seen. Entrance tickets can be purchased online.

Opium Mar

Passeig Maritim de la Barceloneta, 34;
65/557-6998; www.opiumbarcelona.com;
Sun.-Thurs. 11pm-5am, Fri.-Sat. 11pm-6am;
€20 cover

Opium Mar is a split-level restaurant, cocktail bar, and nightclub rolled into one, with a seafront terrace where 24-hour party people lounge on daybeds until dawn. Situated among a strip of clubs close to the exclusive Hotel Arts, this chic nightspot attracts a cosmopolitan clientele and gets very crowded on summer nights. World-renowned DJs—among them David Guetta, Bob Sinclar, and Jason Derulo—regularly take to the decks here, playing primarily house beats. Sign up for the guest list or reserve for dinner to skip the queue, and go glam.

SANTS, LES CORTS, AND LA ZONA ALTA

CLUBS
Bikini

Avinguda Diagonal, 547; 93/322-0800;
www.bikinibcn.com; Thurs. midnight-5am,
Fri.-Sat. midnight-6am, Sun. 7pm-2am;
€6-15 cover

A mainstay on Barcelona's nightlife scene, Bikini is one of the city's oldest clubs, founded in 1953. Adele and Kylie Minogue have graced the stage of this slick club and concert hall in recent years, although it generally hosts more low-key performances. Concerts take place early evening before the club kicks off, spinning house, commercial, salsa, and R&B records until the early hours. Attracts an uptown crowd with prices to match. Guest list discounts available.

Festivals and Events

There's always something to celebrate in Barcelona. Throughout the year, the city hosts a huge range of festivals, popular with locals and visitors alike, from celebrating patron saints to global music gatherings.

SPRING
Diada de Sant Jordi

Various locations, Las Rambla; Apr. 23

Catalonia's patron saint, St. George, is celebrated on April 23, which also happens to coincide with World Book Day (both Shakespeare and Cervantes died on this date). The two collide in the day's traditions: Women give men a book, and men give women a rose. Book and flower stalls are set up across the city, but La Rambla is a particular hive of activity. Several buildings open their doors to the public today, including the Government Palace (Palau de la Generalitat de Catalunya, Plaça de Sant Jaume, 4).

Diada de Sant Jordi

are also available (around €85). Book early, as tickets sell out quickly.

SUMMER

Sónar

Various locations; mid-June; sonar.es; €155 for a three-day ticket

This three-day music festival brings some of the world's best electronic acts to Barcelona and draws an international crowd who make the trip to Barcelona specifically for the festival. It is split into two distinct parts—daytime Sónar, held in the Fira Montjuïc conference center (Avinguda de la Reina Maria Cristina), and nighttime Sónar, held in the Fira Gran Via L'Hospitalet (Av. Joan Carles I), south of the city. Previous performers include New Order, The Chemical Brothers, Björk, and Kraftwerk.

Sant Joan

Barceloneta beach; June 23-24

This popular feast day kick-starts summer with bonfires on the beach and the crackle of fireworks across the city on the evening of June 23. One of the best places to experience Sant Joan is down on the beach, where an all-night party draws crowds of revelers and musicians to the seafront to drink, dance, and dodge firecrackers until dawn. If you're up for it, head to the beach early (before 9pm) to get a good spot. Similar parties take place across Spain.

Barcelona Pride

Various locations; end of June; www.pridebarcelona.org

Barcelona's Pride festival takes place in late June/early July, with concerts, activities, and cultural events across the city, all celebrating diversity. The main concert stage is situated on the

Easter/Holy Week

Various locations

You're most likely to spot Good Friday processions in the Barri Gòtic, near the Catheral or La Rambla. Easter Monday is also a public holiday in Barcelona, and it is when children eat the *Mona de Pascua*, a sponge cake or chocolate egg consumed at Easter, and traditionally gifted to children by their godfather. Expect to see lots of wonderful window displays in bakeries around the city.

Primavera Sound

Parc del Fòrum (Carrer de la Pau, 12); end of May-beginning of June; www.primaverasound.com; three-day ticket €215, day ticket €85

This is one of Barcelona's most famous music festivals. Some of the world's biggest pop, rock, indie, and alternative acts have played at Primavera Sound, including The Cure, The Pixies, Public Enemy, Patti Smith, Arcade Fire, and Neil Young. A full weekend pass costs around €215 and can be booked online via the Primavera Sound website. Day tickets

Avinguda de la Reina Maria Cristina, between Plaça de Espanya and the Palau Nacional in Montjuïc. The weeklong festivities end with a lively march along the length of Avinguda del Paral·lel, starting at the Jardins de les Tres Xemeneies and finishing at Plaça d'Espanya.

Festival Cruïlla

Parc del Fòrum; July; www.cruillabarcelona. com; three-day ticket €120, day ticket €75

One of the city's most diverse music festivals, Cruïlla welcomes acts from around the world to its three stages in Parc del Fòrum. It is also more under-the-radar than Sónar and Primavera Sound, making for smaller crowds and a more local vibe. Recent performers have included Jack White, Seasick Steve, Damien Marley, and Fatoumata Diawara.

Circuit Festival

Various locations; mid-August; www.circuitfestival.net

One of Europe's biggest gay festivals, Circuit attracts partygoers from far and wide for 10 days of music, clubbing, and diverse events across the city. The highlight is a 12-hour waterpark party held at Illa Fantasia in Vilassar de Dalt (outside the city).

Festa Major de Gràcia

Gràcia; mid-August

Residents of the Gràcia neighborhood spend months creating street decorations for this weeklong festival, which kicks off on August 15. Each street is decorated according to a theme, and prizes are awarded for the most original designs. Throughout the week, there's a whole range of festivities; by night there are outdoor concerts, and a general party atmosphere rules, and by day cultural traditions prevail,

including all the usual suspects—*castells* (human towers), *correfoc* (firerunning), *gegants* (giants), and more. Once the Gràcia festival draws to a close, a similar event takes off in the neighborhood of Sants.

FALL
Diada Nacional de Catalunya

Various locations; Sept. 11

Catalonia's national day commemorates the fall of Barcelona during the War of the Spanish Succession on September 11, 1714. It has been celebrated since the late 19th century, although it was banned during Franco's dictatorship. In recent years, it has been adopted as a day of demonstrations for Catalan independence and has a decidedly more political tone than other local festivals.

La Mercè

Various locations; Sept. 24; www.lameva.barcelona.cat/merce/en

Barcelona's biggest annual festival celebrates the feast day of Our Lady of Mercy (known as *La Mercè*), the city's co-patron saint. Festivities begin a few days before the main feast day of September 24, with live performances and parades across the city, including *castells* (human towers), processions of *gegants i capgrossos* (giant papier-mâché models), and lots of dancing of the *sardana*, Catalonia's traditional dance. Hundreds of free events are spread across plazas, parks, and streets—check the festival's website for a full program.

WINTER
Epiphany

Various locations; Jan. 5-6

In Spain, Los Reyes Magos (the Three Kings) traditionally bring children their Christmas presents. Children in

Barcelona wait in excited anticipation for January 5, when the Three Wise Men arrive from the East bearing gifts and parade through the city center (known as La Cabalgata). The festivities usually kick off at around 4:30pm, when the kings arrive in Port Vell by boat and are greeted by the mayor of Barcelona. From 6pm, the Three Kings begin their parade, a magical spectacle of color, music, and dance, which concludes near the Magic Fountain in Montjuïc.

Festes de Santa Eulalia

Various locations; Barri Gòtic, Feb. 12
La Mercè may steal the show, but the feast day of Barcelona's co-patron saint, Santa Eulàlia, sees traditional popular culture take to the streets to celebrate the city's annual winter festival.

Carnival

Various locations; February/March
Carnival takes place before Ash Wednesday, a last hurrah of fun, frolics, and excitement before the 40 days of Lent in the run-up to Easter. The Carnival begins with *Dijous Gras* or "Greasy Thursday," and includes a weekend of local carnival parades, including one in the Ribera area of the old town, *La Taronjada*, which takes place on Sunday and concludes with a huge battle of orange balloons and confetti at the end of the route.

Performing Arts

BARRI GÒTIC AND LA RAMBLA

FLAMENCO

Los Tarantos

Plaça Reial, 17; 93/304-1210;
www.masimas.com/tarantos;
shows at 7:30pm, 8:30pm, 9:30pm daily;
additional 10:30pm show from Jun.-Sept.;
€15

Los Tarantos presents short, sharp bursts of flamenco in a Plaça Reial basement. Many Andalusian and local legends have performed here since it was founded in 1963, and while tourist-oriented, the intimate venue manages to retain a sense of authenticity. The music and dance shows last 30 minutes, ideal for a brief, good-value introduction to Spain's most passionate art form.

THEATER

Gran Teatre del Liceu

La Rambla, 51-59; 93/485-9900;
www.liceubarcelona.cat; prices vary

The program at Barcelona's opera house, the Gran Teatre del Liceu, combines new works and classical productions. The season runs from September until June and sees the permanent orchestra and chorus perform alongside internationally renowned soloists. Ballet also forms an important part of the theater's activities, and contemporary musicians—from Bob Dylan to Van Morrison—make regular appearances, while the Petit Liceu series introduces children to the world of opera. Seats located in the central area of the upper floors offer the best acoustics and are cheaper than the lower floors. Subtitles available. Purchase tickets in advance; tickets to the 2,292-seat theater are coveted.

EL RAVAL
CONCERTS
JazzSí

Carrer de Requesens, 2; 93/329-0020; www.tallerdemusics.com/jazzsi-club; from 6:30pm daily; €6-€10

Part of the Tallers de Músics school in Raval, JazzSí presents big talent on a small stage. A creative platform for up-and-coming and professional artists, this laid-back, intimate venue has a daily program of live music, from Cuban and jazz, to pop, rock, and blues sessions. The flamenco nights on Friday and Saturday are always a hit (8:45pm, €10 with one drink included).

CINEMA
Filmoteca de Catalunya

Plaça de Salvador Seguí, 1-9; 93/567-1070; www.filmoteca.cat; Tues.-Fri. 5pm-10pm, Sat.-Sun. 4:30pm-10pm; €4

The Filmoteca de Catalunya is a cultural institution dedicated to the preservation and celebration of film. Situated deep in the Raval, this cast concrete monolith transformed its dense urban surroundings into a contemporary plaza that extends into the ground-floor ticket hall. From here, film fanatics descend to the subterranean screens, where original-language world cinema is programmed in themed cycles, or explore the exhibition spaces, which present temporary shows that relate cinema to history and the arts. Grab a pre-show bite to eat at the popular terrace cafe, La Monroe (Plaça de Salvador Seguí, 1-9; 93/441-9461; lamonroe.es).

LA RIBERA/EL BORN
FLAMENCO
Palau de Dalmeses

Carrer de Montcada, 20; 93/310-0673; www.palaudalmases.com; from €25

Palau de Dalmases makes an atmospheric setting for the hour-long flamenco performances that take place here daily (6pm, 7:30pm, and 9:30pm). Tucked away on Carrer de Montcada amid a string of medieval noble residences, this Baroque palace is worth a visit in itself. Shows include traditional flamenco song, dance, guitar, and *cajón* (box drum), and jazz and opera performances also take place on Wednesday and Thursday, respectively, at 11pm.

CONCERTS
Palau de la Música Catalana

Carrer Palau de la Música, 4-6; 93/295-7200; www.palaumusica.cat; prices vary

The only auditorium in Europe that is illuminated entirely by natural sunlight, the Palau de la Música Catalana is an acoustic and decorative wonder. Home of the Orfeó Català choir, more than 300 musical performances take place each year below the incredible stained-glass skylight, ranging from symphonic and chamber music to jazz, flamenco, and *cançó* (Catalan song). Many of the world's best soloists and orchestras have performed here since the inauguration of this Modernista masterpiece in 1908, from Montserrat Caballé to Ella Fitzgerald. If you experience only one live music venue in Barcelona, make it this one.

THEATER
La Puntual

Carrer de l'Allada-Vermell, 15; 63/930-5353; www.lapuntual.info; shows at Fri. 6pm, Sat. noon and 6pm, Sun. noon and 5pm,

occasional additional shows on weekdays;
from €5

One for the kids—La Puntual is a theater dedicated to puppet shows. It's the only one of its kind in the city; all sorts of characters take to the stage each weekend, from traditional marionettes to shadow puppets. Tucked away in El Born, the tiny theater hosts visiting companies, as well as in-house productions that are designed and created locally in the company's workshop. Shows are targeted at children aged 2-9 and are performed in Spanish or Catalan, and occasionally in English.

L'EIXAMPLE
CABARET
Gatsby Barcelona
Carrer de Tuset, 19; 93/700-4453;
www.gatsbybarcelona.com; Wed.-Thurs.
9pm-2:30am, Fri.-Sat. 9pm-3am; €70

Gatsby Barcelona is an Art Deco-style tribute to F. Scott Fitzgerald's debauched protagonist. The black and gold doors to this clandestine, so-much-more-than-dinner establishment are hidden within a dingy mall, but they open onto a world of Twenties razzle-dazzle. The contemporary Spanish menu is average and pricey, and there is a minimum spend of €70 per head, compensated for somewhat by the live cabaret show throughout the evening. After midnight, it becomes a cocktail lounge and dance floor. Book in advance and dress smartly.

MONTJUÏC AND POBLE-SEC
DANCE
Tinta Roja
Carrer de la Creu dels Molers, 17;
93/443-3243; www.tintaroja.cat;
Wed.-Sat. from 8:30pm; from €3

A quirky bar and theater tucked away in Poble-sec, the tiny Tinta Roja takes its inspiration from the classic Argentine tango club. Housed in a former urban dairy, the over-the-top boudoir décor of the café-concert space recalls bygone Buenos Aires. Tango is the raison d'être, although the program is nearly as eclectic as the decor, and also includes jazz, circus, flamenco, poetry, theater, and English-language improv.

Mercat de les Flors
Carrer de Lleida, 59; 93/256-2600;
www.mercatflors.cat; Mon.-Fri. 11am-2pm,
4pm-7pm; from €8

Mercat de les Flors is the city's primary platform for contemporary dance. Built for the 1929 International Exposition, the Noucentisme-style building was later a flower market, before the theater was established in 1983. The theater's program is devoted to movement arts, from the traditional to the experimental. Situated around the expansive Plaça Margarita Xirgu at the foot of Montjuïc, it forms part of the *Ciutat del Teatre* (City of Theater), together with the Teatre Lliure and Institut del Teatre.

CONCERTS
Sala BARTS
Av. del Paral·lel, 62; 93/324-8494;
www.barts.cat; prices vary

Opened in 1892, Sala BARTS was the first theater in the infamous Paral·lel district, although it has been remodeled and renamed many times. In its current reincarnation, BARTS (Barcelona Arts on Stage) presents a diverse program, from music, comedy, and dance to theater, magic, and circus acts. It's worth checking the listings for emerging and established musicians on low-key tours; Neneh Cherry, Macy Gray, ELO, and The Vamps have all played this intimate venue in recent years.

Palau Sant Jordi

Passeig Olímpic, 5-7; 93/426-2089,
www.palausantjordi.cat; prices vary

One of the key venues of the 1992 Olympic Games, Palau Sant Jordi is the largest indoor arena in Spain, with a capacity of nearly 18,000 and a distinctive domed roof. Today, this multi-purpose space hosts superstar musicians and cultural events of epic proportions, from Madonna and Metallica to Disney on Ice and Cirque du Soleil. Sant Jordi Club, a smaller venue annexed to the main arena, presents a more low-key line-up.

THEATER
El Molino

Carrer de Vila i Vilà, 99; 93/205-5111;
www.elmolinobcn.com; shows from 9pm;
from €15

Barcelona's answer to the Moulin Rouge, El Molino opened in 1898, when the theater district of Paral·lel was in its heyday. For nearly a century, debauched cabaret shows took to the legendary stage. Having closed its doors in 1997, the theater raised its curtain once more after an extensive redesign (2007-2010) and now offers contemporary burlesque that still captures the essence of this mythical establishment. The theater bar, which has a terrace just behind the windmill sails, is also a nice spot for a cocktail.

Teatre Grec

Pg. de Santa Madrona, 36; 93/413-2400,
www.barcelona.cat/grec; from €15

An open-air theater hidden amid beautiful formal gardens, the Teatre Grec was built for the 1929 International Exposition on the site of a former quarry. The Greek-style amphitheatre is carved out of the Montjuïc hillside and is used primarily during the summer months as the main venue for the Festival Grec, an international celebration of performing arts. During the festival, a pop-up restaurant occupies the garden pavilion. The peaceful setting and city views make it worth a visit even outside of theater season.

WATERFRONT
CONCERTS
L'Auditori

Carrer de Lepant, 150; 93/247-9300;
www.auditori.cat; prices vary

Home to the Barcelona Symphony and Catalonia National Orchestra (OBC), L'Auditori is a focal point for music in the city. Classical music dominates the busy agenda, together with some jazz, pop, and the occasional singer-songwriter. Screenings of Hollywood blockbusters accompanied by the OBC offer a fun twist on the traditional orchestra performance. Upstairs, the Museu de la Música de Barcelona (Tues., Wed., Fri., 10am-6pm; Thurs. 10am-9pm; Sat.-Sun. 10am-7pm; €6) houses a collection of instruments from around the world.

SHOPPING DISTRICTS

PASSEIG DE GRÀCIA (L'EIXAMPLE)
Best for: Upscale fashion
Metro: Diagonal or Passeig de Gràcia
Passeig de Gràcia—Barcelona's answer to the Champs-Élysées—is the city's most prominent shopping street, and its most exclusive. Connecting Plaça de Catalunya with Avinguda de Diagonal, this 19th-century boulevard has always been a parade of wealth. Today, this unique architectural heritage is occupied by haute-couture houses, concentrated at the Diagonal end of the street, while toward Plaça de Catalunya, the Spanish high street emerges, and continues into the Barri Gòtic along Avinguda del Portal de l'Àngel. The streets surrounding Passeig de Gràcia—**Rambla de Catalunya, Carrer de Mallorca,** and **Enric Granados**—echo the elegance of the main boulevard and host many independent designers.

PASSEIG DEL BORN AND VICINITY (LA RIBERA)
Best for: Trendy boutiques selling clothes, shoes, accessories
Metro: Jaume I
Beyond the city's main thoroughfares, shops are smaller and each area has its own vibe. In La Ribera, trendy, one-off boutiques populate the tiny streets around **Passeig del Born.**

BARRI GÒTIC
Best for: Authentic, traditional goods
Metro: Liceu or Jaume I
The Barri Gòtic hosts an eclectic mix of artisans, antiques, and old-time establishments selling all sorts, from handmade sweets to traditional hats. Shops are not concentrated on one street or square, but are peppered throughout the neighborhood.

CARRER DE LA RIERA BAIXA (EL RAVAL)
Best for: Vintage and retro treasures
Metro: Liceu or Sant Antoni
El Raval's tendency for alternative subcultures translates to its shopping vibe, with vintage style, retro records, and off-the-wall design haunts ready for those looking to make a statement. This short side street in Raval is the beating heart of retro retail in the city, lined with second-hand stores selling vintage clothing, old records, and everything in between. Rails of pre-loved threads spill onto the street, creating a dynamic market ambience, and there's even an English-speaking hair salon, **La Strada** (13), that specializes in retro cuts. Check out **La Vella Maia** (10) for accessories and one-off handbags, **De Faralaee** (9) for leather and Levis, **Kilostore** (11) to pick 'n' mix by weight, **Motel** (5) for a slice of the 1950s, and **Lullaby** (22) for designer goods.

GRÀCIA
Best for: Alternative design
Metro: Fontana or Diagonal
Gràcia exemplifies some of the same eccentricities as El Raval, but it is decidedly more hipster. Here, hot young designers, ethical fashion, and contemporary artisans reflect the neighborhood's bohemian flavor. Shops are peppered throughout, though Carrer de Bonavista or Carrer de Verdi is a good place to start.

Shopping

For a relatively compact city, the variety of shops in Barcelona is extraordinary. Multinational flagships, international haute-couture, century-old artisans, and unique local design all coexist within a few square miles.

Most shops open between 9am and 10am, and close between 8pm and 9pm. Many of the smaller and more traditional establishments, including the food markets, close in the afternoon between 2pm and 5pm, approximately. Nearly all shops are closed on Sunday.

BARRI GÒTIC AND LA RAMBLA
CLOTHING
Desigual

*Plaça de Catalunya, 9; 93/343-5940;
www.desigual.com; Mon.-Sat. 9am-9pm*

Desigual, meaning "unequal" in Spanish, is famous for its flamboyant, colorful clothing for men and women. The headquarters of the global fashion brand are based in Barcelona, with branches across the city and a flagship store on Plaça de Catalunya. The bold, asymmetrical (hence the name) designs and kaleidoscopic prints are instantly recognizable and capture the city's playful character.

SHOES AND ACCESSORIES
La Manual Alpargatera

*Carrer d'Avinyó, 7; 93/301-0172;
www.lamanualalpargatera.es; Mon.-Fri.
9:30am-8pm, Sat. 10am-8pm; from €12*

The first espadrilles store in Barcelona, La Manual Alpargatera opened in 1941 and soon became a symbol of the city. Catering to locals, tourists, and celebrity clients (Ralph Lauren and Jean-Paul Gaultier have both picked up a pair here), the artisan shoemaker offers a wide variety of espadrilles: traditional styles originating from different areas of Catalonia (and beyond), as well as more modern interpretations and custom-made designs. The signature espadrilles, a simple slip-on with a canvas upper, are still made in the workshop at the back of the shop.

Guantería y Complementos Alonso

*Carrer de Santa Anna, 27; 93/317-6085;
Mon.-Sat. 10am-10pm*

Time stands still in this emblematic glove and accessory shop. The beautiful wooden shopfront is filled with leather gloves, delicate mantillas, and traditional fans, while inside, attentive staff and antique display cabinets maintain retail traditions from the last century. Founded in 1905, this is one of a dying breed; stop by to experience it.

Sombrerería Obach

*Carrer del Call, 2; 93/318-4094;
www.sombreriaobach.es; Mon.-Fri.
10am-2pm, 4pm-8pm; Sat. 10am-2pm,
4:30pm-8pm*

There's a hat for every occasion at Sombrerería Obach. Classic headpieces of all shapes and sizes seem to float in the old-fashioned window display of this time-honored gentleman's hat shop, from Stetsons and Panamas to traditional berets. Wrapping around a corner in the heart of the Barri Gòtic, Sombrerería Obach oozes old-school elegance and has formed part of the neighborhood's retail heritage for nearly a century.

LOCAL DESIGN
La Nostra Ciutat

Carrer del Pi, 11; 93/156-1539;
www.lanostraciutat.co; Mon.-Sun., 11am-9pm
daily

Support the city's creative community at La Nostra Ciutat, a design store offering locally made artisan crafts of all sizes, shapes, and budgets. Dozens of reasonably priced graphic prints line the walls, while an eclectic collection of jewelry, stationery, keyrings, mugs, bags, and more fill the warehouse-style space, located in the heart of the Barri Gòtic. There is also a smaller branch in El Raval (Carrer del Dr. Dou, 11; 93/158-8313; Mon.-Sat. 11am-3pm, 4pm-9pm).

FOOD AND WINE
La Colmena

Plaça de l'Àngel, 12; 93/315-1356;
www.pastisserialacolmena.com;
9am-9pm daily

Pastisseria La Colmena is the city's oldest sweet shop, and has stood in its current location since 1868. This family-run traditional store still handcrafts its signature hard-boiled sweets (*bolados*) in a range of unique flavors following a century-old recipe (from €15 per box). Its beautiful interiors and shopfront are worth a visit alone—historical stores of this kind are disappearing fast in the city— but you can also satisfy your sweet tooth with an array of delicacies, including *panellets* (traditional marzipan cakes), *ensaïmadas* (Mallorcan pastry), truffles, and homemade chocolates.

VINTAGE
L'Arca

Carrer dels Banys Nous, 20; 93/302-1598;
www.larca.es; Mon.-Sat. 11am-2pm,
4:30pm-8:30pm; from €30

L'Arca is a treasure trove of antique textiles, wedding dresses, vintage fashions, lace, accessories, and costume jewelry. The carefully curated collection of heirlooms and hand-me-downs specializes in vintage bridal wear, with revamped dresses that date back as far as the 1920s. The boutique also offers its own bridal collection inspired by bygone eras, vintage evening wear, an impressive kimono rack, and a cabinet full of traditional fans. Brides-to-be: find your "something old" amid the haul.

DEPARTMENT STORES
El Corte Inglés

Plaça de Catalunya, 14; 93/306-3800;
www.elcorteingles.es; Mon.-Sat.
9:30am-10pm

Spain's answer to Selfridges or Macy's, El Corte Inglés offers a wide range of quality products, from fashion, food, and furniture to music and makeup. As the country's principal department store, it is a Spanish institution with more than 90 stores nationwide. There are six branches in Barcelona, with the largest occupying the northeast side of Plaça de Catalunya. Don't miss the views from the ninth-floor café.

EL RAVAL
LOCAL DESIGN
Orígens

Carrer del Carme, 39; 93/277-9521;
www.origensbcn.com;
Mon.-Sat. 11am-2pm, 4pm-8pm

Orígens sources modern and traditional arts and crafts produced by local artisans. Reuse, recycling, and responsible consumption are at the heart of the shop's ethos, and the collection of accessories and homewares demonstrates a commitment to eco-friendly and socially conscious design. The timber shelves of this tiny corner store are piled high with all kinds of

BEST SOUVENIRS

Desigual Barcelona

CLOTHING

Just like its architecture, Barcelona's attitude to fashion is original and daring. Spanish fashion talents that have made it big across the globe have flagship stores in Barcelona, including **Desigual** (Plaça de Catalunya, 9) and **Etnia** (Carrer de l'Espasería, 1-3), and there's a vivacious scene of young designers.

LEATHER AND ESPADRILLES

Alongside the fashion-forward houses, artisans continue to practice traditional craftsmanship passed down through the generations. Here, as across Spain, hand-made leather goods are especially high quality, primarily shoes and handbags, as well as handmade lace and *espardenyes* (espadrilles); **La Manual Alpargatera** (Carrer d'Avinyó, 7; 93/301-0172; www.lamanualalpargatera.es; Mon.-Fri. 9:30am-8pm; Sat. 10am-8pm) is the place to pick up a pair of these rope-soled shoes, originally worn by Pyrenean peasants.

FOOD ITEMS FROM LOCAL MARKETS

Food shopping in Barcelona is a sensory experience. Most experience it firsthand at **La Boqueria** market, just off La Rambla, though this is just one of a city-wide network of neighborhood markets—39 in all. (Also recommended: **Mercat de Sant Antoni** or **Mercat de Santa Caterina.**) Each one lies at the heart of the local community, where chefs hand-pick locally grown artichokes and fishmongers flog the catch of the day. Put away the camera and stock up on olives, jamón, cheese, or something more adventurous if you have kitchen facilities; your daily shop is one way to truly join the locals. Across the city, traditional gourmet food shops and bodegas, such as **Bodega Maestrazgo** and **Queviures Múrria,** are also worth keeping an eye out for.

original products, from recycled rubber rucksacks and hand-woven baskets to wooden watches, postcards, and pottery. There's another branch with the same opening hours in the Barri Gòtic (Carrer de Sant Felip Neri, 1; 93/463-8341).

Nuovum

Carrer del Pintor Fortuny, 30; 93/412-6411; nuovum.com; Mon.-Sat. 11am-2:30pm, 4pm-8:30pm

Nuovum provides a platform for up-and-coming local designers. Jewelry, bags, sunglasses, and original accessories, mostly designed and made in Barcelona, are beautifully displayed within the wooden honeycomb shelving. What started out as an online venture now has two shops in the city—this is the original, the second is in El Born (Carrer de la Bòria, 23; 93/319-9424; Mon.-Sat. 11am-8:30pm). The paper vase by Octaevo is a popular, transportable gift to take home.

VINTAGE
Holala! Plaza
Carrer de Valldonzella, 2; 93/302-0593; holala-ibiza.com; Mon.-Sat. 11am-9pm

A veritable nirvana for any follower of vintage fashion, this second-hand superstore presents unique clothing handpicked from flea markets and closets across the world, including a lot of American hand-me-downs. Each piece must pass a strict quality test, so whether you're after crushed velvet, military gear, or retro denim, it's likely to be in good condition. The store also stocks vintage furniture, video games, skateboards, surfboards, and a whole host of accessories.

MUSIC
Discos Revólver
Carrer dels Tallers, 13; 93/302-1685; www.discos-revolver.com; Mon.-Sat. 10am-9pm

Crammed with vinyl LPs, CDs, memorabilia, and artwork, Discos Revólver is the quintessential independent record store. With two outlets on the youthful Carrer dels Tallers (Revólver Records at number 11 belongs to the same owner), this is the place for some good old-fashioned crate digging, especially if you're a fan of indie, pop, and rock. Revólver's founders are active in the local music scene, hosting the occasional live concert and

coordinating International Record Store Day in the city every April.

LA RIBERA/EL BORN
CLOTHING
Ivori
Carrer dels Miraller, 7; 93/137-0264; www.ivoribarcelona.com; Mon.-Sat. 11am-8:30pm

Made in Barcelona is the maxim at Ivori. Creations by local young talents fill the pretty backstreet boutique in El Born, complemented perfectly by the intricate 19th-century ceiling and ivory-washed walls. Founder and designer Carola Alexandre selects a unique yet affordable range of women's clothing, shoes, handbags, and accessories, ensuring they're all 100 percent Catalan designed and made, to present alongside her own original collection.

SHOES AND ACCESSORIES
Beatriz Furest
Carrer de l'Espartería, 1; 93/268-3796; www.beatrizfurest.com; Mon.-Sat. 11am-9pm

Beatriz Furest combines Catalan design and Italian leather to create an irresistible range of women's accessories. Coming from a family of fashionistas who founded the Furest menswear brand in 1898, the designer learned the tricks of her trade in the family's traditional workshops and founded her own brand in 1996. At once classic and contemporary, Furest's beautifully crafted handbags capture Barcelona's street style.

Etnia Barcelona
Carrer de l'Espasería, 1-3; 93/018-6614; www.etniabarcelona.com; Mon.-Sat. 10am-8pm, Sun. noon-8pm

Etnia Barcelona creates painfully cool shades that are popular with the A-list.

This designer eyewear brand draws its inspiration from the art world—collections often revolve around one specific artist, be it Da Vinci, Klimt, or Raphael—and its angular, scratch-proof mineral lenses have been sported by the stars. The interior of the brand's flagship store is light and bright, and you can test out your new specs at the rooftop bar.

Vialis

Carrer de la Vidrieria, 15; 93/319-9491; www.vialis.es; Mon.-Sat. 10:30am-9pm

Simple, timeless shapes and hand-stitched details characterize the range of traditional women's shoes at Vialis. Handmade in Spain using vegetable-tanned leather, the distinctive designs bear a natural finish that reveals the tones and textures of the material. Founded in 1996 by Jaume Serramalera, there are several outlets in the city, including local shoe store Casas, which bought the brand in 2015. This branch in the Born is where it all began.

L'EIXAMPLE

CLOTHING

Santa Eulalia

Passeig de Gràcia, 93; 93/215-0674; www. santaeulalia.com; Mon.-Sat. 10am-8:30pm

Suiting and booting bourgeois *Barceloneses* since 1843, Santa Eulalia is one of the city's oldest haute-couture fashion houses. Three floors of exquisite clothing, shoes, and accessories, for both men and women, are impeccably presented in the glamorous William Sofield-designed shop. The collection includes select luxury labels, including Dior, Chanel, Givenchy, and Stella McCartney, as well as its own line of prêt-à-porter for women and bespoke tailoring for men. Spy the seamstresses in action

through a window into the workshop. If all that fashion leaves you famished, there's a fabulous café lounge and terrace at the back of the shop, serving breakfast, lunch, and plenty of bubbly (11am-8pm; €16.50-€22).

Aïlanto

Carrer d'Enric Granados, 46; 93/451-3106; ailanto.com; Mon.-Sat. 11am-2pm, 4pm-8pm

Fine, floaty, and feminine—that's the signature look from Ailanto, a haute-couture house founded in 1995 by Basque brothers Iñaki and Aitor Muñoz. Known for its geometric patterns, colorful prints, and delicate fabrics, the brand's original designs have become a regular on the international catwalk. This is one of just two exclusive womenswear boutiques (the other is in Madrid).

Sita Murt

Carrer de Mallorca, 242; 93/215-2231; www.sitamurt.com; Mon.-Sat. 10am-8:30pm

A "natural chic" style characterizes the creations of Sita Murt, womenswear that is at once simple and sophisticated, with loose necklines, changing volumes, and contrasting materials. Targeted at young working women, the collection caters to all occasions, from comfy knitwear and casual tops to silk pants and day dresses. The brand was founded by a local, Carmen "Sita" Murt, and is now run by her children.

Teresa Helbig

Carrer de Mallorca, 184; 93/451-5544; www.teresahelbig.com; by appointment only

Local talent Teresa Helbig specializes in women's haute couture and bridal fashion. Helbig learned to sew at her mother's kitchen table and keeps a close eye on her studio's creations today, made and sold in the exclusive atelier that she founded in 1997. Exquisite craftsmanship and deceptively simple styles with extraordinary detailing characterize her collection. The clientele includes the likes of Halle Berry, Taylor Swift, and Gwen Stefani.

SHOES AND ACCESSORIES

Lupo

Passeig de Gràcia, 124; 66/710-0790; www. lupobarcelona.com; Mon.-Sat. 10am-8:30pm

Founded in 1920 in Barcelona, Lupo creates luxurious bags and accessories made with soft Spanish leather. From slouchy holdalls to elegant purses, the original designs draw their inspiration from the city, its art, and the organic shapes of Gaudí. The *abanico* style, which imitates a Spanish fan, is the store's signature shape. Each exquisite handbag is crafted with care and designed to last.

Bimba y Lola

Passeig de Gràcia, 55-57; 93/215-8188; www. bimbaylola.com; Mon.-Sat. 10:30am-9pm

Named after the founders' greyhounds, Bimba y Lola is a young fashion brand from Galicia that is right on trend. Color, pattern, and bold prints lend a youthful aesthetic to the collection, which specializes in handbags but also includes women's clothing. The brand has become one of the fastest-growing labels in the world since it was founded in 2005 by two sisters from Galicia, with more than 200 stores in 17 countries. This branch is part of the Bulevard Rosa mall.

Tous

Passeig de Gràcia, 99; 93/467-5959; www.tous.com; Mon.-Sat. 9:30am-8:30pm

Tous is a Catalan jewelry, accessory, and fashion brand founded in 1920.

The brand is immediately recognizable for its teddy bear logo, which was introduced in the 1980s by Rosa Oriol, daughter-in-law of the founders. The bear is present throughout the collection of original designs in different shapes and forms. There are 16 branches in the city; this is the flagship store.

Camper

Rambla de Catalunya, 122; 93/217-2384; www.camper.com; Mon.-Sat. 10am-9pm; from €75

This contemporary footwear company from Mallorca creates relaxed yet refined styles for men, women, and children that blur the boundary between smart and sportswear. Each Camper store is unique; the sleek Rambla de Catalunya branch is the largest in Spain and includes the first Camper One space, which enables customers to participate in the design process.

FOOD AND WINE

Queviures Múrria

Carrer de Roger de Llúria, 85; 93/488-3355; www.murria.cat; Tues.-Fri. 10am-8pm, Sat. 10am-2pm, 5pm-8pm

With a beautiful shopfront and interiors that recall the grocery stores of yore, this gourmet-style delicatessen offers a mouthwatering selection of artisan cheeses, Iberian ham, foie, caviar, smoked fish, oils, coffees, canned delicacies, wines, and champagnes. Emblematic establishments like Queviures Múrria are under threat due to rising rents in the city, and many have already closed. Look for the antique adverts in the window—the Anís del Mono poster was designed by famous local artist Ramon Casas.

BOOKS

Llibreria Altaïr

Gran Via de les Corts Catalanes, 616;
93/342-7171; www.altair.es;
Mon.-Sat. 10am-10:30pm

This centrally located, travel-focused bookshop was born to fuel your wanderlust. Guidebooks, globes, and travel literature line the shelves, while antique maps adorn the walls. Altaïr Viatges, an in-house travel agency at the rear of the shop, can give you a helping hand.

COME IN English

Carrer de Balmes, 129-Bis;
93/453-1204; www.libreriainglesa.com;
Mon.-Fri. 9:30am-8:30pm, Sat.
9:30am-2pm, 4:30pm-8pm

The city's most extensive selection of English-language books is available at COME IN. Stocking everything from biographies and classics to new releases and children's literature, the bookshop has become a reference for anybody interested in the English language since it was founded in 1984. With friendly staff on hand to guide you through the vast catalog, this is a favorite with foreign residents in the city.

LOCAL DESIGN

Jaime Beriestain

Carrer de Pau Claris, 167; 93/515-0779;
beriestain.com; Mon.-Fri. 10am-9pm, Sat.
11am-9pm, Sun. 11:30am-7:30pm

Chilean designer Jaime Beriestain has created some of the hippest interiors in town, including the Almanac hotel, and his self-named restaurant and concept store pays homage to all the things he holds dear. Art, design, and grandma's cooking come together in an inviting, sage-green, timber-floored space, filled with geometric prints, Fifties-style furniture, and an eclectic collection of homewares you'll want to take home. Once you're done browsing, sink into a deeply comfortable armchair and order a mini banoffee pie. Pure style.

GRÀCIA, PARK GÜELL, AND BEYOND

CLOTHING

Colmillo de Morsa

Carrer de Vic, 15; www.colmillodemorsa.
com; Mon.-Fri. 11am-2:30pm, 4:30pm-7pm,
Sat. 11am-3pm

This creative young label has been causing a stir on the local and national catwalk since it was founded in 2009 by Elisabet Vallecillo and Javier Blanco. Colmillo de Morsa's (meaning "walrus tusk") minimalistic collections combine organic fabrics with Nordic influences to create responsible women's fashion, made in Barcelona. Think delicately printed beasties, floaty silk, and a muted palette of natural tones. Timeless and unique, yet affordable.

Coshop

Carrer d'Astúries, 4; 93/128-3214; coshop.es;
11am-8:30pm daily (8pm on Sunday)

Coshop is a community of eco-conscious local fashion designers. The flagship store in Gràcia supports new talent, offering commercial space to those working with organic, sustainable, and recyclable fabrics. All designed and made locally, the range of mostly women's clothing also includes bridal. The pickpocket-proof Urbanita bag is a bestseller. Unique pieces at reasonable prices.

ACCESSORIES

Koetània

Carrer de Goya, 8; 93/511-7221; koetania.
com; Mon. 5pm-8pm, Tues.-Fri. 11am-2pm,
5pm-8pm, Sat. 11am-2pm

Founded in 2011 by local duo Marta

Blanco and Daniel Bellido, Koetània crafts handmade contemporary jewelry, specializing in personalized wedding bands. Prospective clients can view the skilled artisans in action in the open workshop and become involved in the creative process. Book an appointment online if you're looking for a unique piece for the big day.

MONTJUÏC, POBLE-SEC, AND SANT ANTONI

MALLS

Las Arenas de Barcelona

Gran Via de les Corts Catalanes, 373-385; 93/289-0244; www.arenasdebarcelona.com; Jun.-Sept. Mon.-Sat. 10am-10pm, Oct.-May Mon.-Sat. 9am-9pm

A former bullring in Plaça d'Espanya, Las Arenas is a contemporary shopping center with three circular floors of high-street shops, as well as a gym, cinema, restaurants, and roof terrace. The original Neo-Mudejar façade was retained when the 1900 building was transformed by British architect Richard Rogers in 2011. Temporary exhibitions and expositions take place in the domed space on the top floor. Don't miss the 360-degree views from the roof terrace, which can be accessed from inside or via the external glass elevator (€1).

MARKETS

Mercat de Sant Antoni

Carrer Comte d'Urgell, 1; 93/423-4287; www.mercatdesantantoni.com; Mon.-Sat. 8am-8pm

Occupying an entire block in the Sant Antoni neighborhood, the Mercat de Sant Antoni is one of the oldest and largest local markets in the city. A cast-iron, cross-shaped structure designed by Antoni Rovira i Trias in 1882, the market houses 250 stalls selling a diverse range of products, from fresh vegetables, fish, and meat to clothes, shoes, and homewares. The market reopened in 2018 following a nine-year renovation project, which suffered lengthy delays due to the medieval city wall and counter wall that run beneath the building. To view these massive constructions, enter from Carrer de Manso and head to the basement. On Sunday mornings, enthusiastic collectors of all ages gather around the outside of the market between 8:30am and 2:30pm to source and swap secondhand books, coins, magazines, comics, postcards, records, cava bottle tops, and stamps.

WATERFRONT

MARKETS

Els Encants

Carrer de los Castillejos, 158; 93/246-3030; www.encantsbcn.com; Mon., Wed., Fri. and Sat., 9am-8pm

One of the oldest flea markets in Europe, the Mercat dels Encants moved to a dazzling new home in 2013 and has settled in surprisingly well. The soul of the old market lives on as buyers barter with vendors, their bounty sprawling across the floor, just as they have for centuries. The purpose-built, three-story structure accommodates 500 stalls of varying sizes, harboring a treasure trove of antiques, homeware, furniture, fabric, tools, electronics, and more. All the action is reflected in the extraordinary mirrored canopy, amplifying the buzz of the marketplace. It's a fun place to procure unique souvenirs.

WHICH BEACH?

- **Easiest to reach:** Platja de Sant Miquel, Platja de la Barceloneta

- **Best for families:** Platja de la Nova Icària, Platja del Bogatell

- **Best for watersports:** Platja de Sant Sebastià, Platja de Sant Miquel

- **LGBTQ+ friendly:** Platja de la Mar Bella

- **Near bars and restaurants:** Platja de la Barceloneta, Platja del Somorrostro

- **Less crowded (relatively speaking):** Platja de la Nova Icària, Bogatell, Platja de la Mar Bella. Note that all of Barcelona's beaches are crowded in summertime.

Recreation and Activities

✪ BEACHES

A beach and city break rolled into one: It's one of Barcelona's greatest calling cards. Almost 5 kilometers (3 miles) of golden sands stretch from Barceloneta, where the city meets the sea, all the way to the Forum, with numerous beaches strung along the seafront. In summer, there's a constant holiday vibe, with thousands of bikini-clad bodies stretched out before a promenade lined with restaurants and *xiringuitos* (beach bars) to beat the band. But it's even better to come here for a stroll when it's not sunbathing weather, when the warmth of the sun on a crystal clear winter's day casts long shadows from the palm trees right along the front—the perfect antidote to the dense cityscape and cultural overload.

Platja de la Barceloneta

Pg. Marítim de la Barceloneta,
metro: L4-Barceloneta; bus: 45, 59, D20
This is the city's oldest and busiest beach, and is actually three beaches in one. It's not the most relaxing nor the cleanest stretch of sand, but it has a contagious, effervescent vibe that needs to be sampled.

Platja de Sant Sebastià refers to the southernmost, and slightly quieter, stretch of sand, in front of the glamorous, sail-shaped W Hotel. Nudists and surfers (when the conditions are right) flock to this area, and several new bars and restaurants here have given this end of the beach a new lease on life.

Platja de Sant Miquel, named after the local church of Sant Miquel del Port, is the busiest section. Situated in front of Plaça del Mar and close to the bus stops where beachgoers arrive from the center, this section is also popular for watersports, such as paddle surfing. Look out for Rebecca Horn's *l'Estel ferit* along this stretch, a 10-meter-high (33-foot) sculpture comprising four steel cubes, which pays tribute to the old fishing district.

Continuing north, **Platja de la Barceloneta** is named after the adjacent neighborhood. This is traditionally where *Barceloneses* came to eat fish and paella. Today, the promenade is packed with eateries of every kind, seasonal beach bars, and an array of characters trying to make a living out of the tourism buzz, from professional sandcastle builders and street sellers (known as *manteros*) to would-be waiters flogging *cervezas* or mojitos made on the hoof.

Platja del Somorrostro

Passeig Marítim de la Barceloneta, 32, metro: L4-Ciutadella | Vila Olímpica; bus: 36, 45, 59, 92, D20, V21, V27

Platja del Somorrostro is sandwiched between Platja de la Barceloneta and Port Olímpic, and overlooked by the glistening metallic scales of Frank Gehry's giant fish sculpture. Wider than the Barceloneta beaches but equally as popular, this final stretch of sand is lined with exclusive bars and clubs that attract an international crowd day and night. It wasn't always so glamorous, though. *Somorrostro* was the name of a shantytown that stood right here little more than 50 years ago. Look for the commemorative plaque on the promenade wall, which depicts an aerial view of the beach in the 1950s, almost unrecognizable today.

Platja de la Nova Icària and Bogatell

Passeig Marítim de la Nova Icària / Passeig Marítim del Bogatell; metro: L4-Ciutadella | Vila Olímpica, L4-Llacuna; bus: H16, 59

Beyond Port Olímpic, the beaches become more spacious and less crowded, and have a more local vibe. With plenty of leisure amenities, including climbing frames, volleyball courts, and table tennis, these beaches are great for families and those who can't lie still. Platja de la Nova Icària comes first; its proximity to the Olympic Port ensures that a range of food and watersports are close at hand. Neighboring Platja del Bogatell is the widest,

longest, and most pleasant stretch of sand along the whole beachfront. The two beaches are flanked by a promenade and green space, beyond which lies Vila Olímpica (at the Nova Icària end), a residential area where the athletes were accommodated during the 1992 Olympic Games. The neighborhood of Poblenou lies parallel to Platja del Bogatell.

Platja de la Mar Bella

Passeig Marítim de la Mar Bella; metro: L4-Poblenou, L4-Selva de Mar; bus: 26, H16, V27

Platja de la Mar Bella is the next beach heading north from Bogatell. This beach is particularly popular with the LGBTQ+ crowd, and there is an area for nudists. Food options are few in this area, but it's a popular choice for sports and there is a skate park on the promenade.

WATERSPORTS
Moloka'i SUP Center

Carrer de Meer, 39; 932/214-868; www.molokaisupcenter.com; Tues.-Sat. 10am-7pm, Sun. 10am-6pm; rental from €15 per day, classes from €25

Specializing in Stand Up Paddle, this Barceloneta center will have you walking on water in no time. Any age group or fitness level can learn to ride the calm Mediterranean waters with Moloka'i, which provides quality equipment and experienced trainers. Paddle surfs and normal surf equipment is also available for rental only.

JetScoot

Moll de la Ronda; 93/252-8514; www.jetscoot.com; from €30

If you're looking for an adrenaline rush, make your way to JetScoot in Port Fòrum, where you can try your hand at flyboarding, hoverboarding,

Platja de la Nova Icària

parasailing, wakeboarding, jet-skiing, and more.

Barcelona Watersports

OceanOne Port Vell; 626/071-561; barcelonawatersports.es; 10am-9pm daily; from €65

This British-run center in the swanky OceanOne Port Vell offers RYA (Royal Yachting Association) training in PWC, powerboat, motorboat, and sail, as well as specializing in trips, rides, and charters for tourists, corporate and group events (from €65 per person).

PARKS AND GARDENS

MONTJUÏC, POBLE-SEC, AND SANT ANTONI

Jardins de Mossèn Costa i Llobera

Carretera de Miramar, 38; Nov.-Mar. 10am-7pm daily, Apr.-Oct. 10am-9pm daily

More than 800 succulent species inhabit the Jardins de Mossen Costa i Llobera, an unlikely oasis clinging to the sea-facing side of Montjuïc. This unique collection of exotic plants hail from desert, subdesert, tropical, and high mountain regions around the world and together represent one of Europe's biggest gardens specializing in cacti. Arranged in terraces that step down the mountainside, the gardens afford magnificent sea and port views through the spiny trunks of this slightly surreal setting.

Jardins de Joan Maragall

Avinguda de l'Estadi, 69; 93/292-4212; Sat.-Sun. 10am-3pm; free

Centered around the 1929 Palauet Albéniz—the official Barcelona residence of the Spanish royal family—the Jardins de Joan Maragall are fit for a king. Tree-lined paths and lush lawns give way to broderie flower beds, ornamental sculptures, and water features, reaching a crescendo in front of the main façade of the modest Neoclassical palace. A green, serene hiatus from the city, these elegant landscaped gardens remain largely undiscovered and are open only at the weekend.

WATERFRONT
Parc Diagonal Mar

Carrer de Llull, 362; Dec.-Feb. 10am-6pm daily, Mar. and Nov. 10am-7pm daily, Apr. and Oct. 10am-8pm daily, May-Sept. 10am-9pm daily

Designed by starchitects EMBT (Enric Miralles and Benedetta Tagliabue), Parc Diagonal Mar is a futuristic urban space built for the 2004 Universal Forum of Culture. The park was designed to connect Avinguda Diagonal with the seafront via a maze of paths branching off a sinuous spine. The 14-hectare space is divided into seven distinct recreational zones, all connected by water, and includes a large children's play area, a lake, and a central plaza. A sprawling metallic sculpture weaves its way through the whole park like the unwieldy roots of a gargantuan tree.

SANTS, LES CORTS, AND LA ZONA ALTA
Parc de Collserola

www.parcnaturalcollserola.cat

The tree-studded hills surrounding Mount Tibidabo belong to the Parc de Collserola, the world's largest metropolitan park, which is home to many hiking routes. The most accessible is the Carretera de les Aigües, a 10-kilometer (6-mile) walking and cycling trail that sits on a shelf above the city, traversing the mountainside from Sant Pere Màrtir in the south to the Carretera de la Rabassada in the north.

To reach Tibidabo, take the FGC train (L7) or bus numbers H4, V13, or V15 to Avinguda Tibidabo, switch to the 196 bus, and then the Tibidabo Funicular (€7.70/€4.10 when purchased with a ticket to Tibidabo Amusement Park). To join the Carretera de les Aigües path, take the FGC train (S1 or S2) to Peu del Funicular, then switch to the Vallvidrera Funicular and alight at the Carretera de les Aigües stop.

FOOTBALL
SANTS, LES CORTS, AND LA ZONA ALTA
FC Barcelona

Camp Nou stadium, C. d'Aristides Maillol, 12; www.fcbarcelona.com; tickets from €69; metro: Collblanc

Football is more than a sport in Spain; it is a religion. FC (Football Club) Barcelona is one of the country's top teams; it plays on weekends during the season (August-May) at the Camp Nou stadium.

Matches (90 minutes) are lively, with singing, horn honking, and general merriment; the waving of the unofficial Catalan flag, the *est e lada* (the "starred flag"—flown by supporters of Catalan independence), is a common sight. The atmosphere is family-friendly, and you shouldn't worry about taking older children to a match. Fans tend to wear the blue and claret team colors. The atmosphere is family-friendly, and you shouldn't worry about taking older children to a match.

The stadium opens 90 minutes ahead of kick-off on match days—it is worth getting to the stadium nice and early to enjoy the build-up and find your seat in plenty of time. The stadium, open to the elements, can get cold in winter, so take layers for extra warmth. The cheaper seats higher up in the stadium tend to be more filled with tourists and fewer regular attendees. You'll find many of the local fans sitting behind the goals or lower down, closer to the pitch.

Alcoholic drinks are not sold inside the stadium, which only offers alcohol-free beer in the run-up to and during the match, and you are not allowed to bring alcohol into the stadium. Fans are free to bring food and soft drinks—in fact, most local fans do so, with some of the most common snacks being satisfyingly big baguette sandwiches filled with ham and cheese. (There are snack stalls inside the stadium, but there is not a great amount of choice, so bring a little picnic and you'll fit right in.)

It's best to book tickets in advance; they usually become available on the team's official website (www.fcbarcelona.com/tickets/football/football-tickets) around four weeks before matches. Tickets can also be booked on TicketMaster (www.ticketmaster.es), which sells tickets at the official price. Bear in mind that match days and times are often not confirmed until around two weeks beforehand, so it could be a good idea to wait until they are officially confirmed than risk a change and miss the match.

The best way to get to the stadium is by metro. Get off at Collblanc or Les Corts. The road between, the Travessera de les Corts, is lined with bars where fans can stop for a pre-match beer and get into the spirit.

SPA

LA RIBERA/EL BORN
Aire Barcelona

Passeig de Picasso, 22; 93/295-5743;
beaire.com; Sun.-Thurs. 9am-midnight,
Fri.-Sat. 9am-2am; from €38

Although the city never formed part of Al-Andalus, AIRE Barcelona has a distinctly Arabic flavour. This deluxe spa is housed in the vaulted basement of an 18th-century warehouse in El Born, a tranquil underground lair inspired by the bathing traditions of ancient civilizations. The "thermal tour" includes a series of pools, a steam room, a flotarium (salt bath), and a "bath of a thousand jets," all set within candle-lit, exposed brick caverns: the perfect hideout from the city chaos above. For an extra treat, a range of tantalizing massages and rituals delight the senses.

TOURS

For all tours listed below, guides speak English.

CITY TOURS
Hidden City Tours

65/558-5156; www.hiddencitytours.com;
available daily; €18

Hidden City Tours leverages tourism to create jobs for the homeless, with each tour led by a member of the city's homeless community. History and contemporary culture is interwoven with the guide's individual story. There are five routes, from the classic sights of the Gothic Quarter to a gritty exploration of life on the streets of El Raval. An excellent opportunity to leave a positive footprint on the city. Tours are private and are available daily; email lisa.grace@hiddencitytours.com to reserve.

ART AND ARCHITECTURE
Barcelona Architecture Walks

Passatge del Hort de Velluters, 5;
68/249-7208;
www.barcelonarchitecturewalks.com;
"Urbanism," Wed. 4pm; "The Sea," Sat.
10:30am; "Gaudí," Tues., Fri., and Sun.
10:30am; "The Market," Thurs. 10:30am;
"The Future," Mon. 4pm; €35 (2.5-3 hours)

In a city famous for its urban design and architecture, who better to show you around than a local architect? Designed for beginners and buffs alike, these urban walking tours prompt a new appreciation for the built environment and how it embodies the city's history. Choose from five regular tours on topics ranging from Gaudí to Enric Miralles. Special tours geared toward archi-geeks are available on request. Founded by local studio Miel Arquitectos, the team of professional, practicing architects is passionate about architecture and the city.

Barcelona Street Style Tour

www.barcelonastreetstyletour.com; walking tours: El Raval, 10am, 4:45pm daily; El Born and Barrí Gòtic, 2pm daily; free (with donation); bicycle tour: Poblenou, 10am daily, €23; reservations essential

Barcelona's city's streets are an authentic outdoor gallery for those who know where to look. The knowledgeable Street Style guides offer an intriguing insight into the context and changing landscape of street art in the city. There are two walking routes—El Born/Barrí Gòtic (meet at Arc de Triomf) and El Raval (meet at MACBA)—and a bicycle tour of the former industrial area of Poblenou, taking in all kinds of street art from large-scale contemporary murals and sculptures to posters, stenciled art, and tagging. Street art workshops are also available; email tours@barcelonastreetstyletour.com for more information.

HISTORY
Barcelona and the Spanish Civil War

66/347-6009; info@spanishcivilwartours. com; daily except Wed. and Sun., 10am-2:30pm (mid-Jun.-mid-Sept.: 9am-1:30pm); €30/under 15s €15

Led by Barcelona-based historians Nick Lloyd and Catherine Howley, this 4.5-hour walking history lesson follows a chronological route through the Barri Gòtic, revealing the events of 1936-1939, from a failed military coup and libertarian revolution, to catastrophic air raids, murder, and mass exodus. The tour provides harrowing but essential context for understanding the city today, as well as Catalonia's current political situation. The tour includes two lengthy stops, allowing the group to examine a range of original artifacts. Numbers are limited; email to reserve in advance.

BOAT TOURS
Catamaran Orsom

Portal de la Pau, 1; 93/441-0537; barcelona-orsom.com; from €15.50

Soak up miles of skyline on the 22.8-meter (75-foot) Orsom Catamaran during a 90-minute cruise along the Barcelona coast. Sunbathe in the giant hammock sun loungers aboard the midday sailing (€15.50, 2:30pm) or channel Ibiza vibes on the sunset cruise (€19.50, times vary), which glides gently across the Mediterranean to the sounds of live jazz and chill beats. The sailing season runs from April until mid-October. Cruises set sail from Port Vell, close to the Columbus Monument.

Las Golondrinas

Moll de Drassanes; 93/442-3106; lasgolondrinas.com; from €7.70

Las Golondrinas has been running pleasure boat trips since 1888. Today, a traditional fleet of double-decker wooden boats, as well as several modern catamarans, offer a range of tours. The 40-minute tour of the Port of Barcelona (€7.70) explains maritime life in the city, past and present, while the 90-minute scenic sail along Barcelona's coastline (€15.20) gives passengers a unique skyline perspective. In summer, there is also a live-music cruise that sets sail in the evening, and a water taxi service to Port Fòrum. There is also a combined ticket for the 90-minute cruise that includes entrance to the Barcelona Aquarium (€28). Sailings operate year-round, starting at approximately 11am and finishing at 6:30pm (earlier in winter). Discounts available online.

HELICOPTER TOUR
Cat Helicopters

Passeig de l'Escullera; 93/224-0710; cathelicopters.com; Nov.-Mar Mon.-Fri. 9am-6pm, Sat. 10am-5pm, Sun. 10am-3pm, Apr.-Oct. 10am-7pm daily; from €79

Take in Barcelona's unique urban layout from above with a whistle-stop aerial tour. The circular Sky Tour (€125) follows the Barcelona beachfront along to the Fòrum, comes round past Torre Glòries and the Sagrada Família, then along Avinguda Diagonal to Camp Nou, before heading back over Plaça d'Espanya and Montjuïc. Alternately, the Costa Tour (€79) sticks to the shoreline, with views of the Columbus Monument and Barceloneta. It's possible to extend the Sky Tour to include the stunning Montserrat mountain range for €340 per person.

CLASSES
COOKING
Bear on Bike

Carrer de la Riereta, 15; 63/306-6986; www.bearonbike.es; 10am Tues.-Sat. (reserve online); €80 (4.5-hours)

Buy. Cook. Eat. That's the order of events at the Bear on Bike immersive cookery class. It begins with a tour of La Boqueria market, where an Australian-Italian couple, Ella and Alberto, share tips for choosing great produce and stock up on local,

seasonal ingredients from their favorite stalls. Then it's back to Espai EGG, an offbeat gastronomic space deep in El Raval to learn a few new tricks while preparing a delicious, three-course lunch that goes beyond the typical Spanish cookery classes (no paella here). A grazing board of charcuterie, cheese, and olives and biodynamic wine tasting keeps participants going until the feast is ready.

Foodie Experience

Passatge Madoz, 6; 68/521-0102; www.foodiexperiencebcn.com; Mon.-Wed. 6pm-9pm, Thurs.-Fri. noon-3pm; €65 (3 hours)

Learn how to prepare quintessential Spanish dishes with sisters Angels and Carmen, who bring their family's culinary traditions to the table together with a healthy measure of fun. The hands-on cookery class takes place in a beautiful, bright space just off La Rambla. Participants prepare five traditional recipes, including a family-sized paella, while chef Angels shares tips and techniques, as well as local foodie knowledge. When the banquet is prepared, the group sits

Bear on Bike cooking class

down together with a glass of home-made sangria or organic wine and tucks in.

WINE TASTING
Blend and Bottled

Carrer de Lluís el Piadós, 6; 62/820-0284;
www.blendandbottled.com;
Tues.-Sat. 1pm-7pm; from €15

Allow Dutch oenophile Claartje van den Bogaard to guide you through the world of vines and wines. Based in a cozy studio near Arc de Triomf, aficionados can learn how to navigate a local wine list, sampling vinos from across the country, at the "Taste of Spain" experience (Fri.-Sat. 5pm, €49). Or take a more relaxed approach with the walk-in wine flights—a guided selection of Spanish wines to swirl, sniff, and sip at your own pace (€15-€35). Pair with some artisan cheeses and charcuterie and let the conversation flow.

Accommodations

An intimate B&B in a restored Modernista building, an exclusive clandestine enclave tucked away in the Gothic Quarter, high-level indulgence in the city's tallest skyscraper, or boutique-on-a-budget digs in a local neighborhood—whatever your style or budget, there's a place for it in Barcelona. With more than 70,000 hotel beds and countless more hostels, guesthouses, and apartments, visitors are truly spoiled for choice. Nevertheless, the beds fill up quickly, so reserve as far in advance as possible, especially at peak times. Many hotels require a two-night minimum stay on weekends during peak season.

Thousands of **apartment rentals** are available across the city, both privately through peer-to-peer platforms, such as Airbnb, and via established rental companies and hotel booking websites. In order to rent out an apartment for short-term stays in Barcelona, landlords require a license from the city council. If you do rent a private apartment, it is worth checking that the landlord is in possession of the correct license; illegal holiday lets are at the center of a row over tourism and are driving rental prices up for residents.

Besides fulfilling the primary purpose of providing a bed for the night, many of the city's high-end hotels have become an integral part of the city's social life. In their Michelin-starred restaurants and skyline terraces, you're just as likely to bump into aspirational locals as hotel residents.

WHERE TO STAY

Though the endless options can be overwhelming, Barcelona is a compact city with an excellent transport system, so wherever you choose to stay, getting around is straightforward and easy.

Barri Gòtic: The Barri Gòtic is packed with tourists but oozes historical charm, and some of the city's most alluring accommodations are concealed behind its thick stone walls.

El Raval: Across La Rambla, El Raval has a lively bohemian vibe, although it can feel a little too edgy at night.

La Ribera: Just a stone's throw

from the waterfront, the Ciutat Vella is the city's oldest district, where many sights are buried amid its quaint, narrow streets. Within the Ciutat Vella, La Ribera is the best all-rounder for streetlife, shopping, eating, and drinking.

L'Eixample: By far the largest district in the city, L'Eixample has the largest range of accommodation, covering all budgets. The central area around Passeig de Gràcia is very well located for all the major sights—most are within a 30-minute walk—though traffic can be noisy. Many hotels in this part of town occupy late-19th or early-20th-century buildings and exude fin-de-siècle elegance.

Gràcia: At the top end of Passeig de Gràcia, visitors can live like a local in the old village of Gràcia, enjoying its vibrant squares and hip cafés. Several boutique hostels offer a refreshing alternative for those on a budget.

Montjuïc, Poble-sec, and Sant Antoni: If you want to feel immersed in local neighborhood life, Sant Antoni and Poble-sec tick that box, and are strategically located between the greenery of Montjuïc and the winding lanes of the Ciutat Vella.

Waterfront: The extensive waterfront area suits those who want to concentrate on the beach, ideally in summer; the skyscraper hotels here offer opulence with a view. And if you want to combine beach life with a neighborhood ambience, Poblenou is the place, though it is a

little further away from the main tourist attractions.

Sants, Les Corts, and La Zona Alta: Accommodation in uptown Barcelona tends to be loftier and leafier than its downtown counterparts. Gardens and pools are the norm in this part of town, though it's a little farther from the sights and city life.

BARRI GÒTIC AND LA RAMBLA

€100-150
Hotel Catalonia Avinyó
Carrer d'Avinyó, 16; 93/270-2170;
www.cataloniahotels.com; €140 d
Hotel Catalonia Avinyó is situated at the heart of the Gothic Quarter, just a stone's throw from Plaça Sant Jaume, La Rambla, and Plaça Reial. This modern three-star hotel fulfills all the basics with a bit to spare. The 83 guest rooms are simple but clean and there's a generous continental spread for breakfast. Ask the helpful staff for a room overlooking the lush internal courtyard, which tend to be quieter than street-facing rooms. The small rooftop pool, jacuzzi, and terrace are perfect for cooling off in the height of summer.

Denit Hotel
Carrer d'Estruc, 24; 93/545-4000;
www.denit.com; €140 d
Nearly all the main sights are within walking distance of Denit Hotel, a no-nonsense, three-star stay in the very heart of the city. This clean,

minimalist hotel makes a comfortable resting point come evening—hence the name *de nit* (meaning "by night")—although leisure facilities are few. The 36 guest rooms are small but well designed, with stark white walls softened by pale wooden furnishings; natural light is limited. The very reasonable buffet breakfast is served in the basement restaurant.

OVER €250
Hotel Neri
Carrer de Sant Sever, 5; 93/304-0655; hotelneri.com; €290 d

Overlooking the atmospheric Plaça Sant Felip Neri, Hotel Neri is an exclusive hideaway in a magical corner of the city. Clean, contemporary finishes allow the historical fabric of the building to shine, while every luxury is catered for in the 22 sophisticated guest rooms, some with private terraces. Six apartments are also available in the building opposite. The city's only Relais & Chateau property, Neri is a haven of peace in the heart of the bustling Gothic Quarter—the only thing missing is a pool. Pedestrian access only; transfers can be arranged.

The Wittmore
Carrer de Riudarenes, 7; 93/550-0885; thewittmore.com; €375 d

In a tiny alleyway of the Gothic Quarter, a smartly dressed doorman welcomes guests into old-world luxury with a distinctly British feel at The Wittmore. Hardwood paneling, classic chandeliers, tartan wallpapers, and velvet furnishings create an exclusive, enigmatic ambience throughout, from the fireside lounge to the small rooftop pool and terrace. Twenty-two rooms of varying sizes overlook the interior patio and have limited natural light, although it only accentuates the

mood. Downstairs, The Witty restaurant serves up rich bistro classics and opens onto a vertical garden. No photos, no pets, no children.

Soho House
Plaça del Duc de Medinaceli, 4; 93/220-4600; sohohousebarcelona.com; €290 d

Soho House is a hip private members' club with all the trimmings. Founded in London in 1995, the Barcelona branch channels an English country house style with a Catalan twist, and opened to much fanfare in 2016. Luxury treats await on every floor. The basement houses a private cinema and the farmhouse-style Cowshed spa, complete with pool; there's a swanky club lounge, a gym, and two restaurants, while the rooftop pool and bar is the place to spot celebs, with magnificent views over Port Vell. Rooms are modest but extremely well equipped: go for the "Medium Corner" if your budget allows.

EL RAVAL
€150-250
Barceló Raval
Rambla del Raval, 17-21; 93/320-1490; www.barcelo.com; €160 d

Shrouded in a diaphanous steel mesh, this 10-story, elliptical design hotel opened in 2008, and acted as a catalyst for regeneration in the area. Hot pinks, oversized lampshades, and 1970s-inspired furnishings set a funky, eclectic tone to the social spaces. The 182 rooms are, thankfully, a little more low-key—upper floors have the best views but are also the most expensive. The Sunday brunch buffet (€25) is popular with locals. Don't miss the 360-degree terrace bar; the pool may be miniscule but the views are mighty.

Hotel España

Carrer de Sant Pau, 9-11; 93/550-0000;
www.hotelespanya.com; €180 d

One of the oldest hotels in the city, Hotel España began life as a 19th-century inn. It was given a Modernista makeover in 1903 by Domènech i Montaner, and has recently been upgraded for the 21st century with the addition of a rooftop pool and bar. Located at the more refined end of Carrer de Sant Pau, just off La Rambla, the 82 modern guest rooms are small but swish. Dine like Gaudí in the traditional Fonda España restaurant, followed by al fresco cocktails and live music up top.

Casa Camper

Carrer d'Elisabets, 11; 93/342-6280;
casacamper.com/en/Barcelona; €240 d

Tucked away on an unassuming narrow street, Hotel Casa Camper cocoons its guests in understated luxury. Conceived by Mallorcan footwear company Camper, the brand's signature red runs throughout the contemporary interiors and spacious guest rooms, all of which have both a lounge and bedroom area. A complimentary round-the-clock buffet, gym and laundry service, and a mobile hotspot to take out and about, top off the attentive but relaxed service. There's no pool, but the skyline terrace has views of Tibidabo. Downstairs, continue the discreet luxury experience at Dos Palillos, a Michelin-starred Asian fusion restaurant.

LA RIBERA/EL BORN

€100-150

Chic & Basic Born

Carrer de la Princesa, 50; 93/295-4652;
chicandbasic.com; €110 d

This aptly named hotel is a boutique-on-a-budget option, just a 3-minute walk from the Museu Picasso. One of seven in the city from this hip hotel franchise, the white, minimalist rooms here are small but stylish. Handy extras include "help yourself" coffee and bicycle rental. You should know your roommate intimately, though—the in-room glazed shower cubicles leave little to the imagination. The color-changing LED mood lights and curtains are gimmicky but fun. Go for a street-facing room with balcony; interior rooms are dark.

Hotel Banys Orientals

Carrer Argenteria, 37; 93/268-8460;
www.hotelbanysorientals.com; €140 d

Just steps from the beautiful basilica of Santa Maria del Mar, Hotel Banys Orientals is well located in the heart of El Born. Simple but stylish with monochrome interiors, this boutique-budget hotel scores highly on the price-quality scale. The 43 guest rooms are small but comfortable, many with four poster beds and small balconies. Ask for a room facing the side street—Carrer de l'Argenteria can get noisy at night. The ground-floor restaurant, Senyor Parellada, serves traditional Catalan fare at reasonable prices and is popular with locals.

Hotel Rec

Carrer del Rec Comtal, 19; 93/556-9960;
hotelrecbarcelona.com; €140 d

Named after a Roman watercourse that once ran along this street in El Born, the adults-only Hotel Rec opened in 2018. This brand-new building features 99 bright guest rooms and a clean, contemporary aesthetic. It's all happening on the sunny rooftop terrace, where you can while away summer afternoons by the pool or sample craft beer at a free masterclass. Downstairs, the Fismuler restaurant offers modern market cuisine and is run by three former chefs from Ferran Adrià's elBulli. Book through the website for complimentary extras.

€150-250
Yurrban Trafalgar
Carrer de Trafalgar, 30; 93/268-0727; yurbbantrafalgar.com; €160 d

It's the complimentary extras at Yurbban Trafalgar that make this contemporary, 67-room hotel stand out, including Finna bike rental, a smartphone with city maps, laundry service, and a daily wine and cheese happy hour. Sleek furnishings and quirky wall coverings contrast a primarily grayscale palette throughout the hotel's eco-conscious interiors. Located between Plaça d'Urquinaona and the Arc de Triomf, Yurbban's eighth-floor rooftop pool and terrace elevates guests high above the low-rise Born neighborhood—ideal for a sundowner with splendid city views. Next door, the more exclusive **Yurbban Passage** (Carrer de Trafalgar, 26; 93/882-8977; www.yurbbanpassage.com; €255 d) offers a similar experience, with the addition of a spa and gym.

L'EIXAMPLE
€100-150
TOC
Gran Via de les Corts Catalanes, 580; 93/453-4425; tochostels.com/barcelona; private rooms from €140; dorm beds from €32

"All the bling without the sting": that was 50 Cent's verdict when he filmed a HostelWorld advert at TOC Barcelona in 2016. Chic interiors and thoughtful, practical design run throughout this boutique hostel next to Plaça de la Universitat, which offers shared dorms (6/8-person) and private suites (2/4-person). Suites are compact but comfortable, while each bunk-bed sleeping pod is complete with sockets, reading light, and shelves. Soak up the afternoon sun and the young, laid-back vibes by the outdoor pool and terrace, the social hub in summer.

La Casa Gran B&B
Avinguda Diagonal, 439; 63/689-7429; lacasagranbarcelonabb.com; €90 d

Housed in an early-20th-century listed building, La Casa Gran B&B is an intimate, welcoming pied-à-terre on one of the city's main thoroughfares. Opened in 2013, Victor and Anna make convivial hosts, passionate about sharing their local knowledge with those who are lucky enough to reserve one of their four simple, yet elegant, guest rooms. An organic, continental breakfast, which includes Anna's homemade cakes, is served on the generous private terrace—a rare commodity in this town.

Praktik Bakery
Carrer de Provença, 279; 93/488-0061; hotelpraktikbakery.com; €110 d

Wake up to the smell of freshly-baked bread at Praktik Bakery, located just a block away from Gaudí's La Pedrera. One of four design hotels from the Praktik brand, each with a unique theme, the popular Baluard bakery is located on the ground floor of this boutique-on-a-budget hotel—a great spot for breakfast. The 74 small but chic guest rooms are adorned with white tiles, white-painted wood, and black fixtures, with the odd splash of color, each one offering Crabtree & Evelyn toiletries and rain-effect showers.

Room Mate Emma

Carrer del Rosselló, 205; 93/238-5606;
room-matehotels.com; €125 d

The Madrid-based Room Mate group has a handful of design-oriented, boutique-on-a-budget hotels across the city—Room Mate Emma was the first. Located three blocks from Passeig de Gràcia, a futuristic lobby welcomes guests into this playful, hip hotel with a youthful vibe. Rounded furniture, backlit walls, and bold splashes of hot pink continue the *Jetsons* aesthetic throughout the 56 guest rooms. Suites have their own terrace; avoid the interior rooms. A generous breakfast is served until midday.

Casa Mathilda

Carrer Roger de Lluria, 125-127;
93/532-1600; casamathilda.com; €140 d

A welcoming bed and breakfast close to La Pedrera, Casa Mathilda occupies the first floor of a classic Eixample apartment block. Guests can enjoy breakfast (€9) or complimentary fresh fruit in the cozy living room, or wind down with an early evening vino on the sunny terrace. The 14 compact but well-planned guest rooms fall into three categories according to location—interior courtyard facing, street-facing, and rooms with a terrace. Each one includes a natural-fiber mattress and bathrobes. Reception is open 8am-8pm; late check-in can be arranged.

€150-250
the5rooms

Carrer de Pau Claris, 72; 93/342-7880;
the5rooms.com; €160 d

German fashion designer Yessica Delgado Fritz founded the5rooms in 2004, with the desire to offer an alternative to the city's traditional hotels. Inspired by her own travel experiences, she converted a five-bedroom, 19th-century apartment into a boutique B&B with nine spacious doubles, three junior suites, and two self-catering apartments, all with generous bathrooms. Exposed brick walls, contemporary furnishings, and unique art pieces set a stylish backdrop for this friendly home from home, where guests share tips at the communal breakfast table.

Casa Bonay

Gran Via de les Corts Catalanes, 700;
93/545-8070; casabonay.com; €195 d

A temple to all things cool and Catalan, Casa Bonay is a hip design hotel housed within a 19th-century building with high ceilings and original tiled floors. The 67 light-filled guest rooms are adorned with bespoke design flourishes by local artisans. Yoga mats, sun loungers, and outdoor showers are among the extras found in the exclusive terrace rooms. The rooftop **Chiringuito bar** (93/545-8076; Mon.-Fri. 6pm-11:30pm, Sat.-Sun. 1:30pm-11:30pm) is a leafy spot for a cold drink, while downstairs the **Libertine bar** (93/545-8076; Sun.-Thurs. 11:30am-1am, Fri.-Sat. 11:30am-1:30am), **Satan's Coffee Corner** (8am-6pm), and the **King Kong Lady** restaurant (685/582-314; Tues.-Sat, 8pm-midnight), which serves a fusion of exotic flavors, are popular with locals.

Hotel Pulitzer

Carrer de Bergara, 8; 93/481-6767;
hotelpulitzer.es; €200 d

It doesn't get much more central than the Hotel Pulitzer, located just off Placa de Catalunya. A sleek mid-range option with 86 modest but modern guest rooms, as well as five "Extra" large rooms and one suite with terrace, the hotel's contemporary interiors are adorned with original artworks, prints, and hardwood furnishings. The leafy rooftop terrace attracts both locals and hotel guests, hosting regular live music and DJs sessions from May to September, albeit with limited views and no pool. Downstairs, The Greenhouse (93/463-6116; set lunch menu Mon.-Fri. 1pm-4pm €19.50, Sat.-Sun. €25) restaurant offers vegetable-focused fine dining. Book through the website for complimentary extras.

✪ Axel Hotel Barcelona

Carrer d'Aribau, 33; 93/323-9393; axelhotels.com; €160 d

Situated at the heart of Barcelona's gay district (known as Gaixample), Axel Hotel is "hetero-friendly," but caters primarily to male clientele. The rooftop terrace, with its pool, jacuzzi, and Sky Bar, has a party vibe, while the urban spa and gym are popular with the adult-only guests. Floral flourishes contrast chic neutral interiors throughout the 105 comfortable guest rooms, with four suites boasting terraces. The friendly, impeccably dressed staff are clued-in on the city's LGBTQ+ scene.

✪ Margot House

Passeig de Gracia, 46; 93/272-0076; margothouse.es; €200 d

Hide away in minimalist luxury at Margot House, occupying one of Barcelona's most privileged addresses. Concrete surfaces, whitewashed walls, and locally produced timber furnishings bedeck the nine chic guest rooms, four of which offer views of Gaudí's Casa Batlló, located opposite. The Japanese-Scandinavian aesthetic continues throughout the spacious library, kitchen, and breakfast areas, where attentive staff prepare light bites on request. Brompton bike rental and a self-published guide book in each room complete the discreet boutique experience. It's easy to miss the entrance; look for the plaque next to the buzzer.

OVER €250

Majestic Hotel & Spa

Passeig de Gràcia, 68; 93/488-1717; hotelmajestic.es; €325 d

Opened in 1918, smack bang in the middle of Passeig de Gràcia, this neoclassical building emanates classic charm and counts Picasso and Hemingway among its former guests. A grand piano and opulent marble lobby welcome guests, leading to two elegant restaurants and a piano bar. Elsewhere, there's a spa, a gym, and a rooftop pool and bar, offering views over the city's most elegant boulevard. The 275 modernized rooms vary from the modest deluxe doubles to penthouse suites of up to 400 square meters (4,300 square feet); ask to be located on one of the upper floors, facing Passeig de Gràcia.

Cotton House Hotel

Gran Via de les Corts Catalanes, 670; 93/450-5045; hotelcottonhouse.com; €300 d

The former headquarters of the Cotton Producers' Guild, the lavish Cotton House Hotel pays homage to its material namesake in everything from the room names to the plush decor. Guests are greeted with cava as they enter an extravagant world of marble, wrought-iron staircases, coffered ceilings, and geometric-tiled floors. Opened in 2015 by Marriott Hotels, this five-star hotel includes a rooftop pool, terrace, and library, and offers afternoon tea. Nearly all 83 elegant rooms have balconies, apart from the Panama rooms, which are a little tight.

Almanac

Gran Via de les Corts Catalanes, 619-621; 93/018-7000; almanachotels.com; €450 d

Rest in opulent luxury at the Almanac, the newest addition to Barcelona's inventory of high-end hotels. Muted and gold tones run throughout the Art Deco-inspired interiors, with oak and walnut accents emanating an air of 1920s sophistication. Each capacious guest room is equipped with the latest smart technology and white marble bathrooms, complete with bespoke scents and walk-in showers. "Cube" rooms have a quirky chaise-lounge built into the protruding bay window, while up top, a multi-tiered roof terrace is perfect for a sundowner with city views.

GRÀCIA, PARK GÜELL, AND BEYOND
€100-150
Generator Barcelona

Carrer de Còrsega, 373; 93/220-0377; generatorhostels.com; private rooms €125; dorm beds from €32

A stylish, colorful renovation of a 1960s office building, Generator Hostel Barcelona offers shared and private accommodation on the edge of Gràcia. Quirky chill-out lounges are dotted throughout the large, social hostel, each one with a unique ambience. Downstairs, the vibrant *Fiesta Gràcia* bar, inspired by the famous neighborhood festival, serves food and drink all day and is decorated with hundreds of lanterns. The penthouse apartment and premium twins boast private terraces with city views; rooms on the sixth floor or above are quieter.

Casa Gràcia

Passeig de Gràcia, 116; 93/174-0528; casagraciabcn.com; private rooms €130; dorm beds from €35

The ultimate hostel-hotel hybrid, Casa Gràcia brings together the best of both in a hard-to-beat location at the top of Passeig de Gràcia. Hip and inherently Instagrammable, it offers a range of simple accommodation including six-bed dorms, private rooms, and apartments, all with private bathrooms; rooms with balconies are larger and lighter. Naturally the social hub is the underground bar, with anything from TED Talks to stand-up comedy on the nightly agenda. Mariah Carey shot a Hostelworld ad here in 2018: "Even Divas are believers."

✪ Pol & Grace Hotel

Carrer de Guillem Tell, 49; 93/415-4000; polgracehotel.es; €140 d

The Pol & Grace Hotel is one Spanglish couple's happy ever after. Off the beaten track but still well connected, this modern hotel is on the edge of Gràcia, where guests can sample the local neighborhood vibe. The compact rooms are bright and functional, while upstairs a rooftop terrace offers ample chillout space. On the ground floor, an information board, book exchange, and co-working space create a lively social hub. A mobile phone loaded with maps and data is provided in each room, and friendly staff are on hand to help plan your trip.

MONTJUÏC, POBLE-SEC, AND SANT ANTONI
€100-150
✪ Hotel Market

Carrer del Comte Borrell, 68; 93/325-1205; www.hotelmarketbarcelona.com; €120 d

Just steps from the market of Sant

Antoni, Hotel Market is an excellent chic-on-a-budget option, with lofty ceilings, grand chandeliers, and hardwood finishes. Standard rooms vary in size, noise levels, and views; ask for one with a balcony overlooking the street. Superiors are spacious and junior suites boast outdoor terraces. On the ground floor, an elegant restaurant serves modern Catalan dishes, and the Cocktail Bar Rosso spills out onto a side-street terrace.

B-Hotel
Gran Via de les Corts Catalanes, 389-391; 93/552-9500; www.b-hotel.com; €120 d

B-Hotel punches above its weight, easily surpassing expectations for a three-star hotel. Located at the busy interchange of Plaça de Espanya, it is well connected for seeing the sights, yet offers a different perspective at the foot of Montjuïc. The cool, contemporary vibe inside culminates with the relaxed rooftop terrace, where guests can soak in the infinity pool. The 84 spacious guest rooms are comfortably furnished with a crisp, minimalistic aesthetic. The café culture and buzzing community hubs of Sant Antoni and Poble-sec are within walking distance. Very handy for airport and rail connections.

€150-250
Hotel Brummell
Carrer Nou de la Rambla, 174; 93/125-8622, www.hotelbrummell.com, €180 d

Situated at the foot of Montjuïc, Hotel Brummell is an understated urban retreat. Mellow social spaces are dotted throughout, from the terrace and plunge pool to the shady restaurant patio. Rooms are chic but compact, with some offering rare glimpses of city greenery, while each penthouse includes a terrace and outdoor

hot tub. Brompton bikes and free yoga classes complete the boutique experience.

WATERFRONT
€100-150
Hostal Poblenou B&B
Carrer del Taulat, 30; 93/221-2601; hostalpoblenou.com; €99 d

Make yourself at home at Hostal Poblenou, a friendly oasis of calm just off the popular Rambla de Poblenou. Six modest but comfortable guest rooms, each one named after a famous artist, are housed within a renovated early-20th-century building, with original tiled floors and high ceilings. The Dalí and Picasso rooms are particularly pleasant, overlooking the sunny terrace where breakfast is served. Well connected to the center and just an 8-minute walk from Platja del Bogatell, this B&B is ideal for a beach break in the city.

OVER €250
W Barcelona
Plaça De La Rosa Dels Vents, 1; 93/295-2800; w-barcelona.com; €349 d

The sail-shaped silhouette of Ricardo Bofill's W Hotel dominates the skyline along Barcelona's beachfront. With more than 500 guest rooms, several gourmet restaurants, pools, and unrivaled views of the sea and city, this luxury resort has everything that its rich and fabulous clientele could possibly need—at a price, of course. The outdoor pools at the base of the hotel host lively weekend parties in summer, while the 26th-floor Eclipse Bar (93/295-2800; www.eclipse-barcelona. com) is a special, albeit pretentious, place for a sundowner. Taxis are your best bet for getting around come evening; it is a 20-minute walk from Barceloneta metro station.

Hotel Arts

Carrer de la Marina, 19-21; 93/221-1000;
hotelartsbarcelona.com; €380 d

Live the champagne lifestyle at Hotel Arts, 44 floors of exclusive luxury, located within one of Barcelona's tallest buildings. Operated by Ritz Carlton, this vertical resort overlooks the Olympic port and Barceloneta beach, catering for your every need with a Mediterranean-view infinity pool, luxury spa, high-end boutiques, and no fewer than six restaurants, including the two-Michelin-starred Enoteca by Paco Perez (93/483-8108; enotecapacoperez.com; Tues.-Fri. 7:30pm-10pm, Sat. 1pm-3pm, 7:30pm-10pm; tasting menu €190). The 483 bright and modern guest rooms boast incredible views; extravagant suites are on the higher floors (above the 19th). If big-time luxury is your thing, this is where it's at.

SANTS, LES CORTS, AND LA ZONA ALTA

€150-250

Primero Primera

Carrer del Dr. Carulla, 25;
93/417-5600; primeroprimera.com;
€195 d

Get a taste of uptown Barcelona living at Primero Primera, situated in one of Barcelona's most affluent neighborhoods. A chic Fifties block close to Les Tres Torres FGC station, this 30-room boutique hotel offers a calm respite from the downtown chaos, set amid lush gardens with an outdoor pool. Dark wood and vintage furnishings lend an air of timeless elegance to this authentic high-class home run by the Pérez Sala family, who live on the first floor (hence the name). Balcony rooms have garden and pool views.

Information and Services

TOURIST INFORMATION

Turisme de Barcelona (www.barcelonaturisme.cat; 93/285-3834) has a number of tourist offices, located at strategic points across the city, and also has a comprehensive website. There are seven tourist information offices in Barcelona—including in both terminals of Barcelona-El Prat Airport, as well as the city's main railway station, Estació de Sants—and 10 information kiosks dotted across the city. The main city center offices are:

- Plaça de Catalunya (Plaça de Catalunya, 17-S; 93/285-3834; 8:30am-9pm daily): Located beneath the square, this large information office also provides VAT refund services.
- Plaça Sant Jaume (Carrer de la Ciutat, 2; Mon.-Fri. 8:30am-8pm, Sat.-Sun. 9am-3pm).
- Catedral (Plaça Nova, 5; Mon.-Sat. 9am-7pm, Sun. 9am-3pm): Located on the ground floor of the Col·legi Oficial d'Arquitectes de Catalunya (COAC) opposite the Cathedral.

POLICE

- General emergency line: 112 (fire, police, ambulance)
- Guàrdia Urbana: 092
- Medical emergencies: 061
- For general governmental information: 012, www.gencat.cat

The Guàrdia Urbana police station on La Rambla caters specifically for tourists (La Rambla, 43; 93/256-2477 or 93/256-2478; ajuntament.barcelona. cat/guardiaurbana), though incidents can be reported at any police station, either Mossos d'Esquadra (regional police) or Guàrdia Urbana (municipal police).

HOSPITALS AND PHARMACIES

The main hospitals in Barcelona are:

- Hospital Clínic (Carrer Villarroel, 170; metro: Hospital Clínic)
- Hospital del Mar (Passeig Marítim 25-29; metro: Ciutadella | Vila Olímpica)
- Hospital de la Santa Creu i Sant Pau (Sant Antoni Maria Claret, 167; metro: Guinardó | Hospital de Sant Pau)
- Hospital Vall d'Hebron (Passeig de la Vall d'Hebron, 119-129; metro: Vall d'Hebron)

There are many pharmacies in the city center, indicated by a red or green cross sign outside. Many are open all day, though some close for lunch between 2pm and 5pm, and most are closed on Sundays. Out of hours, there are several 24-hour pharmacies across the city, or visit www.farmaguia.net to find out which pharmacies are on call (*farmàcies de guàrdia*).

- Farmàcia Torres (Carrer de Aribau, 62; 93/4539-220; www.farmaciaabierta24h.com; open 24 hours; metro: Universitat)
- Farmàcia Laguna (Carrer de Provença, 459; 93/455-1207; open 24 hours; metro: Sagrada Familia)

LUGGAGE STORAGE

There are left-luggage services (*consigna*) at the main transport interchanges (Sants Railway Station, Barcelona-Nord Bus Station), as well as dozens of independent providers across the city. Locker Barcelona (Carrer Estruc, 36; lockerbarcelona. com; €4-13) is conveniently located close to Plaça de Catalunya, and can be reserved online in advance.

WIFI

Barcelona city WiFi is easy to use centrally, but usually works only if you're stationary. Each time it is used, you will be required to sign in again. Many cafés and restaurants offer free WiFi, which is normally more reliable.

Transportation

GETTING THERE

AIR

Located 12 kilometers (7.5 miles) southwest of the city, Barcelona-El Prat (BCN; 90/240-4704; aena-aeropuertos.es) is the region's largest airport. The airport has two terminals, T1 and T2, which are situated 4 kilometers (2.5 miles) apart. There is a free shuttle bus that runs between the terminals every 6-7 minutes, 24 hours per day; it takes approximately 10-15 minutes. It's a green bus that stops just outside Terminal 1, and outside Terminal 2B (under the bridge). It is advisable, however, to travel directly to the correct terminal.

Terminal 1 (T1) operates 70 percent of flights, including transatlantic flights and most national airlines. It is a large terminal with ample facilities. Terminal 2 (T2) is the airport's original terminal, and is now a base for low-cost airlines, serving mostly European destinations. It is divided into three parts: T2A, T2B, and T2C. The latter is used exclusively by easyJet.

Options for getting to the city center include:

Bus

Aerobús (aerobusbcn.com) operates direct transfers to the city center (35 minutes; €5.90 one way, €10.20 return within 15 days). There are two lines: A1 (serving Terminal 1) and A2 (serving Terminal 2), both of which stop at Plaça d'Espanya, Gran Via-Urgell, Plaça Universitat, and Plaça de Catalunya. With departures every 5-10 minutes from 5:35am until 1am, every day of the year, this is the most convenient way to travel to the center. In Terminal 1, buses depart from underneath the terminal building (downstairs from Arrivals), while in Terminal 2, buses depart outside T2B—look for the blue bus. There is a ticket machine beside both bus stops, or tickets can be purchased on board. If you are planning to alight before Plaça de Catalunya, keep an eye on the screen inside the bus as stops are not always announced.

Transports Metropolitans de Barcelona (TMB) run a public bus line (number 46) to Avinguda Paral·lel from Terminal 2 (note that this is a metro or bus ride from Plaça de Catalunya), valid with a single (or T-10) metro ticket. This is the cheapest way to get to the city and the journey takes approximately 35 minutes, stopping 16 times en route. TMB also operates a night bus from Terminal 1 to Plaça de Catalunya (35 stops, 42 minutes).

Train

Terminal 2 is on the commuter railway line (R2), operated by Rodalies de Catalunya. Services run every 30 minutes to Barcelona Sants (20 minutes) and Passeig de Gràcia (27 minutes). A footbridge connects Terminal 2A with the airport's railway station. Passengers arriving in Terminal 1 must take the airport shuttle bus to Terminal 2. A new shuttle train between Terminal 1 and the city center is expected to be open by the end of 2020.

Metro

In 2016, the airport was connected to the city's metro system via line 9 (L9), with a station in each terminal. The Terminal 1 station is underneath the airport, while the Terminal 2 station is adjacent to the railway station (across the footbridge from the airport building). The L9 terminates at the Zona Universitària metro station at the upper end of Avinguda Diagonal; to reach the city center, passengers must change at Torrassa (L1), Collblanc (L5), or Zona Universitària (L3). Unless your destination is located along the L9, the metro is not as convenient as the bus or train connection for traveling to the center.

Taxi

A taxi from the airport to the city center costs approximately €25-30 and takes 25-30 minutes. There are taxi stands outside all terminals.

TRAIN

The city's main railway station is **Estació de Sants,** situated in the Sants neighborhood, west of the city center. If traveling to Barcelona from elsewhere in Spain, or the south of France, it's quite likely that you will arrive in Barcelona by train. The **AVE** high-speed rail service, operated by Renfe (www.renfe.com), offers direct connections to Barcelona from Zaragoza and Madrid (2.5 hours; €32-€127). There are also direct daily international services to Barcelona from 15 cities across France, including Paris (6.5 hours), Lyon (5 hours), Marseille (4.5 hours), and Toulouse (3 hours 15 minutes), from €35. These services are a collaborative effort between the Spanish and French high-speed rail services: the AVE and TGV (operated by SNCF). Cheap fares can be found if booked in advance.

Train is the quickest and easiest form of public transport to Barcelona from other urban areas in Catalonia. Barcelona is connected to Girona, Lleida, Tarragona, and Figueres by high-speed rail, while the regional rail network, Rodalies de Catalunya (www.rodalies.gencat.cat), operates commuter and medium-distance services that connect many areas of the region to Barcelona. Most regional services stop at Estació de Sants, and some make additional stops at other stations in the city, including Passeig de Gràcia, Clot, La Sagrera, and the Estació de França.

BUS

There are long-distance bus routes to Barcelona from all over Spain and Europe. International connections across mainland Europe are operated by Eurolines (90/240-5040; www.eurolines.es) and Flixbus (www.flixbus.com). There are no direct bus services from London, though connections via Paris do exist.

National services are operated by Alsa (90/242-2242; www.alsa.es) and include direct daily connections to Barcelona from all major Spanish cities as well as a direct international service from Montpellier. Within Catalonia, a handful of bus companies operate the regional network. Traveling by bus can be the only way to reach Barcelona by public transport from some parts of the region.

Barcelona's main bus station is Estació de Nord (Carrer d'Alí Bei, 80; barcelonanord.cat), situated in an an old railway station building dating from 1861. Most national bus connections depart from here. Buses also depart from outside the city's main railway station, Barcelona Sants (Plaça dels Països Catalans, 1-7; 93/495-6020; www.adif.es), primarily international services. Some regional bus services depart from bus stops elsewhere in the city.

CAR

Arriving to Barcelona by car is fairly straightforward. There are two key ring roads: the Ronda Litoral, which runs parallel to the seafront, and the Ronda de Dalt, which skirts the opposite side of the city, at the foot of the Collserola hills. Between the two Rondas, there are two major thoroughfares that cross the city—Gran Via and Diagonal—which you are likely to encounter on your journey at some point.

GETTING AROUND

Barcelona's public transport system is extensive, efficient, and cheap, and it's the best way to get around the city. Transports Metropolitans de Barcelona (TMB; www.tmb.cat) runs 10 metro lines, more than 100 bus routes, several tram routes, a funicular, and two cable cars. The integrated fare system means that travel cards can be used across all modes of transport, and a free transfer from one mode to another is permitted within a period of 1 hour and 15 minutes.

METRO

Metro services operate from 5am to midnight Monday to Thursday, Sundays, and public holidays; 5am to 2am on Friday; and nonstop on Saturday. A single journey costs €2.20. The excellent value T-10 ticket is valid for 10 journeys, costs €10.20, can be used by multiple passengers, and is interchangeable between different modes of transport (bus, tram, etc.). The Hola BCN multi-day unlimited travel pass is available for 2-5 days, ideal for those intent on covering the length and breadth of the city by public transport. Note that the whole city is within zone 1 (zones 2-6 cover areas outside the city limits). Tickets can be purchased at the self-service ticket machines located in every metro station.

BUS

Barcelona's public bus network connects all the city's districts and the metropolitan area with more than 100 routes. The network is run by the TMB and prices are per metro system above (single journey €2.20). Note that T-10 tickets cannot be purchased on board. Running times vary by route, but most services begin between 5am and 8am, and end between 10pm and 11pm. Running times and frequency of service are posted at the bus stops. Pick up a bus map at any metro station, or download the TMB app.

There are 17 night buses that run between 10pm and 6am, indicated by an "N" in front of the number. All night buses pass through Plaça de Catalunya (except the N0), where transfers can be made.

In recent years, the city has been consolidating bus routes in order to streamline the system. The new routes begin with "D," "V," and "H," and represent lines that traverse the city diagonally, vertically, and horizontally, with respect to the city map as viewed with the coast running along the bottom. Standard number bus routes represent more convoluted, pre-existing routes.

TMB also runs the city's official hop-on, hop-off tour bus, the **Barcelona Bus Turístic** (www.hola-barcelona.com). For first-timers and those in a hurry, this is the easy, leg-saving option. There are three distinct lines covering the most important city sights accompanied by an audio guide available in 16 languages.

TRAIN

Suburban trains are run by **Ferrocarrils de la Generalitat de Catalunya** (FGC). All lines start and terminate at Plaça de Catalunya and pass through several stops within the city en route to suburbs and nearby towns. Services are regular and can be accessed using a metro ticket (check zone before boarding if traveling to outlying areas).

CAR AND TAXI

Taxis in Barcelona are cheap and plentiful. They can be flagged anywhere across the city and paid for by card or with cash. Between midnight and 6am on weekends and public holidays, there is an additional charge of €2, and there is a surcharge on Fridays, Saturdays, Sundays, and public holidays between midnight and 6am.

After a short appearance in the city, Uber no longer operates in Barcelona, due to restrictions introduced by the Catalan government. Cabify, a similar service founded in Madrid, also pulled its services temporarily due to the legislation but has recently returned, albeit with a much-reduced fleet. To use the service, download the Cabify app and sign up. The first journey must be reserved 15 minutes in advance, and thereafter as required.

Although it is perfectly feasible to drive around Barcelona, it is neither necessary nor recommended to rent a car while visiting the city. Parking is limited and expensive, and driving etiquette can be disorienting; the roundabout at Plaça d'Espanya, for example, is particularly chaotic. Public transport is so efficient (and so cheap), it hardly warrants the inconvenience.

BICYCLE

Barcelona has a bicycle sharing system—**Bicing**—but it is only available to residents. There are, however, numerous rental companies for all kinds of two-wheeled vehicles. The city's network of bicycle lanes is steadily expanding and cycling is recommended except in very crowded areas, such as the narrow streets of the Barri Gòtic. The city council has introduced restrictions regarding the use of some novelty forms of transport, including electric scooters and Segways. Check the current regulations with the rental shop before setting off.

SITGES

One of Spain's original resorts,

Sitges is famous for its beaches, vibrant gay night-life, and year-round holiday ambience. A coastal town just 35 kilometers (22 miles) southwest of Barcelona, this is where the city comes to play. Buff bodies pack the shoreline in summer, while in the depths of winter, one of Spain's wildest Carnival celebrations transforms the town into one big street party—just one item in a busy festival calendar. Despite the debauchery, Sitges manages to stay classy, with grandiose Modernista villas and chic boutiques dotting the whitewashed

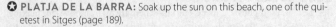

HIGHLIGHTS

✪ **CARRER PRIMER DE MAIG:** Also known as "Sin Street," this busy strip is at the heart of the town's vibrant nightlife scene (page 185).

✪ **PLATJA DE LA BARRA:** Soak up the sun on this beach, one of the quietest in Sitges (page 189).

✪ **CARNIVAL:** Shimmy through the streets at one of the most extravagant Mardi Gras celebrations this side of the Atlantic (page 190).

streets of the picturesque old town, culminating in an elegant beachfront promenade.

ORIENTATION

Sitges's town center is compact and eminently walkable, centered unofficially around **Plaça Cap de la Vila.** The whole of the central area is commonly referred to as the **old town**— bound by Avinguda Sofia and the seafront to the west and south, and Avinguda d'Artur Carbonell and Carrer de Rafael Llopart to the north and east—though the oldest part lies in the narrow lanes that surround the **Església de Sant Bartomeu i Santa Tecla,** known as the **Vila Vella.** This is the town's highest point, which presides over the busy beachfront from a rocky perch known as **La Punta.**

Down by the sea, the town runs parallel to the breezy **promenade.** More than a dozen **beaches** lie along the south-facing shoreline. Opposite the Platja de la Ribera, **Carrer Primer de Maig,** also known as "Sin Street," is the place to party, with **Plaça de la Indústria** marking the epicenter of Sitges' vibrant gay nightlife scene.

PLANNING YOUR TIME

Sitges makes a great day trip from Barcelona; there are four trains per hour that take just 35 minutes. A day in Sitges generally revolves around the beach, wandering the charming old town, and long, lazy lunches. There are many interesting sights, but it is generally more about soaking up the holiday vibe or experiencing one of the town's famous festivals. Most sights in Sitges are closed on Mondays and public holidays.

Sitges enjoys its own microclimate, with warm summers and mild winters. The town is busiest during July and August, but there is a lot going on throughout the year, and the town is just as busy during **Carnival** in February/March, and the **Sitges Film Festival** in October, as it is at the height of summer.

As well as the standard Spanish and Catalan public holidays, Sitges has two local holidays that celebrate the town's patron saints, **Sant Bartomeu** (August 24) and **Santa Tecla** (September 23). During peak times and on weekends throughout the year, hotel and restaurant reservations are essential.

Itinerary Idea

ESSENTIAL SITGES

Beaches, shops, nightlife, cuisine, culture—there are many motives for making the trip to Sitges. Your perfect itinerary will depend a little on when and why you go, but the following route encompasses a little something for everyone. Whatever the weather, it's worth getting there early, by around 10am, particularly in summer, when there's fierce competition for a spot on the beach.

1 Step off the train and look up at Sitges **railway station,** the first stop along the Ruta dels Indians, on arrival. The station building dates from 1881, which was the same year that the first section of this line was inaugurated, funded by a group of Catalans established in Cuba. Spot marvelous mansions as you stroll toward Plaça Cap de la Vila in the town center.

2 Next, delve into the narrow streets of the old town, reemerging to face the sea in front of the **Església de Sant Bartomeu i Santa Tecla,** the town's most emblematic landmark.

3 Spend an hour or two contemplating the town's artistic spirit at **Museu del Cau Ferrat,** former studio and home of Modernista painter Santiago Rusiñol, and the adjacent **Museu de Maricel.**

4 Descend the stairs from La Punta (outside the Església de Sant Bartomeu i Santa Tecla), and tuck into fresh seafood at **Fragata,** sitting alongside the medieval bastion.

5 Walk off the lunchtime feast along the bustling seafront **promenade.** Find a spot on the beach for the afternoon.

6 Switch to **Platja de Sant Sebastià,** the beach on the opposite side of the old town, and let the afternoon drift into evening with a cocktail in hand on the terrace of **Vivero Beach Club Restaurant.**

7 Wander back through the old town and treat yourself to some retail therapy in the chic boutiques along **Carrer Major.**

8 Join the locals for a casual dinner at **El Cable,** one of the town's favorite tapas bars.

9 Round off the perfect Sitges day on a high at Hotel MiM's **Sky Bar.**

Itinerary Idea

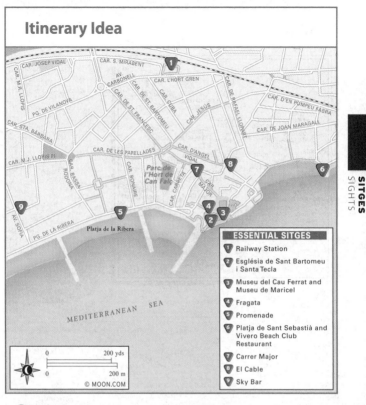

Sights

Sitges's main cultural sights are concentrated in the oldest part of town, the **Vila Vella,** where an 11th-century castle is said to have stood on the site of the present town hall. Sights are generally closed on Mondays and public holidays.

ESGLÉSIA DE SANT BARTOMEU I SANTA TECLA

Plaça de l'Ajuntament, 20; 93/894-0374

The asymmetrical silhouette of the Església de Sant Bartomeu i Santa Tecla (Parish Church of Saint Bartholomew and Saint Tecla) is the town's most emblematic image. Built upon a medieval bastion and the remains of two earlier churches (one Romanesque and one Gothic), the seafront Baroque landmark has undergone many modifications since it was built in the 17th century.

Inside, the parish church has three naves, flanked by side chapels containing many beautiful altarpieces, the most important of which is the Renaissance centerpiece dating from 1499, situated behind the main altar. This is the work of Neapolitan artist Nicolás de Credença and represents

177

Sitges

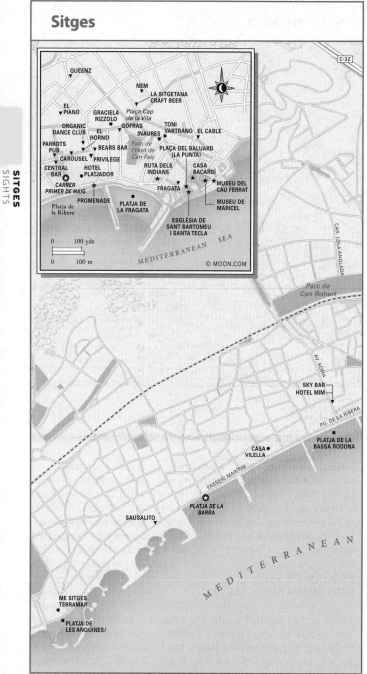

QUEENZ

NEM

LA SITGETANA
CRAFT BEER

EL
PIANO

GRACIELA
RIZZOLO

Plaça Cap
de la Vila

ORGANIC
DANCE CLUB

GOFRAS

EL
HORNO

TONI
VARTRANO   EL CABLE

INAURES

PARROTS
PUB

BEARS BAR

Parc de
l'Hort de
Can Falç

PLAÇA DEL BALUARD
(LA PUNTA)

CAROUSEL   PRIVILEGE

CENTRAL
BAR

HOTEL
PLATJADOR

RUTA DELS
INDIANS

CASA
BACARDÍ

CARRER
PRIMER DE MAIG

FRAGATA

MUSEU DEL
CAU FERRAT

MUSEU DE
MARICEL

Platja de
la Ribera

PROMENADE

PLATJA DE
LA FRAGATA

ESGLÉSIA DE
SANT BARTOMEU
I SANTA TECLA

0   100 yds

0   100 m

MEDITERRANEAN SEA

© MOON.COM

C-32

Parc de
Can Robert

AV. SOFIA

SKY BAR
HOTEL MIM

PG. DE LA RIBERA

CASA
VILELLA

PLATJA DE LA
BASSA RODONA

PASSEIG MARÍTIM

PLATJA DE LA
BARRA

SAUSALITO

MEDITERRANEAN

ME SITGES
TERRAMAR

PLATJA DE
LES ANQUINES/

CAR. LOLA ANGLADA

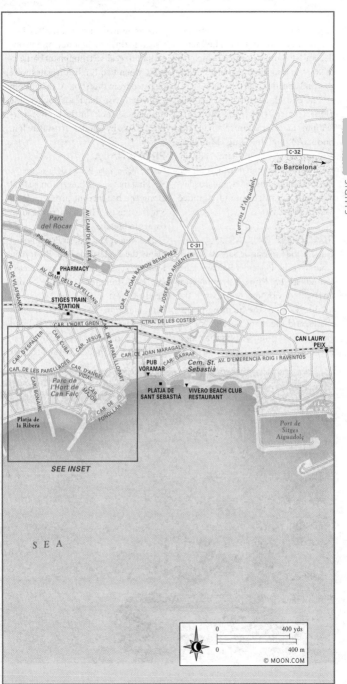

SEE INSET

SEA

Parc del Rocar

PG. DE RONDA

AV. CAMÍ DE LA FITA

PG. DE VILAFRANCA

PHARMACY

AV. CAMÍ DELS CAPELLANS

STIGES TRAIN STATION

CAR. DE JOAN RAMON BENAPRÈS

AV. JOSEP MIRÓ ARGENTER

C-31

C-32

To Barcelona

Torrent d'Aiguadolç

CTRA. DE LES COSTES

CAR. L'HORT GREN

CAR. D'ESPALTER

CAR. CUBA

CAR. JESÚS

CAR. DE RAFAEL LLOPART

CAR. DE JOAN MARAGALL

CAR. GARRAF

AV. D'EMERENCIÀ ROIG I RAVENTÓS

CAN LAURY PEIX

PUB VORAMAR

Cem. St. Sebastià

CAR. DE LES PARELLADES

CAR. D'ÀNGEL VIDAL

CAR. BONAIRE

Parc de l'Hort de Can Falç

CAR. MAJOR

CAR. DE FONOLLAR

PLATJA DE SANT SEBASTIÀ

VIVERO BEACH CLUB RESTAURANT

Platja de la Ribera

Port de Sitges Aiguadolç

0   400 yds
0   400 m

© MOON.COM

179

Sitges's two patron saints, to whom the church is dedicated. The highly decorative Baroque organ, completed in 1699, is also of note; images of angels and apostles adorn its sides.

The church is only open for religious services (Sept.-Jun Mon.-Fri. 7:30pm, Sat. 8pm, Sun. 9am, 11am, noon, 7:30pm; Jul.-Aug. Mon.-Fri. 7:30pm, Sat. 8pm, Sun. 9am, 11:30am, 7pm, 8pm), although during summer, the local museums (www.museusdesitges.cat) organize sporadic guided tours and activities.

PLAÇA DEL BALUARD

Outside the Església de Sant Bartomeu i Santa Tecla, Plaça del Baluard (also known as La Punta) provides an unrivalled vantage point over the Mediterranean, the bustling promenade, and the many beaches strung along the seafront. This is the oldest part of Sitges, where six cannons were once mounted in a former bastion. One remains *in situ* today, and its inscription recalls a triumphant battle in 1797, when two English frigates were defeated from this spot. At the bottom of the staircase that leads down to the promenade, look for the bronze mermaid statue by Catalan artist Pere Jou.

PROMENADA

Passeig Marítim and Passeig de la Ribera
Soaking up the sea breezes on a stroll along the beachfront promenade in Sitges is a must. This is where the town comes to breathe.

Starting at Plaça de la Fragata, just below the Església de Sant Bartomeu i Santa Tecla, it's a flat and pleasant 2.5-kilometer (1.5-mile) stroll heading west toward the ME Sitges Terramar hotel. The initial stretch, called Passeig de la Ribera, is lined with restaurants, hotels, and lively terraces. After Avinguda Sofía it becomes

Església de Sant Bartomeu i Santa Tecla

Passeig Marítim, and from there on in, the promenade gets quieter and more open. One beach runs into another right along the seafront, while across the road, the lively sidewalk gives way to impressive mansions and gardens, many of which were built by wealthy returning emigrants.

CASA BACARDÍ

Plaça de l'Ajuntament, 11; 93/894-8151; casabacardi.es; Mon.-Sat. noon-2pm, 4pm-8:30pm, Sun. noon-2pm, 4pm-7:30pm; €12/€10 students and over 65s

Sitges is the birth town and family home of Facundo Bacardí Massó, founder of one of the world's most famous rums. Born to a family of bricklayers in 1814, Bacardí emigrated to Cuba in 1830 as one of the town's so-called "*indians*" (emigrants who sought their fortune in the Americas). He established his first distillery in 1862 in Santiago de Cuba, where he perfected unique blends of the sugarcane-based spirit and revolutionized the rum-making process.

Casa Bacardí is a permanent visitor center housed in the Mercat Vell (old market), just beside the town hall in Sitges. The guided discovery tour (Tues.-Sat. 4pm; 45 minutes; €10) delves into the turbulent history of the brand and its owners, explains the production process, and—the best bit—finishes in the lounge bar with a tasting session of three cocktails, and the chance to learn how to make the perfect mojito. On the last Friday of every month, there is also a Mixology Masterclass (2-2.5 hours; €35; over 18s only) led by professional bartenders, where visitors learn to measure, mix, blend, and savor nine cocktails. Lots of fun, especially on a rainy day.

MUSEU DEL CAU FERRAT
(Cau Ferrat Museum)

Carrer de Fonollar, 6; 93/894-0364; museusdesitges.cat; Mar.-Jun. and Oct. Tues.-Sun. 10am-7pm, Jul.-Sept. Tues.-Sun. 10am-8pm, Nov.-Feb. Tues.-Sun. 10am-5pm; €10/€7 students and children aged 13-16/€5 pensioners/free for under 13s; free for everyone on the first Wednesday of the month; ticket includes access to Museu de Maricel

Cau Ferrat is the former home and studio of Barcelona-born artist Santiago Rusiñol (1861-1931), one of the pioneers of the Catalan Modernisme movement. Situated next door to the Museu de Maricel, the museum is a treasure trove of paintings, drawings, ironwork, sculpture, furniture, glass, and ceramics. It combines Rusiñol's eclectic personal collection of ancient art and antiques, along with his own work and that of his contemporaries, including Ramon Casas and Pablo Picasso.

Rusiñol set up his studio here in 1893, when he bought a seafront house in the heart of the old town, and transformed it into a temple of

Museu del Cau Ferrat is situated in the pretty Vila Vella.

RUTA DELS INDIANS

In the early 19th century, a wave of emigration swept across Catalonia. Bound for the Americas—mainly Cuba and Puerto Rico—many young locals set sail in search of fortune (and were known here as "indians"). Those who returned home built grand, colonial-style mansions (*cases d'indians*) in an eclectic mix of styles—primarily Neoclassicism, Modernisme, and Noucentisme—and also invested in local infrastructure. Evidence of this can be spotted in several Catalan port towns, including Sitges. The following route explores the architectural legacy left by the town's prodigal sons.

Plaça Cap de la Vila

- Start at the **railway station.** The station building dates from 1881, which was the same year that the first section of this line was inaugurated, funded by a group of Catalans established in Cuba.

- Head toward the town center along **Carrer de l'Illa de Cuba,** keeping an eye out for majestic mansions along the way, particularly numbers 31 and 35.

- Turn right onto Carrer de Sant Gaudenci, and then left onto **Carrer de Sant Bartomeu,** spotting more grandiose houses along **Carrer de Sant Bartomeu** (numbers 28, 24, 8, and 1), all of which belonged to illustrious *sitgeanos.*

- At the end of the street, turn right onto **Plaça Cap de la Vila,** where at number 2 you will find one of the town's most emblematic *cases d'indians*, recognizable by its clock tower decorated with mosaic tiling.

- Emerge onto the seafront, where many Modernista masterpieces face the Mediterranean along **Passeig de la Ribera.** Look for numbers 3 (Villa Lola), 15 (which was built by one of the founders of Vichy Catalán), 18, 20, 22, and 29.

- Make your way back to the old town, stopping by the following Neoclassical buildings en route: Carrer de la Davallada, 12, and Carrer de Port Alegre, 2 and 9.

- Finally, learn about Sitges's most famous expatriate at **Casa Bacardí,** and round things off with a refreshing mojito.

Modernisme. Fascinated by Gothic motifs, he created an intense, Neo-Gothic-Modernista interior, with intricate stained glass, coffered ceilings, and hand-painted ceramics; he even embedded Gothic elements from the ancient castle of Sitges into the building's façade.

Cau Ferrat became a meeting point for artists, musicians, and writers involved in the Modernisme movement. In his will, Rusiñol left the museum to the town of Sitges, and it opened to the public in 1933, preserving the artistic spirit of the founder. It is accessed from the adjacent building, Can Rocamora, which is also the access point for the Museu de Maricel.

MUSEU DE MARICEL
(Maricel Museum)

Carrer de Fonollar; 93/894-0364; museusdesitges.cat; Mar.-Jun. and Oct. Tues.-Sun. 10am-7pm, Jul.-Sept. Tues.-Sun. 10am-8pm, Nov.-Feb. Tues.-Sun. 10am-5pm; €10/€7 students, children aged 13-16/€5 pensioners/free for under 13s; free for everyone on the first Wednesday of the month; ticket includes access to Cau Ferrat

The Maricel Museum houses a vast collection of Catalan art spanning a thousand years (10th-20th centuries). Located next to Rusiñol's Cau Ferrat, the seafront museum forms part of a Noucentista complex built between 1910 and 1918, which lends a majestic tone to the old town. The same ticket is valid for the Museu de Maricel and Cau Ferrat, and together they form an unexpected cultural haven.

The museum takes visitors on a whistle-stop tour through the major art movements of the last millennium. There are sculptures and altarpieces belonging to the Romanesque and Gothic periods, ceramics and furniture from the Renaissance and Baroque, and paintings representing Neoclassicism, Romanticism, and Realism. Revered local artists appear in the halls dedicated to Modernisme, Noucentisme, and the 19th-century Luminist school of Sitges, and don't

Museu de Maricel

miss the striking murals of Josep M. Sert, inspired by the Great War. But perhaps the most memorable moment comes in the light-filled "mirador" space, where three figures (by Joan Rebull) dawdle against an almost surreal backdrop of sea and sky.

The Noucentista complex continues across the street with the splendid **Palau de Maricel,** used primarily for cultural and private events. Guided tours of the palace are available on Sundays (11am in English, noon in Catalan, 1pm in Spanish; €5; 45 minutes), and there is a program of al fresco moonlit concerts during summer.

Food

Fresh fish and seafood top the menu in most traditional restaurants in Sitges, with *arròs a la sitgetana*—a rice dish that combines shellfish with meaty ingredients—being the local take on paella. On the weekends, day trippers from Barcelona fill the town's many eateries, particularly in waterfront spots; reservations are a must.

Despite the seafood focus, Sitges's most typical dish is actually a winter salad, *xató*, which consists of curly endive, cod, tuna, anchovies, eggplant (aubergine), and black olives. The salad is dressed with a rich vinaigrette made from red peppers, chilis, toasted almonds, and garlic, and is served between November and March. The town's most renowned beverage is a dessert wine, *malvasia*, which has been produced on the grounds of the old Hospital de Sant Joan since the 18th century.

SPANISH AND CATALAN
✪ Fragata

Passeig de la Ribera, 1; 93/894-1086;
www.restaurantefragata.com; 1pm-4:30pm,
8:30pm-12:30am daily; €16.90-€26.50

Superbly located just below the church of Sant Bartomeu and Santa Tecla, Fragata is a Sitges institution, serving traditional Catalan fare. Modern interiors, white tablecloths, and attentive service set an upmarket ambience for the high-quality, beautifully presented cuisine; paella is the highlight. Book a table on the terrace alongside the medieval bastion to keep an eye on the action along the seafront promenade. Excellent price-quality ratio.

Vivero Beach Club Restaurant

Paseo Balmins, s/n; 93/894-2149;
www.elviverositges.com; Tues.-Sat.
1pm-4pm, 8pm-11pm, Sun.-Mon. 1pm-4pm;
€14.85-€26.90

Clinging to the rocks at the end of Platja de Sant Sebastià, this beach club and restaurant has the finest location in all of Sitges. Seafood dominates the menu, but if that doesn't tempt you, the upstairs terrace is the ideal spot for an afternoon cocktail, complete with sun loungers and day beds. The location comes at a price, though it's not hugely more expensive than other waterfront restaurants.

Can Laury Peix

Avinguda del Port d'Aiguadolç, 49;
93/894-6634; www.canlaury.com;
12:30pm-11:30pm daily; €15.50-€20

Perched on the edge of the glitzy marina, Can Laury Peix is a classic seafood restaurant in the Port d'Aiguadolç. A bright, elegant spot with a fabulous portside terrace, this is the place to while away a sunny afternoon, tucking into fresh fish and some of the best paella in town. It's a 20-minute walk from the hubbub of the town center (follow the coastline beyond Platja de Sant Sebastià), but it is a pleasant stroll and the food is worth it.

TAPAS
Nem

Carrer de l'Illa de Cuba, 9; 93/894-9332;
www.nemsitges.com; Tues.-Fri. 7:30pm-11pm,
Sat. 1:30pm-3pm, 7:30pm-11pm; €5-€7

A foodie favorite on a Sitges side street, Nem offers a short but delectable menu of fusion tapas, made to share. The monthly menu of delicately prepared, seasonal dishes—such as roasted cod with pea purée, fresh peas, and black pudding, or sea bream sashimi with soy jelly, ginger, and chives—borrows

chocolatey indulgence of Gofras

flavors from across the globe, and is served in an intimate space at very reasonable prices. Reservations advised.

⊗ El Cable

Carrer Barcelona, 1; 93/894-8761;
elcable.cat; Mon.-Fri. 7pm-11:30pm,
Sat.-Sun. noon-3:30pm, 7pm-11:30pm; €1-€8
There's always a buzz at El Cable. Situated just one block from Sant Sebastià beach, this traditional, family-run tavern opened in 1940 and is rightfully considered one of the best tapas bars in town. There's rarely any elbow room—patrons perch on window sills outside—so get there early if you want to bag a table. The *patatas bravas* are legendary, and make sure you try the *cojonudos* (fried quail's egg, chorizo, and red pepper) and the "McCable" (mini burger with brie and green pepper).

SWEETS
Gofras

Carrer de Sant Pau, 2; 93/894-9558;
Oct.-mid-Jun. Sat.-Sun. 4pm-9pm,
mid-Jun.-Sept. 4pm-11pm daily
Sitges may not be the obvious place to find the world's best Belgian waffles, but Gofras (meaning "waffles" in Catalan) is certainly a contender. Served warm with a variety of toppings—from Nutella and cream to banana and Baileys—these wonderful, gridded squares of messy, chocolatey indulgence are delicious and fun to eat.

Bars and Nightlife

Sitges is a small town with a big reputation when it comes to going out. It is especially popular with the gay crowd, though most places are welcoming to all. The buzz starts early, as sun worshippers round off a lazy beach day with a chilled beer on the terraces of Plaça de la Indústria. By midnight the bars are packed, particularly in summer. The fun tends to focus on barhopping from one lively joint to the next, with certain venues offering live entertainment, from dancers and drag queens to singers and strippers.

NIGHTLIFE DISTRICT
⊗ Carrer Primer de Maig

Carrer Primer de Maig, also known as "Carrer del Pecat" (meaning "Sin Street"), is at the heart of the action. This infamous, pedestrianized street is lined with pubs, clubs, and disco bars, with blaring music, drinks, dancing, and a raucous ambience until the early hours. The side streets branching off the main strip are also packed with bars, while another hub of activity can be found around Carrer de Sant Bonaventura.

BARS AND PUBS
Pub Voramar

Carrer de Port Alegre, 55; 93/894-4403; www.pub-voramar.com; Mon.-Tues. and Thurs. 3:30pm-1:30am, Fri. 3:30pm-2am, Sat.-Sun. noon-2am

This lively cocktail bar overlooking Platja de Sant Sebastià has been serving up cocktails by the sea since 1956. This family-run watering hole was originally a fisherman's warehouse belonging to the founder's grandfather, and maintains a distinct nautical theme. The mojitos, caipirinhas, and piña coladas are especially good (and generous)—perfect for a summer's evening on the terrace.

La Sitgetana Craft Beer

Carrer de Sant Bartomeu, 10; 93/809-9435; lasitgetana.cat; Mon.-Fri. 6:30pm-11:30pm, Sat.-Sun. noon-3pm, 6:30pm-11pm

A low-key locale buried in the old town, La Sitgetana serves artisan craft beers brewed on site. Pale ale, brown ale, IPA, lager, or Bavarian wheat beer—whatever your taste, there's a local brew for you. With warm timber finishes and an intimate atmosphere, this is a find for any craft beer fan.

Parrots Pub

Plaça de la Indústria, 2; 93/894-1350; www.parrots-sitges.com; Mar.-Oct. and Carnival: 5pm-3am daily

Parrots is at the heart of Sitges's gay nightlife scene. Situated on Plaça de la Indústria along the famous "Sin Street" strip, its rainbow-colored terrace is a popular people-watching spot. Owned by the Parrots Group, which

also has a hotel, restaurant, and bar just across the square, it's a cheap and cheerful spot with table service and a lively atmosphere.

Sausalito

Passeig Marítim, 55; www.sausalitositges. com; Jun.-Aug. 10:30am-8pm daily, until 7pm early Sept., Easter-May and mid-Sept.-mid-Oct. weekends only, closed mid-Oct.-Easter

Sausalito is a chic beach bar with all the trimmings—drinks, snacks, sun loungers, WiFi, massages, and showers—for those who want to be waited on hand and foot (at a price). Situated in a former boathouse, built into the promenade wall along Platja de la Barra, sun-worshippers can take a break from the heat with a cold beer on the terrace, or rent a sun lounger and set up camp for the day (book in advance). A glass of cava as the sun goes down rounds off the perfect beach day.

Carrer Primer de Maig in the daytime

LIVE MUSIC AND ENTERTAINMENT
El Piano

Carrer de Sant Bonaventura, 37; 93/814-6245; www.elpianositges.com; 10:30pm-3am (daily during Carnival, Easter, May-Sept.; select weekends Oct.-Apr., check website for details); no cover

A showbiz buzz fills the air at El Piano, a music bar full of fun and feel-good

GAY SITGES

Sitges has been known as a bohemian artists' retreat ever since the Modernista painter Santiago Rusiñol set up shop here in the late 19th century, bringing with him a merry band of artists, poets, dancers, composers, and playwrights. It soon became one of the first tourist destinations in Spain, which opened the small fishing village to the world and paved the way for the liberal, cosmopolitan society that populates the town today. This progressive outlook has long since established Sitges as a gay-friendly hub, and even during Franco's fascist regime, it continued to push the boundaries. Since the 1980s, both the town and its tourism sector have grown exponentially, and today it is the most popular gay destination in Spain, particularly among young men.

BARS AND CLUBS

Everywhere in Sitges is gay-friendly, but there are a number of venues, facilities, and events that specifically cater to the local and visiting gay community. Gay bars and clubs are central to Sitges's vibrant nightlife scene, which is centered around **Carrer Primer de Maig** (aka "Sin Street") and **Carrer Bonaire.** Popular bars include **Parrots Pub** (Plaça de la Indústria, 2), **Privilege** (Carrer Bonaire, 24), **Central Bar** (Plaça de la Indústria, 5), **Bears Bar** (Carrer Bonaire, 17), **El Horno** (Carrer Joan Tarrida, 6), and **Carousel** (Carrer de Joan Tarrida, 14), which tend to close around 3am, after which time the party continues at the **Organic Dance Club** (Carrer Bonaire, 12). While hetero-friendly, the male-only ambience in these bars and clubs can be intense.

FESTIVALS

The gay community plays an active role in all the town's major festivals, but there are two particular events that attract visitors from across Europe: **Gay Pride** in June (www. gaysitgespride.com), a 10-day party that culminates with a flamboyant parade, mirroring similar events across the world, and **International Bears Week** in September (www.bearssitgesclub.org), which is one of the most popular festivals of its kind in Europe, attracting more than 5,000 visitors.

RESOURCES

For more information on gay Sitges, visit www.gaysitgesguide.com (or download the app) and www.gaysitgeslink.org.

vibes. Classic showtunes, sing-along videos, chart music, and cheese will have you singing and dancing all night long. Regular live performances from West End stars add an extra touch of razzle-dazzle to the camp, theatrical atmosphere. Friendly staff embrace guests with a warm welcome in this intimate venue, where you can't help but have a good time.

✪ Queenz

Carrer d'Espalter, 2; 93/894-0712; queenzdinnershow.com; 8:30pm-midnight Fri.-Sat. (Thurs.-Mon. Jun.-Sept., fewer shows throughout the year, check website for details); €44.50

Dinner, drag, and dancing—Queenz is quite the experience. The evening starts at 8:30pm with a glass of cava and a three-course meal. As dinner concludes, the fun really begins as drag, theater, and humor come together for an hour-long spectacle full of fun and laughter. The show finishes around midnight, when it's time for the audience to hit the dance floor, where anyone can be queen for a night. Shows are more frequent during the summer months, and sell out well in advance. Reserve online.

Platja de la Fragata

Beaches

No fewer than 17 golden beaches are strung along the coastline, most of which are within walking distance of the town center. On the face of it they are all quite similar, but each one has its own character and ambience, whether small, large, lively, quiet, family-friendly, gay, sporty, or naturist.

Most beaches have the basic facilities—toilets, showers, lifeguards, sun lounger rental, ramp access—and many also offer watersports, massage services, and beach bars. The fine sand is clean and the shoreline has a regular, low gradient, making for shallow, warm waters that are ideal for children.

Half of the beaches are located along the seafront promenade, between Església de Sant Bartomeu i Santa Tecla and the ME Sitges

Terramar hotel—effectively one long strip divided into several coves by man-made breakwaters. The beaches closest to the town center are the busiest, and can be very crowded during the summer months. Arrive early if you want to claim a spot. If you're planning to make a day of it, it is worth renting sun loungers and an awning, especially during July and August, when the sun is strong and finding somewhere to lay your towel on the sand can be nearly impossible.

Platja de Sant Sebastià

This is where you'll find the locals. A traditional fisherman's beach northeast of the iconic church and old town, Sant Sebastià is overlooked by a charming row of sea-view apartments and a lively promenade. It measures 205 by 20 meters (673 by 66 feet)

and is popular with families. Showers here are card-operated; cards can be bought at the beach bar and include 400 seconds.

Platja de la Fragata
Situated right below the iconic Church of Saint Bartholomew and Saint Tecla, Fragata is full of life and buzzing with young people. With more sand than nearby strands, sports are popular here, particularly volleyball, soccer, and watersports. There are no sun loungers, umbrellas, or awnings available for rent.

Platja de la Bassa Rodona
This is the main gay beach in town. Everyone is welcome, but be prepared to bare all alongside scores of buff male bods and the odd naturist, too. Centrally located along the seafront promenade (in front of Pic-Nic), this beach is sandwiched between Platja de la Ribera and Platja de l'Estanyol and is similar in character to its neighbors—long and narrow, with

all the key facilities and plenty of sun loungers and umbrellas for rent.

✪ Platja de la Barra
This is one of the largest beaches along the Sitges seafront and, given that it is a 20-minute walk from the center, it is also one of the quietest. Protected by four artificial islands, the water here tends to be calm and it is popular with local families. Don't miss Sausalito for a beachside beverage or bite to eat.

Platja de les Anquines
A shell-shaped cove at the western extreme of the Sitges coastline, in front of the ME Sitges Terramar hotel. Fewer sunseekers make it this far along the promenade, so it is considerably quieter than more central areas. There is also more sand, and the beach is protected by breakwaters. Nootka Kayak and Paddle Surf (93/810-0256; www.nootka-kayak.com) is a great place to try out your sea legs. This beach is a 30-minute walk along the seafront promenade, or a quick taxi ride.

Shopping

Sitges is an affluent town and it shows. Considering its size, it has an impressive range of shops, from high street stores to designer boutiques, catering to locals as well as the well-heeled tourists the town attracts. Most shops are within a 5- to 10-minute walk from Plaça Cap de la Vila, where Carrer de les Parellades, Carrer Jesús, Carrer de Sant Francesc, and Carrer Major intersect. Branch off onto any of these streets and you will find an abundance of shops. Carrer Major is the main shopping street, which continues

on as Carrer de Sant Francesc heading north from Plaça Cap de la Vila.

Traditional opening hours generally apply (10am-2pm, 5pm-8pm), but as Sitges is a resort town, some shops open late and on Sundays. During low season, opening hours are often reduced.

CLOTHING AND ACCESSORIES
Graciela Rizzolo
Carrer de les Parellades, 18; 93/894-1064; gracielarizzolo.com; Mon.-Fri. 10:30am-2pm,

5pm-8:30pm, Sat. 10:30am-9pm, Sun. 11am-8:30pm

Graciela Rizzolo has been assembling the latest looks for the women of Sitges for more than 20 years. The fashion house began with collections designed and made in-house, which has expanded over the years to include carefully selected brands. With high-quality clothing, shoes, and accessories, affordable prices, and something for all occasions, it's a worthwhile alternative to the high street. A second store located at Passeig de la Ribera, 31 has a more summery vibe.

Toni Vartrano

Carrer Major, 28; 93/811-3229; tonivartrano.com; 11am-9pm daily

This long-established fashion store brings on-trend apparel to the discerning, fashion-conscious male. Vartrano's designs (nearly half of the collection is designed in-house) follow the latest tendencies, but always with a distinctly Mediterranean style and a hint of British restraint. The result is a unique collection of quality clothing that is particularly popular with Sitges's gay community. The ladies' collection is next door.

JEWELRY
Inaures

Carrer Major, 25; 93/894-7076; www.inaures.com; Tues.-Sat. 10:30am-1:30pm, 5pm-8:30pm

Monika Hellwig and Aurora Artés delicately handcraft unique pieces of jewelry in this gallery and workshop. The duo met at the Massana School of Art in Barcelona, and opened Inaures in 1994, producing mainly earrings, rings, and necklaces for women, and a small selection of male jewelry. They work with silver, gold, precious stones, resin, glass, and colorful enamels, and their designs has been exhibited internationally.

Festivals and Events

Sitges has a year-round holiday vibe, largely due to a jam-packed festival calendar. Barely a weekend goes by when there isn't some sort of celebration taking place, each one unique in its own right. The main events are covered below.

FEBRUARY/MARCH
✪ Carnival

Floats, feathers, divas, and drum beats—the Sitges Carnival is one of the most extravagant Mardi Gras celebrations this side of the Atlantic. Celebrated in many parts of the Christian world during the week leading up to Ash Wednesday, Carnival was traditionally a preparation period for Lent. Over the years, it has evolved into a bombastic blowout of hedonistic fun that reaches a climax on Shrove Tuesday (Mardi Gras).

Prohibited throughout Franco's dictatorship, today Carnival is celebrated across Spain, but is at its most sensational in Santa Cruz de Tenerife, Cádiz, and Sitges. It is an exuberant and colorful affair. The fun begins on Thursday with the arrival of *Carnestoltes*, the Carnival King, who takes over the town and invites revelers to join him in his debauched pursuits. Together with the Carnival Queen, he heads up the parades until his downfall on Ash Wednesday, when the festival concludes with a funeral procession in his honor.

During the almost week-long extravaganza, more than 250,000 partygoers flock to Sitges for one of the wildest parties of the year. A busy agenda of festivities runs throughout the week, from gastronomic fairs, live music, and street parties, to mask-making workshops and pets in fancy dress. The biggest parades (and party nights) are the *Rua de la Disbauxa* (Debauchery Parade) on Sunday night and the *Rua de l'Extermini* (Extermination Parade) on Tuesday night. There's a family-friendly parade during the day, but come evening, it's a raucous show of flamboyant floats and scantily clad performers leaving a glittering trail of revelry in their wake.

Accommodation in Sitges must be booked several months in advance. Extra bus and train services run between Barcelona and Sitges throughout the festival, but be prepared to stand. Don't forget your fancy dress.

MARCH
Barcelona-Sitges International Vintage Car Rally

www.rallybarcelonasitges.com

The International Vintage Car Rally sees dozens of classic vehicles cruising down the Garraf coast in a showcase of vintage glam. Every year since 1959, enthusiasts gather from far and wide to participate in the Barcelona-to-Sitges rally, driving cars and motorcycles made before 1929, and even donning period dress for the occasion. The parade starts in Plaça Sant Jaume, Barcelona, then follows the scenic coast road to Sitges, terminating at Port d'Aiguadolç around midday. Thereafter, the cars are displayed

Sitges Carnival

in Plaça de la Fragata amid a festive atmosphere.

AUGUST
Festa Major
www.sitgesfestamajor.cat; Aug. 19-26

Sitges celebrates Saint Bartholomew, co-patron of the town, with one week of festivities revolving around his feast day on August 24. All the usual traditions can be enjoyed—*gegants, correfoc, castellers, sardanas*—as well as street parties, live music, processions, gastronomic events, and a seaside fireworks display on the evening of August 23. Santa Tecla (Sept. 22-23), a smaller, more family-oriented version

of the Festa Major, is held in honor of the town's co-patron saint.

OCTOBER
International Fantastic Film Festival of Catalonia
www.sitgesfilmfestival.com; early Oct.

A 10-day feast of fantasy and horror films held in early October, this is one of Spain's most prominent cinema festivals and attracts an international posse of Hollywood elite, from Quentin Tarantino to Guillermo del Toro. The town embraces the horror fest with ghoulish delight—there's even an annual zombie walk.

Accommodations

There are accommodation options for all styles and pockets in Sitges, though broadly speaking, it tends to be expensive in comparison to the surrounding area. Advance booking is advised throughout summer and during the town's main festivals, but there are excellent deals available if traveling off-peak, even at some of the most expensive hotels.

Hotel Platjador
Passeig de la Ribera, 35; 93/894-5054; www.platjadorhotelsitges.com; €131 d

An old favorite along the seafront, Hotel Platjador is simple but has a stellar reputation and excellent off-season deals. The rooms are spotless and cheery (go for a sea view), the breakfast is hearty and served until noon, there's an outdoor swimming pool and a rooftop bar, and it's smack-bang in the heart of things. But above all, the friendly staff go the extra mile for their

guests, such as complimentary wine in the minibar. It may look a little old-fashioned—hence the three-star rating—but the price-quality ratio here is excellent.

Hotel MiM
Avenida Sofía, 12; 93/811-3500; www.hotelmimsitges.com; €189 d

This eco-conscious boutique hotel is owned by Lionel Messi, and embodies many of the luxuries a superstar footballer might be accustomed to: a soothing spa, plush interiors, and a prime location close to the beach. The 77 guest rooms are bright and spacious, with picture windows framing sea and Sitges views. The highlight is the rooftop pool and Sky Bar (May-Oct. Thurs.-Sun. noon-midnight, Apr. noon-8pm, mid-Mar. Sat.-Sun. noon-6pm), a magical spot to round off the day. It's pricey and a tad pretentious, but the stunning 360-degree views and

Ibiza-style ambience make it worth stopping by.

✪ Casa Vilella

Passeig Marítim, 21; 93/524-0200; www.hotelcasavilella.com; €250 d

Relive the early 20th century's glory days at this beachfront mansion, designed by Gaudí disciple Joan Rubió i Bellver in 1919. Boasting a superb location along the seafront, just 10 minutes from the old town, Casa Vilella is a boutique beachside stay with Noucentisme charm and friendly, four-star service. The 14 plush guest rooms are tastefully furnished, though guests are more likely to spend their time by the pool in the lush gardens or sipping a sea-view sundowner on the chic, chill-out terrace.

ME Sitges Terramar

Passeig Marítim, 80; 93/894-0050; www.melia.com; €215 d

Recently taken over by Meliá, this 1930s beachfront hotel has had a refreshing makeover and emanates luxury chill-out vibes, from rooftop DJs to poolside yoga. The 213 guest rooms are spacious and bright with soft, contemporary furnishings in neutral tones; many feature balconies with spectacular Mediterranean views. Situated at the far end of Passeig Marítim, it's a good 30-minute walk along the seafront to the center of town, though with a spa, two outdoor pools, an oyster bar, a restaurant, and a private beach club, it's tempting to stay put.

Information and Services

TOURIST INFORMATION

The tourist information center in Sitges is adjacent to the railway station (Pl. Eduard Maristany, 2; 93/894-4251; www.sitgestur.cat; mid-Oct.-mid-Jun. Mon.-Fri. 10am-2pm, 4pm-6:30pm, Sat. 10am-2pm, 4pm-7pm, Sun. 10-2pm, mid-Jun.-mid-Oct. Mon.-Sat. 10am-2pm, 4pm-8pm, Sun. 10am-2pm).

POLICE

For minor incidents, contact the municipal police force, the **Policía Local** (Carrer Samuel Barrachina; 93/811-0016). For major incidents, contact the regional police force, the **Mossos d'Esquadra** (Carrer la Devesa; 93/657-1700). Thefts can be reported at either police station.

HOSPITALS AND PHARMACIES

The primary care center in Sitges, the **Centre d'Atenció Primària (CAP)**, is open 8am-9pm daily (Carrer Samuel Barrachina, 1; 93/894-7578). Outside of these hours, the nearest public hospitals are **Hospital Residència Sant Camil-Seu** in Sant Pere de Ribes (Ronda Sant Camil, s/n, Sant Pere de Ribes; 93/896-0025; www.csg.cat; 8am-9pm daily) and **Hospital Sant Antoni Abat** in Vilanova I la Geltrú (Carrer de Sant Josep 21-23, Vilanova i la Geltrú; 93/893-1616; 8am-9pm daily), a 10- and 20-minute drive from Sitges, respectively. Both hospitals operate a 24-hour emergency service.

At least one pharmacy remains open 9am-11pm every day—check the local council's website (www.sitges.

Sitges's busy beachfront promenade

cat) to find out where. Outside of these hours, there is no on-call pharmacy in Sitges. For urgent supplies, an on-call pharmacy is open 24 hours in both Vilanova i la Geltrú and Sant Pere de Ribes.

LUGGAGE STORAGE

Hotels in Sitges normally offer luggage-storage services, but there are a couple of options for day trippers, including **Mail Boxes Etc.** (Carrer de la Bassa-Rodona, 7; 93/811-4294; www.mbe.es) and **Luggage Storage Sitges** (Carrer de Sant Gaudenci, 17; 93/178-0010; Mon.-Sat., 10am-8pm; €5 per item). The latter is run by **Hello Apartments Sitges** (www.helloapartmentssitges.com).

WIFI

There's no public WiFi network in Sitges, but visitors can connect for free in the tourist information center next to the train station. Most bars offer free WiFi for customers.

Transportation

GETTING THERE

From Barcelona, the quickest and easiest way to get to Sitges is by train. Services leave every 15 minutes from three stations in Barcelona—Estació de França, Passeig de Gràcia, Estació de Sants—and take between 35 minutes and an hour.

PLANE

Barcelona-El Prat Airport is just 28 kilometers (17 miles) northeast of Sitges. **MonBus** (93/893-7060; www.monbus.cat) runs direct bus transfers from the airport to Sitges every 30 minutes (6:50am-11:50pm) from Monday to Friday, and every hour at the weekend (8:50am-10:50pm). During the winter months (mid-Oct.-mid-Apr.), services run every two hours on Sundays. The journey takes 25 minutes and costs €7.10 (includes a surcharge of €3 for single fares to or from the airport). The MonBus bus stop is at Terminal 1 (T1). There is a free shuttle bus between terminals.

If going to the airport by train, passengers must change at El Prat de Llobregat (one stop from the airport) for Sitges. Services from the airport run every 30 minutes (5:42am-11:38pm). From El Prat de Llobregat, the R2 Sud services runs every 30 minutes to Sitges and takes 24 minutes. The airport train station is situated opposite Terminal 2 (T2), and is connected to the terminal via a footbridge.

TRAIN

Trains depart Barcelona for Sitges approximately every 15 minutes from 5am until midnight. The main service is the R2 Sud (R2S) commuter line, operated by Rodalies de Catalunya, which originates at Estació de França and stops at Passeig de Gràcia and Estació de Sants en route. The R13, R14, and R15 follow the same route. The journey takes approximately 60 minutes from Estació de França, 45 minutes from Passeig de Gràcia, and 35 minutes from Sants, and costs €4.20 each way.

Sitges railway station is a 5-minute walk from Plaça Cap de la Vila in the heart of the old town.

BUS

Buses depart Barcelona for Sitges approximately every 30 minutes (6:30am-11:20pm) from Monday to Friday throughout the year, and every hour on the weekend (8:20am-10:20pm). During the winter months (Oct. 12th-Easter), services run every two hours on Sundays (9:20am-11:20pm). The journey takes between 45 and 55 minutes, depending on how many stops are made en route, and costs €4.10. Not all buses stop at the airport. Operated by MonBus (93/893-7060; www.monbus.cat), the starting point for the service in Barcelona is the bus stop at Ronda de la Universitat, 33, close to Plaça de Catalunya. There is another stop on Carrer de Sepúlveda with Carrer del Comte d'Urgell, and another in Plaça Espanya. The Sitges stop is in front of Parc Can Robert on Passeig de Vilafranca, just a 7-minute walk from Plaça Cap de la Vila.

MonBus also operates a night bus between midnight and 5am. Six buses run from Sunday to Thursday, and eight on Friday and Saturday (Jun.-Sept.). In winter (Oct.-May), there are fewer services (three from Sunday to Thursday, six on Friday and Saturday).

CAR

From Barcelona, drive 40 kilometers (25 miles) southwest on the C-32 highway to reach Sitges. The drive takes approximately 40 minutes. The C-32 is a toll road, costing €6.93 each way, and passes through several tunnels beneath the Garraf Massif, a coastal mountain range between Barcelona and Sitges. Alternatively, take the scenic, coastal route, the C-31, which branches off from the C-32 after Castelldefels. There is no toll, though the road is a little windy and the journey takes approximately 50 minutes.

Parking in Sitges can be difficult. Some streets have free parking (not generally in the center), while blue zones indicate metered on-street parking (along the seafront, for example). Public and private car parks are available around town.

GETTING AROUND

Sitges is a small, compact seaside town, best explored **on foot.**

TAXI

Taxi stands are situated at the railway station (Carrer Salvador Mirabent), at the Centro Comercial Oasis (Carrer de la Sínia Morera), on the Passeig Marítim at the junction with Avinguda Sofía, and at the Meliá Sitges (Carrer de Joan Salvat Papasseit, 38). During the summer, there are additional taxi stands situated outside the ME Sitges Terramar (Passeig Marítim, 80) and the Hotel Platjador (Passeig de la Ribera, 35), at opposite ends of the seafront promenade.

To order a taxi, call **Sitges Taxi Association** (93/894-3594 or 93/894-1329; www.taxi-sitges.com).

LEAVING SITGES

The last train back to Barcelona from Sitges leaves at 10:25pm, while the last day-time bus service leaves at 10pm from Monday to Friday and 9pm at the weekend. MonBus operates a night service between midnight and 5am, approximately, with more services at weekends and during the summer.

From Sitges, visitors can travel on to Tarragona (by train).

MONTSERRAT

Montserrat, meaning "serrated mountain," is so much more than a monastery—it's a geological phenomenon. Approaching it from afar is nothing short of breathtaking: A supernatural, saw-like silhouette shoots up from the horizon, its pink-tinged stony tentacles extending heavenward. It's little wonder it has been recognized for its celestial qualities. This extraordinary mountain is one of the symbols of Catalonia and has been an important place of pilgrimage for more than 1,000 years. Halfway up, an 11th-century Benedictine Abbey is nestled among the

HIGHLIGHTS

⊕ **MONESTIR DE SANTA MARIA DE MONTSERRAT:** Visit the venerated statue of the Virgin and Child, famously known as Black Madonna, and listen to the heavenly voices of the Escolania Boys' Choir (page 201).

⊕ **MONASTERY TO SANT JERONI TRAIL:** Make the 2.5-hour trek to this spectacular lookout point, the summit of the singular massif of Montserrat (page 206).

peaks of Montserrat

⊕ **ROCK CLIMBING IN PARC NATURAL DE LA MUNTANYA DE MONTSERRAT:** Scaling the needles and pinnacles of Montserrat is an exhilarating way to admire one of Catalonia's most unique landscapes. Guided tours are available (page 207).

mountain's creases and folds, in honor of the Virgin of Montserrat, who reportedly appeared to shepherds here in the 9th century. At the top, the surreal pinnacles of the Parc Natural de la Muntanya de Montserrat form a singular landscape to which one can instantly attribute some of Gaudí's fantastical forms. Listen to the euphonic Escolania Boys' Choir in the Basilica or hike on high among the rocky turrets; either way, you'll find yourself a little closer to heaven.

ORIENTATION

Montserrat's jagged pinnacles can be spotted from Barcelona on a clear day, 50 kilometers (30 miles) northwest of the city. Measuring 10 kilometers by 5 (6 miles by 3), the solitary massif has a maximum elevation of 1,236 meters (4,055 feet), although it appears much higher.

Just over halfway up the mountain (720 meters/2,400 feet), the Abbey of Our Lady of Montserrat is nestled into a cliff shelf and can be accessed by road, cable car, or rack railway. The monastery is a self-contained complex comprising the Basilica, the Museu de Montserrat, the multimedia Espai Audiovisual, living accommodation for monks, the Escolania de Montserrat, and tourist and pilgrim facilities (hotel, restaurants, shops, medical center, police station, and tourist information).

From the monastery, the Funicular de Santa Cova (closed at the time of writing) takes visitors downhill toward the sacred spot where the Virgin is said to have appeared in the 9th century. The Funicular de Sant Joan, on the other hand, transports visitors to the top of the mountain and the magnificent Parc Natural de la Muntanya de Montserrat.

PLANNING YOUR TIME

Montserrat is a popular and easy day trip from Barcelona. Half a day is enough to explore the monastery, though it's worth making a day of it to experience the sublime beauty of the mountain's natural park. The Escolania Boys' Choir performs at the monastery at 1pm on weekdays, 6:45pm from Monday to Thursday, and Sundays at noon and 6:45pm. There are no performances on Saturdays or from mid-June until mid-August when the school is closed for summer holidays (check www.escolania.cat for exact dates)

Montserrat is busiest on weekends and during July and August. April 27 is the feast of the Virgin of Montserrat, a special day in the monastery. The religious celebrations begin on the evening of April 26, and continue throughout the following day, accompanied by traditional Catalan festivities, including *castellers* (human towers), music, and *sardana* dancing. Note that on feast days and holy days, the opening hours and choir's schedule may be altered.

Montserrat is exposed to the elements and has a unique climate affected by its shape. The average temperature is 13-14ºC (55-57ºF), and it is not uncommon for the mountain to disappear into thick fog. Several microclimates can exist simultaneously across the mountain. At the top, it can be cold and windy, yet in areas with little shade, you will find yourself exposed to the sun (avoid midday hiking in summer). If you're planning to hike, bring sunscreen, a sun hat, layers, and plenty of water.

Itinerary Idea

ESSENTIAL MONTSERRAT

To make the most of your day, leave Barcelona by 9am, buy your transport tickets in advance, and take note of the train schedule. There are a couple of generic restaurants in the monastery complex, although bringing a picnic to enjoy in this beautiful setting is a better (and cheaper) option. There is also a simple hotel, but visitors normally return to Barcelona to sleep.

This full-day itinerary combines the best of the mountain's physical and metaphysical elements, guaranteed to leave you feeling uplifted. Wear comfortable (hiking) shoes and pack a picnic, sunscreen, and plenty of water.

1 Arrive early and catch the Aeri de Montserrat cable car to the monastery, if your nerves allow it.

2 Spend the morning exploring the Monestir de Santa Maria de Montserrat, starting with the Espai Audiovisual.

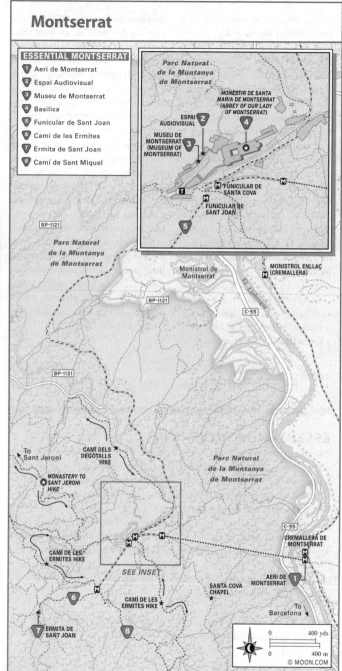

Montserrat

ESSENTIAL MONTSERRAT

1. Aeri de Montserrat
2. Espai Audiovisual
3. Museu de Montserrat
4. Basilica
5. Funicular de Sant Joan
6. Camí de les Ermites
7. Ermita de Sant Joan
8. Camí de Sant Miquel

Parc Natural de la Muntanya de Montserrat

MONÈSTIR DE SANTA MARIA DE MONTSERRAT (ABBEY OF OUR LADY OF MONTSERRAT)

ESPAI AUDIOVISUAL

MUSEU DE MONTSERRAT (MUSEUM OF MONTSERRAT)

FUNICULAR DE SANTA COVA

FUNICULAR DE SANT JOAN

BP-1121

Parc Natural de la Muntanya de Montserrat

Monistrol de Montserrat

MONISTROL ENLLAÇ (CREMALLERA)

El Llobregat

BP-1121

C-55

BP-1121

To Sant Jeroni

CAMÍ DELS DEGOTALLS HIKE

MONASTERY TO SANT JERONI HIKE

Parc Natural de la Muntanya de Montserrat

C-55

CREMALLERA DE MONTSERRAT

CAMÍ DE LES ERMITES HIKE

SEE INSET

SANTA COVA CHAPEL

AERI DE MONTSERRAT

To Barcelona

CAMÍ DE LES ERMITES HIKE

ERMITA DE SANT JOAN

0   400 yds
0   400 m
© MOON.COM

MONTSERRAT
ITINERARY IDEA

3 Marvel at the surprisingly broad collection of art housed in the **Museu de Montserrat**, a hidden gem filled with masterpieces.

4 Enter the **Basilica**, the monastery's centerpiece, and pay your respects to the Virgin of Montserrat. Then take a seat and let the angelic voices of the famous Escolania Boys' Choir lift you up. (Performances are at 1pm on weekdays, noon on Sundays.)

5 Leaving the spiritual sanctuary behind, take the **Funicular de Sant Joan** to the top of the mountain and prepare for another transcendent experience amid this surreal landscape.

6 Join the **Camí de les Ermites** trail, following signs for Sant Joan, and discover the remains of the mountain's many hermitages.

7 Pause for a picnic by the **Ermita de Sant Joan,** taking in remarkable views of the Earth from above.

8 Follow the **Camí de Sant Miquel** (part of the Camí de les Ermites) back down to the **monastery,** as the golden afternoon light illuminates the glorious peaks.

Monastery Complex

SIGHTS
✪ MONESTIR DE SANTA MARIA DE MONTSERRAT (Abbey of Our Lady of Montserrat)

Abadia de Montserrat; 93/877-7701; www.montserratvisita.com, www. abadiamontserrat.net; 7:30am-8pm daily

Conceived as a sanctuary for the Virgin of Montserrat, co-patron saint of Catalonia, the Benedictine Abbey of Montserrat is the region's most important religious center. It was founded in 1025, two centuries after the Virgin Mary is said to have appeared to local shepherds, and has been active for nearly 1,000 years, during which time the monastery complex has been extended and rebuilt several times. Although temporarily abandoned during various wars, it continues to function today, with a congregation of more than 80 monks who maintain Montserrat as a place of pilgrimage and prayer.

The abbey's centerpiece, the **Basilica of Montserrat,** is home to the venerated statue of the Virgin and Child, famously known as *La Moreneta* (or "Black Madonna") due to the color of her skin. Pilgrims have flocked here for centuries to pray before the carving, which is thought to date from the 12th century. The statue, which measures just 95 centimeters (just over 3 feet) in height, is enthroned in a silver altarpiece situated in the Cambril de la Mare de Déu, on the upper level of the Basilica's apse. Worshippers are invited to visit

ESCOLANIA BOYS' CHOIR

Montserrat has long since been considered a center of cultural importance, and is home to the Escolania Boys' Choir, one of the oldest boys' choirs in Europe, dating from the 14th century. The boys are trained and educated at the prestigious Escolania institute, having successfully passed an arduous selection process, and their celestial voices accompany religious ceremonies and prayers in the **Basilica.** The choir sings at 1pm on weekdays, 6:45pm from Monday to Thursday, and Sundays at noon and 6:45pm. Performance times may vary in accordance with special religious celebrations. Their otherworldly chorus moves even the most stoic mortals, and it is worth making sure you arrive on time for their **daily recital** (except Saturdays).

the shrine and pay their respects; there's often a queue to the right of the Basilica's main entrance (8am-10:30am, noon-6:15pm daily, plus 7:15pm-8pm mid-Jul.-Sept.).

Originally a 16th-century Gothic structure, the Basilica was rebuilt following the Peninsular War (1807-1814), and again following the Spanish Civil War (1936-1939). As a consequence, it represents a curious amalgamation of architectural styles, with Gothic and Renaissance forms, Neoclassical choir stalls, Modernista ornamentation, and a Plateresque Revival façade, much of which was completed in the 20th century. Inside, the Basilica's exquisite decor was shaped by some of Catalonia's most gifted 20th-century sculptors, among them Josep Llimona i Bruguera, Josep Maria Subirachs (best known for the Passion Façade of La Sagrada Familia), and Antoni Gaudí. Elsewhere, the monastery complex comprises living quarters for monks, an art museum, and tourist and pilgrim facilities.

MONTSERRAT MONASTERY COMPLEX

La Moreneta (Black Madonna) sits above the altar in the Basilica of Montserrat.

Santa Cova Chapel

MUSEU DE MONTSERRAT
(Museum of Montserrat)

Abadia de Montserrat; 93/877-7745;
www.museudemontserrat.com;
10am-5:45pm daily (until 6:45pm mid-Jun.-
mid-Sept. and weekends Mar.-Oct.); €8

Don't miss the monastery's impressive art collection, which is housed in this museum beneath the main square and can easily go unnoticed. Despite losing much of its cultural heritage during the Napoleonic Wars, the monastery has accumulated a valuable collection of more than 1,300 pieces spanning thousands of years. An Egyptian mummy, Gothic altarpieces, and rare works by Caravaggio, El Greco, Picasso, and Monet are among the treasures that can be found within. Audio guides are available to help you navigate (€2.20). Free entry on April 27.

ESPAI AUDIOVISUAL

93/877-7777; 9am-5:45pm daily
(weekends until 6:45pm); €5.50

The story of Montserrat—mountain, monastery, and sanctuary—comes to life in this multimedia space, located opposite the tourist information center. Visitors can walk through a thousand years of history, learn about the mountain's geology, and find out what life in the monastery is like today. It's an innovative and insightful experience.

OUTSIDE THE COMPLEX
Santa Cova Chapel

Located below the monastery complex, Santa Cova (meaning "holy grotto") is where Our Lady of Montserrat is said to have appeared to shepherds in the 9th century, prompting the evolution of Montserrat as a religious sanctuary. A 17th-century chapel is built into the mountain on the spot where the visions occurred.

This peaceful refuge can be reached via the cliff-edge Camí de la Santa Cova path (45-minute walk, 1.4km/0.9mi). Accessed via steps that descend next to the Cremallera de Montserrat (rack railway) station, the path plummets down the mountainside from the monastery and offers magnificent views over the surrounding area. Alternatively, the Funicular de la Santa Cova can take you part of the way there. From the Santa Cova station, it's a 20-minute walk to the grotto and chapel. Along the way, there's a series of Modernista sculptures dedicated to the 15 Mysteries of the Rosary, including works by Antoní Gaudí and Josep Puig i Cadafalch. Return via the same route; a popular option is to walk down and get the funicular on the way back.

Note that the Funicular de la Santa Cova was closed at the time of writing. Check the website (www.cremallerademontserrat.cat) for current status.

Parc Natural de la Muntanya de Montserrat

Oficina del Parc Natural de la Muntanya de Montserrat, Monestir de Montserrat, Plaça Abat Oliva; 93/835-0644 or 93/828-4007; muntanyamontserrat.gencat.cat

Rising from the low-lying surroundings like a dramatic rupture in the Earth's crust, the Montserrat massif is one of nature's wonders. Some 50 million years ago, this area was submerged under water and formed part of a large river delta. Rocks, pebbles, and decaying organic matter accumulated here, fusing together over time to form the mountain's foundations. A shift in the earth's plates exposed this conglomerate of sedimentary rock to the elements, which, over millions of years, shaped the incredible landscape present today.

Parc Natural de la Muntanya de Montserrat (Montserrat Mountain Natural Park) was declared a natural park in 1987, and a huge variety of flora and fauna reside amid the mountain's unique finger-like rock formations. The uppermost area is a strictly protected nature reserve, while the rest of the mountain falls within the natural park and can be experienced in many different ways.

Funicular de Sant Joan

The whole mountain lies within the natural park, and it is possible to hike from the base to the summit. However, if combining your visit with a visit to the monastery, it is best to start from the monastery complex and head for the top of the mountain. Follow one

panoramic view from Sant Jeroni, Montserrat's highest peak

of the hiking trails leading up from the monastery, or take the Sant Joan funicular.

FUNICULAR DE SANT JOAN

The Sant Joan funicular railway transports passengers between the monastery and Pla de les Taràntules at the top of the mountain, which is a common starting point for hiking in the natural park. The steep, six-minute journey is an experience in itself, offering panoramic bird's-eye views of the monastery and mountain.

The funicular runs every 12 minutes from 10am daily (every 20 minutes Nov.-Mar.). The last outward/return journey varies according to season as follows: Nov.-Mar. 4:30pm/4:50pm, Apr.-mid-Jun. and mid.-Sept.-Oct. 5:24pm/5:50pm, weekends Apr.-Jun. and Sept.-Oct. 5:48pm/6:10pm, mid-Jun.-mid-Sept. 6:24pm/6:50pm. The funicular usually closes for maintenance during

January. Check www.cremallerade-montserrat.cat for current timetables. Tickets cost €13 round-trip (€8.75 one way), purchased at the station.

At the top of the Funicular de Sant Joan, the Aula de Natura (nature center) has an informative exhibition on the history of the mountain and its climate, flora, and fauna. From here, scan the gnarly skyline and see what shapes you can spot—many of the peaks have been christened over the years for their lifelike forms, such as the Cat, the Elephant, and the Mummy.

HIKING

There are numerous hiking trails across the Montserrat massif, starting at various access points. The following routes all begin in the monastery complex. Before setting off, visit the tourist information center and pick up a map. Respect this area of natural wonder; don't stray from the marked paths and take your trash with you.

✪ Monastery to Sant Jeroni

Distance: 7 kilometers (4.3 miles), loop
Duration: 2 hours 30 minutes
Effort Level: Moderate

Walk among the extraordinary stone pillars of Montserrat, following this classic route to the mountain's highest peak, Sant Jeroni (1,236 meters/4,055 feet). Allow extra time for a picnic stop and plenty of photo opportunities along the way.

Take the Funicular de Sant Joan up to Plà de les Taràntules. From the station, take the path on the right, passing under a small bridge, and follow signs for Sant Jeroni. On the left, you'll pass by four huge turrets, known as the *Gorres*; the tallest one, Gorra Frígia (1,153 meters/3,782 feet) is topped by a cross. Follow the path to the head of the valley, making a detour en route to enjoy magnificent vistas from the Serra de les Paparres viewing point.

The path then enters a forest and crosses the Santa Maria stream via a wooden footbridge. When the path splits, go left and continue to the summit of Sant Jeroni (the path on the right returns to the monastery). Halfway up, pause at the Mossèn Cinto viewing point before continuing to the top where, on a clear day, magnificent views stretch from the Pyrenees to Mallorca. After reaching the summit, return via the same path until you reach the fork once more, then follow the other path downhill to the monastery.

Longer option: More seasoned hikers can leave out the funicular and combine with the Hermitage Route to make one long hike (10 kilometers/6 miles). To do so, follow the Hermitage Route until you reach Plà de les Taràntules, then switch to the Sant Jeroni route and head for the summit.

Camí de les Ermites (Hermitage Path)

Distance: 7 kilometers (4.3 miles), round-trip
Duration: 2 hours
Effort Level: Easy

The Camí de les Ermites rises gently up Montserrat's scenic slopes, leading hikers to discover the remains of three old hermitages on the southern face of the mountain. Starting in the monastery complex (Plaça de l'Abat Oliva), follow the Camí de Sant Miquel, which passes by the lower station of the Funicular de Sant Joan, toward the Sant Miquel chapel. Just before reaching the chapel, there's a path on the left leading to the Sant Miquel cross; the awe-inspiring views make it worth the short detour. Continue past the chapel to the crossroads at Pla de Sant Miquel, then follow the signs for Sant Joan uphill to Plà de les Taràntules, in front of the upper station of the Funicular de Sant Joan.

Keep left on the Sant Joan trail, which passes by the Ermita de Sant Joan (hermitage of Sant Joan) en route to Sant Onofre, which is embedded in the cliff-face. Finally, climb "Jacob's ladder" to the ruins of the Santa Magdalena hermitage. Return via the same route or take the Funicular de Sant Joan back down to the monastery from Plà de les Taràntules.

Camí dels Degotalls

Distance: 3.2 kilometers (2 miles), round-trip
Duration: 50 minutes
Effort Level: Easy

This mini hike is suitable for all. The route starts opposite the monastery's self-service restaurant, and runs parallel to the road (BP-1121). It's an easy, leafy stroll through lush vegetation, where evergreen oaks, yew, and white maple trees provide refuge on a hot day. The path runs alongside a calcareous rock face that descends from Pla de la Trinitat, a natural plain situated 200 meters (656 feet) above the path, and continues until the "Degotalls" point (approximately 25 minutes). Along the way, there is a series of monuments dedicated to famous Catalan artists and writers, and views that stretch over the Llobregat valley to the Pyrenees. Return via the same route.

✪ ROCK CLIMBING

Montserrat is a climber's paradise. Scaling its coarse conglomerate needles and pinnacles is an exhilarating way to experience one of Catalonia's most unique landscapes. There are more than 5,600 climbing routes of different levels amid the massif's weathered spires, including some of the best single- and multi-pitch routes in Spain. The activity in Montserrat is strictly regulated to help preserve endangered species; some areas are prohibited during mating season, for example. There are heavy fines for disobeying mandatory rules. **Guies de Muntanya Montsettat** is one of many offering rock-climbing options (from €60).

VIA FERRATA

A hybrid between a hiking trail and a climbing route, a *via ferrata* doesn't require any technical climbing knowledge or experience, but it is a step up from the average mountain hike in terms of physical challenge. Steel cables normally run parallel to these adventure trails, as well as iron rungs, ladders, and bridges, to aid and secure climbers along the way. There are several such trails in Montserrat, the most popular being the *Ferrada de les Dames*. **Guies de Muntanya**

Ermita de Sant Joan along the Camí de les Ermites (Hermitage Path)

Montserrat offers guided *via ferrata* tours (€180 for a group of four); hikers should be fit and healthy, wear hiking shoes and suitable clothing, and bring food and drink for the day.

GUIDED TOURS
Guies de Muntanya Montserrat
60/806-1995;
www.guiesdemuntanyademontserrat.cat;
€50-€200
This team of professional guides is passionate about Montserrat and offers a variety of dynamic ways to discover its exceptional natural beauty: rock climbing, hiking, orienteering, *via ferrata*, trail running, and specialized tours (including geology and biology). Private guided activities and courses for all ages and levels are led by multilingual instructors who are experts in the environment of Montserrat and place emphasis on protecting it. The company operates throughout the year; guides arrange a meeting point in advance (normally the monastery), and equipment and insurance are included.

Information and Services

TOURIST INFORMATION
The tourist information center in Montserrat is located beside the Cremallera de Montserrat (rack railway) station (93/877-7777; www.montserratvisita.com; Oct.-Feb. Mon.-Fri. 9am-5:45pm, Sat.-Sun. 9am-6:45pm, Mar.-Sept. 9am-8pm daily).

POLICE
The regional police force, the Mossos d'Esquadra, have a station within the monastery complex (Plaça de l'Abat Oliva).

HOSPITALS AND PHARMACIES
The monastery has a small medical center located in Plaça de l'Abat Oliva, next door to the Mossos d'Esquadra station. For medical emergencies, patients are transferred to the Hospital Sant Joan de Déu in Manresa (Carrer Sant Joan de Déu; 93/875-9300), a 30-minute drive (25 kilometers/16 miles) from Montserrat. The Creu Roja (Red Cross) has a station in Monistrol de Montserrat (Carrer de Balmes, 19; 93/238-2236) at the foot of the mountain, with a volunteer mountain-rescue team.

The nearest pharmacy to Montserrat is also in Monistrol de Montserrat, just across the Llobregat river from the train station: Farmacia de Montserrat (Carrer del Pont, 31; 93/835-0129; Mon. and Sat. 9am-1pm, 4:30pm-8pm, Tues.-Fri. 9am-1:30pm, 4:30pm-8pm).

LUGGAGE STORAGE
There is no luggage storage service in Montserrat.

WIFI
Montserrat has a free public WiFi network.

hiking trail to Sant Jeroni

Transportation

GETTING THERE

The best way to get to Montserrat from Barcelona is by train. Hourly trains depart from **Barcelona-Pl. Espanya** and connect with the **Aeri de Montserrat** (cable car) or the **Cremallera de Montserrat** (rack railway) to make the final leg of the journey to the monastery. Combined tickets are available. From the monastery it is possible to access other areas of the mountain via hiking trails and funicular railways.

TRAIN

Montserrat is on the R5 commuter railway line (Barcelona-Manresa), which is operated by **FGC** (*Ferrocarrils de la Generalitat*). Hourly trains depart Barcelona's **Plaça d'Espanya** station for Montserrat from 5am until 10:30pm daily. The journey takes just over one hour and costs €5.25 one way. There are two stops in Montserrat, **Aeri de Montserrat** and **Monistrol de Montserrat**; the former is opposite the Aeri de Montserrat cable car station, while the latter connects with the rack railway (Cremallera de Montserrat), both of which will take you to the monastery, halfway up the mountain.

CABLE CAR

The **Aeri de Montserrat** (93/835-0005; www.aeridemontserrat.com; €7.50 one-way, €11.50 round-trip) cable car is the quickest way to reach the monastery from the foot of the mountain, taking just five minutes to make the steep 1,350-meter (4,429-foot) journey. Inaugurated in 1930, the cable car has stood the test of time and affords spectacular views as it ascends.

209

COMBINED TICKETS FOR REACHING MONTSERRAT

Three different combined tickets are available online or to buy at Plaça d'Espanya. Before setting off from Barcelona, decide between the cable car and rack railway, as this will dictate which ticket you buy and where you will need to get off the R5 train. Both modes of transport take you to the same place and cost the same, so it is entirely up to your personal preference. The cable car is quick and fun but involves standing, while the rack railway is slower but more comfortable and accessible. Note that tickets are not interchangeable between the cable car and the rack railway, as they are operated by different companies.

the Aeri de Montserrat cable car

The **Trans Montserrat** (€31.60) includes all transport tickets (metro in Barcelona, round-trip train from Pl. Espanya to Monistrol de Montserrat, round-trip ticket for the rack railway or cable car, round-trip ticket for the Sant Joan and Santa Cova funiculars), as well as entry to the Espai Audiovisual. The **Tot Montserrat** (€50.95) is the most comprehensive option and includes all transport (as above) as well as entry to the Espai Audiovisual and Museu de Montserrat, and a buffet lunch. Finally, the **Montserrat Expres** (€35.65) includes a round-trip train ticket from Pl. Espanya to Monistrol de Montserrat, a round-trip ticket for the rack railway or cable car, and a backpack containing an MP3 audio guide, an open-air museum guide, and some local biscuits, known as *carquinyoli*.

Cabins depart every 15 minutes from 9:40am until 7pm daily from March until October (Nov.-Feb. Mon.-Fri. 9:40am-5:15pm, Sat.-Sun. 9:40am-6:15pm). The lower station is located just opposite the Aeri de Montserrat railway station. Free parking is available at the cable car station.

RACK RAILWAY

Operated by FGC, the **Cremallera de Montserrat** (93/252-1480; www.cremallerademontserrat.cat; €6.60 one-way, €11 round-trip; €7.20/€12 in high season) is a rack railway that transports passengers from the town of Monistrol de Montserrat to the monastery. The 5-kilometer (3-mile) journey takes 15 minutes, and it's a gentle ride that offers multiple perspectives over the surrounding landscape. Trains depart the Monistrol de Montserrat station every 20 minutes from 8:48am, stopping at Monistrol-Vila en route to Montserrat. The last outward/return journey varies according to season as follows: weekdays Nov.-Mar. 5:48pm/6:15pm, weekdays Apr.-mid-Jun. and mid.-Sept.-Oct. and weekends Nov.-Mar. 6:48pm/7:15pm, daily mid-Jun.-mid-Sept., weekends Apr.-mid-Jun., and mid.-Sept.-Oct.: 7:48pm/8:15pm). Coming from Barcelona by train, get off at Monistrol de Montserrat FGC railway station and change to the rack railway line. Plentiful free parking is available at the Monistrol-Vila station.

BUS

The cheapest way to get to Montserrat is by bus. **Autocares Julià** (93/261-5858; autocaresjulia.com) runs a daily service, departing at 9:15am (arrives 10:40am) from Carrer de Viriat, next to Sants Railway Station in Barcelona (€5.10 one way), which drops passengers at the monastery.

CAR

From Barcelona, drive 36 kilometers (22 miles) northwest on the A-2 highway, exiting at junction 582A onto the C-55. The A-2 is a toll road; this section costs approximately €4.50 one way. Follow the C-55 for approximately 13 kilometers (8 miles), then turn onto the BP-1121, a windy road that leads uphill to Montserrat (7 km/4 mi). The drive is 60 kilometers (37 miles) and takes approximately one hour.

There is limited parking available beside the monastery (400 spaces). The car park lines the road leading up to the monastery—it's a 15-minute walk uphill from the spaces that are furthest away; it's open 24 hours and costs €6.50 per day. Alternately, there is free parking available beside both the cable car and rack railway stations at the base of the mountain.

GETTING AROUND

The monastery sits on a cliff shelf halfway up the mountain. The complex is flat, accessible, and eminently walkable. From the monastery, there are two funicular railway lines (one of which is closed as of 2019) that take visitors to the most emblematic sites elsewhere on the mountain. It is equally possible to reach these sites via the natural park's many hiking trails.

Both funiculars are operated by the Ferrocarrils de la Generalitat de Catalunya (www.cremalleradentmontserrat.cat); combined tickets are available to connect with the Montserrat Rack Railway and the train to Barcelona.

LEAVING MONTSERRAT

The last rack railway departs the monastery for Monistrol de Montserrat at 6:15pm (weekdays Nov.-Mar.), 7:15pm (weekdays Apr.-mid-Jun. and mid-Sept.-Oct.; weekends Nov.-Mar.), or 8:15pm (daily mid-Jun.-mid-Sept.; weekends Apr.-mid-Jun. and mid-Sept.-Oct.). The last cable car leaves at 6:30pm daily Mar.-Oct. (Nov.-Feb. Mon.-Fri. 5:15pm, Sat.-Sun. 6:15pm). Both connect with the train to Barcelona (R5); the last service leaves Monistrol de Montserrat at 10:41pm and Aeri de Montserrat at 10:45pm. The last bus leaves Montserrat at 6pm (Jun.-Sept.) or 5pm (Oct.-May) from the coach car park beside the Mirador dels Apòstols (the self-service restaurant).

If traveling by car, it is possible to combine this day trip with a visit to the popular resort town of Sitges, an hour's drive from Montserrat.

TARRAGONA

The port city of Tarragona was

once the most important Roman settlement on the
Iberian Peninsula. Today, a legacy of architectural
monuments stands as testament to its glorious
past, including a stunning seaside amphitheater
and the 26-meter-high (85-foot) Les Ferreres aqueduct. Upon these ancient foundations, successive
chapters of the city's history evolved, from medieval to Modernista. The imposing Roman walls
still enclose the historic quarter, where the hilltop
12th-century cathedral is surrounded by winding streets that unravel onto wide 19th-century

HIGHLIGHTS

✪ AMFITEATRE ROMÀ (ROMAN AMPHITHEATER): Tarraco's ancient arena is set against a spectacular Mediterranean backdrop (page 218).

✪ CATEDRAL DE TARRAGONA: The city's crowning glory sits at the highest point of the Part Alta (page 222).

✪ LES FERRERES AQUEDUCT: Walk along the top of this aqueduct, a marvel of Roman engineering on the outskirts of the city (page 226).

avenues and the Balcó del Mediterràni viewing point.

ORIENTATION

Tarragona's historic center, Part Alta ("highest point"), is literally its highest point. This once-walled Roman settlement remains the soul of the city, particularly around Plaça de la Font, where bustling café terraces lie before the City Hall. At the base of the Part Alta, two parallel thoroughfares, the Rambla Vella and Rambla Nova, mark the transition point to the modern city.

Tarragona's waterfront is awkwardly separated from the city by railway lines, so access is a little convoluted. The fisherman's neighborhood of El Serrallo lies south of the train station. Just north of the port are Platja del Miracle, the city's main beach, the Balcó del Mediterràni lookout point, and the Roman amphitheater. There are more attractive stretches of sand north of the city, accessible by bus.

PLANNING YOUR TIME

Tarragona is frequently visited as a day trip from Barcelona. One day is enough to see the highlights and get a taste of the city, though you'll do it at a more leisurely pace in two days. If visiting on the weekend or during the Santa Tecla festival (September 14-24), it is advisable to make restaurant and accommodation reservations in advance. A handful of sights close on Mondays (including the Amfiteatre Romà, except during summer). The Catedral de Tarragona is closed on Sunday during certain times of the year. If you'd like to take a guided tour of the cathedral, reserve at least 48 hours in advance via email (info@catedraldetarragona.com) or telephone.

As well as the standard Spanish and Catalan public holidays, Tarragona has two local public holidays that honor the city's patron saints: Sant Magí (August 19) and Santa Tecla (September 24).

TARRAGONA

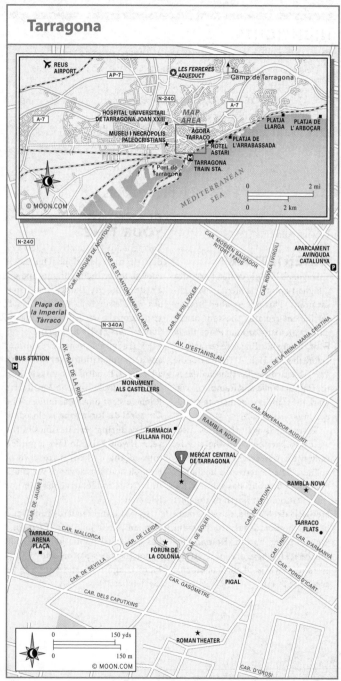

Tarragona

REUS AIRPORT

✈ LES FERRERES AQUEDUCT

To Camp de Tarragona

AP-7

N-240

A-7

A-7

HOSPITAL UNIVERSITARI DE TARRAGONA JOAN XXIII

MUSEU I NECROPOLIS PALEOCRISTIANS

MAP AREA

ÀGORA TARRACO

PLATJA LLARGA

PLATJA DE L'ARBOÇAR

HOTEL ASTARI

PLATJA DE L'ARRABASSADA

TARRAGONA TRAIN STA.

Port de Tarragona

MEDITERRANEAN SEA

0   2 mi

0   2 km

© MOON.COM

N-240

CAR. MARQUÉS DE MONTOLIU

CAR. DE ST. ANTONI MARIA CLARET

CAR. DE PIN I SOLER

CAR. MOSSÈN SALVADOR RITORT I FAUS

CAR. ROVIRA I VIRGILI

APARCAMENT AVINGUDA CATALUNYA

Plaça de la Imperial Tàrraco

N-340A

AV. D'ESTANISLAU

CAR. DE LA REINA MARIA CRISTINA

BUS STATION

AV. PRAT DE LA RIBA

MONUMENT ALS CASTELLERS

RAMBLA NOVA

CAR. EMPERADOR AUGUST

FARMÀCIA FULLANA FIOL

1 MERCAT CENTRAL DE TARRAGONA

RAMBLA NOVA ★

CAR. DE FORTUNY

TARRACO FLATS ●

CAR. DE JAUME I

CAR. MALLORCA

CAR. DE LLEIDA

CAR. DE SOLER

CAR. UNIÓ

CAR. D'ARMANYA

TARRACO ARENA PLAÇA

CAR. DE SEVILLA

FÒRUM DE LA COLÒNIA ★

PIGAL ●

CAR. PONS D'ICART

CAR. GASÒMETRE

CAR. DELS CAPUTXINS

0   150 yds

0   150 m

ROMAN THEATER ★

CAR. D'OROSI

© MOON.COM

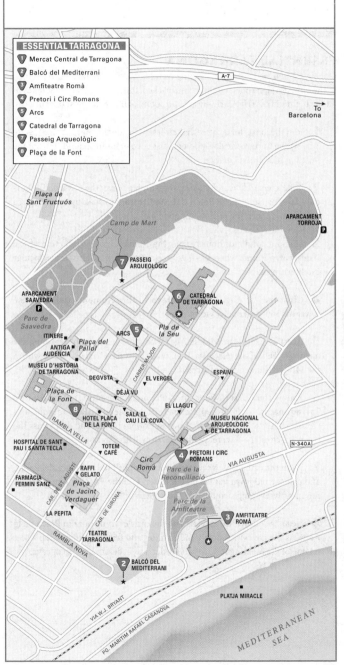

ESSENTIAL TARRAGONA

1 Mercat Central de Tarragona
2 Balcó del Mediterrani
3 Amfiteatre Romà
4 Pretori i Circ Romans
5 Arcs
6 Catedral de Tarragona
7 Passeig Arqueològic
8 Plaça de la Font

Plaça de Sant Fructuós

Camp de Mart

A-7

To Barcelona

APARCAMENT TORROJA

7 PASSEIG ARQUEOLÒGIC

APARCAMENT SAAVEDRA

Parc de Saavedra

6 CATEDRAL DE TARRAGONA

Pla de la Seu

ITINERE
ANTIGA AUDENCIA
MUSEU D'HISTÒRIA DE TARRAGONA

Plaça del Pallol

5 ARCS

CARRER MAJOR

DEGVSTA
EL VERGEL
ESPAIVI

Plaça de la Font
DÉJÀ VU

8

HOTEL PLAÇA DE LA FONT
SALA EL CAU I LA COVA

EL LLAGUT

MUSEU NACIONAL ARQUEOLÒGIC DE TARRAGONA

RAMBLA VELLA

N-340A

HOSPITAL DE SANT PAU I SANTA TECLA

TOTEM CAFÉ

Circ Romà

4 PRETORI I CIRC ROMANS

VIA AUGUSTA

FARMÀCIA FERMIN SANZ

RAFFI GELATO

Plaça de Jacint Verdaguer

LA PEPITA

CAR. DE ST. AGUSTI

CAR. DE GIRONA

Parc de la Reconciliació

Parc de la Amfiteatre

3 AMFITEATRE ROMÀ

TEATRE TARRAGONA

RAMBLA NOVA

2 BALCÓ DEL MEDITERRANI

PLATJA MIRACLE

VIA W.J. BRYANT

PG. MARITIM RAFAEL CASANOVA

MEDITERRANEAN SEA

TARRAGONA

Itinerary Idea

ESSENTIAL TARRAGONA

One day, 2,500 years of history—time travel is possible in Tarragona. Return to the city's Roman roots with this jam-packed, full-day itinerary that takes in all the highlights. Arrive early, by around 10am, to make the most of your visit.

1 Join the locals for a coffee and croissant inside the Mercat Central de Tarragona to start the day, and peruse the colorful fresh food stalls of the bustling Modernista market.

2 Take a leisurely wander along the Rambla Nova, the city's main thoroughfare, pausing at the Balcó del Mediterrani to soak up sweeping sea views—and touch the railings for good luck.

3 Spend a couple of hours exploring Roman Tarraco, starting at the Amfiteatre Romà, where gladiators once fought, set against a spectacular Mediterranean backdrop.

4 Cross the Via Augusta to the Pretori i Circ Romans, and climb the tower for 360-degree city views.

5 Fast-forward to the Middle Ages with a pre-lunch amble through the narrow streets of the Part Alta, then savor seasonal Catalan cuisine within the 14th-century cavern of Arcs restaurant.

6 Follow the Carrer Major up to Pla de la Seu and the Catedral de Tarragona, which represents a magnificent blend of Romanesque and Gothic styles. Allow at least an hour to explore inside, and don't miss the beautiful cloister—a secret garden bursting with fragrance.

7 From the cathedral, weave your way downhill toward Plaça del Pallol, and exit the old town via Portal del Roser. Join the Passeig Arqueològic for an early-evening stroll beside the Roman walls.

8 Head back downhill and soak up the early evening buzz in Plaça de la Font, as the day winds down and families and friends gather. Grab a seat on one of the bustling terraces and order a well-deserved glass of cava.

ROMAN TARRACO

In Roman times, Tarraco (modern-day Tarragona) was the provincial capital of Hispania Citerior—the largest province in the Roman Empire—and a major administrative, mercantile, and military base in Roman Spain.

The Roman city was founded in the 2nd century BC, as the first and oldest Roman settlement on the Iberian Peninsula. It began as a military base. The defensive city walls, which were nearly 4 kilometers (2.5 miles) long, were the first Roman construction. Over the next 400 years, Tarraco became one of the most influential cities in the Roman world, reaching its peak in the 2nd century AD.

The city's status was reflected in its fine architecture—the **Circus, Amphitheater, Theater,** and **Local Forum** are among the monumental edifices constructed during Tarraco's golden era. The administration of the province was conducted from the mighty **Provincial Forum,** built in the 1st century BC. At the highest point stood the **Temple of Augustus** (where the cathedral stands today), dedicated to the emperor who once lived in the city.

statue of Caesar Augustus in Tarragona

Today, 2,000-year-old ruins are dotted across town as testament to Tarragona's Roman heritage. Together they paint a vivid picture of the grandeur of the former provincial capital.

VISITING TARRAGONA'S ROMAN SITES

Tarragona's Roman sites are managed by the **Museu d'Història de Tarragona,** or MHT (Carrer dels Cavallers, 14; 97/724-2220; museu.tarragona.cat). Entrance to a single site costs €3.30 (€1.70 students and over 65s; free for under 16s), though it is worth investing in a combined ticket if you intend to visit more than a couple. There are two kinds of combined tickets: four sites (€7.40/€3.65) or all sites (€11.05/€5.50). Audio guides are available via QR codes posted at each site, and the **Imageen** augmented-reality app allows users to swipe between scenes from the present day and the Roman city.

To grasp the extent of Tarraco at its peak, drop in to the **Antiga Audencia** (Plaça del Pallol, 3; 97/729-6100; museu.tarragona.cat) and view the extensive scale model of the Roman city in the 2nd century AD. Both the Antigua Audencia and the **Volta del Pallol** in the square outside once formed part of the Provincial Forum.

TARRACO VIVAL FESTIVAL

Every May, Tarragona returns to its Roman roots during the **Tarraco Viva** festival (www.tarracoviva.com), a cultural celebration that breathes life into the city's ancient stones. Reenactments of all aspects of Roman life—theater, gladiators, cuisine, writings, engineering, fashion—take place across the archaeological sites during a dynamic few days that recall Tarraco's former glory.

Sights

TOP EXPERIENCE

✪ AMFITEATRE ROMÀ
(Roman Amphitheater)

Parc de l'Amfiteatre Romà; 97/724-2579; museu.tarragona.cat; Apr.-Sept. Tues.-Sat. 9am-9pm, Sun. 9am-3pm (plus Jun.-Aug. Mon. 9am-3pm), Oct.-Mar. Tues.-Fri. 9am-7:30pm, Sat. 9am-7pm, Sun. 9am-3pm; €3.30/€1.70 students and over 65s/ free for under 16s

The Romans chose a spectacular seafront setting for their most important entertainment venue: the amphitheater. The elliptical structure was constructed in the 2nd century, partly carved into the rocky coastline outside the city walls, next to the Via Augusta, Hispania's main highway. As the site of epic gladiator battles, bloody confrontations with wild beasts, and public executions, the amphitheater could hold up to 14,000 spectators, seated according to social status in stands divided into three horizontal sections. Sections of both the north stand, carved into the rock, and the south stand, supported by concrete vaults, are still clearly visible today. The action took place in the central arena, under which subterranean galleries held animals and gladiators before they were released onto the stage.

In AD 259, Bishop Fructuoso and his deacons were burned at the stake within the stadium during the persecution of Christians. A Visigothic basilica and cemetery were built on the site in the 6th century to honor their martyrdom. In the 12th century

Epic gladiator battles took place before 14,000 spectators in the Roman amphitheater.

Subterranean tunnels and vaulted chambers supported the stands of the Roman Circus.

this was replaced by the Romanesque church of Santa Maria del Miracle, the remains of which sit incongruously among the Roman ruins.

Access to the amphitheater is via the Parc de l'Amfiteatre Romà de Tarragona, gardens that spill down the hillside in concentric curves, echoing the form of the structure below. Pause to admire the borders planted with species common in Roman times, together with an explanation of what they were used for. The visit itself is short; explanatory panels are placed throughout the site.

PRETORI I CIRC ROMANS (Roman Circus)

Plaça del Rei-Rambla Vella; 97/722-1736; museu.tarragona.cat; Apr.- Sept. Tues.-Sat. 9am-9pm, Sun. 9am-3pm (plus Jun.-Aug. Mon. 9am-3pm); Oct.-Mar. Tues.-Fri. 9am-7:30pm, Sat. 9am-7pm, Sun. 9am-3pm; €3.30/€1.70 students and over 65s/ free for under 16s

Thirty thousand fans once cheered from the stands of the Roman Circus, as two- and four-horse chariots raced recklessly around the track. Built between AD 81 and 96, the stadium was in use until the 5th century, although today only a small portion of the 325-meter (1070-foot) circuit remains; the rest is hidden underneath 19th-century buildings stretching as far as Plaça de la Font. The long subterranean tunnels and vaulted chambers that supported the structure run directly underneath the city above, and are better preserved than the stand itself. The eastern side can be explored from within the archaeological site, but several vaults can also be spotted amid the city streets, on Plaça Sedassos and Carrer Ferrers, along Carrer Trinquet Vell, and in Plaça de la Font.

At the corner of the 1st-century complex, an underground passageway leads to the Praetorium, a Roman tower that stood at the corner of the vast Provincial Forum and which housed a staircase that connected it to the circus and lower city. In the 12th century, it was used as a palace for the Crown of Aragon, and later as a prison. Enter the complex from Plaça del Rei and climb to the terrace for 360-degree views.

the remains of the 1st-century Roman Circus

PASSEIG ARQUEOLÒGIC (Archaeological Promenade)

Avinguda Catalunya, 1A; 97/724-5796; museu.tarragona.cat; Apr.- Sept. Tues.-Sat. 9am-9pm, Sun. 9am-3pm (plus Jun.-Aug. Mon. 9am-3pm), Oct.-Mar. Tues.-Fri. 9am-7:30pm, Sat. 9am-7pm, Sun. 9am-3pm; €3.30/€1.70 students and over 65s/ free for under 16s

The Roman wall that surrounds Tarragona's historic quarter is the oldest Roman construction still preserved outside Italy. The Passeig Arqueològic, or Archaeological Promenade, runs alongside the most significant sections of wall that remain. It's a pleasant green ribbon that sits between the immense ancient structure and outer defensive bastions, which were built during the 18th-century War of Succession.

The walls were the first great construction undertaken by the Romans in Tarraco and began as a wooden fortification around a military base. Construction was completed in the second century, measuring 3.5 kilometers (2.2 miles) and reaching as far as the harbor. Approximately 1,100 meters (3,600 feet) of wall still stands today.

Points of interest along the promenade include the **Archbishop's Tower,** which has Roman foundations but is otherwise representative of medieval defense architecture. Further along, the **Minerva Tower,** dedicated to the Roman goddess, houses what is believed to be the oldest Roman sculpture and inscription in the Iberian Peninsula. You can also spot 18th-century cannons, a bronze statue of Augustus, and a statue of the Capitoline Wolf amid the greenery.

To enter the Passeig Arqueològic, exit the old town to the west via the Portal del Roser and turn right. The 45-minute walk concludes at the eastern extreme of the old town, just behind Plaça de l'Antic Escorxador. Explanatory panels accompany the leisurely stroll.

FÒRUM DE LA COLÒNIA (Colonial Forum)

Carrer de Lleida; 97/724-2501; museu. tarragona.cat; Apr.-Sept. Tues.-Sat. 9am-9pm, Sun. 9am-3pm (plus Jun.-Aug. Mon. 9am-3pm), Oct.-Mar. Tues.-Fri. 9am-7:30pm, Sat. 9am-7pm, Sun. and public holidays 9am-3pm; €3.30/€1.70 students and over 65s/free for under 16s

The Colonial Forum was the social and political hub of Roman life. Dating from around 30 BC, the forum comprised a vast central square surrounded by public and religious buildings, including the judicial basilica, the *curia* (meeting place of the municipal council), temples, and shops,

More than one kilometer of Roman wall still stands today.

which were known as *tabernae*. It is thought that the forum was in use until at least the end of the 3rd century.

Once the beating heart of Tarraco, little is left of the Colonial Forum. When the city expanded in the 19th century, the remnants of many Roman buildings were destroyed. Today, the small portion of the forum that remains seems like a peculiar anachronism hemmed in by modern residential blocks, where neighbors air their laundry above a scattering of ancient stones.

The archaeological site is divided into two sections, linked by a footbridge. In the larger section, accessed from Carrer de Lleida, evenly spaced columns trace the footprint of the basilica, the largest building in the complex. The curia would have been located within the basilica, while a series of small rooms ran along each side. Across the footbridge, the ancient street layout is visible, as well as the foundations of several houses and columns from the Capitoline temple.

Explanatory panels guide visitors around the site, which can be visited in approximately 30 minutes.

The Colonial Forum was once the hub of Roman life.

ROMAN THEATER

A few streets south of the Forum lies the Roman Theater, built in the time of Augustus. Even less remains of this

221

structure, though the three basic elements can be identified: the *cavea* (seating), part of which was built into the hillside, the *orchestra* (a semicircular area reserved for dignitaries), and the *scaena* (stage). The rest of the volume is represented by a skeletal steel structure. Though not open to the public, the ruins can be viewed from a purpose-built platform overlooking the site, together with explanatory text and images.

✪ CATEDRAL DE TARRAGONA

Pla de la Seu; 97/722-6935; www.catedraldetarragona.com; Jun. 12-Sept. 10 Mon.-Sat. 10am-8pm, Sun. 3pm-8pm, Sept. 11-Oct. 31 Mon.-Sat. 10am-7pm, Mar. 18-Jun. 10 Mon.-Sat. 10am-7pm, Nov. 2-Mar. 17 Mon.-Fri. 10am-5pm, Sat. 10am-7pm; €5/€4 students and over 65s/€3 children aged 7-16/ free for children under 7

The city's most emblematic building sits at the highest point of the Part Alta. This prominent site has been a place of worship for nearly 2,000 years. Construction on the cathedral, dedicated to Saint Thecla, began in 1171, and the site was consecrated in 1331, though work continued long after.

Stylistically, the cathedral sits somewhere between the Romanesque and Gothic, and incorporates elements of both. This is particularly evident in the ornate principal façade overlooking Pla de la Seu, which features an intricate Gothic portal in the center, flanked by two Romanesque doorways on either side. Don't miss the 4th-century Roman sarcophagus situated above the right-hand portal, which depicts scenes from the life of Christ.

Although unfinished—the Black Death cut the project short in 1348—the façade, with its glorious, 11-meter (36-foot) rose window, has become a symbol of the city and can be spotted

Catedral de Tarragona

Mercat Central

simple tour covers the cathedral and cloister (€8, 45 minutes), while the complete tour also includes Roman ruins and the bell tower (€15/€10 over 65s and children aged 7-16, 90 minutes). For tours, reserve at least 48 hours in advance via email (info@catedraldetarragona.com) or telephone.

MERCAT CENTRAL DE TARRAGONA

Plaça de Corsini; 97/789-7888;
Mon.-Sat. 8:30am-9pm

Built in 1915, Tarragona's central market is a fine example of 20th-century civic architecture. It was designed to centralize market stalls distributed across the city, and opens onto the pleasant Plaça de Corsini, where children play and locals gather for an afternoon drink.

The imposing stone-and-cast-iron construction was designed by Josep Maria Pujol i de Barberà in the Modernista style, evident in decorative flourishes throughout, from the typeface of the building's signage to the intricate ironmongery and ceramic-clad roof. Inside, the building is divided into three sections. Most of the 47 market stalls flaunt tempting fresh produce; you'll find colorful arrays of fruit, vegetables, meat, and cheese, and a glistening selection of sea creatures. Fishmongers skillfully gut the daily catch while local chefs handpick seasonal wild mushrooms to the beat of the butcher's cleaver—it's always a sensorial experience. Cafés and bars are dotted around the edge, while a handful of tapas bars are situated in the central area, together with high tables where diners can perch. This combination of grazing and grocery shopping makes for an animated marketplace, full of vitality. Outside on Plaça de Corsini, temporary markets

from afar. The cathedral's interior is magnificent. Weighty cruciform columns rise solemnly along either side of the central nave to a rib-vaulted ceiling, creating an unexpected sense of amplitude, heightened by colorful dapples of light dancing across the bare stone. The central nave is lined with spectacular 15th-century choir stalls, featuring floral, mythological, and animal motifs carved from Flanders oak. Up ahead, the white marble altar dates from the 13th century and is one of the finest examples of Catalan Romanesque sculpture, while the exquisite alabaster retable that presides over the altar is a 15th-century Gothic masterpiece, featuring sculptures of St. Thecla, the Virgin Mary, and St. Paul.

Exit to the left of the altar, and emerge into the beautiful cloisters that surround a peaceful garden filled with fragrant roses and orange blossoms. Gothic ribbed vaults sit alongside decorative Romanesque capitals in the cloisters; look for the curious carving that depicts a group of rats burying a cat! The Diocesan Museum is housed in a series of rooms around the cloisters and exhibits medieval and modern religious art and sculptural works originating in the area.

An audio guide (€2) and two guided tours are available in English; the

set up shop throughout the week— clothes on Tuesday and Thursday, and antiques on Friday.

Between 2007 and 2017, the market underwent a massive renovation project, restoring it to its former glory and incorporating a large supermarket in the basement. Grab a breakfast coffee and croissant at one of the cafés and soak up the morning market buzz or drop by for a quick bite at one of the tapas bars later in the day.

RAMBLA NOVA
Rambla Nova, Passeig de les Palmeres

Modeled on Barcelona's famous Rambla, Tarragona's Rambla Nova is a tree-lined boulevard, with a central, pedestrianized promenade, flanked by traffic on either side. Unlike the original, however, this "new" Rambla remains the focal point of city life, lined with terraces, shops, restaurants, and offices, where locals go about their day-to-day activities.

Laid out in 1854 following the demolition of the 16th-century city walls, the thoroughfare runs from the Balcó del Mediterrani to the Plaça de la Imperial Tàrraco. Statues and monuments are dotted along the way—most notably, the **Monument als Castellers** at the intersection with Carrer del Pare Palau, an almost life-size reproduction of a human castle, one of Tarragona's proudest cultural traditions.

BALCÓ DEL MEDITERRANI

At the eastern end of Rambla Nova, the Balcó del Mediterrani is a lookout point perched 40 meters (131 feet) above the Mediterranean Sea, offering sweeping panoramic views over the Platja del Miracle beach, the ancient Roman amphitheater, and the city's large industrial port. The wrought-iron railing is a symbol of the city and an iconic spot for locals; legend says that touching the railings brings good luck.

Balcó del Mediterrani

MUSEU NACIONAL ARQUEOLOGIC DE TARRAGONA
(National Archaeological Museum of Tarragona)

Tinglado 4, Moll de Costa; 97/723-6209; www.mnat.cat; Oct.-May Tues.-Sat. 9:30am-6pm, Sun. 10am-2pm, Jun.-Sept. and Easter 9:30am-8:30pm, Sun. 10am-2pm; €4.50/€3.50 for under 25s, over 65s, and families

The National Archaeological Museum of Tarragona (MNAT) contains thousands of artifacts from Roman Tarraco found in the surrounding area, including mosaics, jewelry, bronze, ceramic, and sculptural remains, many of which were discovered over the last 150 years due to the urban expansion of the modern city. Artifacts span eight centuries of Roman Tarraco. Don't miss the beautiful, 2nd-century mosaic of Medusa.

The museum headquarters in Plaça del Rei is closed for renovation until 2022. In the meantime, the museum has relocated to Tinglado 4, a former passenger terminal in the port. Here, visitors can view the Tarraco/MNAT exhibition, a condensed history of Tarraco featuring 207 of the museum's most representative exhibits.

The MNAT also manages the Paleochristian Museum and Necropolis, and the Roman Theater of Tarragona. The MNAT entrance ticket also includes access to the Early-Christian Museum and Necropolis.

MUSEU I NECRÒPOLIS PALEOCRISTIANS
(Paleochristian Museum and Necropolis)
Avinguda de Ramón y Cajal, 84; 97/721-1175; www.mnat.cat; Jun.-Sept. Tues.-Sat. 10am-1:30pm, 4pm-8pm, Sun. 10am-2pm, Mar.-May and Oct. Tues.-Sat. 9:30am-1:30pm, 3pm-6pm, Sun. 10am-2pm, Nov.-Feb. 9:30am-1:30pm, 3pm-5:30pm, Sun. 10am-2pm; €4.50/€3.50 over 65s and under 25s/ free for children under 8 and with a Museu Nacional Arqueològic de Tarragona ticket

More than 2,000 tombs populate this Roman city of the dead, discovered in 1923 on the banks of the Francolí River. The Early Christian necropolis is one of the best-preserved late Roman cemeteries (3rd-5th centuries AD) in the Roman Empire, and reveals much about life and death in Tarraco more than 1,500 years ago. It is thought that Bishop Fructuosus and his deacons, Augurius and Eulogius, who were burnt alive in the amphitheater in AD 259, are buried here. The remains of a basilica built in their honor, and the presence of Christian symbols on many of the tombs, are testament to the Roman conversion to Christianity.

Les Ferreres Aqueduct on the outskirts of the city

❂ LES FERRERES AQUEDUCT

N-240 toward Lleida (4 kilometers/2.5 miles from Tarragona); 97/734-2069; www.pontdeldiabletarragona.com

Water was supplied to the Roman city of Tarraco via two long aqueducts. The first was 50 kilometers (31 miles) long and was fed by the Gaià River, while the second was fed by the Francolí River and measured 15 kilometers (10 miles) in length. The surviving 217-meter (712-foot) stretch of aqueduct known as the Pont del Diable, or Les Ferreres Aqueduct, belonged to the latter and is situated 4 kilometers (2.5 miles) west of the city. The spectacular two-tiered structure of arches bridges a ravine and stands 26 meters (85 feet) tall at its highest point. This feat of Roman engineering was constructed using large ashlars (square-cut stones) without mortar and is thought to date from the 1st century. Visitors can walk along the top of the aqueduct, in the channel where water once flowed toward the city. Guided tours are available in English (Mon.-Fri. 10am and noon; 90 minutes; €5).

The easiest way to reach the aqueduct is by car; it can actually be seen from the AP-7 motorway. A taxi from the city center costs approximately €12-15 one way. By public transport, bus numbers 5 and 85, both of which depart from Prat de la Riba in the city center in the direction of Sant Salvador, stop within walking distance of the aqueduct.

Food

This port city has a long tradition of fresh seafood, and is particularly known for its *peix blau* (blue fish), primarily sardines, anchovies, and mackerel. Grilled langoustines, *arròs negre* (rice cooked in squid ink), *arrossejat* (seafood rice or noodles cooked paella-style in fish stock), and mussels from the Ebro delta are among the typical fare found in the area—the fishermen's district, El Serrallo, is a good place to sample it. Of particular note is the romesco stew. Romesco normally refers to a cold dip made from garlic, red peppers, tomatoes, bread, and almonds, but in Tarragona it is also a fish casserole based on the same ingredients.

With the seasons come different flavors and produce. The xarró de Tarragona, for example, is a vegetable and pork broth served with pasta or noodles that is popular in winter. However, the region is most famous for its calçots, which can be enjoyed from January to April. Originating in the neighboring city of Valls, these sweet spring onions are barbecued and eaten dipped in romesco sauce. You can order *calçots* at restaurants, and it's also common for people to cook them at home.

SPANISH AND CATALAN
Restaurant Arcs

Carrer de Misser Sitges, 13; 97/721-8040; restaurantarcs.com; Tues.-Sat. 1pm-4pm, 8:30pm-11pm; €17-€22, weekday set lunch menu €25

Dine beneath perfectly preserved 14th-century arches in Arcs, an inviting restaurant hidden away on a tiny street near the cathedral, where chef-owner Carlos Llobet personally

seafood paella at El Llagut

greets his guests. The menu is divided into two parts: seasonal dishes and house classics, all of which represent Catalan cuisine with a lavish, innovative twist, such as the Iberian pork loin roasted with coconut milk, vermouth, almonds, ginger, lime, and honey. The weekday lunch menu (€25) includes three courses, wine, water, and coffee—or, for a splurge, try the eight-course tasting menu (€42) served with wine pairings (€17).

✪ Degvsta

Carrer dels Cavallers, 6; 97/725-2428; www.degvsta.com; Mon. 1:30pm-4pm (closed Mondays in summer); Tues.-Sat. 1:30pm-4pm, 9pm-11pm; €10-€19.50, weekday set lunch €16

This hidden gem is tucked away amid the medieval streets of the Part Alta. A handful of retro-styled dining rooms are slotted in between the ancient stone walls and wooden beams. There are two private rooms, a beautiful patio, and a wine cellar where guests are invited to select a bottle. Made

with local, seasonal ingredients, the contemporary Spanish cuisine is just as memorable—think grilled pork loin with eggplant hummus, smoked eel tartar, and veal tataki with glazed shallots and Asturian cheese. The friendly, welcoming staff complete the experience.

El Llagut

Carrer de Natzaret, 10; 97/722-8938; elllagut.com; Sun.-Mon. 1pm-4pm, Tues.-Sat. 1pm-4pm, 8:30pm-midnight; €13-€21, weekday set lunch menu €15

Paella is the specialty at El Llagut, a cozy seafood restaurant on a pleasant old town square. There are plenty of varieties to choose from—such as the lobster rice stew or black rice with prawns—though the daily catch, fresh from the sea, is also a good choice. Pair it with some fried artichokes and a crisp, local white wine, and while away the afternoon, just as the locals do. Reserve in advance and request a table on the relaxed terrace in Plaça del Rei.

TAPAS
✪ Espaivi

Plaça del Fòrum, 13; 67/226-6894;
Tues.-Sun. 2pm-4pm, 7pm-11pm, Fri.-Sat.
until midnight, Nov.-Dec. and Mar., closed
Sun. eve, Jan.-Feb. closed Sun. eve and Tues.
and Wed. afternoon; €8-€18

An intimate corner of Plaça del Forum, the exposed stone walls of Espaivi are, as the name suggests, lined with an exquisite collection of wines. Seasonal, market cuisine based on local produce and slow food principles fills the menu, which changes often and features mouth-watering dishes such as artichokes with foie and jamón, croaker ceviche, and grilled skirt steak. Portions are generous—order several dishes to share—and don't be shy about asking for help when selecting your tipple. Finish off with the popular *Bombete*—a melt-in-the-mouth filo pastry parcel filled with vanilla cream.

CAFÉ
La Pepita

Plaça de Mossèn Cinto Verdaguer, 9;
69/949-3448; Mon.-Sat. 8am-midnight;
€4-€13, weekday set lunch €9
(main course and drink)

This quirky, all-day café is furnished with antique cinema seats, colorful flowerpots, and a bicycle hanging from the ceiling. Slip into a booth and order up the breakfast special (coffee and a mini sandwich, €1.70), or soak up the evening ambience from the terrace with a selection of tapas and *tostadas* for dinner. The house special is the *pepita*—a filo pastry sandwich available with a range of fillings.

VEGETARIAN
El Vergel

Carrer Major, 13;
97/706-4850;
elvergeltarragona.com;
1pm-11pm daily; €12-€18

Situated on the first floor of an early-20th-century building in the historic quarter, El Vergel's seasonal menu features flavorsome, organic, vegan dishes: think vegan chorizo, black trumpet risotto, and seaweed soup. Nordic decor and original floor tiles set a calming backdrop for this clean, green cuisine, which is tempting to carnivores and herbivores alike. A set menu is served at lunch (1pm-3:30pm) and dinner (8:30pm-11pm), and a range of sweet and savory snacks, organic teas, and specialty coffee is available between 3:30pm and 8pm.

DESSERTS
Raffi Gelati

Plaça de Mossèn Cinto Verdaguer, 1;
97/713-9721;
www.raffagelati.com;
10am-9pm daily

One of three branches in the city, Raffa Gelati Ice and Coffee produces homemade gelato and was founded in 1958 by an Italian couple, who were the first to introduce authentic Italian ice cream to Tarragona. Their nephew continues the tradition, and has added coffee, cakes, sandwiches, crepes, and more to the repertoire at this tiny outlet on the corner of Placa de Mossèn Cinto Verdaguer. Ideal for breakfast or a cooling ice cream, to be enjoyed on the terrace.

Bars and Nightlife

Plaça de la Font has plenty of bars and eateries to start the evening. A small tip: What is known as a *clara* (shandy) in Barcelona is called *champú* in Tarragona. If you order a *clara*, you will most likely receive a mixture of beer and soda water, rather than lemonade.

BARS
Déjà Vu
Baixada de la Misericòrdia, 16; 97/713-9441; dejavutgn@gmail.com; Mon.-Fri. 7pm-3am, Sat.-Sun. 11am-3am

A cozy bar beneath an ancient stone archway, Déjà Vu is popular day and night. At the weekend, around midday, partake in the popular "vermut hour," when locals meet for a glass of fortified wine, olives, and crisps (€2), or stop by for an early evening aperitif, when you'll pay €1.50 for a glass of wine or beer, served with a delectable *montadito* (canapé on toast). After dark, the friendly bar staff mix up reasonably priced jam-jar cocktails and oversized gin-and-tonics.

CLUBS AND LIVE MUSIC
Sala el Cau i La Cova
Carrer del Trinquet Vell, 2; 97/723-9812; Mon.-Thurs. 11pm-5am; Fri.-Sat. 11pm-6am; cover varies

Roman barrel vaults dating from the 1st century create a unique setting for this live music venue and club. Situated beneath Baixada de la Misericòrdia, these ancient archways once supported the stands of the Roman Circus, which ran right across this part of the city. A legendary venue since 1969, local and national musicians of all genres regularly take to the stage here, and once the concert is over, the venue becomes a club with two rooms—one dedicated to pop, one techno.

Totem Café
Rambla Vella, 15; 63/087-2924; Wed.-Thurs. 10pm-2:30am, Fri.-Sat. 10pm-3am; no cover

Totem Café is a local favorite for after-dinner drinks and dancing. Conveniently close to the lively Plaça de la Font, this two-story disco bar is the place to keep the party going after things wind down on the square. DJs spin commercial tracks as revelers of all ages mingle beneath the disco ball. There are occasional themed nights, and live football matches are often shown on the big screen before the night kicks off.

HUMAN CASTLES OF CATALONIA

A human castle, or *castell*, is a thing of beauty: A balancing act of up to 10 tiers and 200 people, it's a tremendous display of coordination and teamwork. Bodies of all shapes, sizes, and ages are the construction materials for these precarious structures. Brows sweat and shoulders ache as the tower begins to appear, tier-by-tier, according to precise choreography and timing. The crowd holds its breath as the tiny *enxaneta*—the final piece of the jigsaw, usually a young child— clambers to the top and raises a hand. There's a collective sigh of relief as traditional music rings triumphantly through patriotic Catalan hearts.

Building human castles (*castells*) is a proud local tradition.

This curious Catalan tradition was declared an example of Cultural and Intangible Heritage of Humanity by UNESCO in 2010. Its origins lie in Valls, 20 kilometers (12 miles) north of Tarragona, though the tradition actually evolved from a Valencian folk dance, the *Ball de Valencians*, which arrived in Catalonia in the 18th century. (The *Ball de Valencians* finished by raising one of the dancers into the air.)

Castells were very popular during the second half of the 19th century but went into decline in the early 1900s and almost disappeared. As Spain transitioned to democracy in the second half of the 20th century, the tradition took off once more, and for the first time spread beyond the local area, becoming a symbol of Catalan identity. Popularity has continued to flourish until the present day, with more than 70 *colles* (clubs) and 10,000 *castellers* (castle-builders) practicing this blend of culture and acrobatics across Catalonia.

CASTELL PERFORMANCES

The unofficial season runs from mid-June until the end of October, though castells can be seen throughout the year.

A typical performance consists of three human castles and a farewell pillar by each participating club (there are normally three). *Castellers* dress in white trousers, a black waist sash, a white-spotted red bandana, and a shirt specific to their *colla* (club). The clubs take turns building their towers, accompanied by traditional music played on the *gralla* (a Catalan wind instrument) and drum. There is no clear winner or loser, though each club strives to build the most complex structure.

The tradition often forms part of a local festival, such as **La Mercè** and **Santa Eulàlia** in Barcelona, **Santa Tecla** (Sept. 14-24) and **Sant Magí** (Aug. 14-19) in Tarragona, and on the **National Day of Catalonia** (Sept. 11).

In Tarragona, there are regular human castle displays across town from June until October. Related activities include witnessing practice sessions and even taking part! Also in Tarragona, the **Concurs de Castells**—a prestigious human tower competition—is organized by the city council and held in the **Tarraco Arena Plaça** (Carrer de Mallorca, 18) every two years during the first weekend of October. More than 40 clubs from across the region are judged by the difficulty of their constructions in front of 6,000 spectators. Go to eng.concursdecastells.cat for tickets, which are required to attend the event.

Recreation and Activities

BEACHES

Long stretches of fine, golden sand characterize the Costa Daurada (Golden Coast) in southern Catalonia, which stretches from Cunit in the north to Alcanar in the south. Around Tarragona, 10 pleasant beaches are strung along 15 kilometers (10 miles) of coastline heading north. Most of the beaches are easily accessible, both in terms of transport and disabled access, and have good facilities, such as showers, bars, and restaurants. With shallow waters and a gently sloping shoreline, this is a relaxed, family-friendly area, ideal for sun-worshippers in summer or a leisurely stroll at any time of year.

Platja Miracle

This is the main city beach. It is separated from the center by train tracks, which makes it a little awkward to reach; at the time of writing a new footbridge was under construction. Otherwise, the best route starts along Via Augusta, just east of the Parc de l'Amfiteatre. Take the steps that descend toward the sea, connecting with Baixada Miracle until you reach the underpass on Carrer de Mestre Benaiges. It's a 10-minute walk. As far as city beaches go, Platja Miracle is reasonable, but there are more pleasant options nearby.

Platja de l'Arrabassada

Platja de l'Arrabassada offers the best balance between clean, calm sands and

Platja de l'Arrabassada

proximity to the city. Easily reached by bus (numbers 8, 11, or 12 from Rambla Vella), or a 25-minute walk from the town center, this blue-flag, family-friendly beach is 550 meters long and 65 meters wide (1,804 by 213 feet) and has good facilities.

Platja Llarga

The longest beach in the area, Platja Llarga boasts 3 kilometers (2 miles) of fine sands. This beach is located further north than Platja de l'Arrabassada and can be reached by the same buses (8, 11, 12).

Platja de L'arboçar

Also known as Cala Waikiki or Cala Fonda, this is a small but beautiful cove, reminiscent of the Costa Brava. Considered the nicest beach in the area, part of its beauty is down to its seclusion; there is no development and no facilities, and it is popular with nudists. Make sure you bring a picnic and some water.

Getting there takes time as it can only be reached on foot. By public transport, take the number 12 bus from Rambla Vella to La Mora (25 minutes). Once there, head toward Torre de la Móra, a 16th-century tower at the southern end of the beach, then follow the woodland trail to Platja de L'Arboçar (20 minutes). By car, park in La Mora and follow the same path. It can also be accessed via a woodland trail at the northern end of Platja Llarga.

WALKING TOURS

Itinere

Baixada del Roser, 8; 97/723-9657; www.turismedetarragona.com; €24-€45

Itinere is a group of knowledgeable, friendly guides with 20 years of experience who offer private walking tours of the city. There are two standard routes: the "Petit Comité" (2 hours, €25, entrance to Roman Circus included), a family-friendly tour of Roman and medieval Tarragona, and "Tarragona Hidden Gems" (3 hours, €45, entrance to Cathedral included), which covers the highlights and delves beneath the surface to reveal some of the city's ancient secrets. Led by passionate Tarragona native Xavi Mejuto, members of the team happily share their local knowledge and offer a meet-and-greet service for those traveling from Barcelona and farther afield.

Àgora Tarraco

Passeig Marítim Rafael Casanova, 1; 97/724-8866; agoratarraco.com

Àgora Tarraco offers two walking tours: the "Tarraco Virtual Reality Experience" (10am, 11:30am, 1pm, 5pm daily; 90 minutes; €20, entrance to amphitheater included) with VR glasses, and "Huellas de Tarraco," meaning "Traces of Tarraco" (2 hours, €10, Jul.-Aug. Sat.-Sun. 11am). During winter, tours must be booked in advance and do not run on Sundays.

Festivals and Events

Throughout the year, Tarragona hosts a variety of traditional, cultural, and gastronomic festivals.

MARCH/APRIL
Easter

Solemn processions through the city take place throughout **Holy Week**—a tradition that dates back to at least 1550. The main event is the Holy Burial Procession on **Good Friday**, when more than 4,000 people parade religious floats through the Part Alta.

MAY
Tarraco Viva

www.tarracoviva.com

This festival celebrates the city's Roman heritage with historical re-enactments of life in Tarraco—gladiator fights, theater, music, dance—performed amid the ancient ruins of the city. A gastronomic festival of ancient Roman cuisine, **Tarraco a Taula,** runs alongside Tarraco Viva. Some events require tickets, which can be bought online.

AUGUST
Sant Magí

Aug. 14-19

The city celebrates its co-patron saint with a lively procession through the Part Alta filled with local cultural tradition, including the *gegantons negritos* (black giants), dwarves, *bastoners* (stick dancers), and, of course, *castells* (human castles).

Tarragona returns to its Roman roots during the annual Tarraco Viva festival.

SEPTEMBER
Santa Tecla
Sept. 14-24

Every September, the city celebrates its patron saint, Santa Tecla, with a 10-day, citywide festival. This is the liveliest time of the year in Tarragona, reaching a climax on the feast day itself, September 23. The celebrations date back to 1321, when the relics of the saint's arm arrived in the city from Armenia.

During the festival, *Tarraconenses* fill the streets with festivities, including *castells*, live music, traditional dance, fireworks, and a party atmosphere that continues long into the night. On September 23, the sacred arm is paraded through the streets of the old town as part of the festival's most significant ceremonial procession, the *Seguici Popular,* accompanied by traditional music and dance, bells ringing, and a whole host of giants, animals, and mythical creatures. The procession culminates at the cathedral, dedicated to Santa Tecla, where much ado is made of returning the saint's arm to its resting place inside. For more information, see santatecla. tarragona.cat.

If you're not around for the festivities, the **Casa de la Festa** (Via Augusta, 4; 97/722-9930; Jun. 24-Sept. 24 Thurs.-Fri. 10am-1pm, Sat. 11am-2pm, 5pm-8pm, Sun. 11am-2pm, Sept. 25-Jun. 23 Thurs.-Fri. 9am-1pm, Sat. 10am-2pm, 5pm-8pm, Sun. 10am-2pm; free) captures the spirit of revelry all year round. The festive rituals are explained in three exhibition halls, illustrated with artifacts and elaborate costumes, which are stored here to be ready for the next year.

OCTOBER
Concurs De Castells
Tarraco Arena Plaça, Carrer de Mallorca, 18; eng.concursdecastells.cat

The best *colles* (human castle groups) from across Catalonia compete in the most important competition of the season, held every two years on the first weekend of October. Tickets are required and can be purchased online.

Accommodations

Despite a recent surge in popularity, the range of accommodation in Tarragona leaves a lot to be desired. Nevertheless, there are still many options for a short stay. The majority of the sights are in or close to the Part Alta, the city's old town, so it is advisable to choose accommodation within walking distance. The city center offers a mixture of mid-range hotels, hostels, and tourist apartments.

Pigal
Carrer del Cardenal Cervantes, 6; 97/750-6818; hotelpigal.com; €60 d

A warm welcome awaits at Pigal, the best budget option in town. The convivial host, Xavier, is a fountain of local knowledge and goes the extra mile to ensure that guests get the most out of their stay in his hometown. Just a six-minute walk from the railway station, the hotel is centrally located in a 19th-century building with an eye-catching sea-blue façade. Rooms are basic but spotless with private bathrooms, original floor tiles, and a shabby-chic aesthetic that lends character to an otherwise stark interior.

Tarraco Flats

Carrer Méndez Núñez, 5; 97/707-1997; www.tarracoflats1890.com; €55 d (2-night minimum stay)

Live like a local in Tarraco Flats, a block of 14 charming apartments located just off Rambla Nova. Original tiled floors, lofty ceilings, and period carpentry exude 19th-century elegance throughout this recently restored building. Apartments vary in size, accommodating between two and eight people, each one equipped with a kitchen and AC. Check-in is carried out electronically, so don't expect a warm welcome—although it's perfect for those looking for an independent pied-a-terre in the city center. Choose an apartment facing the inside of the block, as the street can be noisy late at night.

Hotel Plaça de la Font

Plaça de la Font, 26; 97/724-6134; hotelpdelafont.com; €78 d

Conveniently close to all the main sights, this simple, three-star hotel sits on a vibrant square in the old town, which fills with locals in the evening. The 20 spotless guest rooms are basic but comfortable and bright, each one adorned with an inspirational photograph of the local area. Rooms at the front have a small balcony overlooking the square. Breakfast and half-board options are available, although there is a plethora of eateries on the doorstep.

Hotel Astari

Via Augusta, 95-97; 97/723-6900; www.hotelastari.com; €89 d

A 10-minute walk from the historic center, the modern Hotel Astari feels like a cross between a beach and a business hotel. The outdoor swimming pool and lounge area is the main attraction, followed by its proximity to the beach—Platja del Miracle and Platja de l'Arrabassada are within easy walking distance. The 83 guest rooms are simple but comfortable; go for a sea view room with terrace.

Round off a day of sightseeing with an early evening glass of *cava* in Plaça de la Font.

Information and Services

TOURIST INFORMATION

Tarragona is served by two tourist information centers. The **principal office** is located near the cathedral in the heart of the old town (Carrer Major, 37; 97/725-0795; turisme@tarragona.cat; Oct.-Jun. 22 Mon.-Fri. 10am-2pm, 3pm-6pm, Sat. 10am-2pm, 3pm-7pm, Sun. 10am-2pm, Jun. 23-Sept.23 10am-8pm daily, Sept. 24 10am-2pm). The second tourist information center is located in a **small booth** along the pedestrian promenade of Rambla Nova (Rambla Nova; 97/725-0795; Nov.-Mar. Mon.-Sat. 10am-2pm, 3pm-6pm, Sun. 10am-2pm, Apr.-Jun. 22 and Oct. Mon.-Sat. 10am-2pm, 4pm-7pm, Sun. 10am-2pm, Jun. 23-Sept. 24 Mon.-Sat. 10am-2pm, 4pm-8pm, Sun. 10am-2pm, additional Sun. hours during Aug., 4pm-8pm).

Both centers provide tourist and cultural information about Tarragona, free city maps, tourist brochures, accommodation guides, and train and bus schedule information. Tarragona's official tourism website, www.tarragonaturisme.cat, is also an excellent resource. There are four, self-guided themed routes—Roman, Early Christian, Medieval, and Modernista—that allow visitors to learn about the most important periods of the city's history. Information can be found online and at the visitor centers.

A third **information center** is dedicated to tourism in Catalonia, and is run by the regional tourism board (www.catalunya.com). It is located just off Rambla Nova, one block from the city tourist office listed above (Carrer de Fortuny, 4; 97/723-3415; ot.tarragona@gencat.cat; Mon.-Fri. 10am-2pm, 3pm-6:30pm, Sat. 10am-2pm). The office also assists non-EU tourists to apply for a VAT (sales tax) refund (Mon.-Fri. only).

POLICE

- Guàrdia Urbana emergency line: 092
- Mossos d'Esquadra emergency line: 112

For minor incidents, contact the municipal police force, known as the **Guàrdia Urbana** (Carrer de l'Arquebisbe Pont i Gol, 6; 97/724-0345). To report a theft, visit one of the tourist offices for assistance. For major incidents, contact the regional police force, the **Mossos d'Esquadra** (Carrer Dr. Mallafré Guasch, 7; 97/792-2970).

HOSPITALS AND PHARMACIES

Tarragona has two public hospitals, both of which have 24-hour emergency services.

Hospital de Sant Pau i Santa Tecla (Rambla Vella, 14; 97/725-9900; www.xarxatecla.cat) is centrally located on Rambla Vella, on the edge of the Part Alta. The emergency number is 97/725-9914. **Hospital Universitari de Tarragona Joan XXIII** (Carrer del Dr. Mallafré Guasch, 4; 97/729-5800; www.icscampdetarragona.cat) is the city's largest hospital and is situated on the edge of town, northwest of the city center. The emergency number is 97/729-5800.

There are many pharmacies in the city center, indicated by a red or green cross sign outside. Many are open all day, though some close for lunch between 2pm and 5pm, and most are closed on Sundays. Outside regular hours, visit www.farmago. cat to find out which pharmacies are on call (*farmàcies de guàrdia*); there are normally two. This information is also published in the daily newspapers and posted on pharmacy doors across the city. Central pharmacies with long opening hours include **Farmàcia Fullana Fiol** (Carrer Cristòfor Colom, 1; 97/721-4517; 9am-10pm daily) and **Farmàcia Fermin Sanz** (Rambla Nova, 55; 97/722-1430; Mon.-Fri. 8am-9pm, Sat.-Sun. 9am-10pm).

LUGGAGE STORAGE

There are no luggage storage services in any of Tarragona's transport hubs. The **main tourist information center** (Carrer Major, 37) offers a limited service for free.

WIFI

There is free public WiFi across the city. The network is TGN_et_connecta.

Transportation

GETTING THERE

Located 100 kilometers (62 miles) southwest of Barcelona, the best way to get to Tarragona is by train, which takes approximately one hour from Barcelona.

PLANE

Reus Airport (REU) is located 7 kilometers (4.3 miles) west of Tarragona and handles charter flights and low-cost airlines traveling to European destinations. The **Hispano Igualdina** bus company (90/229-2900; www.igualadina.com) runs a direct airport transfer service between Tarragona Bus Station and Reus Airport (20 minutes, €3); the timetable varies seasonally. A one-way taxi journey to Tarragona city center takes around 15 minutes and costs approximately €20-€25.

Catalonia's principal airport, **Barcelona–El Prat,** is located 82 kilometers (51 miles) northeast of Tarragona. There is a direct bus service between Barcelona-El Prat and Tarragona, operated by **Plana** (97/721-4475; www.busplana.com; 60-80 minutes; €13 one way/€23.95 return), which runs several times a day. Check website for current timetable. Barcelona-El Prat can also be reached by train (www.renfe.com), changing at Barcelona Sants.

TRAIN

There are two railway stations in Tarragona. Regional services connect Barcelona with Tarragona's **main station,** which is located close to the seafront, within easy walking distance of the city center. Various operators offer dozens of daily services from Barcelona (Barcelona França, Passeig de Gràcia, and Barcelona Sants) to Tarragona, from €7.55 one way (approximately one hour). Tickets can be bought online or at the station; be sure that you get on the right train, as tickets are only valid for the chosen operator.

The alternative train station, **Camp de Tarragona,** is situated 12 kilometers (7.5 miles) north of the city and was purpose-built for the high-speed train (AVE) that runs between Barcelona and Madrid. From Barcelona, the AVE takes 40 minutes to arrive in Camp de Tarragona. A shuttle bus, run by Plana (97/721-4475; www.busplana.com; €2), connects the Camp de Tarragona station with Tarragona's bus station. Services between Barcelona and Camp de Tarragona (from €10.50 one way) are quicker but more expensive than those that run between Barcelona and Tarragona's city-center railway station. It is hardly worth paying extra, however, given that any time saved en route from Barcelona is offset by the transfer to Tarragona city center. If you need a taxi from Camp de Tarragona, call **Agrupación Taxi Estación Camp de Tarragona** (61/634-7775). The trip via taxi takes about 15 minutes and costs €23-€28.

BUS

Tarragona's bus station is located just off Plaça de la Imperial Tàrraco—a major traffic interchange in the city center—behind the Hotel SB Ciutat de Tarragona. There are local and regional services connecting the city with most towns in the region, including approximately six daily services from Barcelona Estació del Nord (90 minutes; €8.90), which are operated by Alsa (www.alsa.es).

CAR

Tarragona is 100 kilometers (62 miles) southwest of Barcelona. From Barcelona, take the C-32 heading southwest until it merges with the AP-7 motorway, then exit at junction 33 onto the N-240 toward Tarragona. Five hundred meters (1,640 feet) before

the junction, there is a lay-by and car park from which the Roman Pont del Diable (Les Ferreres Aqueduct) can be viewed and visited.

An alternative route from Barcelona is to take the C-31 highway heading southwest along the coast, passing by Sitges on the way. As the C-31 terminates at El Vendrell, take the N-430 carriageway toward Tarragona. This route is slower but has no road tolls and follows the path of the Roman Via Augusta, passing several archaeological sites en route, including the Arc de Berà (a triumphal arch near the town of Roda de Berà), the Roman quarry of El Mèdol, and the Torre dels Escipions (a funerary tower 6 kilometers/4 miles north of Tarragona).

There are several public car parks in the city that are open 24 hours, with a set price of €5.50 per day. The first 2.5 hours are charged at €0.037 per minute, after which the daily rate applies. The most central car parks are **Aparcament Avinguda Catalunya** (Av. Catalunya, 7; underground), **Aparcament Saavedra** (Carrer Josepa Massanes, 4; underground, accessed from Av. Catalunya), and **Aparcament Torroja** (Passeig de Torroja, 24; open air, just north of the Part Alta).

On-street parking is available by zone—make sure you check the color and signage. Blue zones are available to visitors for a maximum stay of two hours, Mon.-Sat. 9am-2pm, 4pm-8pm (€0.75 for 30 minutes; €1.10 for one hour; €3 for two hours). Outside of these hours, parking is free. The same applies to green zones, though the timetable is slightly different: Mon.-Fri. 9am-2pm, 4pm-8pm. For more information, visit aparcament-stgn.cat.

GETTING AROUND

Tarragona is a compact city and most sights can be reached on foot. Vehicular traffic is restricted within the historic center (known as the Part Alta) where the major sights are located, though an efficient bus network exists, which is handy for visiting sights and beaches beyond the center. Driving in Tarragona is straightforward and hassle-free, though it is unlikely you will use the car to get around, except if visiting sights outside the city center.

PUBLIC TRANSIT

Tarragona has an efficient and extensive network of buses, run by EMT Tarragona (L'Empresa Municipal de Transports de Tarragona; 90/036-5114), which serves the city and the surrounding area. A single journey costs €1.50. If you plan to spend a few days in the city and/or visit local beaches and sights beyond the city center, it may be worth buying the Targeta 20/90 travel card (€16), which is valid for 20 journeys within 90 days by multiple users. Travel cards can be purchased at the EMT office (Carrer de Soler, 4), in the bus station, or at newspaper kiosks and *estancs* (tobacco shops) around the city. Single journeys can be purchased on board (cash only, no notes larger than €10 are accepted). There is no metro system in Tarragona.

TAXI

Taxis can be easily flagged on the street or at one of the many taxi stands in the city, including the railway station, bus station (Rambla Vella, 14, outside the Hospital de Sant Pau i Santa Tecla), and Rambla Nova, 71 (outside the Alexandra Aparthotel). Taxi companies include Agrupación Radio Taxi (97/722-1414, 97/723-6064; www.taxi-tarragona.com), Autolux (65/042-8577, 90/210-5052; www.taxisautolux.com), Taxi 24 H Tarragona (69/833-0808; www.taxi24htarragona.es), and Taxi Tarraco (64/226-9752, 65/377-3396).

LEAVING TARRAGONA

The last train back to Barcelona leaves Tarragona at 10:15pm (11:10pm in summer), while the last bus to Barcelona leaves at 9:10pm.

GIRONA

Girona is situated at the conflu-ence of four rivers and has served as a crossroads for many civilizations. Today a thriving provincial capital, the city's urban fabric is an elegant balance of old and new. Crowned by the eclectic cathedral and the medieval city walls, the beautiful *Barri Vell* (old town) tumbles down the east bank of the river Onyar, where colorful façades are reflected in its glassy surface. Across several bridges, the modern city continues with chic boutiques, plentiful plazas, and a menu of museums

HIGHLIGHTS

✪ **CATEDRAL DE GIRONA:** Girona's most emblematic building embodies centuries of the city's history (page 244).

✪ **EL CALL:** Explore a medieval maze of cobbled lanes where the city's prosperous Jewish community once lived (page 250).

✪ **EL CELLER DE CAN ROCA:** Sample mind-blowing, Michelin-starred cuisine in one of the world's best restaurants. Just be sure to reserve in advance (page 254)!

that is almost as appealing as the city's famous culinary scene.

ORIENTATION

Girona is a compact and walkable city. Most of the city lies on the banks of the Onyar. The hilly east bank has always been the heart and soul of the city. Today, the Barri Vell (old town, located on the east bank) is still partially surrounded by the ancient city walls and encompasses the most extensive and best-preserved Jewish quarter in Europe. Most of Girona's sights are hidden amid the tightly knit urban fabric that rises from the bustling Rambla de Llibertat and culminates with the towering Cathedral.

No fewer than 11 bridges connect this ancient labyrinth to the newer, flatter neighborhood of Mercadal on the west bank of the Onyar. Across the river, 19th-century buildings line the elegant streets that form the modern hub of city life around Carrer de Santa Clara and Plaça de la Independencia.

PLANNING YOUR TIME

Girona is well connected to Barcelona and is a popular day trip from the city. It is also a worthwhile detour en route to the Costa Brava or La Garrotxa. One day is enough to cover Girona's highlights and get a feel for the city. An overnight stay will give you the chance to sample the reputable local cuisine. (Reserve up to 11 months in advance for a table at El Celler de Can Roca.)

Museums and monuments are generally open Monday to Saturday 10am-6pm (Mar.-Sept. 7pm or 8pm), and 10am-2pm on Sundays and public holidays. Some are closed Mondays, except during July and August. Entrance is free at most museums on the first Sunday of the month. Many also open their doors for free on the Dia Internacional dels Museus (International Day of Museums, normally mid-May), July 25, September 11, and October 29.

The high season in Girona is July and August, although the busiest week of the year is mid-May, when the Temps de Flors (www.gironatempsdeflors.cat) festival fills the streets with flowers and the city is at its most beautiful. Girona has two local public holidays: Sant Jaume (July 25) and Sant Narcís, patron saint of the city (October 29). The latter is celebrated with the Fires de Sant Narcís (firesdegirona.cat), a 10-day, citywide

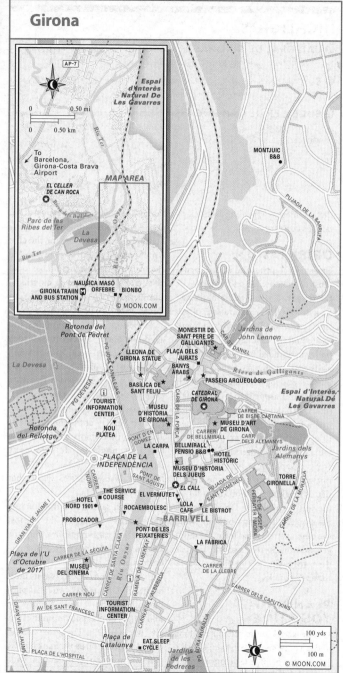

Girona

festival. If you plan to visit during either festival, make sure you reserve accommodation well in advance.

Girona has a mild climate and is pleasant to visit year-round, something that is reflected in the hotel prices, which remain relatively constant. Temperatures in summer can rise well into the 30s (80s-100s in Fahrenheit). The average temperature in winter is around 8°C (46°F), though it can drop below zero (32°F).

Itinerary Idea

ESSENTIAL GIRONA

Get a taste of Girona's past and present, from the medieval secrets of the Barri Vell to the city's gastronomic ingenuity. You'll need the whole day to tackle this itinerary, so plan to arrive early. (Fortunately, the city is less than 40 minutes by train from Barcelona, and the last train back doesn't leave until around 9pm.) Restaurant reservations should be made in advance, especially if you hope to swap out the dinner option for world-renowned fine dining at **El Celler de Can Roca.**

1 Start the day with a visit to the **Museu d'Història dels Jueus** and learn about the medieval city's prosperous Jewish community.

2 Let history bring the streets to life as you lose yourself in **El Call,** an atmospheric labyrinth of narrow lanes, hidden patios, steps, and archways.

3 Wind up in the impossibly picturesque **Pujada de Sant Domenec** and join the locals for lunch at **Le Bistrot.**

4 Delve once more into the medieval maze, this time emerging next to the imposing **Catedral de Girona**—a mishmash of the Romanesque, Gothic, and Baroque. Spend an hour exploring inside. The €7 ticket also includes entrance to the Basílica de Sant Feliu.

5 Descend the 86 steps outside the Cathedral and peep inside the **Basílica de Sant Feliu,** the city's oldest church. If you'd like to return to Girona some day, stop by Plaça de Sant Feliu and kiss *el cul de la lleona,* the rear end of the limestone lioness statue in the plaza. Refuel here with a quick *cortado* at one of the coffee shops in the plaza.

6 Walk the walls, contemplating city panoramas and distant Pyrenean peaks from the **Passeig Arqueològic,** which runs along the top of Girona's medieval boundary.

7 Sample the city's famous culinary scene with dinner at **Bionbo,** an informal gastrobar that fuses Catalan roots with global flavors.

Itinerary Idea

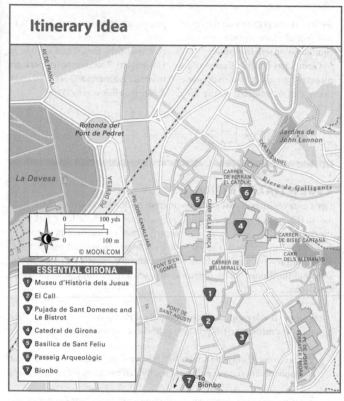

ESSENTIAL GIRONA

1. Museu d'Història dels Jueus
2. El Call
3. Pujada de Sant Domenec and Le Bistrot
4. Catedral de Girona
5. Basilica de Sant Feliu
6. Passeig Arqueològic
7. Bionbo

Sights

Girona's main sights are concentrated in the Barri Vell, the ancient heart of the city, where Roman remains hide amid medieval lanes and 19th-century buildings. Generally, Girona's museums do not offer guided tours, but English audio guides are available via the *visitmuseum* app, which is free to download.

The Episcopal ticket is a combined entrance ticket to the Cathedral, Art Museum, and the Basilica of Sant Feliu. It costs €10 and can be purchased at any of the three sights.

✪ CATEDRAL DE GIRONA

Plaça de la Catedral; 97/242-7189; www.catedraldegirona.cat; Apr.-Jun. and Sept.-Oct. 10am-6:30pm daily, Jul.-Aug. 10am-7:30pm daily, Nov.-Mar. 10am-5:30pm daily; €7, €5 students and over 65s, free for under 7s

Girona's colossal cathedral, dedicated to Santa Maria, is a veritable palimpsest of the city's history and architectural styles through the centuries. Behind the imposing Baroque façade, a Gothic body is built upon Romanesque foundations, with many more ancient secrets buried in the strata below. Situated at the highest point of the city, the site has been a place of worship for more than 2,000 years—a Roman temple, an early Christian church, and a Moorish mosque all once stood in this spot.

Today's cathedral was constructed between the 11th and 18th centuries. The eclectic structure rises from Plaça de la Catedral—a stately setting that some may recognize as the Great Sept of Baelor in King's Landing (*Game of Thrones*, season six), which was based here. From the plaza, climb the grand staircase to reach the somber interior, which contains the world's widest Gothic nave and a wealth of artistic and architectural treasures.

All that remains of the original 11th-century Romanesque cathedral is the Charlemagne bell tower, completed in 1117, and the double-columned cloister; notice the mythical beasts and biblical scenes splendidly carved into the capitals. In the 14th century, the Cathedral was enlarged in the Gothic style to include the 23-meter-wide (75-foot) nave, which is only surpassed in width by the nave of St. Peter's in the Vatican. At the apse, this single nave splits into three, encircling the high altar and Charlemagne's chair (bishop's throne), carved from white Pyrenean marble. Local legend says that if a couple sit on the throne together, they will marry, and if a single person sits on it, he or she will remain single—though you're unlikely to get the opportunity to test the theory!

In the early 17th century, the Baroque façade and staircase were added, although the finishing touches were not completed until the 1960s. A 40-minute audio guide is included with the entrance ticket—a recommended aid for exploring Girona's most emblematic building. Make

Catedral de Girona

the 12th-century Banys Àrabs (Arabic Baths)

sure you pop into the museum at the end of the tour, where the 11th-century Tapís de la Creació (Tapestry of the Creation), a rare masterpiece of Romanesque needlework, portrays the seven days of creation. The €7 entry fee also covers the Basílica de Sant Feliu, while the €10 Episcopal ticket includes entry to both churches, as well as the Girona Art Museum.

BANYS ÀRABS
(Arabic Baths)

Carrer Ferran el Catòlic; 97/219-0969; www.banysarabs.org; Mar.-Oct. Mon.-Sat. 10am-7pm, Sun. 10am-2pm, Nov.-Feb. 10am-2pm daily; €2/€1 students, under 16s, over 65s, people with disabilities

Built by King Alfons I in 1194, the Arabic Baths are situated between the Cathedral and the Basílica de Sant Feliu, in the heart of the medieval city. Rebuilt in the 13th century, following French raids that all but destroyed it, the building formed part of a convent from the 17th century until 1929, when it was handed over for public use.

The highlight is the former changing room, the Apodyterium. Orientated around a central octagonal pool, the room is top lit by a domed roof lantern, supported by slim columns with intricate natural motifs. From here, bathers progressed through a sequence of spaces and pools of varying temperatures—the Frigidarium, Tepidarium, Caldarium—some of which are better preserved than others. Unfortunately, the baths are no longer in use, but a quick wander through this millennial building (allow 15 minutes) proves that the simple pleasures in life haven't changed much.

BASÍLICA DE SANT FELIU

Pujada de Sant Feliu, 29; 97/220-1407; www.catedraldegirona.cat; Mon.-Sat. 10am-5:30pm, Sun. 1pm-5:30pm; €7/€5 students and over 65s/free for under 7s

The oldest church in the city, the Basílica de Sant Feliu was built over the resting place of Sant Feliu (Saint Felix), a 4th-century martyr. Its slender bell tower traces a distinct silhouette on the city's skyline, situated just downhill from the Catedral de Girona. Like its big sister, the building is a mishmash of Romanesque, Gothic, and Baroque styles.

Basílica de Sant Feliu

Today's basilica was constructed between the 12th and 16th centuries and encompasses a Romanesque layout (12th-13th centuries), a Gothic vaulted roof (14th-15th centuries), and a Baroque façade (16th century). As the church was originally outside the city walls, it was fortified for protection, something that is evident in its extra-heavy stone construction. Among the abundant artifacts found here, make sure you spot the eight late-Roman and early-Christian sarcophagi in the sidewalls of the apse, as well as the 14th-century recumbent Christ, a Gothic alabaster sculpture. The complimentary, 20-minute audio guide will point you in the right direction.

The other must-see is the 18th-century chapel and sarcophagus of Sant Narcís (Saint Narcissus), the city's patron saint. The legend of Saint Narcissus and the Flies is one of Girona's finest. Following a French invasion in 1285, the church was ransacked and the tomb of Narcissus desecrated. When the invaders encountered the saint's remains, a swarm of killer flies was reportedly unleashed upon them, causing them to retreat with many fatalities. In honor of the miraculous flies, insect images can be found across the city, including small fly sculptures on the corner of **Carrer de les Mosques** (Street of the Flies), just steps from the basilica.

LLEONA DE GIRONA STATUE

This limestone lioness is situated on a pedestal in the Plaça de Sant Feliu, at the northern end of the Barri Vell. Each day, dozens of tourists totter up a handful of steps to plant a smacker on the feline's buttocks—local legend says that all those who kiss ass will return to the city one day, or possibly never leave.

The statue in Plaça de Sant Feliu is a replica: The original *lleona de Girona,* said to date from the 12th century, lives in the Museu d'Art de Girona. The lioness has become a symbol of the city; renowned local chefs, the Roca brothers, have even created an ice pop in its honor . . . a tempting alternative to a stony smooch.

MUSEU D'HISTÒRIA DE GIRONA
(Girona History Museum)

Carrer de la Força, 27; 97/222-2229; www.girona.cat/museuhistoria; Tues.-Sat. 10:30am-5:30pm (until 6:30pm May-Sept.), Sun. 10:30am-1:30pm; €4/€2 students and pensioners/free for children under 14; free entrance first Sunday of the month

The Museu d'Història de Girona presents a comprehensive rundown of the city's evolution, starting with the first

FLOWER POWER

Temps de Flors

Every May, Girona bursts into bloom as the **Temps de Flors** festival (www.girona-tempsdeflors.cat) flourishes in the streets. Imaginative floral installations adorn every nook and cranny of the old town, transforming the city into a platform for creativity, where the flowers take center stage.

More than 150 monuments, patios, gardens, and historic spaces are filled with arrangements, with many private properties opening exclusively for the event— a unique opportunity to catch a glimpse of the city's hidden treasures. The crafty greenfingers behind this efflorescent invasion push the boundaries of floral art with their colorful creations, from the flamboyant to the abstract, hoping to impress the judges.

A full agenda of events runs alongside the festival, from markets, workshops, and music, to photography competitions and guided tours.

DON'T MISS

The grand Baroque staircase that lies before the Catedral de Girona is, undoubtedly, the festival's centerpiece. Each year, a bright, flower-filled carpet cascades down the 86 steps that lead to the imposing structure—a must-see and logical starting point from which to explore one of Spain's prettiest festivals.

Inside the Cathedral, the **Romanesque cloister** showcases another artistic installation, while just steps away, beautiful blossoms transform the 12th-century **Banys Àrabs.** Other festival highlights include the **Basílica de Sant Feliu, Jardins dels Alemanys,** and the **Torre Gironella,** from which you can catch a bird's-eye view of the city in bloom.

FESTIVAL TIPS

· Make restaurant and hotel reservations in advance.

· Visit at the beginning of the festival (on a weekday, if possible) when the flowers are still fresh.

· Eat a good breakfast or take a packed lunch, so you can continue wandering the artistic creations when the crowds disperse for lunch (1pm-4pm).

· Pick up a plan of the exhibitions from the tourist information center (Rambla Llibertat, 1).

human remains found in the area right up to the transition to democracy after Franco's dictatorship. Located in the heart of the Barri Vell, the museum is housed in a former Capuchin monastery, which has remnants of the Roman city wall in the basement.

Fourteen exhibition rooms over four floors reveal the story of Girona in chronological order. The first three rooms explore the Roman city of Gerunda, founded in the 1st century BC—note the impressive pavement mosaic dating from AD 300.

Head across the cloister to enter Girona's most glorious period, the Middle Ages (8th-15th century, rooms 4-7), when it gained importance as a royal and episcopal city.

On the second floor (rooms 8-9), the story continues with the Modern period (16th-18th centuries), marked by a series of devastating sieges and wars, while the third floor (rooms 10-13) covers the contemporary period (19th century onward). Artifacts and photographs from the 20th century give sobering insight into city life under Franco. The exhibition finishes on a more upbeat note, with a room dedicated to the *sardana*, Catalonia's national dance, which originates in the province of Girona.

MUSEU D'ART DE GIRONA
(Girona Art Museum)

Pujada de la Catedral, 12; 97/220-3834; museuart.com; Mon.-Sat. 10am-6pm (7pm May-Sept.), Sunday 10am-2pm; €4.50/€3.50 under 25s, over 65s, and people with disabilities/free for children under 8

The Girona Art Museum, located inside the grandiose Palau Episcopal, next to the Cathedral, houses what is considered to be the most important art collection in the province of Girona. The permanent collection spans 1,000 years and encompasses 8,500 objects, but Romanesque and Gothic art are the highlights.

Visitors can peruse a millennium of art, from intricate Romanesque carvings and remarkable Gothic altarpieces, through to Baroque sculptures, 19th-century Romanticism, and works by Modernista master Santiago Rusiñol. The most outstanding pieces (originally from two different Spanish monasteries) include an embossed silver 10th-century altar and a polychrome beam that features a detailed illustration of a 12th-century clerical procession.

A visit to the museum is also an opportunity to explore the former bishop's palace, which was built over the course of four centuries (12th-16th). Within these heavy stone walls, many spaces still bear witness to their original function, including the Throne Room, the Episcopal Prison, and the Bishop's Chapel. The lush garden and viewing point are also worth seeking out.

PASSEIG ARQUEOLÒGIC
(City Walls)

Banys Àrabs to Plaça de Catalunya; open during daylight hours

Until the early 19th century, Girona was a walled city. The first walls were built by the Romans in the 1st century BC, when they founded the city of Gerunda and protected it with a mighty fortress. These giant square-cut stone blocks laid a solid foundation for the city and can still be spotted across the Barri Vell—check out the Portal de Sobreportes (the Roman city gateway located between Carrer de Ferran el Catòlic y Plaça de la Catedral) and the lower part of the walls around Torre Gironella and Jardins dels Alemanys.

city views from the top of the medieval walls

Today, this majestic medieval boundary is one of the most striking historical elements of the city. Visitors can walk along the top of the walls, contemplate the city from the many lookout towers, and rest their gaze on the hilly western horizon, just as *gironeses* have done for centuries. Stretching along the eastern limits of the old town, the promenade represents the longest remaining section of Carolingian Wall in Europe. Starting opposite the Banys Àrabs at the northern end, steps lead up to the ramparts through lush gardens between the Cathedral and the Galligants River. From here, it is a 40-minute stroll along the walls to the endpoint near Plaça de Catalunya, with several access points in between.

Look for traces of the city's history along the way, including marks left by sieges and war. These ancient stones are also where many local legends set their scene, from the legend of Torana—a Jewish woman once imprisoned in the Gironella tower—to the stone witch of the Cathedral, a curious gargoyle said to be a petrified witch.

✪ EL CALL
(Jewish Quarter)

The word *call* comes from the Latin term *callis* (meaning "street"), and is used in Catalonia to refer to the Jewish quarters of medieval cities. In Girona, the Jewish quarter was located in the oldest part of the medieval city, and stretched all the way from the Cathedral to Plaça del Correu Vell, and from Carrer de la Claveria to the river. Inhabited from the mid-12th century, the Call's location and prosperity made it one of the most notable Jewish districts in Europe, and a symbol of the importance of the Jewish culture in Girona.

Until the late 14th century, the Call was a place of peaceful coexistence, where both Jews and Christians lived and worked, but in 1391, a wave of anti-Semitic violence spread across Spain, which marked the beginning of the end for Girona's Jewish community. The Call was attacked and diminished, and by the mid-15th century it had become a marginal ghetto to which Jews were confined. Torture, persecution, and inquisition ensued, leading ultimately to the expulsion of the Jews from Spain in 1492.

Today it is one of the best-preserved Jewish quarters anywhere—a magical labyrinth of narrow lanes, stairs, and passageways that twist and turn their way around the city's ancient heart. Imagine life in Jewish Girona as you wander along the Call's main street, Carrer de la Força—a visit to the Museu d'Història dels Jueus will help. As well as being more extensive than Barcelona's Call, Girona's Jewish quarter is prettier, cleaner, and better preserved; photo opps are aplenty.

El Call

Tip: As you explore, keep your eyes peeled for a narrow slot in the stone to the right of the ancient front doors—this is where the Mezuzah, a small, rolled-up parchment containing Bible verses, was placed by Jewish residents to fulfil the mitzvah (commandment) to "write the words of God on the gates and doorposts of your house" (Deuteronomy 6:9). Thirteen such slots have been identified in Girona, including one located just opposite the Museu d'Història dels Jueus. Unusually, this particular example is located to the left of the entrance to number 17, Carrer de la Força.

MUSEU D'HISTÒRIA DELS JUEUS
(Museum of Jewish History)

Carrer de la Força, 8; 97/221-6761; www.girona.cat/call; Sept.-Jun. Tues.-Sat. 10am-6pm, Sun.-Mon. 10am-2pm, Jul.-Aug. Mon.-Sat. 10am-8pm, Sun. 10am-2pm; €4/€2 students and pensioners/ free for children under 14; free entrance first Sunday of the month

Situated in the heart of the Jewish Call, the Museu d'Història dels Jueus is dedicated to recovering, studying, preserving, and disseminating the Jewish history of Girona and Catalonia.

The museum contains 11 galleries. Inside, the story begins with the origins of Girona's Jewish community, from ancient times to their arrival in the city, thought to be around the 9th century. Maps and models explore the rise and fall of Girona's Jewish Call, while subsequent rooms detail Jewish culture in medieval Catalonia, as well as the community's contribution to medieval science, literature, and philosophy. Of particular interest is the collection of tombstones, inscribed with Hebrew epitaphs, from the Jewish cemetery of Montjuïc, just north of the city center.

The final area recalls the decline of Girona's Jewish community, and the horrors endured as peaceful coexistence turned to violence and persecution from the 14th century onward. At the conclusion of the permanent exhibition, there is a contemplative patio

CROSSING THE ONYAR RIVER

No fewer than 11 bridges connect the **Barri Vell** to the Mercadal neighborhood on the west bank of the Onyar. In particular, you might want to seek out **Pont de les Peixateries,** designed by none other than Gustave Eiffel. Painted façades animate the waterfront—a classic photo opp.

where visitors can visit the *mikveh* (women's bath).

MONESTIR DE SANT PERE DE GALLIGANTS
(Monastery of Sant Pere de Galligants)

Carrer de Santa Llúcia, 8; 97/220-2632; www.macgirona.cat; Tues.-Sat. 10am-6pm (7pm May-Sept.), Sun. 10am-2pm; €4.50/€3.50 under 25s, over65s, families, and people with disabilites/free for children under 8

The 12th-century Monastery of Sant Pere de Galligants is one of the most remarkable Romanesque sites in all of Catalonia. The monastery is thought to have been founded in the 10th century, though the existing building was constructed around 1130. A small monastery in a unique urban setting, it fell into decline after the 16th century and was eventually abandoned in 1836.

Situated on the banks of the Galligants River, at the northern extreme of the Barri Vell, the Benedictine abbey is most famous for the decorative capitals found in the basilica's central nave and cloister. These intricate sculptures depict biblical, natural, and mythical motifs. Some have been attributed to the elusive Master of Cabestany, an anonymous sculptor active across France, Northern Catalonia, and Tuscany during the second half of the 12th century. The religious complex is also notable for its Lombard-style, eight-sided bell tower, and its unusual, asymmetrical plan.

Entrance to the monastery is free on the last Tuesday of the month from October to June. It is currently home to the Girona branch of the **Museu d'Arqueologia de Catalunya** (Museum of Archaeology of Catalonia). The museum occupies the former church and cloister and contains archaeological materials found across the province of Girona, dating from prehistory to the Middle Ages.

MUSEU DEL CINEMA
(Museum of Cinema)

Carrer de la Sèquia, 1; 97/241-2777; www.museudelcinema.cat; Sept.-Jun. Tues.-Sat. 10am-6pm, Sun. 10am-2pm, Jul.-Aug. Mon.-Sat. 10am-7pm, Sun. 10am-2pm; €6/€3 students and pensioners/ free for under 16s

Girona's Museum of Cinema is dedicated to the history of the moving image, as told through the extensive collection of Catalan amateur filmmaker Tomàs Mallol. Mallol was a passionate cinephile who spent decades researching and acquiring objects from the pre-cinema era and the early days of cinema. The award-winning museum was created in 1998 to house Mallol's collection, considered the most important of its kind in Spain, and has continued to grow as more valuable collections have been donated.

Centrally located in the Mercadal neighborhood, the museum's permanent exhibition takes visitors on a chronological journey through the evolution of the moving image, from 17th-century Chinese shadow puppets to contemporary cinema. Thousands of cameras, accessories, film rolls, photographs, drawings, and publicity materials open a window into the cinematic experiences of generations past—a goldmine for any cinema buff.

Interactive exhibits invite all the family to get behind the scenes. An hour and a half is enough to get the overall picture, though there's plenty of opportunity to delve deeper if desired.

Food

Thanks in part to its diverse landscapes—*mar i muntanya* (sea and mountain)—the province of Girona is internationally renowned as a creative hub of gastronomic innovation. The city, as the provincial capital, encapsulates this reputation, bringing exciting, avant-garde cuisine to the table across a wide range of eateries, including one of the world's best restaurants, El Celler de Can Roca.

SPANISH AND CATALAN
Le Bistrot
Pujada de Sant Domènec, 4; 97/221-8803; www.lebistrot.cat; 1pm-1am daily; €8-€15
Tucked away in a picturesque corner of the old town, Le Bistrot is a local institution with a lively, old-time atmosphere. The inexpensive, Catalan fare includes *embotits* (cured meats), *canelons* (Catalan take on Italian cannelloni), and an impressive selection of salads as well as the house special, the *pizza de pagès*. The latter comes in more than 20 eccentric varieties, such as the *botifarra de perol amb reducció de ratafia* (sausage with a sweet wine reduction). The set lunch menu (€16 Mon.-Fri., €25 Sat.-Sun.) is replete with authentic Catalan classics.

Bionbo
Carrer del Carme, 75; 97/229-9309; www.bionbo.com; Tues.-Wed. 1pm-4pm, Thurs.-Sat. 8:45pm-11:15pm; weekday set lunch menu €12.50, tasting menu €27
A 10-minute walk south of the city's main attractions, this informal gastrobar embodies the spirit of Girona's gastronomic ingenuity at a price to suit all pockets. Using local, seasonal ingredients, the menu fuses Catalan roots with global flavors, such as leek confit, osmotized potatoes, and fermented vegetables. Choose from two incredibly reasonable options: a three-course set menu at lunchtime on weekdays, or the seven-course surprise tasting menu served evenings (Thurs.-Sat.) and Saturday lunchtime. Reservations are essential and must be made by telephone (Mon.-Sat. 10am-1pm).

Probocador
Carrer de les Hortes, 7; 97/229-8074; probocador.com; Sun.-Mon. 1pm-4pm, Wed.-Sat. 1pm-4pm, 8:30pm-11pm; €13-20, weekday set lunch menu €17
A bright and welcoming locale close to Plaça de la Independència, Probocador serves delicious interpretations of local and Mediterranean classics. The veal cheek cannelloni is a sumptuous riff

the best avocado toast in town at La Fábrica

on the simple Catalan dish, while the baked monkfish and grilled steak filet are hard to beat. With attentive service and generous portions at very reasonable prices—the *menú del día* is exceptionally good value—it is little wonder the place is buzzing. Curiously, a bomb shelter is buried beneath the restaurant, built during the Spanish Civil War to protect up to 750 people from fascist air raids.

FINE DINING
✪ El Celler de Can Roca

Carrer de Can Sunyer, 48; 97/222-2157;
cellercanroca.com; tasting menus €190/€215

Three talented brothers with three Michelin stars: El Celler de Can Roca is one of the most acclaimed restaurants on the planet. Joan, Josep, and Jordi—head chef, sommelier, and pastry chef, respectively—are renowned for their creative, avant-garde take on traditional Catalan cuisine. Local ingredients come together in a surreal fusion of flavors and mind-blowing techniques, such as the caramelized olives picked directly from a bonsai tree or the freeze-dried oyster shell with oyster tartar. Twice named the world's best restaurant, reservations are like gold-dust for this once-in-a-lifetime experience. Each month's tables are released online 11 months in advance, at midnight on the first day of the month. To get there, take a taxi from the city center.

CAFÉS AND BRUNCH
La Fábrica

Carrer de la Llebre, 3; 97/229-6622;
www.lafabricagirona.com; 9am-3pm daily;
€3-€14

Retired professional cyclist Christian Meier and his wife Amber opened this hip cafe in 2015, and it has quickly become the place to have brunch in Girona. The Canadian couple's passion for what they do shines through in all the details—from the wholesome menu to the feel-good ambience and bicycle-themed decor. Colorful servings of avocado toast, chia pudding, seedy breakfast bowls, and grilled vegetables feed the happy vibes of this cyclists' favorite. The excellent specialty coffee can also be sampled at the sister cafe, Espresso Mafia (Carrer de la Cort Reial, 5; espressomafiagirona.com).

DESSERTS
Rocaembolesc
Carrer de Santa Clara, 50; 97/241-6667; www.rocambolesc.com; Sun.-Thurs. 11am-9pm, Fri.-Sat. 11am-11pm; €3-€5:50

If you can't get a reservation at El Cellar Can Roca, fear not, you can get a taste for the Roca brothers' whimsical creations at their very own ice cream factory, located on the west side of the river. Original flavors surprise and delight—the baked apple is particularly good—while the quirky popsicles are full of fun. Try the "Icephone" (yogurt, liquorice, and lime) or the "Cul de la lleona" (apple and bergamot sorbet), a frozen sculpture of Girona's famous lioness in Plaça de Sant Feliu.

Bars and Nightlife

For a city of just 100,000 inhabitants, Girona has a diverse selection of bars, pubs, and clubs, most of which are open Wednesday to Saturday. It's a university town, so there's always more of a buzz during term time (especially Thursdays), with much of the merriment focused around Plaça de la Independència on the west bank of the river.

BARS AND LIVE MUSIC
Lola Café
Carrer de la Força 7; 62/979-4360; Wed.-Sat. 11pm-3am; no cover

The contagious rhythms of live Catalan rumba are belted out several nights a week at this classic bar and live-music venue, a cozy, intimate space nestled amid the medieval lanes of Girona's old town. Baroque-style decor and fresh cocktails set the tone for foot-stomping tunes that will have you dancing until the early hours. As well as rumba, Lola offers her fair share of '80s, '90s, and English hits. Good vibes and good music.

VERMOUTH
El Vermutet
Carrer Bonaventura Carreras I Peralta, 9; 61/970-5300; Wed. 7pm-10:30pm, Thurs.-Sat. noon-3pm, 7pm-10:30pm, Sun. noon-3:30pm

Rub shoulders with the locals at El Vermutet, a tiny corner bar bursting with bonhomie in the heart of the Barri Vell. This is the place to drink vermouth in Girona, and is at its best around midday on Saturday and Sunday, when the feel-good spirit spills out onto the adjacent square. Order a homemade vermouth, accompany with anchovies, olives, and crisps slathered with Espinaler sauce, and enjoy.

CLUBS
Nou Platea
Carrer de Jeroni Real de Fontclara, 2; 97/222-7288; Thurs. 11pm-5am, Fri.-Sat. midnight-6am; €10 cover (one drink included)

A theater-turned-club near Plaça de la Independència on the west side of the river, Nou Platea has been pumping out floor-fillers since 1992, and is the place to dance until dawn. It's a large space that retains traces of its former life—the stage curtain still hangs overhead—with a bar and dance floor on the ground floor and chill-out sofas upstairs. Music ranges from pop, rock, and commercial to pachanga, reggaeton, and techno, depending on the night.

Recreation and Activities

CYCLING

Girona has become something of a cycling mecca and counts dozens of professional cyclists from around the world among its residents. The climate, terrain, and overall quality of life have attracted some of the sport's biggest names and, as a result, a thriving biking community has emerged, as well as a micro-industry serving cycling enthusiasts on two-wheeled vacations.

CYCLING TOURS AND RENTALS
The Service Course
Carrer Nord, 10; 97/266-5406; theservicecoursegirona.com; 9am-5pm daily

A one-stop shop for all your cycling needs, The Service Course was founded by retired professional cyclist Christian Meier and his wife, Amber, with the objective of offering a world-class cycling experience. As well as high-end retail and rentals (from €55

cycling in Girona

per day), there are guided rides (half-day €90, full day €170), sports massage (1 hour, €45) and lactate testing (€180) available. All the details are taken care of—there's a full-time mechanic, bike wash and storage, lockers, showers, and airport transfers—so that you can focus on enjoying the dream cycle vacation.

Eat Sleep Cycle
Carrer del Vern, 3; 97/264-9131; www.eatsleepcycle.com; Jul.-Aug. 8am-1pm, 5pm-8pm daily, Sept.-Jun. 9am-2pm, 4pm-7pm daily

Eat Sleep Cycle's team of biking enthusiasts offer tours for cyclists of all abilities throughout the year. Tours range from one-day (from €50) or self-guided routes exploring the local surroundings, to mini-breaks (from €299) and week-long trips (from €869) that cover the Costa Brava, Pyrenees, and beyond. There's a free weekly shop ride every Monday at 10am, and rental bikes (€25-75 per day) are available. At the Girona-based hub, you can have your bike serviced, book a sports massage, or peruse a selection of high-end cycling gear. Check social media for regular events organized by the team.

TOURS
Girona Trips
68/663-9272; www.gironatrips.com; from €15

Led by passionate local guide Miquel Roger i Badosa, Girona Trips specializes in private tours of the city (€15) and the province of Girona (€35-€65). There are walking tours to cover all interests, from the medieval Jewish quarter to *Game of Thrones* filming locations and contemporary gastronomy. Visitors are greeted at the railway station or hotel, and transport is provided for tours further afield; options include the Costa Brava and Besalú, among others. Reserve online.

Shopping

Girona's shopping scene is small but varied, ranging from traditional stores to independent boutiques and designer fashion. In the Barri Vell, shops are centered around Rambla de la Llibertat and Carrer de les Ballesteries. On the other side of the Onyar, Carrer de Santa Clara and Carrer Nou are lined with chic boutiques, while the main high street stores can be found along Carrer Bisbe Lorenzana, Carrer de Joan Maragall, and Carrer Migdia.

TOYS
La Carpa
Carrer de les Ballesteries, 37; 97/221-2002; lacarpa.cat; Mon.-Sat. 10:30am-1:30pm, 4:30pm-8pm

La Carpa is exactly what a toy shop should be—a higgledy-piggledy Aladdin's cave of delightful surprises covering every surface. Each and every product in this family-run store, from puppets and puzzles to books, bears, and building blocks, is selected with care. You'll even find locally produced

La Carpa

JEWELRY
Nausica Masó Orfebre
Carrer de la Rutlla, 16; 97/221-7955;
www.nausicamaso.com; Mon.-Fri.
10am-2pm, 5pm-8pm

Situated in the city's main shopping district, the quirky jewelry designs in this small boutique are the work of Nausica Masó, granddaughter of the illustrious local architect Rafael Masó (1880-1935). Recycled precious metals and chunky stones are crafted into organic and geometric shapes, many of which are inspired by the work of Masó's grandfather. If you like what you see, visit Rafael Masó's birthplace museum, Casa Masó (Carrer de les Ballesteries, 29; 97/241-3989; www. rafaelmaso.org; €6), a masterpiece of Noucentisme overlooking the Onyar River.

wooden pieces amid this unique collection. Step inside beneath a suspended solar system and let your inner child run free. Magic.

Accommodations

Although small, there's something to suit all budgets in Girona; the converted historic properties in the Barri Vell are particularly special. If you're staying at the top end of the old town, near the Cathedral, it's wise to take a taxi to your accommodation, as it is a steep climb through the cobbled streets, and bring earplugs—the bells ring every 15 minutes around the clock.

Hotel Nord 1901
Carrer Nord, 7-9; 97/241-1522;
www.nord1901.com; €126 d

Centrally located next to Plaça de la Independència, and just a stone's throw from the old town, this family-run, four-star hotel is well priced; its spacious interiors are both stylish and inviting, and the friendly staff offers impeccable service. The pièce de résistance, however, is the leafy garden and pool—the best place to retreat after sightseeing in the summer heat. The hotel also manages two blocks of beautifully appointed one- and two-bedroom apartments: Apartments Nord 1901 (Carrer del Nord, 8-10), located opposite the hotel, and Apartments Força 1901 (Carrer de la Força, 17), just across the river in the heart of the old town.

Hotel Històric
Carrer de Bellmirall, 4A; 97/222-3583;
www.hotelhistoric.com; €113 d

The hilltop Hotel Històric represents an authentic slice of Girona's history, just 100 meters (330 feet) from

Pujada de Sant Domènec

Déjà vu? For *Game of Thrones* fans, the narrow alleyways of Girona's enchanting Barri Vell are likely to feel very familiar. Many scenes from season six of the popular HBO drama were shot in the Catalan city, so don't be surprised if a wander through the labyrinthine medieval streets prompts flashbacks to the free city of Braavos or Oldtown . . . or was it King's Landing? The correct answer is all three. Guided *GoT* tours of the city are available, but if you prefer to do it yourself, visiting these locations may jog your memory . . .

- **El Call:** The labyrinthine streets of Girona's medieval Jewish quarter set the scene for the free city of Braavos, where a blind Arya Stark begged on the streets (Carrer del Bisbe Josep Cartañà) and was attacked by the Waif.

- **Catedral de Girona:** The grandiose staircase that leads to the Cathedral doubled as the exterior of the Great Sept of Baelor in King's Landing, where Jaime Lannister confronts the High Sparrow.

- **Plaça dels Jurats:** Situated opposite the Monestir de Sant Pere de Galligants, the outdoor theater in Braavos was based in this square, where Ayra watches a play about the Lannister family.

- **Banys Àrabs:** Arya hides here while fleeing from the Waif.

- **Pujada de Sant Domenec:** Ayra tumbles down these stairs, in front of Le Bistrot, into a crate of oranges, while the Waif looks on from above.

- **Monestir de Sant Pere de Galligants:** The inside of this former monastery appears as the Citadel in Oldtown, where Samwell Tarly wants to train as a Maester.

the Cathedral. Built on Roman foundations, many of the hotel's exposed stone walls date from the 8th and 9th centuries, though it has been sensitively remodeled to balance contemporary comforts with ancient character. Each of the 13 guest rooms varies in size, style, and facilities, many featuring four-poster beds and antique furniture. Get a taxi with your luggage—it's a steep climb to reach this hotel.

Bellmirall Pensio B&B

Carrer de Bellmirall, 3; 97/220-4009;
bellmirall.eu; €89 d

Bellmirall has been welcoming travelers to sleep amid its medieval stones since 1961. This family-run guesthouse is adorned with arts and crafts handmade by the founders, Ana and Isidre, and has seven simple but unique rooms that ooze antiquated charm (both shared and private bathrooms available). Located just steps from the Cathedral on the edge of the old Jewish quarter, the bells ring out through the enchanting narrow streets as guests enjoy an al fresco breakfast in the patio.

✪ Montjuic B&B

Carrer de L'11 de Setembre, 1; 97/242-7771;
www.montjuicbb.com; €108 d

Situated north of the city center, this luxury hillside feels like a country retreat, replete with little luxuries—Egyptian cotton, rain showers, outdoor pool, log fire—that make for an extra-special stay. Picture windows frame city and mountain views, and some of five rooms open onto a private terrace or garden. The accommodating host, Carmen, prepares a delectable homemade breakfast and eagerly shares her local knowledge. The only catch is the 20-minute uphill walk from the old town, although the L1 bus stops nearby.

Information and Services

TOURIST INFORMATION

The city's main **tourist information center** (Rambla de la Llibertat, 1; 97/201-0001, 97/222-6575; www.girona.cat/turisme; Nov.-Mar. Mon.-Fri. 9am-7pm, Sat. 9am-2pm, 3pm-7pm, Sun. 9am-2pm, Apr.-Oct. Mon.-Fri. 9am-8pm, Sat. 9am-2pm, 4pm-8pm, Sun. 9am-2pm) is located on the banks of the Onyar River at the foot of the old town. The center provides all the usual information—maps, timetables, sights, events, advice—and can arrange VAT refunds for non-EU tourists.

A second **tourist information center,** close to the Pont de Sant Feliu, can assist with making reservations (Carrer Berenguer Carnicer, 3; 97/221-1678, 97/201-1669; puntdebenvinguda@ajgirona.cat; Nov.-Mar. Mon.-Fri. 9am-3pm, Sat.-Sun. 9am-2pm, Apr.-Oct. Mon.-Fri. 9am-7pm, Sat. 9am-2pm, 4pm-7pm, Sun. 9am-2pm). There is also a tourist information office in the arrivals hall of **Girona Airport** (97/218-6708; ot.aeroportgirona@gencat.cat; 8am-8pm daily).

POLICE

For minor incidents, contact the municipal police force, the **Guàrdia Urbana** (Carrer Bacià, 4; 97/241-9092). To report a theft, go to the **citizens' advice office** (OAC; Gran Via Jaume I, 57; 97/218-1610; open 24 hours, 365 days). For major incidents, contact the regional police force, the **Mossos d'Esquadra** (Carrer Vista Alegre, 5; 97/218-1600; www.gencat.cat/mossos).

HOSPITALS AND PHARMACIES

Hospital Universitari de Girona Doctor Josep Trueta (Avenida

França; 97/294-0200) is the city's main hospital, situated north of the center. The principal hospital in the province of Girona, **Hospital de Santa Caterina** (Carrer del Dr. Castany; 97/218-2600), is also located nearby in Salt. Both are approximately 2.5 kilometers (1.6 miles) from the city center and have 24-hour emergency services.

Normal opening hours for pharmacies are Mon.-Fri. 9am-1pm and 4:30pm-8pm, and Sat. 9am-1:30pm. Outside of these hours, 24-hour on-call pharmacies are listed on the doors of all pharmacies when closed, and on this website: www.cofgi.org/farmacies/farmacies-de-guardia.

LUGGAGE STORAGE
There are luggage lockers at the railway station available to all (6am-11pm daily; €3.50-€5 per day).

WIFI
Girona has free WiFi service in public spaces. The network is called "Girona Free Wi-Fi" and is available in more than 170 points across the city (museums, public buildings, streets). Users must register and obtain a password in order to connect, except around the cathedral, where users can log in via Facebook.

Transportation

GETTING THERE
Located 100 kilometers (62 miles) northeast of Barcelona, the best way to get to Girona is by high-speed train (AVE), which takes just 38 minutes from Barcelona. The city can also be easily accessed from the Costa Brava and La Garrotxa.

PLANE
Girona-Costa Brava Airport (GRO) is situated 12 kilometers (7.5 miles) southwest of Girona and handles seasonal charter flights to European destinations, primarily during the summer months (Apr.-Oct.). A one-way taxi journey to the city center costs approximately €30. The region's main airport, **Barcelona-El Prat,** is 110 kilometers (68 miles) southwest of Girona.

Barcelona Bus (90/213-0014; www.sagales.com) runs direct transfers from Girona—Costa Brava Airport (lines 601, 602, 605, 607; 20-30 minutes approx.; €2.75) and Barcelona-El Prat Airport (lines 602, 603; 2-2.5 hours; €19) to Girona city center.

TRAIN
More than 50 trains depart Barcelona's Estació de Sants daily for Girona. The journey takes between 38 minutes and 2 hours 20 minutes, and costs between €8.40 and €31.30, depending on the service. The quickest option is the high-speed train (AVE), while the slowest is the regional service (R1) that runs via the coast. The R11 service and medium-distance (MD) trains are somewhere in between in terms of duration and cost. Very reasonably priced AVE tickets can be reserved in advance.

Girona's **railway station** is located approximately 1 kilometer (half a mile) southwest of the old town. All services arrive here: Regional lines run along an elevated viaduct above the railway station, while the high-speed train line is situated underground and is accessed via a separate, adjacent building. It is an easy 10-minute walk to the city center and 20 minutes to the Cathedral. Alternatively, there is a taxi stand outside the station.

BUS

Approximately seven buses (more in summer) depart Barcelona's Estació del Nord, daily for Girona. The journey (1.5-2 hours) costs €14.50. The route is serviced by both Barcelona Bus (90/213-0014; www.sagales.com) and Alsa (90/242-2242; www.alsa. es). Girona's bus station is located beneath the railway station (Plaça d'Espanya; 97/220-1591).

CAR

From Barcelona, drive 100 kilometers (62 miles) northeast on the AP-7 to reach Girona, exiting at junction 7 or 6B. This is a tolled motorway and costs approximately €8 from Barcelona. The drive takes approximately 1 hour and 15 minutes. The C-35 route is a cheaper, slower alternative.

There are plenty of free parking spaces in Girona. Next to the Parc de la Devesa, at the northern end of the city center, there are two free, 24-hour car parks that are convenient for visiting the Barri Vell. Elsewhere, visitors can park in blue zones (pay at the meter) or in privately run car parks.

GETTING AROUND

Girona is a small, compact city and is best explored on foot.

PUBLIC TRANSIT

There are 11 local bus routes that enable visitors to travel across the city, though only the L7 and L11 enter the Barri Vell. Single tickets cost €1.40 and can be purchased on board.

TAXI

Taxi stands can be found outside the railway and bus station, along Carrer Joan Maragall, and on Avinguda de Ramon Folch, just off Plaça de la Independència. Taxis can be flagged in the street or ordered by telephone (97/222-2323).

LEAVING GIRONA

The last train back to Barcelona leaves Girona at 9:13pm (9:21pm Sat.-Sun.), while the last bus to Barcelona leaves at 6:30pm in winter (mid-Oct.-Apr.), and possibly later in summer (May-mid-Oct.).

Girona is connected to Figueres by frequent buses and trains: 14 minutes by high-speed train (€7) and 30 minutes by regional rail. There are also many bus connections across northern Catalonia, enabling onward travel to the Costa Brava and La Garrotxa. The primary bus company serving the Costa Brava is Sarfa (90/230-2025; compras.moventis.es), with routes right along the coast, including Begur (1.5 hours; €8.35) and Cadaqués (1 hour 45 minutes; €10.80). Teisa (www.teisa-bus.com), on the other hand, runs inland services toward Besalú (1 hour; €4.10) and Olot (60-90 minutes; €7.45).

COSTA BRAVA

Meaning "rugged" or "wild coast," the Costa Brava runs along the northeastern tip of Spain, from Blanes in the south to the French border in the north, encompassing 255 kilometers (158 miles) of remarkable scenery. Windswept rocky headlands, sweeping pine forests, and hidden coves (known as *calas*) characterize these jagged shores, together forming a plethora of dreamy Mediterranean landscapes. This is one of the most beautiful stretches of coastline in Spain, and though mass tourism has

HIGHLIGHTS

✪ **DIVING IN THE ILLES MEDES:** A wealth of underwater life inhabits one of Spain's most important marine reserves (page 283).

✪ **BEACHES NEAR BEGUR:** Unwind by the Med in one of seven crystalline coves around the Begur headland (page 289).

✪ **CAMÍ DE RONDA:** Hike the picturesque stretch of the Costa Brava's coastal path between Calella de Palafrugell and Tamariu (page 294).

✪ **CAP DE CREUS:** Confront nature on this craggy headland, the easternmost point on the Iberian Peninsula (page 299).

✪ **TEATRE-MUSEU DALÍ:** Step into Salvador Dalí's natural habitat and see the world through the eyes of a Surrealist (page 303).

made its mark, there's much more to the Costa Brava than meets the eye.

Populated since prehistoric times, this was where the Greeks and Romans built ancient settlements, where medieval feudal lords ruled from hilltop castles, where avant-garde artists sought refuge and inspiration, and—until recently—where traditional fishing villages lived out a simple, seafaring existence. Today it is a popular summer destination, and there are countless ways to experience its dramatic beauty, by land and by sea. But it is still possible to discover the traditional character and history of the area, from the medieval fortress of Tossa de Mar or the fishing village of Calella de Palafrugell, to the colonial-style mansions of Begur and the whitewashed bay of Cadaqués.

ORIENTATION

The Costa Brava starts in Blanes, 72 kilometers (45 miles) northeast of Barcelona, and twists and turns all the way along the northeastern corner of Catalonia. The Catalan Coastal Range runs parallel to the coast, setting the backdrop for the southern stretch between Blanes and Pals, where tree-clad hills descend into rocky coves, sandy bays, and crystalline waters. Moving north, the landscape grows progressively wilder, as the Pyrenean foothills plunge into the sea at the Cap de Creus headland, the Iberian Peninsula's easternmost point. Dozens of holiday resorts and fishing villages are dotted along the rugged coastline.

The first stop on our tour is Tossa de Mar, 87 kilometers (54 miles) from Barcelona (1 hour 15 minutes by car). From Tossa, the hair-raising coastal road heading north (GI-682) is fabulously scenic, and worth the extra mileage en route to the next stop, the traditional fishing village of Calella de Palafrugell (51 kilometers/32 miles; 1 hour via coastal route). From Calella to the hilltop town of Begur, it's only a 15-minute drive (10 kilometers/6 miles), though again, the coastal route, which skirts the horseshoe bays of Llafranc and Tamariu, is worth the vertiginous drive (25 minutes). The final stretch sees a dramatic change in scenery en route to Cadaqués (72 kilometers/45 miles from Begur; 1

hour 15 minutes by car), a jewel set amid the craggy headland of Cap de Creus. From Cadaqués, it's 2 hours and 15 minutes back to Barcelona (170 kilometers/106 miles) via the AP-7 highway.

PLANNING YOUR TIME

The Costa Brava can be visited as an overnight trip from Barcelona, although it deserves more time if the schedule allows, and is also a popular summer destination in its own right. During July and August, the hottest and busiest months (28C º/82 ºF average), advance hotel and restaurant reservations are a must. Visiting during shoulder season (April-June and September-October) is generally cheaper, cooler, and quieter.

Most holidaymakers choose a base along the coast and spend their days on the beach, making excursions at their leisure—Girona, Figueres, and La Garrotxa are all within reach—though it is equally feasible to make a whistle-stop tour of the highlights. It's possible to reach the Costa Brava by public transport, but to make the most of your trip, a rental car is highly recommended.

Resort towns shut down almost entirely over the winter, with many hotels and restaurants closing from November until March; excellent deals can often be found at hotels that remain open during this period. You can have the place to yourself if you visit during low season, when the winter weather accentuates the coastline's rugged charm, but careful planning is required because of these winter closures.

Itinerary Ideas

This two-day whistle-stop tour covers a lot of ground in very little time (private transport is required) and includes a little bit of everything the Costa Brava has to offer—beautiful beaches, rugged landscapes, food, history, art, and more. Plan carefully, in terms of both timings and reservations—Compartir, Can Climent Platillos, Casa Salvador Dalí, and any accommodations require advance booking—set off early, and be warned: It's a journey that is likely to leave you wanting more.

COSTA BRAVA ON DAY 1

On your first day, you'll hit Tossa de Mar and Calella de Palafrugell before settling down in your hotel in Begur.

1 Spend the morning exploring Tossa de Mar, starting with a wander along the beachfront promenade, and a quick dip if the weather's fine.

2 Conquer the fortified headland, ascending the windy Passeig de Vila Vella all the way to the lighthouse.

3 On the way down, pause for a coffee with a view at Vila Vella Terraza Bar.

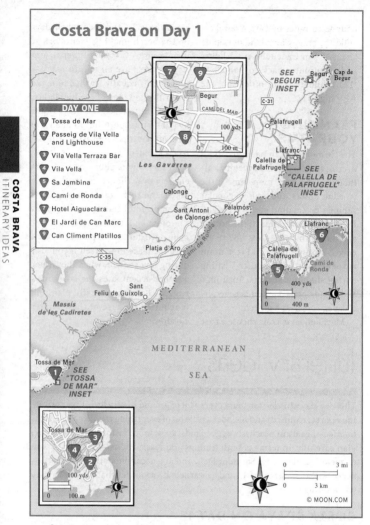

Costa Brava on Day 1

DAY ONE

1. Tossa de Mar
2. Passeig de Vila Vella and Lighthouse
3. Vila Vella Terraza Bar
4. Vila Vella
5. Sa Jambina
6. Camí de Ronda
7. Hotel Aiguaclara
8. El Jardí de Can Marc
9. Can Climent Platillos

© MOON.COM

4 Pass through the medieval defense structures and enter into the Vila Vella (old town), a charming web of narrow streets and stone-built houses.

5 Back on the road, head north along the dizzying coastal road, taking in spectacular views en route to Calella de Palafrugell. When you arrive, tuck in to fresh local fish at Sa Jambina.

6 Walk off the lunchtime feast by following the seafront trail, the Camí de Ronda, from the tiny coves of Calella to neighboring Llafranc and back (a 15-minute walk each way).

7 Back at your car, continue on the vertiginous coast road, skirting the picturesque bays of Llafranc, Tamariu, and Aiguablava on the way to Begur. When you arrive, check in at **Hotel Aiguaclara**, a colonial-style mansion in the heart of the village and one of the first stops on the **Ruta dels Indians** walking tour.

8 Follow the tour and get familiar with the vibrant village center along the way. Finish up with a sundowner at **El Jardí de Can Marc.**

9 Treat your tastebuds to gourmet tapas at **Can Climent Platillos** (advance reservations essential): little plates bursting with big flavors.

COSTA BRAVA ON DAY 2

Leave Begur and continue heading north to **Cadaqués,** ending the day with sunset at **Cap de Creus.**

1 Beat the crowds to the beach at **Platja d'Aiguablava** for a heavenly morning swim or an easy hike along the **Camí de Ronda** trail to Fornells and back.

2 Make medieval **Peratallada** the next stop, and delight in the enchanting cobbled lanes of this fairy-tale village, just a 20-minute drive from Aiguablava. Surprise your senses with the weird and wonderful ice cream flavors at Gelat Artesà de Peratallada.

3 Drive north to Cadaqués, in time for a spot of fine dining at **Compartir.**

4 Get back in the car, hop over to Portlligat, and take a peek inside the Surrealist world of Salvador Dalí, with a visit to his former home, **Casa Salvador Dalí.**

5 Round off the tour at the easternmost point on the Iberian Peninsula, **Cap de Creus,** a 15-minute drive from Cadaqués. Sit back with a drink by the **lighthouse** and marvel at the cape's jagged silhouette as evening draws in.

6 Wind down in the old town of Cadaqués and spend the night in the **Tramuntana Hotel.**

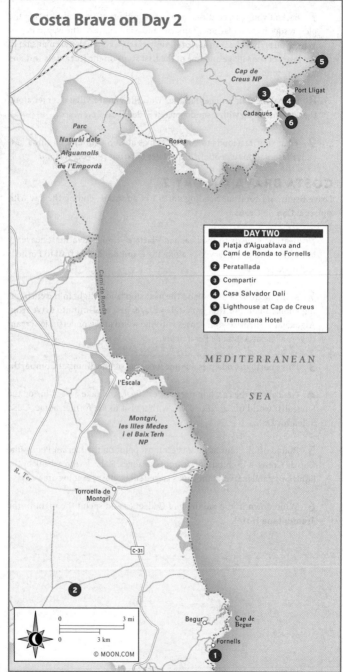

Costa Brava on Day 2

Cap de Creus NP

Port Lligat

Cadaqués

Parc Natural dels Aiguamolls de l'Empordà

Roses

Camí de Ronda

DAY TWO

1. Platja d'Aiguablava and Camí de Ronda to Fornells
2. Peratallada
3. Compartir
4. Casa Salvador Dalí
5. Lighthouse at Cap de Creus
6. Tramuntana Hotel

MEDITERRANEAN

SEA

l'Escala

Montgrí, les Illes Medes i el Baix Terh NP

R. Ter

Torroella de Montgrí

C-31

0   3 mi

0   3 km

© MOON.COM

Begur

Cap de Begur

Fornells

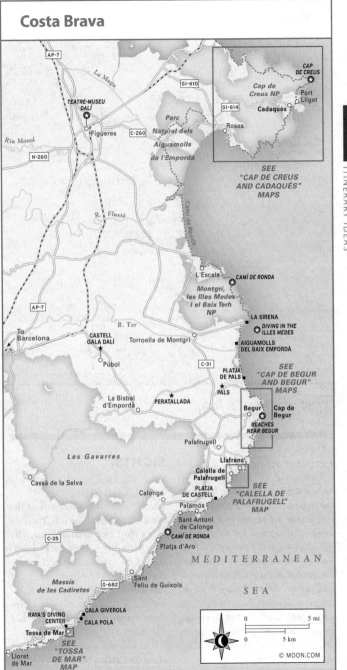

Costa Brava

AP-7

La Muga

TEATRE-MUSEU
DALÍ ★

Figueres

Riu Manol

N-260

C-260

Parc
Natural dels

Aiguamolls
de l'Empordà

GI-610

Cap de
Creus NP

CAP
DE CREUS ☆

Port
Lligat

Cadaqués

GI-614

Roses

SEE
"CAP DE CREUS
AND CADAQUÉS"
MAPS

R. Fluvià

AP-7

R. Ter

To
Barcelona

CASTELL
GALA DALÍ ★

Torroella de Montgrí

Púbol

La Bisbal
d'Empordà

PERATALLADA ★

Les Gavarres

Cassà de la Selva

L'Escala ○

CAMÍ DE RONDA

Montgrí,
les Illes Medes
i el Baix Terh
NP

LA SIRENA ■
☆ DIVING IN THE
ILLES MEDES

■ AIGUAMOLLS
DEL BAIX EMPORDÀ

C-31

PLATJA
DE PALS ■

PALS ★

SEE
"CAP DE BEGUR
AND BEGUR"
MAPS

Begur
☆

Cap de
Begur

BEACHES
NEAR BEGUR

Palafrugell ○

Llafranc ○

Calella de
Palafrugell ■

SEE
"CALELLA DE
PALAFRUGELL"
MAP

Calonge ○

PLATJA
DE CASTELL ■

Palamós ○

Sant Antoni
de Calonge ○

C-35

CAMÍ DE RONDA

Platja d'Aro ○

MEDITERRANEAN

Massís
de les Cadiretes

G-682

Sant
Feliu de Guíxols

SEA

RAYA'S DIVING
CENTER

CALA GIVEROLA

CALA POLA

Tossa de Mar ○

SEE
"TOSSA
DE MAR"
MAP

Lloret
de Mar ○

0   5 mi

0   5 km

© MOON.COM

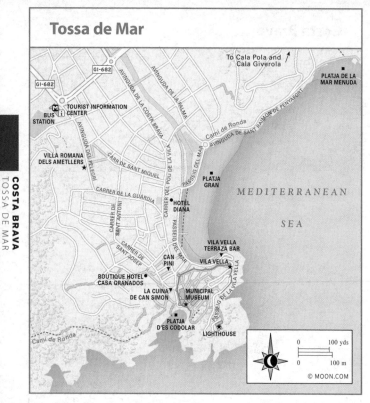

Tossa de Mar

GI-682

GI-682

AVINGUDA DE LA PALMA

AVINGUDA DE LA COSTA BRAVA

TOURIST INFORMATION
CENTER

BUS
STATION

AVINGUDA DEL PELEGRÍ

To Cala Pola and
Cala Giverola

PLATJA DE LA
MAR MENUDA

Camí de Ronda

AVINGUDA DE SANT RAIMON DE PENYAFORT

VILLA ROMANA
DELS AMETLLERS

CARRER DE SANT MIQUEL

CARRER DE LA GUÀRDIA

CARRER DE
SANT ANTONI

CARRER DE
SANT JOSEP

PASSEIG DEL POU DE LA VILA

PASSEIG DEL MAR

PLATJA
GRAN

MEDITERRANEAN

SEA

HOTEL
DIANA

VILA VELLA
TERRAZA BAR

CAN
PINI

VILA VELLA

BOUTIQUE HOTEL
CASA GRANADOS

LA CUINA
DE CAN SIMON

MUNICIPAL
MUSEUM

PASSEIG DE LA VILA VELLA

PLATJA
D'ES CODOLAR

LIGHTHOUSE

Camí de Ronda

0   100 yds

0   100 m

© MOON.COM

Tossa de Mar

Once described by Marc Chagall as a "blue paradise," Tossa de Mar sits on a sweeping, turquoise bay, protected by a rocky, fortified headland. Human life has existed here since the dawn of time, and has worn many guises through the centuries—from Roman farm to medieval fortress and traditional fishing village to bohemian artists' retreat. Today, Tossa is a busy tourist resort that can be a little honky-tonk in places, but it manages to retain some of its historic charm, and with three golden beaches, there is a little something for everyone.

SIGHTS
VILA VELLA (OLD TOWN) AND LIGHTHOUSE

The unmistakable silhouette of the fortified medieval town is Tossa de Mar's most emblematic image. The Vila Vella sits upon a rocky headland at the southern tip of the main beach, protected by heavy walls and defense towers. A 19th-century lighthouse sits at the highest point, where there was once a medieval castle and watchtower.

The only remaining fortified town along the Catalan coast, the Vila Vella citadel was built in the 13th century to protect the town from pirates. Incredibly, the entire perimeter of the walls, four turrets, and three cylindrical towers are still intact.

Inside the walls, the Vila Vella is an enchanting web of cobbled lanes and stone-built houses—a delightful place to explore. Enter beside the imposing clock tower on Carrer del Portal, then weave your way up through the narrow streets, emerging onto the Passeig de Vila Vella. This short footpath, less than a kilometer long, begins at the beach and winds around the headland, right up to the lighthouse. The remnants of the 15th-century church of Sant Vicenç, built upon an earlier Romanesque church, can be spotted en route. On the way back down, follow the Passeig de Vila Vella all the way, pausing to contemplate stunning views across the bay.

VILLA ROMANA DELS AMETLLERS
(Els Ametllers Roman Villa)
Av. del Pelegrí, 5-13; 97/234-0108; www.infotossa.com; 10am-7pm daily; free entrance

Built into the hillside with commanding views of the bay, the Els Ametllers Roman villa (1st century BC-6th century AD) is a classic example of a Roman Mediterranean farm, whose proprietors seamlessly combined a luxurious lifestyle with a working agricultural estate. The remains of the villa were discovered on the edge of the old fishing village in 1914, and it is thought that it was once one of the most important villas in the ancient province of Tarraco.

The villa was divided into two distinct areas that are still clearly visible—living quarters on the upper level, and an industrial zone downhill. At the upper level, the splendor

Tossa's Vila Valla is the only remaining fortified town along the Catalan coast.

of this luxury home is still evident in the exquisite mosaics and stuccos, fine thermal baths, and winter dining room. At the lower level, workshops, grain houses, and storerooms supported the farm's primary activities: cultivating vines and producing wine.

It's a short visit, but a fine opportunity to contemplate the many civilizations that have walked these shores. To discover more about the villa's everyday life, visit the Municipal Museum (Museu Municipal de Tossa de Mar; Plaça Roig i Soler, 1; 97/234-0905; 10am-8pm daily; €3), where many artifacts uncovered here are on display, including pottery, coins, and elegant marble sculptures.

BEACHES

Tossa de Mar has three urban beaches, and many more nearby.

Platja Gran

The main beach in Tossa de Mar, Platja Gran, lies in front of the downtown area and is overlooked by the fortified headland at its southern tip. At 400 meters long and 60 meters wide (1,300 by 200 feet), it is a generous-sized, blue-flag beach with all the usual facilities. A promenade lined with restaurants runs behind the crescent-shaped beach. Parking nearby is scarce.

Platja de la Mar Menuda

Located at the opposite end of town to Platja Gran, La Mar Menuda is a smaller blue-flag beach. At its northern tip, there is a rocky outcrop that surrounds a small cove, which is shallow, calm, and ideal for families. The beach is also popular with divers; there are walk-in dive sites just offshore.

Platja d'es Codolar

This beautiful sandy cove is a pleasant surprise hidden behind the fortified old town. Access it by ducking through a tiny doorway in the ancient walls at Plaça Pintor Roig Soler, or walk along Carrer del Portal.

CALAS NORTH OF TOSSA DE MAR

To reach these beautiful coves just north of Tossa, take the GI-682 toward Sant Feliu for 4 kilometers (2.5 miles), following signs for "Camping Pola." There is also a ferry service from Tossa de Mar. Fondo Cristal (Platja Gran; 97/234-2229; www.fondocristal.com) offers regular glass-bottomed boat services (€17 round trip) to Cala Pola and Cala Giverola. It operates from April to October, with boats leaving approximately every hour between 10am and 4pm (every half hour until 6:30pm in high season). You can walk from one of these *calas* to the other in about 30 minutes, but the walk does go along the main road.

Cala Pola

This tiny sheltered cove is located along a spectacular, windy stretch of coast, just north of Tossa de Mar. Pine and oak forests surround crystal-clear waters to create a natural swimming pool with a family atmosphere.

Cala Giverola

Cala Giverola is bigger but equally as beautiful as its neighbor, Cala Pola. A family-friendly resort with plenty of facilities curves around the shores of Giverola.

RECREATION
DIVING
Raya's Diving Center

Avinguda de Catalunya, 21; 97/234-1147;
www.rayasdiving.com; 9am-6pm

Paco Raya knows the seabed around Tossa like the back of his hand, and is happy to share his knowledge. Raya's offers dives throughout the year by boat or from the shore (subject to weather conditions), as well as a wide range of recreational and professional PADI courses. There are several walk-in dive sites close to the shore in Tossa, which is reassuring for beginners. Three walk-in dives start at €55 (tank and guide included).

FOOD
SEAFOOD
La Cuina de Can Simon

Carrer del Portal, 24; 97/234-1269;
www.restaurantcansimon.com; 1pm-3:30pm,
8pm-10:30pm Tues.-Sun. (closed Tues. in
winter); €28-€48, tasting menus €68/€98

The Lores brothers have been awarded a Michelin star for their take on Catalan cuisine at La Cuina de Can Simon. Originally a fisherman's bar opened by their grandparents just outside the medieval walls, the classic decor speaks of another era, but the artistically presented plates are bang up-to-date. True to the town's fishing tradition, the focus is on fish and seafood—fresh, seasonal, and locally sourced; think urchins, lobster, and cava prawn cocktail.

Can Pini

Carrer del Portal, 12; 97/234-0297;
www.canpini.com; Tues.-Sun. 1pm-4pm,
7pm-11pm; €16.50-€50; set menu €26.50
(lunchtime and evenings before 8:30pm)

Can Pini is a family-run seafood restaurant serving traditional Catalan fare. This is the place to try an authentic seafood paella, salt-crusted sea bass, or the local specialty, *cim i tomba* (monkfish, turbot, and potato stew), though it's not cheap. Inside, there are two dining rooms adorned with paintings by local artists, while the delightful terrace is full of atmosphere. The same family also runs the nearby Braseria Pini, which offers grilled meats and pizza (Carrer del Pont Vell, 5; 97/234-2208; www.canpini.com; 12:30pm-3:30pm, 7pm-10:30pm; €7.50-€30).

BARS AND NIGHTLIFE
Vila Vella Terraza Bar

Passeig de Vila Vella, 4; 97/234-0288;
www.vilavellabartossa.es; Jun.-Sept.
11am-5pm, 7pm-3am daily;
Oct.-May weekends only

An unrivalled spot within the medieval fortifications, the Vila Vella Terraza Bar has the best views in town. Open day and night, it's a shady spot for an afternoon glass of sangria en route to the lighthouse, and come evening time, laid-back cocktails, live music, and twinkling lanterns turn up the romance factor. Tapas are available, too. Prices are reasonable given its privileged location.

ACCOMMODATIONS
Hotel Diana

Plaça Espanya, 6; 97/234-1886; www.
hotelesdante.com; €222 d; open Apr.-Oct.

Hotel Diana's beachfront location is hard to beat. A Modernista mansion built in 1906, its distinctive sea-facing façade overlooks a glorious terrace where breakfast is served, while inside, an air of early-20th-century glamor sweeps through the interiors. Each of the 21 guest rooms is unique and recently renovated; doubles, triples, and stunning four-person suites are available. Go for a sea view.

TOP FESTIVALS ON THE COSTA BRAVA

Besides the regional and national holidays, each town along the Costa Brava celebrates two more public holidays, usually in honor of local patrons. For the towns covered in this book, the local holidays are as follows: Tossa de Mar, January 22 (Sant Vicenç, Tossa's patron saint) and June 29 (Saint Peter and Saint Paul); Calella de Palafrugell, Whitmonday and July 19; Begur, Whitmonday and June 29; Cadaqués, Ash Wednesday and December 18 (Santa Esperança). There are also many cultural festivals and events throughout the year along the coast, particularly in summer.

JANUARY
New Year's Day, Cap De Creus
People from all over the world gather at the Cap de Creus lighthouse, the easternmost point of the Iberian Peninsula, to see the first sunrise of the New Year. Locals dance *sardanes*, and there's hot chocolate for everyone.

JULY AND AUGUST
La Cantada de Habaneras, Calella de Palafrugell
Habaneras are sea shanties that originated in 19th-century Cuba, and were held dearly by those who emigrated there from Catalonia. During summer, these nostalgic lilts are recited up and down the Costa Brava, with the most famous festival taking place in Calella de Palafrugell on the first Saturday in July. In true sailor style, the songs are accompanied with the drinking of *cremat* (burnt rum). The main event takes place in Plaça Port Bo, where a temporary stage and stand is constructed and boats gather. Tickets (€30-€35) go on sale in May. For more information, see www.havanerescalella.cat.

Cap Roig Music Festival, Calella de Palafrugell
A-list stars perform in the magical, seafront setting of Cap Roig at this open-air music festival—the most important of its kind on the Costa Brava. From mid-July until mid-August, just over 2,000 spectators gather nearly every night to witness a stellar lineup play in the spectacular botanical gardens; Sting, Elton John, Andrea Bocelli, and Bob Dylan have all appeared in recent years. Prices vary depending on the show, and tickets often sell out months in advance. For more information, see caproigfestival.com.

Boutique Hotel Casa Granados
Carrer de la Roqueta, 10-12; 97/234-3536; www.hotelcasagranados.com; €278 d; open Apr.-Oct.

A world away from Tossa's touristy downtown, this charming boutique hotel is situated in a quiet, uphill area. The 200-year-old former home of Catalan pianist Enrique Granados offers seven beautifully appointed rooms, with exposed stone, wooden beams, and original features. Downstairs, the sophisticated restaurant serves contemporary cuisine, but the spectacular terraced gardens and swimming pool behind the hotel steal the show.

INFORMATION AND SERVICES

TOURIST INFORMATION
The tourist information center in Tossa de Mar is located next to the bus station (Av. del Pelegrí, 25, Edifici La Nau; 97/234-0108; www.infotossa.com; Nov.-Mar. Mon.-Sat. 9:30am-2pm, 4pm-7pm, Apr.-May and Oct. Mon.-Sat. 10am-2pm, 4pm-7:30pm, Sun. 10am-2pm, Jun.-Sept. Mon.-Sat. 9am-9pm, Sun. 10am-2pm, 5pm-8pm). During summer there is an additional information point on Avinguda de sa Palma, next to the main beach.

POLICE
The municipal police station (**Policia Local**) is located opposite the tourist

Festival Castell de Peralada, Peralada
Set in the gardens of the medieval castle of Peralada (1-hour drive from Begur and Cadaqués), this series of al fresco concerts is dedicated to classical music, opera, and dance, taking place on summer nights throughout July and August. The festival attracts renowned international acts, and also includes some jazz and pop performances. Past performers include Montserrat Caballé, Plácido Domingo, José Carreras, Sara Baras, Woody Allen, Norah Jones, and Dionne Warwick.

Festival de Música Begur
A low-key, affordable festival that has been bringing live music to Begur for over 40 years. Performances cover a wide variety of styles—pop, rock, jazz, soul, classical—held in various venues around town on Fridays in July and August. Some events require tickets. For more information, see www.festivalbegur.cat.

Festival Internacional de Música de Cadaqués
One of the oldest music festivals in Catalonia, the Cadaqués Music Festival offers a wide range of concerts and activities in emblematic spaces across town, including the Church of Santa Maria. For more information, see www.festivalcadaques.cat.

SEPTEMBER
Fira d'Indians de Begur
On the first weekend in September, Begur celebrates its Cuban connections, which date back to a wave of emigration in the 19th century. During the festival, markets, music, costume dress, traditional crafts, and cultural activities come together to celebrate the legacy of those who returned home from the Americas and transformed Begur forever.

Festa Major de Cadaqués
Coinciding with Catalonia's national day (week of September 11), Cadaqués celebrates the final days of summer with its annual local festival, which includes *habaneras* (sea shanties), *sardana* dancing, a *llagut* (catboat) regatta, a "dolls" race (a doll is a traditional jug carried on the head), music, street parties, fireworks, and general merriment.

office in Tossa de Mar (Av. del Pelegrí, 14; 97/234-0135). The nearest regional police station is in Lloret de Mar (**Mossos d'Esquadra**; 97/236-8888; Carrer de Francesc Cambó, 43).

HOSPITALS AND PHARMACIES
For emergencies, the nearest hospital is the **Hospital Comarcal de Blanes,** 16 kilometers (10 miles) away (Accés de la Cala Sant Francesc, 5, Blanes; 97/235-3264; www.salutms.org). For less urgent medical needs, visit the primary care center, the **Centre d'Atenció Primària (CAP)**, in Tossa de Mar (Av. Catalunya; 97/234-1828; Mon.-Fri. 8am-8pm).

There are four pharmacies in Tossa de Mar. **Farmàcia Castelló Cugat** (Avinguda de Ferràn Agulló, 12; 97/234-1303), **Farmàcia Arbussé** (Carrer la Guàrdia, 19; 97/234-0388), **Farmàcia Maria Carmen Lores** (Carrer Enric Granados, 1-9; 97/234-1172), and **Farmàcia Parés** (Rambla Pau Casals, 12; 97/234-0208). To find out which one is on duty after hours, check the notice posted on the door of each pharmacy or visit www.cofgi.org/farmacies/farmacies-de-guardia.

GETTING THERE
The quickest and easiest way to get to Tossa de Mar is by car.

PAELLA

seafood paella

Paella is a rice dish originating in Valencia and is often considered Spain's national dish. In Spain itself it is thought of as a Valencian tradition, though it has been adapted across the country. The original recipe (Valencian) consists of rice, green beans, meat (normally chicken and rabbit), and sometimes snails and artichokes, although perhaps the most well-known variety today is seafood paella, which swaps meat for mussels, prawns, clams, and more.

Named after the large, shallow pan in which it is prepared, paella is cooked with olive oil and flavored with parsley, garlic, and saffron. Spanish cooks start by making a basic *sofregit*—a sauce composed of tomatoes, onion, and olive oil—adding vegetables, seafood, rice, and fish stock, though every household has its own take.

Paella is designed to share, always made to order, and normally requires a two-person minimum. Though traditionally it was eaten straight from the pan, waiters in restaurants normally present the whole paella to the diners, and then take it away to divide it into portions.

Here are some recommendations for where to order paella:

SITGES

- **Fragata:** Excellent price-quality ratio in a superb location, set back from the seafront promenade (page 184).

- **Can Laury Peix:** Bright, elegant spot with a fabulous portside terrace on the edge of the marina (page 184).

TARRAGONA

- **El Llagut:** Cozy seafood restaurant in a pleasant old town square (page 227).

COSTA BRAVA

- **Can Pini:** Authentic and atmospheric family-run restaurant serving local cuisine (page 273).

- **Fiego:** Beachfront seafood dining at its best: simple, fresh, inexpensive, and wonderfully executed (page 282).

- **Toc Al Mar** on Platja d'Aiguablava: Incredibly tasty paella cooked in a wood-fired oven, overlooking the beautiful bay of Aiguablava (page 291).

AVA GARDNER IN TOSSA DE MAR

You might be surprised to find a statue of glamorous star **Ava Gardner** peering longingly over Tossa from the Vila Vella. In 1951, she starred alongside **James Mason** in *Pandora and the Flying Dutchman,* which was filmed in Tossa de Mar, and marked the beginning of Gardner's lifelong affection for Spain. She brought her whirlwind Hollywood lifestyle with her, having an affair with Spanish co-star and matador **Mario Cabré** while being pursued across the Atlantic by her lover, and future husband, **Frank Sinatra**. Tossa took her to its heart, and erected the sculpture (by sculptor Ció Abellí) in 1998, almost 50 years after the film was released.

statue of Ava Gardner

CAR

From Barcelona, drive northeast on the **AP-7** highway. Exit the AP-7 at junction 9A-9B onto the **C-35** toward Vidreres, Lloret de Mar, and Tossa de Mar. From here, there are two options to get to Tossa: exit the C35 at junction 84, and follow the **C-63** toward Lloret de Mar, then the **GI-682** from Lloret to Tossa; or follow the C-35 toward Llagostera, exiting at junction 94 onto the **GI-681**, which takes you over the mountains to Tossa. The latter is normally slightly quicker. The drive takes approximately 1 hour and 20 minutes (107 km/66 mi).

Alternately, take the **C-32** motorway or the **N-II** national road toward Blanes and the Costa Brava. Turn off onto the **GI-600,** then follow the **GI-682** through Lloret de Mar to Tossa de Mar. This route is shorter (91 km/576 mi) but can take longer. Both the AP-7 and C-32 are toll roads (€6-€7).

Parking is plentiful in Tossa, although mostly outside of the town center. There are three free car parks on the outskirts of town, and several more costing between €5 and €12 per day, all of which are within 10-15 minutes walk of the seafront. The more central the car park, the more expensive (up to €42 per day); parking near the beach is nearly impossible. For on-street parking, white and green zones are free (except green on Thursdays); pay at the meter in blue zones.

BUS

From Barcelona, **Sarfa** (90/230-2025; www.sarfa.com) runs regular services to Tossa de Mar from the **Estació del Nord** bus station (1.5 hours; €9.90), some of which originate at **Barcelona-El Prat Airport.** There are 13 daily buses in summer (Jul.-mid-Sept.), and eight the rest of the year. In summer, the first service departs from Estació del Nord at 7:45am, and the last one departs at 12:25am. Otherwise, the first and last services depart at 8:45am and 8:30pm, respectively.

GETTING AROUND

Tossa de Mar is one of the larger towns along the coast. It is perfectly walkable, although there is a rather steep climb up to the lighthouse.

TAXI

There is a taxi stand in front of the tourist information center (Av. El Pelegrí, 25; 97/234-0549 or 97/234-3333; www.taxi-tossa.com).

TOURIST TRAIN

Run by Dicotren (97/234-0241; www.dicotren.com; €6), there are two train routes in Tossa: One loops around the whole town (Bus Station, Beach Promenade, Av. la Palma, Mar Menuda, Av. Joan Maragall, Rbla. Pau Casals, Bus Station; 45 minutes), while the other runs between the beach promenade and the lighthouse (5-10 minutes; every 45 minutes; Mar.-Oct.).

LEAVING TOSSA DE MAR

In summer, the last bus back to Barcelona from Tossa de Mar leaves at 7:40pm, though there are two night buses (2:20am, 4:40am). The rest of the year, the last bus to Barcelona leaves at 6:55pm. For onward travel to Girona or along the Costa Brava, change bus at Llagostera or Lloret de Mar (Sagalés; 97/221-3227; www.sagales.com or Pujol i Pujol; 97/236-4476; www.transpujol.com). There is a direct bus to Girona during summer.

Calella de Palafrugell

The old fishing village of Calella de Palafrugell, a 50-minute drive from Tossa, is strung along a rocky coastline dotted with tiny coves, from the headland of Cap Roig right round to Llafranc, the neighboring bay. Whitewashed fisher's houses with terracotta-tiled roofs curve around the crooked shoreline, embodying a rare, antiquated charm that has long since disappeared in many areas of the coast. Popular with the upper echelons of Catalan society, there's a constant buzz on Calella's tiny beaches come summer, yet it still feels like you've stumbled upon a hidden gem that retains a quaint, traditional spirit.

SIGHTS

JARDÍNS DE CAP ROIG
(Cap Roig Botanical Gardens)

Camí del Rus; 97/261-4582; obrasociallacaixa.org; Apr.-Sept. 10am-8pm daily (but only until 4pm during the festival),

Oct.-Mar. 10am-6pm daily, Jan.-Feb. weekends only; €8/€3 students and over 65s/free under 16s

Exiled Russian colonel Nicola Woevodsky and his aristocratic English wife, Dorothy Webster, chose the headland of Cap Roig, a natural beauty spot just south of Calella de Palafrugell, to create their own slice of paradise on the shores of the Mediterranean.

The couple created these botanical gardens in 1927. At the highest point they built a castle, where they spent the rest of their lives together. Woevodsky, who had a keen interest in architecture, designed the neo-medieval mansion while the lush gardens that surround the castle are the legacy of Webster, a gardening enthusiast. The gardens feature one thousand botanical species from all over the world. Bougainvillea-scented trails, colorful terrace gardens, and palm tree-lined

Calella de Palafrugell

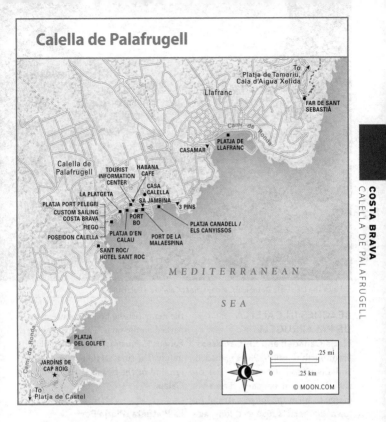

paths wind around the rocky headland, occasionaly revealing spectacular views of the surrounding coastline.

When the couple died, the estate was passed on to the "la Caixa" Foundation, which introduced contemporary sculptures from Spanish and international artists, and continues to maintain the park today. Every summer, a star-studded line-up of musicians performs here during the prestigious Cap Roig Music Festival.

The gardens make a splendid half-day visit, and are at their best in springtime. There's a children's playground and a picnic area, but no refreshments, so come prepared. It can be accessed on foot along the coastal path from Calella de Palafrugell. Ample free parking is available for motorists.

BEACHES AND CALAS

Half a dozen sandy coves sit on Calella's rocky shores, like jewels scattered between craggy outcrops. Connected by coastal paths and lined by traditional houses, it's hard to imagine a quainter Mediterranean scene. Most of the beaches have basic facilities, though space is limited. There are larger beaches nearby—the adjacent horseshoe-bay of Llafranc or Tamariu are great alternatives.

cliffs of the Cap Roig Botanical Gardens, near Calella de Palafrugell

BEACHES IN CALELLA DE PALAFRUGELL

Platja Canadell and Els Canyissos

From north to south, Platja Canadell and Els Canyissos are the first of Calella's urban beaches. The two merge to form the longest strand in town, 200 meters (650 feet) long, accessed via steps. From here, it's a 15-minute walk around the headland to Llafranc.

Port de la Malaespina, Port Bo, and Platja d'en Calau

The next three beaches are essentially one stretch of sand, divided into three areas by rocky outcrops along the shore. This is the most central and busiest beach in town, lined by the seafront promenade, which passes through Calella's emblematic white-porticoed buildings (*voltes*). The first section is Port de la Malaespina, a narrow beach, just 10 meters (33 feet) wide. The middle section, Port Bo, is 100 meters (330 feet) long and is also known as Platja de les Barques due to

the many fishing boats that are often parked on the sand. This is where the famous *Habaneras* festival takes place in July. The final section at the southern end of the beach is Platja d'en Calau.

La Platgeta, Platja Port Pelegri, and Sant Roc

Following the bay around to the south, the next three beaches are small coves cut into the rocks as the land starts to rise toward the headland, and all are accessed by steps. La Platgeta is a small, sandy cove, tucked away between two rocky protrusions. Next up, Platja Port Pelegri is probably the prettiest urban beach in Calella, where old boathouses sit behind golden sands, and clear waters attract snorkeling and diving enthusiasts. It is also one of the more spacious, measuring 75 meters by 30 meters (250 by 100 feet). Finally, Sant Roc (also known as Els Canyers) is a tiny, rocky cove that is good for swimming.

BEACHES AND *CALAS* NORTH OF CALELLA DE PALAFRUGELL

Platja de Llafranc

This beach has a generous stretch of sand in the horseshoe-shaped bay of Llafranc, with a marina at its northern tip. It is situated just north, and within walking distance, of Calella de Palafrugell.

Platja de Tamariu

A sheltered, crescent-shaped stretch of sand in the tiny whitewashed resort of Tamariu, lined with cafés, fish restaurants, and a promenade. Smaller than Llafranc and popular with families.

Cala d'Aigua Xelida

Pine-clad cliffs conceal Cala d'Aigua Xelida, a hidden gem that is only accessible on foot from Tamariu (1.5 km/1 mi). The beach is tiny, but the turquoise waters are ideal for swimming and snorkeling.

CALAS SOUTH OF CALELLA DE PALAFRUGELL

Platja del Golfet

Heading south from Calella de Palafrugell, a half hour ramble along the coastal Camí de Ronda path leads to this incredible cove, where red rock walls plummet into clear waters that reveal a smooth, pebbly seabed. Come prepared, as there are no facilities.

Platja de Castell

Saved from development in the 1990s, this unspoiled beach exudes natural beauty, with golden sands, clear waters, and the ancient ruins of an Iberian settlement nearby. This beach is a 20-minute drive south of Calella de Palafrugell.

RECREATION

DIVING AND SNORKELING

Poseidon Calella

Platja Port Pelegrí; 97/261-5345; www.poseidoncalella.com; Apr.-Oct. 9am-6pm daily

With almost 50 years of experience in diving on the Costa Brava, Poseidon is an institution. Located on the beach in Calella, it offers a great range of dives for all levels, from the walk-in "try dives" for first-timers (€60-€90), to the spectacular Ullastres, Furió Fitó, and Boreas wreck dive sites (€12-€35). The center offers a full range of PADI certifications, including an e-learning option that allows you to complete the theory in advance. There are also daily snorkeling trips in summer, suitable for all the family (www.poseidonboat-tours.com; 2 hours; €20/€15 under 12s).

SAILING

Custom Sailing Costa Brava

Platja Port Pelegrí; 63/561-5172; www.customsailingcb.com; Thurs. 11:30am-4:30pm, Fri. 11:30am-6pm, Sat.-Sun. 11am-6pm

Some of the best bits of the Costa Brava are only accessible from the sea, and Custom Sailing's fleet of small boats can take you there. Based in an old boathouse along Platja Port Pelegrí, the company offers boat rentals, with or without skipper (from €185), boat trips, on-board gastronomy, sport fishing, wakeboarding, waterskiing, and paddle surfing.

FOOD

SPANISH AND CATALAN

Sa Jambina

Carrer Bofill i Codina, 21; 97/261-4613; sajambina@hotmail.es; Tues.-Sun. 1:30pm-3:30pm, Fri.-Sat. 8:30pm-10:15pm; €22

Prepare for an authentic taste of the Mediterranean at Sa Jambina, a

DIVING ON THE COSTA BRAVA

scuba diving off the Medes Islands

The Costa Brava's rugged coastline extends well below sea level. Sharp cliffs, shipwrecks, colored coral, and more than 600 species of fauna—from groupers, eels, and octopuses to barracudas and eagle rays—inhabit these spectacular underwater landscapes. With excellent weather, good visibility, and a diverse world of Mediterranean marine life to discover, some of Spain's best diving opportunities can be found along the coast. There are dives to suit all levels, from introductory sessions to wreck and night diving, and with water temperatures ranging from 12.8ºC in winter to 20.8ºC in summer (55ºF-70ºF), it's possible to dive year-round with a wetsuit. More than 34 dive schools operate in the area, together forming the **Association of Diving Centers on the Costa Brava** (www.submarinismocostabrava. com), which is an excellent source of information. Here are some of the best sites for diving:

first-rate seafood restaurant that uses fresh, local ingredients. Located one block from the beach, traditional flavors, fresh ideas, and great wines make for an almighty feast, Spanish style. The oven-baked fish and rice dishes are the specialty here. It's not cheap, but the quality is outstanding. Leave room for dessert.

✪ Fiego

Platja Port-Pelegrí; 97/261-5996; open Easter-Oct. Fri.-Sat. 10am-1am, Sun.-Thurs. (except Tues.) 10am-7pm; €15

Fiego is traditional beachfront dining at its best: simple, fresh, and wonderfully executed, from grilled fish, mussels, and clams to Basque-style hake and (the highlight) seafood paella. It's a casual, no-frills joint, popular with local families and full of life, with a combination of quality, service, and price that is hard to beat. Reserve and ask for a table on the terrace. For lunch, this means adding your name to the chalkboard when you arrive in the morning.

✪ ILLES MEDES

Level: All levels
Dive school: La Sirena, L'Estartit

Located a mile off the coast of L'Estartit, the Medes Islands archipelago consists of seven uninhabited islets and forms part of the Montgrí, Medes Islands, and Baix Ter Natural Park—one of the most important marine reserves in the western Mediterranean. Dives of varying depths are possible here, with different scenery and marine life to appreciate at each level. The limestone archipelago is also known for its caves and tunnels, although extreme care must be taken in those areas. The largest shipwreck along the Costa Brava, the Reggio Messina, lies close by, and at 28 to 35 meters (92 to 115 feet) is suitable for experienced divers only.

ULLASTRES

Level: All levels
Dive school: Poseidon, Calella de Palafrugell

Two miles off the coast of Llafranc, three underwater mountains start at 8 meters (26 feet) below sea level and reach down to 45 meters (148 feet). Groupers, scorpion fish, and moray eels can be spotted amid colorful gorgonians on the slopes, coves, and passageways of this site.

FURIÓ FITÓ

Level: Experienced
Dive school: Poseidon, Calella de Palafrugell

This submerged massif is one of the Mediterranean's most stunning underwater rock formations. Situated off the Begur headland, its tip is 14 meters (46 feet) below the surface, dropping down to 55 meters (180 feet). Octopus, snapper, lobsters, rays, and sunfish inhabit this colorful wall.

CAP DE CREUS

Level: Experienced
Dive school: Sotamar, Cadaqués

A mountainous underwater landscape lies below sea level around Cap de Creus, where the Pyrenees meet the Mediterranean. The small island of **Massa d'Or** (also known as *Sa Rata*), off the eastern tip of the headland, is the area's most spectacular dive site, with excellent visibility and schools of barracuda. Due to its exposed location and strong currents, it is only suitable for experienced divers, but there are plenty of easier options nearby.

FINE DINING
Casamar

Carrer del Nero, 3, Llafranc; 97/230-0104; hotelcasamar.net; open Easter-Dec.

Tues.-Sat. 1pm-4pm, 8pm-11pm; €19-€38, set menu €52, tasting menu €82

Fine dining is a family affair at Casamar, a Michelin-starred hotel restaurant in Llafranc. Chef Quim Casellas (whose parents own the hotel) presents his take on modern Mediterranean cuisine, from leek cannelloni with prawns to sea cucumber with pil-pil and black truffle. The beautiful setting overlooking the bay tops off the experience. Reserve in advance and ask for a table on the terrace.

BARS AND NIGHTLIFE
Habana Café

Plaça Sant Pere

Situated on the corner of the charming Plaça Sant Pere, Habana Café is a classic hangout for after-dinner drinks, with a terrace that's buzzing until late. Both the name and the delicious mojitos celebrate the Costa Brava's Cuban connections.

3 Pins

Carrer dels Tres Pins; 97/261-4603;
open Easter-Sept. 11am-midnight daily

For a sundowner as evening draws in, 3 Pins occupies the perfect spot. Perched on one of Calella's rocky outcrops, the bar's extensive terrace stretches out beneath three large pine trees (hence the name), as waves crash against the craggy shoreline. Settle in and enjoy the view—service can be slow.

ACCOMMODATIONS

Hotel Sant Roc

Plaça Atlàntic, 2; 97/261-4250;
www.santroc.com; €132 d; three-night
minimum stay; open mid-Jun.-mid-Sept.

Founded in 1955, Sant Roc was one of the first hotels on the Costa Brava. Now run by the third generation of the same family, this welcoming seafront hotel still boasts one of the most splendid locations in the area, with stunning views over the bay of Calella de Palafrugell. The 45 guest rooms are simple but charming—a sea view is a must—and breakfast on the cliff-top, pine-shaded terrace is pretty special.

Casa Calella

Carrer de Codina, 14; 60/812-0601;
casacalella.com; €160 d; four-night
minimum stay

A restored 19th-century house with heaps of charm, Casa Calella sits on the quiet Plaça Església, in the heart of the old fishing village. Simple, elegant decor complements the building's historic charm throughout this boutique guesthouse, which has four spacious guest rooms—two doubles, two suites (2-4 people)—and a relaxing garden, where breakfast is served under a lemon tree. It's just a 5-minute walk to the beach, and nothing is too much trouble for the gracious host, Javier.

Far de Sant Sebastià

Passeig de Pau Casals, 64; 97/230-1639;
www.hotelelfar.com; €220 d

Boundless sea views stretch to the horizon before this clifftop boutique escape. Located next to the lighthouse of Sant Sebastià in Llafranc, nine nautical-style guest rooms are housed within an 18th-century complex, which also includes a hermitage and traditional restaurant, oriented around a charming courtyard. Guests can choose between a sea or landscape view (go for a sea-view room with private terrace) and make use of the exclusive spa at Mas de Torrent Hotel (20-minute drive inland). It's a steep climb from Llafranc, best reached by car.

INFORMATION AND SERVICES

TOURIST INFORMATION

The tourist information center in Calella de Palafrugell is located on the edge of Plaça Port Bo, close to the seafront (Carrer de les Voltes, 4; 97/261-4475; www.visitpalafrugell.cat, turisme@palafrugell.cat; Easter and Oct. Mon.-Sat. 10am-1pm, 4pm-7pm, Sun. 10am-1pm, Apr.-May Sat. 10am-1pm, 4pm-7pm, Sun. 10am-1pm, Jun. and Sept. Mon.-Sat. 10am-1pm, 5pm-8pm, Sun. 10am-1pm, Jul.-Aug. 10am-1pm, 5pm-8pm daily, closed mid-Oct.-Easter).

The main tourist information center in the area is located in Palafrugell and is open throughout the year (Avinguda Generalitat, 33; 97/230-0228; www.visitpalafrugell.cat, turisme@palafrugell.cat; mid-Oct.-Easter Mon.-Fri. 10am-5pm, Sat. 10am-1pm, 4pm-7pm, Sun. 9:30am-1:30pm, Easter-mid-Oct. Mon.-Sat. 10am-1pm, 4pm-7pm, Sun. 9:30am-1:30pm, Jul.-Aug. Mon.-Sat. 10am-8pm, Sun.

9:30am-1:30pm). There are also seasonal information points in Llafranc and Tamariu.

POLICE

The nearest police station is in Palafrugell, where the municipal police station (Policia Local; Avinguda de García Lorca, 31; 97/230-6292) is located next door to the regional police (Mossos d'Esquadra; Avinguda de García Lorca, 20; 97/230-8118). To report a theft, contact the Mossos d'Esquadra. During high season, there is also police presence on the beaches.

HOSPITALS AND PHARMACIES

For emergencies, the Hospital de Palamós (Carrer Hospital, 36, Palamós; 97/260-0160; open 24 hours) is a 20-minute drive away (12 kilometers/7.5 miles). For less urgent medical needs, visit the primary care center, the Centre d'Atenció Primària (CAP), in Palafrugell (Carrer Àngel Guimerà, 6; 97/261-0607; 24 hours).

There is one pharmacy in Calella de Palafrugell—Farmàcia Frigola (Carrer de Pirroig, 23; 97/261-5859; Mon-Sat. 9:30am-1:30pm, 5pm-8pm, Sun. 9am-2pm)—and several more in the surrounding towns. During off hours, one of the pharmacies in Palafrugell is always on call; visit www.cofgi.org/farmacies/farmacies-de-guardia for more information.

LUGGAGE STORAGE

Luggage storage is available at the bus station in Palafrugell (€1.40 all day; Mon.-Fri. 7am-12:15pm, 4pm-6:45pm).

WIFI

There is a free public WiFi network in Palafrugell (Ajuntament.Palafrugell),

but not in Calella itself. Most hotels offer free WiFi.

GETTING THERE

The quickest and easiest way to get to Calella de Palafrugell is by car.

CAR

From Barcelona, drive northeast on the AP-7 highway. Exit the AP-7 at junction 9A-9B onto the C-35 toward Sant Feliu de Guíxols and Platja d'Aro. After Llagostera, the road merges with the C-65, and then the C-31, in the direction of Palamós. Exit the C-31 at Junction 331. Continue straight over two roundabouts, then take the first exit at the third roundabout onto the GI-654 (Avinguda de Palafrugell), following signs for Calella de Palafrugell. Three more roundabouts follow: at the first roundabout, take the first exit onto Avinguda d'Espanya. At the second roundabout, continue straight (second exit), and at the third, take the first exit onto the GIV-6546, and continue to Calella. The drive takes approximately 1 hour and 35 minutes (125 km/78 mi).

In Calella, there is a public multistory car park on the corner of Carrer de Chopitea and Avinguda d'Antoni J. Rovira (Carrer de Chopitea, 29; €0.025 per minute, €12 per day; 10am-midnight daily, summer only), and two open-air car parks at the junction of Carrer de la Costa del Tarongers and Avinguda d'Antoni J. Rovira. Blue zones indicate on-street meter parking (Passeig de la Torre, Plaça de les Teranyines, Carrer del Port Pelegrí).

BUS

From Barcelona, Sarfa (90/230-2025; www.sarfa.com) runs regular services to Palafrugell from the Estació del Nord bus station (2-2.5 hours;

€9.60), some of which originate at Barcelona-El Prat Airport. There are seven daily buses throughout the year, with up to 19 daily services during the busiest weeks of summer. The first service departs from Estació del Nord at 8:30am (7:30am in summer), and the last one departs at 8:15pm (12:25am in summer). To reach Calella de Palafrugell, it is necessary to change to a local bus (line 6) in Palafrugell, or get a taxi—it's just 5 kilometers (3 miles). There is a taxi stand outside the Palafrugell bus station, or reservations can be made in advance.

GETTING AROUND

Calella de Palafrugell is little more than a village, best explored on foot. Nearby beaches and sights can also be reached on foot, following the Camí de Ronda coastal path, although public transport is available during peak season.

PUBLIC TRANSIT

Sarfa runs a local bus service between Palafrugell, Calella de Palafrugell, Llafranc, and Tamariu. During summer there are up to 20 services per day (4-5 during winter), taking approximately 15-20 minutes. From July to September, there is also a sightseeing bus, known as Julivia, that runs along the coast, facilitating easy access to the area's most emblematic points. This service starts and ends in Palafrugell, stopping at Cala Golfet, Cap Roig, Calella, Llafranc, and Tamariu en route. The full loop takes 90 minutes, and there are six services per day (€5).

TAXI

There are several taxi firms that operate a 24-hour, year-round service in the area, including airport transfers and minibuses. Try Taxi Palafrugell (60/951-1071; www.taxipalafrugell.com), Taxis Costa Brava (65/993-6772; www.taxis-costabrava.com), or Taxis Europa (63/913-2633 or 66/950-2809; ww.taxiseuropa.com). Reservations can be made by telephone or online.

LEAVING CALELLA DE PALAFRUGELL

The last bus back to Palafrugell leaves Calella de Palafrugell at 5:30pm in winter and 8:15pm in summer. From Palafrugell it is possible to connect to buses traveling across the Costa Brava, Girona, and Barcelona. The last bus back to Barcelona from Palafrugell leaves at 6:30pm in winter and 9:15pm in summer.

Cap de Begur

To Platja de Pals, Aiguamolls, Del Baix Empordà, and La Sirena

Sa Punta

PLATJA DEL RACÓ

Illa Roja

ILLA ROJA / CALA MORETA

Cala del Rei

SA RIERA

Sa Riera

S'Antiga

Port des Pi

La Coma

Aiguafreda

AIGUAFREDA

SA TUNA

Sa Tuna

CARRETERA DE SA RIERA

SEE "BEGUR" MAP

Begur

GIV-6535

GI-653

GIP-6531

Cap de Begur

Camí de Ronda

GIV-6532

★ *BEACHES NEAR BEGUR*

PLATJA FONDA

Fornells

MEDITERRANEAN

FORNELLS

HOTEL AIGUA BLAVA

SEA

PLATJA D'AIGUABLAVA

CALA D'AIGUA XELIDA

0   .25 mi
0   .25 km

© MOON.COM

PLATJA DE TAMARIU

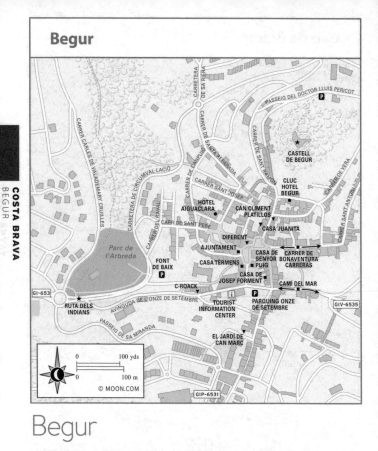

Begur

Map labels:

CARRETERA DE SA RIERA
PASSEIG DEL DOCTOR LLUÍS PERICOT
CASTELL DE BEGUR
CARRER CARLES DE VALDEMARY CRUÏLLES
CARRER DE CAMPING
CARRER DE SANTA REPARADA
CARRER DE SANT RAMON
CARRER DE VERA
CLUC HOTEL BEGUR
CARRETERA DE CIRCUMVAL·LACIÓ
CARRER SANT JOSEP
HOTEL AIGUACLARA
CAN CLIMENT PLATILLOS
CARRER SANT ANTONI
CARRER DE BRAVA
CARR DE SANT PERE
DIFERENT
CASA JUANITA
Parc de l'Arbreda
AJUNTAMENT
CASA DE SENYOR PUIG
CARRER DE BONAVENTURA CARRERAS
FONT DE BAIX
CASA TÈRMENS
CASA DE JOSEP FORMENT
CAMÍ DEL MAR
GI-653
C-ROACK
TOURIST INFORMATION CENTER
PARQUING ONZE DE SETEMBRE
GIV-6535
RUTA DELS INDIANS
AVINGUDA DE L'ONZE DE SETEMBRE
PASSEIG DE SA MIRANDA
EL JARDÍ DE CAN MARC
0 100 yds
0 100 m
© MOON.COM
GIP-6531

Begur

The rugged beauty of the Costa Brava is at its best around the headland of Begur, where jagged cliffs and pine-studded rocky outcrops conceal paradise bays with turquoise waters. This is the chic face of the Costa Brava, where *Modernista* mansions house boutique hideaways and well-to-do *Barceloneses* have their holiday residences. The village itself is a warren of quaint narrow streets, buzzing with holiday spirit around the Plaça de la Vila, while the 11th-century hilltop castle casts a watchful eye over the surrounding county of Baix Empordà and offers superb panoramas of the coast and the Medes Archipelago.

Begur is a 15-minute drive from Palafrugell, or 25 minutes via the scenic coastal road (GIV-6542/GIV-6532).

SIGHTS
RUTA DELS INDIANS
(Walking Route)

www.municipisindians.cat

In the 19th century, scores of emigrants from along the coast set sail for the New World. A plague of phylloxera had hit agricultural crops across Catalonia and times were hard. More than 500 young men from Begur (one quarter of the population at the time) made their way to the Americas, particularly Cuba, in search of a better life.

Known as "indians," many of them found fortune in their new home and, eventually, returned to Begur as wealthy businessmen. They built themselves magnificent, colonial-style mansions, characterized by porticoed galleries and mural paintings, which changed the face of Begur forever. Walk around the center and you will undoubtedly stumble upon their architectural legacy; the following route guides you to the most notable examples.

Start at the Ajuntament (town hall) in Plaça de l'Església, which has a palm tree in the garden and beautiful paintings inside. Detour for a moment to see the Hotel Aiguaclara (Carrer Sant Miquel, 2), known as the Casa Bonaventura Caner i Bataller, which is probably the most majestic of all the *cases indians* of Begur. Head back to the square and notice Casa Térmens (La Fleca bakery), dating from 1869, on the corner opposite the slightly rundown Casa de Senyor Puig (Puig wasn't an "indian" but just liked the style); walk around the side of the building to catch a glimpse of the upstairs portico. Next, pass by the splendid Casa de Josep Forment (Carrer de la Concepcio Pi, 10), en route to Camí del Mar, the best spot from which to view the colonial-style mansions in context. Finally, wander along Carrer de Bonaventura Carreras, where there is a concentration of houses: Casa Josep Pi y Carreras (22), which has an orchard in the garden, Casa Pere Roger (20), which has a double arcade on the rear façade, Mas Carreras (13), Casa de Vicenç Ferrer y Bataller (16), and Casino Cultural (Carrer del Casino, 1). Information plaques accompany the route.

CASTELL DE BEGUR (Begur Castle)

Passeig del Doctor Pericot

Begur's hilltop castle stands proudly above the town. It dates from the early 11th century and was destroyed and rebuilt during the 15th and 16th centuries. It suffered its final ambush during the Napoleonic Wars. Architecturally, there's not much to see at the top, but it's worth the steep, 10-minute climb for the incredible, 360-degree panoramas over land and sea.

✪ BEACHES

The headland of Begur harbors some of the most beautiful coves along the Costa Brava, each with a distinct character and all bursting with natural beauty. Most are tiny bays with a shoreline that descends steeply—something to be aware of with children and non-swimmers. All are within a 10-minute drive of Begur, and during the height of summer, many sun-worshippers arrive early and head home for lunch around 1pm to avoid the midday heat. There's another peak after lunch around 4pm, though bear in mind that most of the beaches are north- or east-facing and are cast into shadow in the early evening. Most beaches have basic facilities, though not all have a lifeguard station.

Driving directions from Begur: To access Aiguablava, Fornells, and Platja Fonda, follow the GIP-6531 and GIV-6532 south from Begur. Arrive early, as parking is limited. To access Sa Tuna and Aiguafreda, follow the GIV-6535 east from Begur.

Peratallada

Fortified medieval villages pepper the landscape of the Baix Empordà county. Crumbling walls, sandstone archways, and cobbled lanes characterize these magical, stone-built hamlets, which are a delight to explore. Of them, Pals and Peratallada are the most visited, and are both within 15 kilometers (9 miles) of Begur. If you like what you see, extend your tour to nearby Palau-sator, Monells, Ullastret, Vulpellac, and Cruïlles.

PALS

The hilltop town of Pals, 6 kilometers (3.7 miles) west of Begur, can be spotted from afar, its historic nucleus presiding over the surrounding pastures, paddy fields, and orchards. This walled town is crowned by the Església de Sant Pere, built between the 10th and 15th centuries, and the 11th-century Torre de les Hores (clock tower), the oldest and best-preserved part of the town's medieval castle. Information plaques guide visitors on a short walking tour around the most emblematic sights of Pals, starting at Ca la Pruna on Carrer de la Creu. A guided tour of the historic quarter in English takes place on Thursday evenings at 8pm throughout July and August (€5). Reserve at the tourist office or visit www.visitpals.com for more information.

PERATALLADA

Meaning "carved stone," Peratallada stays true to its name. Its narrow cobblestone streets and enchanting stone-built architecture bear hardly a trace of the modern world, though it might feel familiar if you're a Kevin Costner fan—some scenes from the 1991 film *Robin Hood: Prince of Thieves* were shot here.

Visitors must park outside the town's walls and explore the fairy-tale village on foot. Follow the beautifully preserved alleys around an 11th-century castle, en route to Plaça de les Voltes—a pretty square, lined by stone archways along one side. Photo opportunities arise every few paces. At the northern tip of the town, pass through one of the town's ancient gateways, Portal de la Virgen; cross the moat and you'll find the 12th-century Romanesque church of Sant Esteve.

A handful of hotels, restaurants, and handicraft boutiques add to the charm. For something sweet, stop by **Cal Tuset** (Plaça de l'Oli, 1B; 97/263-4796; www.caltuset.com), famous for its cupcakes, or cool off with an ice cream from **Gelat Artesà de Peratallada** (Carrer Major, 13; 97/263-4964; www.gelatartesadeperatallada.es; noon-11:30pm daily), which offers an extraordinary array of sweet and savory flavors, including gazpacho and mascarpone with figs.

To access Sa Riera and Illa Roja, follow the Carrer de Sa Riera north from Begur. Illa Roja and Cala Moreta can also be accessed from Platja de Pals via Carretera de la Platja del Racó.

Public transit: From mid-June until mid-September, there are three shuttle-bus routes that connect Begur with the surrounding beaches (€1/€0.50 children aged 5-16 and over 65s). All three originate at Plaça Forga in Begur, outside the pharmacy. Line 1 goes to Sa Riera (every 90 minutes, 10am-8pm), line 2 is for Fornells and Aiguablava (every 90 minutes approx., 10:30am-7:30pm), and line 3 is for Sa Tuna (every 1.5-2 hours, 11am-7pm). All journeys take approximately 15 minutes, and each line includes several stops en route. The return leg commences as soon as the bus arrives at the destination. Visit the tourist information office for details.

Platja d'Aiguablava

Aiguablava is simply beautiful: a perfect cove of soft sand and pine-studded cliffs swooping down to crystalline waters. It's no secret, though, and gets packed in summertime—visit on a weekday or during shoulder season if possible. Toc Al Mar (97/211-3232; www.tocalmar.cat; open daily Mar.-Nov.; €16.80-€39) is an excellent spot for a beachfront paella.

Fornells

The tiny coves of Fornells are difficult to find, hidden amid the creases and folds of the rocky coastline between Aiguablava and Platja Fonda. There are four in total—Cala n'Estasia, Cala Port de ses Orats, Cala d'en Malaret, Cala Port d'Esclanyà—with a mixture of sandy and pebbly shores. Access is via the coastal path, which you can join near Hotel Aigua Blava.

the village of Begur, overlooked by an 11th-century castle

Alternately, snorkel your way from one cove to the next.

Platja Fonda

It's a little tricky to reach Platja Fonda, but its stunning beauty is worth the effort. From the car park, follow a path between the luxury villas that dominate the cliff top, then descend the steps to the grey shingle sand beach. It's east facing and surrounded by cliffs, so go in the morning to make the most of the sun.

Sa Tuna

Old fishermen's houses surround this pretty, stony cove—a welcome discovery at the end of a windy access road. A smaller cove, Cala s'Eixugador, can be reached along the coastal path heading south from Sa Tuna.

Aiguafreda

This little cove is more jetty than beach, and is a popular stop for small boats.

Sa Riera

The most spacious and easily accessible beach on the Begur headland, Sa Riera is a large, crescent-shaped bay with grainy sand, all the usual facilities, a handful of eateries, and a scattering of villas and apartments. On the busiest days of summer, this is the best bet for finding a parking spot and space to enjoy the sun.

Illa Roja/Cala Moreta

Follow the coastal footpath north from Sa Riera and you'll arrive at the nudist beach of Illa Roja and the adjacent Cala Moreta, dominated by a rocky islet just offshore. The view from above is one of the most emblematic images of the Costa Brava. It can also be reached from Platja del Racó/Platja de Pals to the north. No facilities available.

RECREATION

DIVING

La Sirena

Passeig Marítim, 2, L'Estartit; 97/275-0954; www.la-sirena.net; Apr.-Oct 8:30am-7pm daily

The team at La Sirena is serious about diving. Safety-conscious professionals, excellent facilities, and 50 years of experience instill confidence at this dive center—essential when tackling challenging dive sites, such as those in the Illes Medes marine reserve, located a mile offshore. The center offers a range of courses for all levels, as well as guided snorkeling trips. From €37.50.

BIRD WATCHING

Aiguamolls Del Baix Empordà

Ctra. de Sant Pere Pescador to Castelló d'Empúries (GIV-6216, km 13); 97/245-4222; aiguamollsdelemporda.cat; free

Spot more than 300 bird species in this wetland nature reserve, which lies in the Bay of Roses. The park is a mosaic of distinct yet interdependent ecosystems—sea, rivers, beaches, lagoons, meadows, freshwater lakes, and marshes—which are brimming with life and diversity. The best time to bird watch is in the morning or at dusk during migration season (Mar.-May and Aug.-Oct.), although interesting species can be seen year-round. There are seven bird-watching blinds and one tower, as well as a network of trails throughout the park. An information center (El Cortalet; Jan.-Feb. 9am-4pm daily, Mar.-Oct. 9am-6:30pm daily, Nov.-Dec. 9am-5:30pm daily), where binoculars can be rented (€2.50), is located beside the main car park.

FOOD

SPANISH AND CATALAN

Casa Juanita

Carrer Pi iRalló, 7; 97/262-2013;
casajuanita.cat; Easter-Oct. Tues.-Sun.
1pm-4pm, 8pm-11:30pm; €25-35

Feast on incredible fresh fish at Casa Juanita, a tiny, family-run restaurant where waiters present the catch of the day on silver platters for customers' perusal. The chosen fish is prepared with olive oil, tomatoes, onions, and potatoes, sealed up and placed inside the wood-fired oven. Try the frightful-looking but intensely flavored local favorite, *rascassa* (red scorpionfish). Pricey but worth the experience. Reservations advised.

TAPAS

Can Climent Platillos

Carrer Pi i Ralló, 8; 97/262-2502;
canclimentplatillos.com; Mar.-Oct.
Tues.-Sun. 8pm-11:30pm; €6.50-€13.50

Little plates, big impact—that's the verdict on *Platillos* (meaning "little plates"). This tiny, unpretentious bar conjures up delightfully creative gourmet tapas with flavor combinations that you're unlikely to forget. Delectable morsels such as tuna carpaccio with wasabi ice cream, cherry gazpacho, and figs with a foie gras mousse are made for sharing and keep diners coming back for more. Reservations essential.

FINE DINING

Diferent

Plaça de l'Església, 4; 97/262-2872;
www.diferentrestaurant.es; open Mar.-Dec.
only, Tues. 8pm-10:30pm, Wed.-Sun.
1pm-3:15pm, 8pm-10:30pm; €12-€16; set
lunch menu, Wed.-Fri. €25, Sat.-Sun. €30;
evening tasting menu €62

Headed up by the fourth generation of the Caner family—whose classic restaurant, Fonda Caner (Carrer Pi i Rallo, 10; 97/262-2391; www.fondacaner.com), is still going strong—Diferent offers a laid-back, gastronomic adventure. The emphasis is on local produce, which is combined in an artful fusion of Mediterranean flavors, such as the roast veal cannelloni with mushroom béchamel and sheep's cheese, or the pickled foie gras with wine poached pears and honey. The set lunch is particularly good value, though if the budget allows, go for the eight-course tasting menu.

BARS AND NIGHTLIFE

The buzz is always centered on Plaça de la Vila, and any of the terrace bars there are good for a drink and a spot of people-watching, day or night. The following are less obvious choices that you may otherwise miss.

El Jardí de Can Marc

Carrer de la Creu, 10; 97/262-3119;
www.canmarc.cat; open mid-Jun.-Sept. only,
7pm-2am daily

Cocktails, lush gardens, and the best views in town—this is what summer nights were made for. El Jardí de Can Marc describes itself as a "gastro-cocktail chill out," a concept realized in its gourmet tapas, cool cocktails (think elderflower sangria or sea spaghetti gin), and candlelit, sophisticated vibe (over 14s only). Ideal for a pre-dinner sundowner with village, castle, and Mediterranean views, tucked away from the mid-summer hubbub of the center.

C-Roack

Avinguda de l'Onze de Setembre, 8;
97/262-3094; c-roack.com; open
Jun.-mid-Sept. only, Fri.-Sat. 7:30pm-3am,
Sun. noon-3:30pm

The enchanting walled patio of

❂ HIKING THE CAMÍ DE RONDA

Camí de Ronda, Cap de Begur

The Camí de Ronda (or "Costa Brava Way") is a public footpath that traverses the rugged cliffs and picture-perfect *calas* along the length of the Costa Brava. Hikers can discover the coast from another perspective, swim at secluded beaches, and marvel at spectacular views along this scenic trail.

The path dates from the 19th century and was historically used by fisherman, smugglers, police, and anyone who needed to scale this once-remote coastal territory. When mass tourism landed in the late 20th century, development blocked parts of the original paths, but the trail has gradually been restored in recent years. It roughly follows the GR-92 footpath, marked by a red and white line (part of the Grand Randonnée network). The trail consists of 12 stages of easy-to-moderate difficulty, which can be undertaken as a 12- to 15-day hike, or broken down into shorter sections between coastal towns. There's an itinerary to suit every level and timeframe.

When to hike: Shoulder season (late spring, early autumn) is the best time to hike, although it's accessible year-round. July and August are the busiest and hottest months. For earlybirds, setting off at sunrise (around 6am midsummer) makes an uplifting start to the day. Avoid the midday sun if possible (noon-3pm).

What to pack: Sunscreen, hat, water, snacks, swimsuit, towel, mask and snorkel, and hiking or running shoes.

DAY HIKES

The stretch between Palamós and Begur is one of the most scenic parts of the Costa Brava Way, encompassing both wild Mediterranean landscapes and picturesque coastal villages, with many tempting stop-off points along the way. The overall distance is 23 kilometers (14 miles, 7-9 hours), but can be easily broken down into shorter, more manageable sections. Farther north, the spellbinding encounter of land and sea around the headland of Cap de Creus captivates all those who follow the trail through this natural wilderness. By nature, the coastal path is not circular, and the stretches mentioned below can be tackled as an out-and-back venture, or hikers may prefer to take public transport or a taxi back to their starting point upon completion. Unless otherwise stated, the distances and times mentioned are one-way only.

PALAMÓS TO CALELLA DE PALAFRUGELL
10 km/6 mi, 4 hours

Starting in Cala de la Fosca, a beach just north of Palamós, this section of the trail takes in several points of interest en route to Calella de Palafrugell, including the ruins of Castell de Sant Esteve (an 11th-century castle), Platja de Castell, the Poblat ibèric de Castell (ancient Iberian settlement), Cala Estreta (nudist beach), the botanical gardens of Cap Roig, and Platja del Golfet. The terrain is varied and the trail gets busy in summer, but it is a scenic way to access many beautiful beaches.

CALELLA DE PALAFRUGELL TO TAMARIU
7 km/4.5 mi, 2 hours

Probably the most popular day hike along the Camí de Ronda, and also one of the most scenic, this section of the trail is varied, short, and relatively easy. Setting off from the picturesque fishing village of Calella de Palafrugell, the route takes in Llafranc and the Sant Sebastià lighthouse, then follows the cliffs toward Tamariu, with spectacular views en route. Stop at the secluded Cala Pedrosa for a swim. Once in Tamariu, the spectacular Cala d'Aigua Xelida is just an extra 1.5 kilometers (1 mile).

CAP DE BEGUR

There are three distinct sections to the coastal path around the headland of Begur: Platja del Racó to Sa Riera (1.6 km/1 mi, one hour round-trip), Aiguafreda to Sa Tuna (1.5 km/1 mi, 45 minutes round-trip), and Aiguablava to Platja Fonda (2.5km/1.6 mi, 2 hours round-trip). Each one is relatively quick and easy, hopping from one pretty *cala* to the next. It's possible to link the three routes, but it does involve veering inland and navigating some urban areas with minimal signage.

CADAQUÉS TO CAP DE CREUS
7.4 km/4.6 mi, 3 hours

This hike follows an old trail to the Cap de Creus lighthouse. The first stop is Portlligat, former home of Salvador Dalí, just 15 minutes from Cadaqués. From here, the scenic path twists and turns its way around secluded beaches and pebbly coves, with ample opportunity for swimming and picnics. Near the end of the trail, Cala Jugadora is perfect for a refreshing swim.

CAP DE CREUS TO PORT DE LA SELVA
13 km/8 mi, 4 hours

From the Cap de Creus lighthouse, the GR-92 heads inland across the craggy headland, while the Camí de Ronda follows the GR-11 across the northern part of the natural park—one of the most isolated and captivating sections of the trail. Secluded coves and astounding rock formations are aplenty along this stretch, which passes by the delightfully deserted Cala Tavallera en route to Port de la Selva. There is no shade or water available along the way.

C-Roack is an atmospheric spot for an al fresco nightcap. Come here after dinner and delight in the secret garden ambience, sipping gin-and-tonics beneath the hanging lanterns while DJs spin chill-out tunes until the early hours.

ACCOMMODATIONS

Visitors to Begur are spoiled for choice when it comes to accommodation, ranging from 19th-century mansions to fishermen's houses and sleek contemporary hideaways. If you're planning to visit during July or August, book well in advance.

Cluc Hotel Begur

Carrer del Metge Pi, 8; 97/262-4859; cluc.cat; €145 d

Cluc is an intimate boutique hotel in the heart of the village. Twelve compact guest rooms are spread across three floors (upper floors are the quietest) in this carefully restored, 19th-century building which retains much of its original features and charm. A delicious, homemade breakfast is served in the courtyard and the friendly owners, Elena and Santi, help you to make the most of your stay.

Hotel Aiguaclara

Carrer de Sant Miguel, 2; 97/262-2905; hotelaiguaclarabegur.com; €190 d

Tiled floors, high ceilings, and original woodwork are preserved in this 10-bed, colonial-style mansion, which dates from 1866 and is dotted with antique knick-knacks and vintage photographs. Friendly owners Clara and Joan make guests feel at home, with snug social spaces on the lower floors stocked with books, games, and vinyl LPs. Each bright, airy guest room has its own character; two of the first

floor rooms have a private terrace. The hotel restaurant serves simple Mediterranean cuisine and has everyone up dancing on the popular "Vinilos" night every Friday.

Hotel Aigua Blava

Platja de Fornells; 97/262-2058; www. hotelaiguablava.com; €280 d, four-night mininum stay; open mid-Jul.-mid-Sept. only

The four-star, beachfront Hotel Aigua Blava is a classic choice that has it all—an outdoor pool, tennis court, lush gardens, crystal-clear waters, and some of the best views along the Costa Brava. It's a 10-minute drive to Begur, but with the hotel's welcoming atmosphere, gourmet restaurant, and a rocky shoreline of hidden coves to discover, you may be tempted to stay put. Ask for a room with a sea view.

INFORMATION AND SERVICES

TOURIST INFORMATION

The tourist information center in Begur is located in the village center, next to Bar C-Roack (Av. de l'Onze de Setembre, 5; 97/262-4520; visitbegur.cat; summer Mon.-Fri. 9am-2pm, 4pm-9pm, Sat.-Sun. 10am-2pm, 4pm-9pm, winter Mon.-Fri. 9am-2:30pm, Tues. 4pm-8pm, Sat.-Sun. 10am-2pm). The office has an internet connection and a printer.

POLICE

The municipal police station, the Policia Local, is located in the same building as the town hall (Carrer de Francesc Forgas, 1; 97/262-4200), opposite the church. The nearest regional police station (Mossos d'Esquadra) is in Palafrugell (Avinguda de García Lorca, 20; 97/230-8118; www.gencat. cat/mossos).

HOSPITALS AND PHARMACIES

For emergencies, the Hospital de Palamós is a 20-minute drive (Carrer Hospital, 36, Palamós; 97/260-0160; open 24 hours). For less urgent cases, visit the primary care center, the Centre d'Atenció Primària (CAP) in Palafrugell (Carrer Àngel Guimerà, 6; 97/261-0607; open 24 hours).

There are two pharmacies in Begur: Farmàcia Es Mirador (Plaça Forgas, 11; 97/262-3369) and Farmàcia Sònia Torres (Av. Onze de Setembre, 3; 97/262-4243 or 97/262-3760), both open 9am-2pm and 4pm-9pm daily in summer (Mon.-Sat. 9am-1pm, 5pm-8pm; Sun. 10am-1pm in winter). Outside business hours, one of the pharmacies in Palafrugell is always on call; check the notice posted on the door of either pharmacy or visit www.cofgi.org/farmacies/farmacies-de-guardia for details.

LUGGAGE STORAGE

There is no luggage storage service in Begur, except within accommodations.

WIFI

Begur has a public WiFi network, although it is not very reliable. Many bars offer free WiFi to customers.

GETTING THERE

The most convenient way to get to (and around) Begur is by car.

CAR

From Barcelona, drive northeast on the AP-7 highway. Exit the AP-7 at junction 9A-9B and take the C-35 toward Sant Feliu de Guíxols and Platja d'Aro. After Llagostera, the road merges with the C-65, and then the C-31 in the direction of Palamós.

At the Regencós roundabout, take the GI-653 (first exit) to Begur. The drive takes approximately 1 hour and 35 minutes (130 km/81 mi).

Parking is plentiful in Begur, though at the height of summer, it can be difficult to find a spot. The most convenient is the Font de Baix car park, just off Ctra. de Circumvallacio, coming from Regencós. There is also a small multistory parking garage in the center (Parquing Onze De Setembre; Avinguda de l'Onze de Setembre, 1), and the large Sot d'en Ferrer car park on the far side of town (follow Ctra. de Circumvallacio in the direction of Sa Tuna). Blue zones indicate on-street meter parking, while white zones are free. Several empty plots on the edge of town have been converted into car parks, many of which are free. Further information can be found online or at the tourist information office (visitbegur.cat).

BUS

From Barcelona, Sarfa (90/230-2025; www.sarfa.com) runs regular services to Begur from the Estació del Nord bus station (2-2.5 hours; €19.85 one way), some of which originate at Barcelona-El Prat Airport. There are six daily buses in summer (Jul.-Aug.) and three the rest of the year. In summer, the first service departs from Estació del Nord at 8:30am, and the last one departs at 7:30pm. Otherwise, the first and last services depart at 8:30am and 8:15pm, respectively.

GETTING AROUND

Private transport enables greater flexibility for discovering the local area, although it is possible to reach the nearby coastline via shuttle bus in summer. Be aware that there is limited parking available near the beaches, and during high season it fills up quickly.

TAXI

Begur has several taxi companies; among them Taxis Begur (63/098-0895; www.taxibegur.com) offers an English-speaking service, airport transfers, and excursions. There is also a taxi stand located on Carrer de Rosa Puig, across the road from the main bus stop at Plaça Forgas, and another on Avinguda de l'Onze de Setembre (opposite number 14).

LEAVING BEGUR

The last bus back to Barcelona from Begur leaves at 7:20pm in summer, and 6:20pm the rest of the year. The bus stop for Barcelona is in Plaça Forgas, outside the pharmacy. For buses heading north, the bus stop is just across the road. Begur is connected by bus to Girona, Figueres, and towns across the Costa Brava.

Cadaqués

Many creative geniuses have found their inspiration in Cadaqués, set amid the windswept craggy wilderness of the Cap de Creus peninsula, where the Pyrenees crash into the Mediterranean Sea. A charming, whitewashed fishing village nestled in a rocky bay, it retains its allure today. Its most famous resident, Salvador Dalí, spent much of his life in neighboring Portlligat (1 kilometer/0.6 miles northeast of Cadaqués). Visit the artist's hometown of Figueres and the flamboyant Dalí Theatre-Museum en route to Cadaqués to fully understand the influence this area had on the eccentric Surrealist.

SIGHTS

ESGLÉSIA DE SANTA MARIA DE CADAQUÉS
(Church of Santa Maria)

Carrer Portal de Mont, 1-3

A labyrinth of quaint, cobbled streets wind their way up to the Church of Santa Maria, the centerpiece of the old town, which sits at the highest point. From here, enjoy the wonderful view over the terracotta rooftops and glistening bay, dotted with dozens of boats.

Built to replace an earlier church that was destroyed by Turkish pirates in 1534, Santa Maria dates from the 16th century, though some elements were completed much later. The late-Gothic structure houses several Baroque altarpieces, the most important of which is the 23-meter-high (75-foot) gilded sculpture dedicated to the Virgin of Hope behind the main altar, which dates from the 18th century. The 17th-century organ is thought to be one of the oldest in Catalonia. The church only opens to celebrate mass (Sat. 7pm, Sun. 11am), although the altarpiece can be viewed from outside between 10:30am-12:45pm and 4pm-4:45pm daily; audio guides for the old town and church are also available.

Tip: Look for the ancient pavement along Carrer des Call, just up from Plaça Doctor Trèmols, where handmade slate stones are arranged in a herringbone pattern to absorb

Cap de Creus and Cadaqués

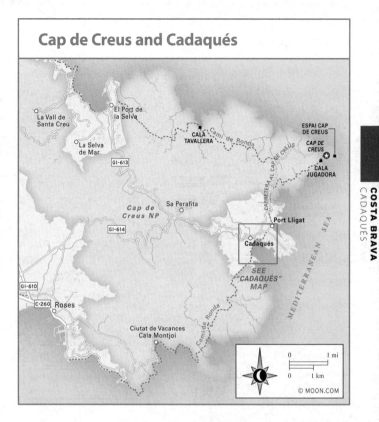

La Vall de Santa Creu
El Port de la Selva
La Selva de Mar
GI-613
CALA TAVALLERA
Camí de Ronda
CARRETERA AL CAP DE CREUS
ESPAI CAP DE CREUS
CAP DE CREUS
CALA JUGADORA
Cap de Creus NP
Sa Perafita
GI-614
Port Lligat
Cadaqués
SEE "CADAQUÉS" MAP
GI-610
C-260
Roses
Camí de Ronda
Ciutat de Vacances Cala Montjoi
MEDITERRANEAN SEA
0   1 mi
0   1 km
© MOON.COM

excess water and prevent people from slipping.

MUSEU DE CADAQUÉS
(Cadaqués Museum)

Carrer d'en Narcís Monturiol, 15;
97/225-8877; museucadaques@gmail.com;
opening times vary according to current
exhibition, check at tourist information; €5

Dedicated to artists who were inspired by, lived in, or worked in Cadaqués, the gallery hosts exhibitions throughout the year, which often focus on the life and work of the town's most famous son, Salvador Dalí. The museum has a permanent collection of work by artists associated with the town, including Richard Hamilton, Pablo Picasso, Ramon Pichot, Joan Miró,

Marcel Duchamp, and Josep Niebla, among others, who also feature in the diverse range of temporary exhibitions hosted here. A visit to the museum is good prep for visiting Dalí's house in neighboring Portlligat.

✪ CAP DE CREUS

The bay of Cadaqués is a white-washed jewel hidden amid the remote, precipitous landscapes of the Cap de Creus headland—the easternmost point on the Iberian peninsula. A desolate frontier of untamed beauty, this is where the craggy pinnacles of the Pyrenees come smashing into the Mediterranean Sea.

Most of this uninhabited wilderness belongs to the **Parc Natural del**

299

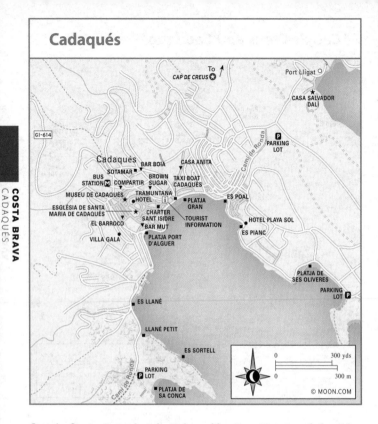

Cadaqués

Cap de Creus. Rugged geological outcrops give way to deep blue creeks, forming a lunar landscape carved by the elements, where only the most hardy fauna and flora survive the fierce tramontane wind. Its isolated, whimsical nature has long since been a source of inspiration—Dalí and friends could often be found roaming its barren ridges—and thanks to its status as a protected area, it remains just as solitary and surreal today.

A windy road leads to the headland's eastern extremity (20-minute drive from Cadaqués), where a 19th-century lighthouse accommodates the Espai Cap de Creus (Carretera Cap de Creus; 87/220-4010; Mar.-Apr. and Oct. Mon.-Sat. 9am-3pm, May-Jun. and late Sept. 10am-3pm daily, mid-Jun.-early Sept. 10am-2pm, 3pm-7pm daily, closed Nov.-Feb.), a visitor center that explains the landscape's evolution and environment. There are numerous ways to explore, including scuba diving tours with Sotamar Diving Center in Cadaques, or hiking a 7-kilometer (4-mile) section of the scenic Camí de Ronda trail that runs along the coast from Cadaqués to the lighthouse. The café next to the lighthouse is the perfect spot to watch the sun set behind the cape's jagged silhouette.

A tourist train, Es Trenet de Cadaqués (65/382-9442; www.es-trenetdecadaques.cat; Easter-Oct.; €10), makes one trip to the Cap de Creus lighthouse from Cadaques at noon, where it stops for 30 minutes. A popular option is to take the train to the lighthouse and walk back to Cadaqués via the coastal trail (7 km/4.5 mi).

BEACHES

Clear blue waters and small, stony beaches are squeezed between rocky outcrops around the bay of Cadaqués. In this quaint setting for a swim, fishing boats rest in front of white-washed houses along these pebbly shores; it's pretty, although quite different from the soft sandy *calas* found farther south along the coast. These tiny coves get busy in summer. To avoid the crowds, head to the untouched shores of Cala Jugadora or Cala Tavallera north of Cap de Creus.

Platja Gran

A statue of Salvador Dalí greets sunseekers as they arrive at Platja Gran, the biggest and most central beach in Cadaqués. Measuring 200 meters long by 20 meters wide (650 by 65 feet), it's a busy, family favorite in summer, with all the usual facilities and two excellent beach bars.

Es Poal and Es Pianc

Heading east from the main beach, these two tiny bays are easily accessible, though small boats are often parked along the shore. Both offer lovely village views. Es Pianc sits in front of the Hotel Playa Sol.

Platja de Ses Oliveres

At the edge of town along the eastern side of the bay, Ses Oliveres is a large, pebbly beach with shallow waters. Along the shore, there is a watersports center and a couple of popular bars that are good for a beachside lunch. Rent a kayak here and venture out to

Cadaques

Casa Salvador Dalí in Portlligat

The rugged beauty of the Costa Brava has been a source of inspiration since time immemorial. Picasso, Chagall, and Miró are among the many famous artists moved by this windswept frontier, though none more so than the prolific and polemic Surrealist, Salvador Dalí. Dalí was born and died in Figueres, and although he spent time in Madrid and Paris, he lived and worked in the area for much of his life.

Three specific locations were particularly influential in the life of this artistic genius: **Figueres,** his hometown and location of the Teatre-Museu Dalí; **Portlligat,** where he lived from 1930 to 1982; and **Púbol,** where he bought a castle for his wife, Gala. Two days are required to complete the triangle and visit all three museums in these locations, though visiting even one of the three opens a window into Dalí's surreal world. For more information on these museums, visit www.salvador-dali.org.

CASA SALVADOR DALÍ (SALVADOR DALÍ HOUSE)
Platja Portlligat; 97/225-1015; www.salvador-dali.org; €12/€8

A lantern-wielding, necklace-wearing polar bear welcomes visitors to the former home of Salvador and Gala Dalí in Portlligat, setting the tone for the multitude of eccentricities in store. Drawn to the area by its landscape, light, and isolation, Dalí lived and worked here from 1930 until 1982.

The house, which began as a fisherman's hut, grew with the couple over half a century, "like a real biological structure [. . .] Each new pulse in our life had its own new cell, its room," as Dalí himself described it. The result is a labyrinthine structure that steps up the hillside, with rooms linked by passageways and random-shaped windows framing views across the bay of Portlligat—views that have a constant presence in his work (his painting "The Persistence of Memory" is one example).

The Dalí residence had three distinct areas for living, working, and public life. The latter took place outdoors, around the courtyards, olive garden, and phallic swimming pool; one can only imagine the soirées. It's a cabinet of curiosities as wacky as the man

the small island of Cucurucuc in the middle of the bay.

Platja Port d'Alguer
Heading west from Platja Gran, the next small bay is Port d'Alguer, which is similar in character to Es Poal and

Es Pianc, and is overlooked by several popular bars.

Es Llané and Llané Petit
Continuing west, the next pair of beaches are Es Llané and Llané Petit, two stony beaches with great views

himself, where stuffed animals and oversized eggs sit alongside Pirelli tires and kitsch artifacts—not forgetting the iconic Mae West sofa.

The visit takes around 50 minutes and is carried out in small groups (unguided), each with an allocated time slot. Tickets must be reserved in advance (online, telephone, or email to pll@fundaciodali.org), and picked up at least 30 minutes before entry time (don't be late).

Getting there: The house is a 15-minute walk from Cadaqués, and can also be reached by car.

✪ TEATRE-MUSEU DALÍ
Plaça Gala-Salvador Dalí, 5, Figueres; 97/267-7500; Nov.-Feb. Tues.-Sun. 10:30am-6pm, Mar. and Oct. Tues.-Sun. 9:30am-6pm, Apr.-Jun. Tues.-Sun. 9am-8pm, Jul.-Sept. 9am-8pm daily, also open 10pm-1am daily during August; €15/€11; advance reservation online advised

Housing a collection of more than 1,500 works, this museum in Dalí's hometown is an extraordinary nerve center of all things Dalí. Every last detail was designed by the artist, whose objective was to invite visitors into his hallucinatory world of Surrealism.

The idea for the museum was conceived in the 1960s, when the mayor of Figueres asked Dalí to donate one of his works to a local gallery. Dalí responded by offering to donate an entire museum. He spent the next decade transforming the Municipal Theater of Figueres, which had been severely damaged during the Civil War, into his last great work. Opening in 1974, the museum appropriated elements of the former theater in true Dalínian fashion, crowned by an iconic glass dome. Paintings, drawings, sculptures, prints, installations, holograms, stereographs, and photographs take visitors on a beautifully choreographed journey through his life's work, culminating with the crypt, the artist's final resting place.

Getting there: Figueres is 40 kilometers (25 miles) from both Portlligat (50-minute drive) and Púbol (35-minute drive). The museum can be visited while on the Costa Brava, but also makes an easy day trip from Barcelona (140 kilometers/87 miles). From Barcelona, the best way to get there is by high-speed train (AVE; 55 minutes; from €10.85), which stops at Figueres Vilafant on the edge of town. A shuttle bus takes passengers to the center.

CASTELL GALA DALÍ
Púbol; 97/248-8655; €8/€6

Built in the 14th century, the medieval castle of Púbol was bought by Salvador Dalí in 1969 as a gift to his wife, Gala. From 1971 until 1980, she spent her summers in this private sanctuary, located on the edge of Púbol, a charming, stone-built village. Dalí envisioned the castle as a continuation of their Portlligat home, but dedicated entirely to Gala: a place where "she would reign like an absolute sovereign." Indeed, Dalí would only visit the castle on receiving a handwritten invitation from Gala.

The Dalís found the castle in a state of disrepair and fell in love with its romantic appeal. As they restored the three-story building, Dalí found many innovative ways of using the crumbling walls and ceilings to create surprising spaces and decorated the interiors with hand-painted frescoes. After Gala passed away in 1982, she was buried in the castle grounds. Dalí moved to the castle and lived there until 1984, when a fire broke out in his bedroom, thought to be a possible suicide attempt. After the fire, he spent the rest of his days living in Figueres.

Getting there: Púbol Castle is a 35-minute drive from Figueres (39 km/24 mi), and 1 hour 15 minutes from Cadaqués (65 km/40 mi).

across the bay. The smaller of the two, Llané Petit, has a short pier and is popular with families.

Es Sortell and Platja de Sa Conca

At the quieter end of town, these two beaches sit on either side of a rocky promontory. Es Sortell is a pebbly beach facing the bay that is connected to a small island via a stone footbridge. Tucked behind the outcrop, Sa Conca is a quiet haven that is popular with nudists.

CALAS NORTH OF CAP DE CREUS

Cala Jugadora

The remote wilderness of Cap de Creus is replete with rocky inlets, secret coves, and islets scattered along the coast—a landscape sculpted by the elements. Many of these beaches are only accessible by sea; of those that can be reached by land, Cala Jugadora is a true gem, and its clear waters a snorkeler's paradise. It's a 30-minute walk from the lighthouse.

Cala Tavallera

Located on the northern shores of the natural park, Cala Tavallera is a remote, pebbly beach with shallow, crystal-clear waters. Arrive on foot, following the GR 11 footpath from Port de la Selva or the Cap de Creus lighthouse (two hours approx.).

RECREATION

SAILING

Taxi Boat Cadaqués

Riba des Poal; 66/638-2852; taxiboatcadaques.com; open May-Oct.

Riding the waves in Taxi Boat's rubber dinghy is a speedy way to see the creeks and crevices of Cap de Creus. The company offers a taxi service to Port de la Selva, Casa Dalí (Portlligat), and more, as well as two-hour outings with a swimming stop and a visit to the Cova de l'Infern (cave and natural swimming pool). Personalized snorkeling trips are also available (max. 11 people)—an opportunity to explore remote, hidden coves, and deep blue waters. Prices range €15-25.

Charter Sant Isidre

Riba Nemesi Llorens; 62/696-0298; chartersantisidre.com; open Easter-Oct.

Set sail around Cap de Creus in style aboard the Sant Isidre, a beautifully restored traditional sailboat built in 1925. The classic tour is a two-hour trip (noon, 5pm, 7pm; €16) along the natural park's coastline, with a 20-minute snorkel stop. The boat is also available for private rental for full or half days, with opportunities to eat, sleep, and enjoy music on board.

DIVING

Sotamar

Avinguda Caritat Serinyana, 17; 97/225-8876; www.sotamar.com; 10am-1pm, 4pm-7pm daily

Sotamar Diving Center organizes excursions to 25 dive sites in the Cap de Creus Natural Park, as well as daily snorkeling excursions (€25). There are sites to suit all levels, from the Llanishen shipwreck just offshore (11-19 meters/36-62 feet) to the spectacular island of Massa d'Or; all diving excursions are guided. The center also offers a wide range of diving courses, from try dives (€60) and free diving (from €30) to SSI Open Water (€390) and professional qualifications.

FOOD

FINE DINING

Compartir

Riera de Sant Vicenç, s/n; 97/225-8482; www.compartircadaques.com; Mar.-Sept. Tues.-Sun. 1pm-4pm, 8pm-10:30pm, Oct.-Feb. Thurs.-Sat. 1pm-4pm, 8pm-10:30pm; tasting menu €70

Opened in 2012 by a trio of el-Bulli alumni (the same team behind Disfrutar in Barcelona), the modern Mediterranean dishes dreamed up here are all designed to share (*compartir* in Spanish). Traditional Catalan flavors are reimagined as unexpected, artful creations—take the marinated sardines with raspberries, beetroot, and pistachios, for example. Set in a pretty courtyard with laid-back, rustic-chic decor.

SPANISH AND CATALAN
Casa Anita

Carrer Miquel Rosset, 16; 97/225-8471; www.casaanitavip.com; Dec.-Sept. 2pm-3:30pm, 8:30pm-10:30pm; €15-€36

There's no printed menu, no wine list, and no prices on display, but you can expect simple, well-executed food, excellent local wines, and a traditional atmosphere at this backstreet bodega. Merrily serving its loyal clientele since 1960, Casa Anita is a family-run restaurant where guests fill up the communal tables and take their pick from the day's specials—the attentive host, Joan, will explain what's on offer. Local langoustines, sardines, and sea bass feature regularly. Advance reservations advisable.

INTERNATIONAL
✪ El Barroco

Carrer des Pla d'en Retalla, 2; 97/225-8632; elbarroco.net; 1pm-3pm, 7:30pm-10pm daily, open Easter-Sept. and during holiday season; €15-€19

Full of knick-knacks and artifacts, El Barroco is as eccentric as its most famous patron, Salvador Dalí, who frequently dined here and even designed the restaurant's logo. The leafy walled patio is the main space in this Lebanese jewel, where platters packed with hot and cold *meze* (tabbouleh, hummus, baba ghanoush, and more), as well as meat skewers, grilled fish, and delicate desserts, delight all those who manage to find it. Expect fragrant spices in the air, and a warm welcome from Sami, the piano-playing, multi-talented host.

BARS AND NIGHTLIFE
Bar Mut

Plaça del Dr. Pont, 12; Apr.-Sept. 10am-midnight daily, Mar. and Oct. weekends only; cash only

A hipster terrace bar with bay views and plenty of people-watching potential, Bar Mut is open all day and is good for a cold white wine, a full-on tapas feast (the innovative menu starts at €3.50), a moonlit nightcap, or all of the above. The mojitos (€6.50) and vermouths are especially good. Soak up the feel-good spirit as the village lights dance across the water. No reservations.

Bar Boia

Avinguda Caritat Serinyana, s/n; 97/225-8651; www.boianit.com; Jun.-Sept. 8:30am-3am daily, Oct.-May 9am-9pm daily

World champion mixologist Manel Vehí serves up mind-boggling cocktails at this classic *xiringuito* (beach bar). A renowned hangout for arty types since 1946, Bar Boia was a favorite of Dalí, Man Ray, Duchamp, and co. ElBulli-trained Vehí, who represents the fourth generation of the bar's founding family, has reimagined the space as a gastrobar, bringing it up to date with his signature tapas and creative concoctions. Order a plankton and sea fennel gin-and-tonic and channel your inner Dalí.

Brown Sugar

Plaça Art i Joia; 65/938-1154; open Easter-Sept. Mon., Wed.-Sun. 6pm-3am, all day Jun.-Aug.

If chilled hippie vibes make you happy, this charming backstreet bar will too. An intimate, cave-like space that spills out onto the street, Brown Sugar serves up inexpensive fruit cocktails and vegan-friendly fare in a cheery ambience with great music (often live). This eclectic hidden gem really comes to life around midnight.

ACCOMMODATIONS

Tramuntana Hotel

Carrer de la Torre, 9; 97/225-9270; www.hotel-tramuntana-cadaques.com; €105 d; open Apr.-Oct.

Tramuntana is an adults-only boutique retreat buried in the old town. A traditional, whitewashed façade gives way to bright, minimalist interiors, with a cool palette, clean lines, and contemporary furnishings. Each of the 11 guest rooms has a private balcony and modern bathroom, while downstairs there's a cozy lounge and a garden terrace beneath the pines. The steep cobbled streets can be challenging to navigate with luggage, but the convivial hosts, Carlos and Rosa, happily pick up guests in their golf buggy.

Hotel Playa Sol

Riba es Pianc, 3; 97/225-8100; www.playasol.com; €220 d; open Mar.-Oct. (five-night min. stay during Jul.-Sept.)

Magnificent views across the bay of Cadaqués are the selling point at Hotel Playa Sol, a long-standing establishment overlooking the tiny Es Pianc beach. There are plenty more perks, though, including an outdoor pool, tennis and basketball courts, and lush gardens where guests can lounge beneath olive trees. Built in the 1960s and recently updated, the interior decor is simple and timeless. Garden rooms are quiet, but nothing compares to the azure panoramas from the sea-view rooms.

Hotel Playa Sol

Villa Gala

Carrer Solitari, 5; 87/222-8000; hotelvillagala. com; €375-€620 d; open Apr.-Dec.

Boutique Villa Gala embraces its guests in discreet luxury. All 14 guest rooms are bright and elegant, enjoying sea and village views, a private balcony or terrace, and a range of extras. Exposed stone, timber furnishings, and white and blue tones are present throughout the contemporary Mediterranean interiors, while outside, the glistening pool and terrace gardens are simply irresistible. It's heaven, if the budget allows.

INFORMATION AND SERVICES

TOURIST INFORMATION

The main tourist information office in Cadaqués is located one block from the seafront, on the ground floor of an 18th-century building where wine used to be produced—look for the vintage grape press (Carrer d'es Cotxe, 1; 97/225-8315; www.visitcadaques.org; summer Mon.-Sat. 9am-9pm, Sun. 10am-1pm, 5pm-8pm, winter Mon.-Thurs. 9am-1pm, 3pm-6pm, Fri.-Sat. 9am-1pm, 3pm-7pm).

POLICE

The municipal police station (Policia Local; 97/215-9343; Carrer Carles Rahola, 9) is located close to Camping Cadaqués. The nearest regional police station is in Roses (Mossos d'Esquadra; Ctra. de les Arenes, Roses; 97/254-1850).

HOSPITALS AND PHARMACIES

For emergencies, the Hospital de Figueres is a 50-minute drive (Ronda del Rector Arolas, Figueres; 97/250-1400; www.salutemporda.cat; open

24 hours). For less urgent cases, visit the primary care center, the Centre d'Atenció Primària (CAP), in Cadaqués (Carrer Nou, 6-10; 97/225-8807; 8am-8pm daily, 24 hours during summer).

There are two pharmacies in Cadaqués: Farmàcia Colomer (Camí Portlligat, 28; 97/225-8932; Mon.-Sat. 9am-1pm, 4:30pm-8pm) and Farmàcia Moradell (Plaça Frederic Rahola, 9; 97/225-8751). To find out which one is on duty outside regular hours, check the notice posted on the door of each pharmacy or visit www.cofgi.org/farmacies/farmacies-de-guardia.

LUGGAGE STORAGE

There is no luggage storage service in Cadaqués, except within accommodations.

WIFI

There is no public WiFi in Cadaqués, but many bars offer free WiFi for customers.

GETTING THERE

The quickest and most convenient way to get to Cadaqués is by car, although there is a direct bus from Barcelona, and a high-speed train service to Figueres.

CAR

From Barcelona, drive northeast on the AP-7 highway. Exit the AP-7 at junction 4 and take the C-260 toward Roses. Before reaching Roses, take the GI-614, following signs for Cadaqués. From here, it's a windy, 30-minute drive over the mountains. In total, the journey takes approximately 2 hours and 15 minutes (177 km/110 mi).

Parking in central Cadaqués is nearly impossible. As you arrive in Cadaqués, veer right onto Carrer de ses Hortes, where there is a 24-hour public car park on the right. There are several informal parking lots on the edge of town—Sa Conc, Platja del Ros, and opposite Cadaqués camp site (Av. Salvador Dalí)—most of which are free. There is limited on-street parking, and it is difficult to find a spot. It is not possible to drive along the narrow streets of the old town; you may need to walk to your accommodation with your luggage.

BUS

From Barcelona, Sarfa (90/230-2025; www.sarfa.com) runs two daily services to Cadaqués from the Estació del Nord bus station (2 hours 45 minutes; €24.95), some of which originate at Barcelona-El Prat Airport. The bus station is on the edge of town (Passatge Taronjeta, 36).

TRAIN

Renfe (90/224-0202; www.renfe.es) runs dozens of daily trains from Barcelona Sants to Figueres, including the high-speed AVE service, which takes just 55 minutes (from €10.85).

From Figueres, take a taxi (Servei De Taxi Figueres; 97/293-2251) or bus to Cadaqués (Sarfa, line 3; 90/230-2025; www.sarfa.com; three daily buses, more in summer; one-hour journey).

GETTING AROUND

The best way to get around Cadaqués is on foot.

TAXI

Local taxi companies offer airport transfers and excursions: Taxi Pepe (69/661-1784; 24-hour; by reservation only between 10pm-7am) and Taxi Ole (62/652-6832). Alternately, Eco Car (Avinguda Caritat Serinyana, 10; 97/225-8592, 61/888-3656, or 67/746-5570; open Easter-Oct.) offers electric golf buggies that can be rented with or without driver, as well as electric bikes.

LEAVING CADAQUÉS

In summer, the last bus back to Barcelona from Cadaqués leaves at 7:45pm. The rest of the year, the last bus leaves at 3:15pm (5pm Sat.-Sun.). For onward travel to Girona or the Costa Brava, change at Figueres.

LA GARROTXA

Over the course of 700,000 years, seismic activity rocked the county of La Garrotxa. Violent eruptions and fiery streams of molten lava shaped and sculpted this extraordinary landscape, which represents the most prominent volcanic field on the Iberian Peninsula. Today, the remnants of that explosive era together form the beautiful Parc Natural de la Zona Volcànica de la Garrotxa, a sea of sleeping giants where sweeping forests and stone-built villages are cradled between the craters. Time stands still in medieval Besalú, cliff-hanging Castellfollit de la

HIGHLIGHTS

✪ **FAGEDA D'EN JORDÀ:** Fall under the spell of this enchanting beech forest, which is particularly beautiful in autumn (page 317).

✪ **HIKING VOLCÀ DEL CROSCAT:** Take a rare peek inside a volcano and into an extraordinary old quarry (page 319).

✪ **WALKING TOUR OF BESALÚ:** Cross the majestic Pont de Besalú and immerse yourself in Besalú's medieval charm (page 327).

Roca, and perfectly preserved Santa Pau, while the regional capital, Olot, is nestled amid four volcanoes. Across the region, kilometer-zero gastronomy known as *cuina volcànica* captures the flavors of the volcanic soil.

ORIENTATION

Garrotxa is a landlocked county in the province of Girona that lies to the west of Figueres and stretches as far as the French border to the north. Physically, the county is roughly divided into two areas by the Fluvià valley, with the cliffy Alta Garrotxa (Upper Garrotxa) to the north, and the Parc Natural de la Zona Volcànica de la Garrotxa to the south.

Olot (113 kilometers/70 miles north of Barcelona) is the county capital and official gateway to the zone, and is well located for exploring the natural park. The park's most interesting features, including the Santa Margarida and Croscat volcanoes and the Fageda d'en Jordà beech forest, are situated between Olot and the pretty town of Santa Pau, 10 kilometers (6 miles) southeast of the capital.

Heading northeast from Olot, Castellfollit de la Roca sits on the banks of the Fluvià river, as does the medieval capital, Besalú. The latter is beyond the park's boundaries,

21 kilometers (13 miles) east of Olot and 133 kilometers (83 miles) from Barcelona. However, Besalú is also a popular base for visitors, given its charm and cultural heritage, and its proximity to the park.

PLANNING YOUR TIME

La Garrotxa can be visited as an overnight or weekend trip from Barcelona, although there is plenty to do for those planning a longer stay, and it makes an excellent base from which to explore the province of Girona.

The area experiences abundant rainfall throughout the year, and cooler temperatures than coastal areas, due to its proximity to the Pyrenees. The average summer high is around 26°C (79°F), while in winter, the driest season, temperatures hover around freezing at night, and 10°C (50°F) during the day. The busiest time of year is October to December, when the autumn colors draw visitors in droves. The park is exceptionally beautiful during this period, but try to avoid weekends throughout October, November, and early December, as hiking trails get very busy and there is often gridlock around the car parks. Easter is also a popular time to visit. During peak times, make hotel and restaurant reservations in advance.

A visit to La Garrotxa usually combines the natural wonders of the volcanic landscape with a healthy helping of culture. Visitors can base themselves in the countryside or sample medieval life in the area's archaic villages. Whatever your preference, everywhere in the park is within a 45-minute drive. Public buses serve the region, but driving is the most convenient way to explore.

Itinerary Ideas

In two days, it is possible to experience the best of La Garrotxa. First concentrate your efforts on exploring the natural landscape, and then move on to the human habitats that exist in its midst. Arrive early from Barcelona on Day 1, or the evening before, and spend two nights at Cal Sastre, a stylish boutique hotel on the village square of Santa Pau.

LA GARROTXA ON DAY 1

Set off early to explore the Parc Natural de la Zona Volcànica de la Garrotxa, following the signposted Itinerary 1 (one of the 28 hiking route "itineraries" in the park) the entire way. This popular 10.5-kilometer (6.5-mile) trail takes in the park's three classic sights.

1 Park in the Santa Margarida car park.

2 From the car park, follow Itinerary 1 to climb the steep slopes of the verdant Volcà de Santa Margarida, and catch your breath by the 11th-century hermitage inside the crater.

3 Leaving Santa Margarida behind, keep hiking along Itinerary 1 to enter the Fageda d'en Jordà beech forest, where leaves dancing in the breeze dapple the rugged forest floor with an almost mystical light.

4 Re-emerging from the woods, follow the path around the Volcà del Croscat, and take a peek beneath the Earth's crust in the fascinating former quarry.

5 As you near the end of the hike, settle in for a post-hike feast at Restaurant Masnou. Make sure you sample the *fesols* (haricot beans), the local specialty.

6 Walk back to the car park and drive to the quaint village of Santa Pau.

7 Check in to Cal Sastre, then spend the late afternoon wandering Santa Pau's tiny medieval streets.

La Garrotxa

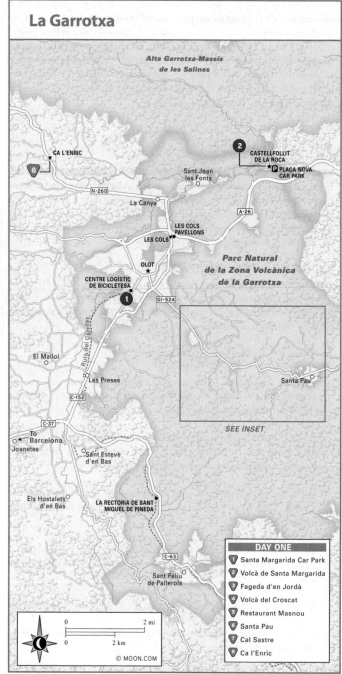

Alta Garrotxa-Massís de les Salines

CA L'ENRIC

8

CASTELLFOLLIT DE LA ROCA

2

★ PLAÇA NOVA CAR PARK

Sant Joan les Fonts

N-260

La Canya

A-26

LES COLS PAVELLONS

LES COLS

OLOT
★

Parc Natural de la Zona Volcànica de la Garrotxa

CENTRE LOGÍSTIC DE BICICLETESA

1

GI-524

Rua del Carrilet

El Mallol

Les Preses

C-152

Santa Pau

SEE INSET

C-37

To Barcelona
Joanetes

Sant Esteve d'en Bas

Els Hostalets d'en Bas

LA RECTORIA DE SANT MIQUEL DE PINEDA

C-63

Sant Feliu de Pallerols

| 0 | | 2 mi |
| 0 | | 2 km |

© MOON.COM

DAY ONE

1. Santa Margarida Car Park
2. Volcà de Santa Margarida
3. Fageda d'en Jordà
4. Volcà del Croscat
5. Restaurant Masnou
6. Santa Pau
7. Cal Sastre
8. Ca l'Enric

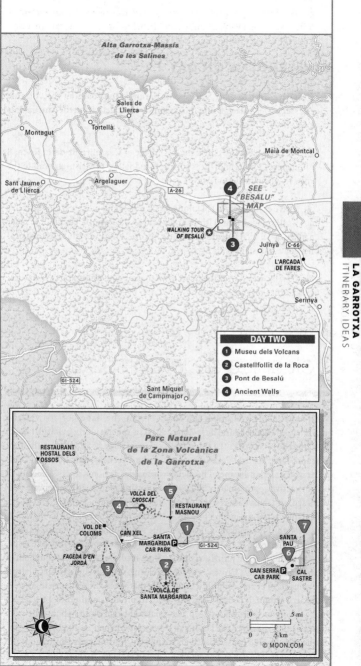

Alta Garrotxa-Massís
de les Salines

Sales de
Llierca

Montagut   Tortellà

Maià de Montcal

Sant Jaume
de Llierca   Argelaguer   A-26

4 SEE
"BESALÚ"
MAP

WALKING TOUR
OF BESALÚ

3   Juïnyà   C-66

L'ARCADA
DE FARES

Serinyà

GI-524

Sant Miquel
de Campmajor

DAY TWO
1 Museu dels Volcans
2 Castellfollit de la Roca
3 Pont de Besalú
4 Ancient Walls

Parc Natural
de la Zona Volcànica
de la Garrotxa

RESTAURANT
HOSTAL DELS
OSSOS

VOLCÀ DEL
CROSCAT   **5**
4   RESTAURANT
MASNOU

VOL DE   CAN XEL   **1**
COLOMS   SANTA   **7**
MARGARIDA   GI-524   SANTA
CAR PARK   PAU
FAGEDA D'EN   **3**   **2**   CAN SERRA   **6**
JORDÀ   CAR PARK   CAL
VOLCÀ DE   SASTRE
SANTA MARGARIDA

0   5 mi

0   5 km

© MOON.COM

313

8 For dinner, splurge at Ca l'Enric in La Vall de Bianya (18 kilometers/11 miles from Santa Pau), a family-run Michelin-starred restaurant that captures the essence of the region's flavors.

LA GARROTXA ON DAY 2

1 Drive over to Olot, and spend the morning roaming the volcanic cityscape. Delve deeper into the region's seismic activity at the Museu dels Volcans.

2 Next up, visit the cliff-hanging village of Castellfollit de la Roca, 8 kilometers (5 miles) northeast of Olot, and follow the leisurely trail to the river to enjoy the best views.

3 Drive east to Besalú (14 kilometers/9 miles) and make a grand entrance across the magnificent 11th-century bridge, the Pont de Besalú. Meander a maze of cobbled lanes in the town's historic core and picture its medieval heyday a thousand years ago.

4 Finally, watch over the town from the ancient walls, and take one last look at the volcanic horizon.

Parc Natural de la Zona Volcànica de la Garrotxa

With more than 40 volcanoes and 20 lava flows, the Parc Natural de la Zona Volcànica de la Garrotxa (La Garrotxa Volcanic Zone Natural Park) is a singular volcanic landscape. The field became active approximately 700,000 years ago, and must have resembled an apocalyptic scene for much of its history, though these ancient cones surrendered their slopes to nature long ago (and there is very little risk of them erupting today). Croscat was the last volcano to erupt, roughly 11,000 years ago, although beneath the surface, stirring tectonic plates keep the area seismically active. The last major earthquake in 1428 caused death and destruction as far away as Barcelona.

From the ashes of its volatile past, a spectacularly beautiful landscape emerged. Situated at the foot of the Pyrenees, this dormant mass of magma is home to 1,178 species of flowering plants, 261 vertebrate animals, and swathes of oak and beech forests nourished by the fertile volcanic soil. Humans, too, have long since inhabited the pockmarked landscape, from medieval settlements built out of volcanic stone to 20th-century quarrying that sliced Croscat open to its core.

To preserve and protect the area's natural beauty and habitat, the park was established in 1982. Today, numerous hiking trails throughout the area (labeled "Itineraries") enable

the Montsacopa volcano at Olot

visitors to explore this fascinating geological terrain and its many sites of interest. Besides exploring on foot, the park makes for a pleasant drive, with plenty of villages and eateries as stopping points. A wonderful alternative is to float above the Earth's crust in a hot air balloon.

VISITING THE PARK

97/227-1600; en.turismegarrotxa.com
The park is always open and entrance is free (aside from parking fees). The most-visited area of the park lies between Olot and Santa Pau, accessed via the GI-524. The towns of Olot and Santa Pau lie within the park's boundaries, as does Castellfollit de la Roca.

PARKING

There are two main car parks in the Parc Natural Zona Volcànica de la Garrotxa, both of which are located between Olot and Santa Pau: Can Serra, just opposite the Fageda d'en Jordà, and Santa Margarida,

located between the Croscat and Santa Margarida volcanoes. Parking fees vary by car park and season. To visit Castellfollit de la Roca, park in the Plaça Nova car park, which is located in the town itself.

TOURIST INFORMATION CENTERS
Olot and Santa Pau

The tourist information center in Olot is at the crossroads of Carrer Dr. Fàbregas with Carrer Sant Rafel (Carrer Dr. Fàbregas, 6; 97/226-0141; www.turismeolot.com; Apr.-Jun. Mon. and Wed.-Sat. 10am-2pm, 4pm-7pm, Sun. 10am-2pm, Jul.-Sept. Mon.-Sat. 9am-2pm, 3pm-7pm, Sun. 9am-2pm, Oct.-Mar. Mon. and Wed.-Sat. 10am-1pm, 4pm-6pm, Sun. 10am-1pm).

The tourist information center in Santa Pau is located in Plaça Major (Plaça Major, 1; 97/268-0349; www.visitsantapau.com; Mon. 10am-2pm, Wed.-Sun. 10am-2pm, 4:30pm-6:30pm; closed Mon.-Fri. during Feb.).

Between Olot and Santa Pau

There are several tourist information centers within the park, including the Can Serra information center in the car park opposite the Fageda d'en Jordà (Ctra. Olot-Santa Pau, km 4; 97/219-5074; Sat.-Sun. 10am-3pm, daily in August; Oct. 12-Dec. 8 Sat.-Sun. 9am-5pm), the Can Passavent information center at the entrance to the Croscat quarry (Ctra. Olot-Santa Pau, km 7; 97/219-5094; 10am-4pm daily), and the Casal dels Volcans information center in Olot (Avinguda de Santa Coloma, 43; 97/226-8112; Tues.-Sun. 10am-2pm). At Can Serra, it is possible to rent carriers for small children.

SIGHTS

OLOT

La Garrotxa's many distinctive qualities come together in Olot, the county capital. Set on the banks of the Fluvià River, on a plain surrounded by mountains, the city is shaped by four volcanoes that sleep amid the striking cityscape. Of them, the Montsacopa volcano lies at the heart of the city, with a 17th-century chapel and two watchtowers around the rim. Climb the volcano, a 30-minute hike, for 360-degree views.

These urban volcanoes are omnipresent in Olot life, from the volcanic materials used to build the city, to its remarkable landscapes and the local earthy cuisine. The town has a long tradition of painting, sculpture, and ceramic, including the 19th-century "Olot School," a group of painters who were inspired by the surrounding terrain. The Museu de la Garrotxa (Carrer de l'Hospici, 8; 97/227-1166; museus.olot.cat; Tues.-Fri. 10am-1pm, 3pm-6pm, Sat. 11am-2pm, 4pm-7pm, Sun. 11am-2pm) has a good representative collection, while the Museu

Fageda d'en Jordà

Santa Pau

dels Volcans (Parc Nou, Avinguda de Santa Coloma, 43; 97/226-6762; museus.olot.cat; Tues.-Sat. 10am-2pm, 3pm-6pm, Sun. 10am-2pm) explores the physical environment of La Garrotxa and its seismic activity.

BETWEEN OLOT AND SANTA PAU
✪ Fageda d'en Jordà

Where once lava flowed from the Croscat volcano, an enchanting beech forest has grown up at an unusually low altitude (550-650 meters/1,800-2,100 feet above sea level), unique for this species in Spain. The forest floor rises and falls with the rugged, undulating lava flow, and craggy hummocks of up to 20 meters (65 feet), known locally as *tossols*, are concealed beneath a leafy carpet. This deep and dense deciduous woodland transforms with the seasons and is particularly beautiful in autumn, when it becomes an awesome mass of rusty hues. Many have fallen under its mystical spell, including Catalan poet Joan Maragall, who wrote a famous verse in its honor. Within the forest, you can visit La Fageda Cooperativa (97/268-1011; www.fageda.com), a social enterprise that produces delicious yogurt and dairy products. Park at the Can Serra car park (Carretera d'Olot a Santa Pau, km 4; 97/219-5074), opposite the woods along the main road from Olot to Santa Pau.

SANTA PAU

Situated in the heart of the natural park, 10 kilometers (6 miles) southeast of Olot, Santa Pau is a beautifully preserved medieval village, famous for its haricot beans (known as *fesols* or *mongetes*). A 13th-century castle watches over the stone houses and narrow lanes of the historic center, which is oriented around Plaça Major. The triangular-shaped plaza is also known as *Firal dels Bous* (Fair of the Bulls), referring to the old cattle market that used to take place here, and has remained relatively unchanged since the 14th century.

Castellfollit de la Roca

CASTELLFOLLIT DE LA ROCA

Perched precariously on top of a 50-meter-high (164-foot) precipice, the village of Castellfollit de la Roca is, quite literally, a cliffhanger. The medieval settlement, built mainly from volcanic rock, clings spectacularly to the edge of a lava cliff along the northern limits of the natural park. The striking crag of basalt columns rises dramatically at the confluence of the Fluvià and Toronell rivers, and represents one of the most extraordinary geological feats in the area. Plaça Josep Pla and the bell tower of the old church offer excellent panoramas over the valley and the tiny medieval town. Wander along the main street (Carrer Major) to the viewing points, or follow the leisurely Itinerary 13 trail to the river. The village is tiny, but there are a handful of places to eat or drink.

Castellfollit de la Roca is a 12-minute drive from Olot. Take the A-26 heading northeast, exiting at junction 79 onto the N-260 for Castellfollit de la Roca (8 kilometers/5 miles).

TOP EXPERIENCE

HIKING

Visitors can discover the natural beauty of La Garrotxa Volcanic Zone Natural Park on foot by following one of the many hiking routes ("Itineraries") signposted throughout the park. There are 28 trails of various lengths, ranging from 30 minutes to 7 hours. Most are well signposted, although maps are useful when following the longer routes. These trails form part of the Itinerània (www.itinerannia.net) network, which covers over 2,500 kilometers (1,550 miles) across the surrounding regions of Ripollès, Garrotxa, and Alt Empordà. Ninety-eight percent of the park is private property; respect the people who live there, and leave no trash.

The first three points of interest listed here (Volcà del Croscat, Volcà del Santa Margarida, and Fageda d'en Jordà beech forest) are the most-visited areas of the park. They can be explored independently, as described here, or combined in a 10.5-kilometer (6.5-mile) hike following Itinerary 1. This popular route takes in all three sights, starting at either the Can Serra (Fageda d'en Jordà) or Santa Margarida car park. A good option is to park at Santa Margarida and follow the Itinerary 1 in a clockwise direction, and on the final leg of the hike, finish with a hearty lunch at Restaurant Masnou.

✪ Volcà del Croscat (Croscat Volcano)

Distance: 2.9 kilometers (1.8 miles), round-trip
Duration: 50 minutes
Effort Level: Easy

Ever wondered what the inside of a volcano looks like? At 190 meters (623 feet), Croscat is the highest and youngest volcanic cone in the area, and one of the highlights of the park. Part of Croscat was quarried until the early 1990s, which cut a clean slice out of the Strombolian volcano, leaving its insides open for exploration—a rare opportunity to peek beneath the Earth's crust.

Starting at the Santa Margarida car park, follow Itinerary 15 across the road towards Restaurant Masnou. At the restaurant, turn left and head uphill, then follow the path to the right, around the base of the volcano. Head downhill to the Can Passavent information center, where there is a permanent exhibition about the volcano, then turn left and discover the former quarry—a geological cross-section that adds a unique and surprising dimension to the hike. Return via the same route.

hiking at the foot of the Croscat Volcano

Volcà de Santa Margarida (Santa Margarida Volcano)

Distance: 3 kilometers (1.8 miles), loop

Duration: 1 hour 20 minutes

Effort Level: Moderate

With a diameter of 1.2 kilometers (0.75 miles), Santa Margarida is the largest volcano in the area. Its wide, meadow-filled crater forms a perfect circle, while lush forests blanket its outer slopes. In the center of the crater lies the curious Romanesque hermitage of Santa Margarida, the volcano's namesake, which dates from the 11th century.

Starting in the Santa Margarida car park, follow Itinerary 1 to the rim of the volcano and down into the crater. It's a moderately steep hike up, and more gentle descent. From the crater, Itinerary 1 continues in the direction of La Fageda d'en Jordà, so unless you are planning to complete the full 10.5-kilometer (6.5-mile) route, walk around the volcano's rim and retrace your steps back to the car park.

Fageda d'en Jordà

Distance: 1.5 kilometers (1 mile), loop

Duration: 35 minutes

Effort Level: Easy

The enchanting Fageda d'en Jordà beech forest can be explored via several walking trails, the easiest of which begins at the Can Serra car park (Carretera d'Olot a Santa Pau, km 4; 97/219-5074), opposite the woods along the main road from Olot to Santa Pau. Itinerary 2, also known as the Joan Maragall trail, is short and relatively flat, and takes hikers into the heart of the beech grove. Setting off from the car park, follow the underpass across the road and descend the steps into the forest. At this stage, Itinerary 1 and Itinerary 2 run parallel. Follow the path to the foot of a large hummock, walking around its

Volcà de Santa Margarida

Vías Verdes greenway

circumference. From here, Itinerary 2 returns to the car park, while Itinerary 1 delves deeper into the woods, eventually emerging towards the Santa Margarida volcano.

Castellfollit de la Roca

Distance: 2 kilometers (1.2 miles), loop
Duration: 45 minutes
Effort Level: Easy

The Itinerary 13 hiking trail is an easy, 2-kilometer (1.2-mile) loop, which passes through the village of Castellfollit de la Roca and down the cliff face to the Fluvià River. It starts and finishes in the Plaça Nova car park in the village. Plaça Josep Pla and the bell tower of the old church offer excellent panoramas over the valley and the tiny medieval town.

CYCLING

The Vías Verdes greenways (www. viesverdes.cat) are disused railway lines that have been adapted for walkers and cyclists across Spain. Part of this network passes through La Garrotxa, running along the old line from Olot to Girona (known as the Carrilet), with many shorter routes that branch off into the surrounding area. Cycling is an enjoyable and eco-friendly way of exploring La Garrotxa's unique landscape, and there are routes to suit all levels. Autumn and spring are the best times to try it. Bikes can be rented in Olot, or in Girona for anyone keen on attempting a longer distance.

RENTALS
Centre Logístic de Bicicletes

Av. Estació, 3; 97/269-2023;
bicicletes.atma.cat

The Logistic Bike Center in Olot offers a complete service of rentals, transfers, and logistics, for short and long routes. Choose from electric, mountain, racing, hybrid, and adapted bikes, match with all the necessary accessories, and then set off on a GPS-guided adventure; or hire an experienced guide and enjoy the ride. Prices range from €6 per hour, €15 for a half day, €20 per day, and €85 per week. The Ruta del

Carrilet cycling trail begins in Olot, although transfers and hotel pick-ups are also available.

TRAILS
Ruta del Carrilet
Distance: 57 kilometers (35 miles)
Duration: 5-6 hours, one-way
Effort Level: Moderate

The Carrilet cycle lane follows in the tracks of the narrow-gauge railway line that once ran between Olot and Girona. It's a straightforward route that crosses the volcanic landscape and many charming towns, with an average downhill gradient of 1.5 percent. The section between Olot and Les Planes d'Hostoles (23.5 kilometers/14.5 miles, 2.5 hours one-way) is the most popular part of the trail, encompassing many points of interest. This section also connects with many other routes, enabling cyclists to branch off and explore the surrounding landscape. La Rectoria de Sant Miquel de Pineda B&B is situated along this route and makes an excellent base for cycling enthusiasts.

HOT AIR BALLOON RIDES
Vol de Coloms
97/268-0255; www.voldecoloms.cat

La Garrotxa Volcanic Zone Natural Park is at its most spectacular when viewed from above, taking in a bird's-eye view of the dormant volcanoes. Vol de Coloms offers early-morning balloon rides (60-90 minutes, from €160) over this remarkable landscape, taking off close to the Croscat Volcano, with views that stretch from the Pyrenees to the Mediterranean on a clear day. Flight and accommodation packages are available (from €170 pp).

FOOD
OLOT AND VICINITY
✪ Les Cols
Carretera de la Canya; 97/226-9209;
lescols.com; tasting menus €105/€150 with
wine, Thursday set lunch menu €20

Les Cols represents a magical collaboration of Olot's finest creative talents: culinary wizard Fina Puigdevall and Pritzker Prize-winning architects RCR, whose avant-garde remodeling of a traditional farmhouse makes a sublime setting for this two-Michelin-starred restaurant. Like the architecture, Puigdevall's 18-course tasting menus combine tradition and modernity, inspired by nature and the surrounding landscape. The experience begins with a tour of the restaurant, before diners embark on a gastronomic journey of the Catalan countryside, as told through a select set of local ingredients, from pig's trotters and wild boar, to truffles, trout, and chestnuts. The result is a well-rounded sequence of dishes that capture the flavors of each season. Reservations essential. To sample Les Cols at a bargain price, go on a Thursday lunchtime (€20); there is no à la carte menu.

Ca l'Enric
Ctra. de Camprodon, Nacional 260,
km 91, La Vall de Bianya; 97/229-0015;
www.restaurantcalenric.cat; Tues.-Sun.
1:15pm-3:15pm, Fri.-Sat. 8:45pm-10:30pm;
€29-€38, tasting menus €85/€110

Located 8 kilometers (5 miles) northwest of Olot, Ca l'Enric began as a 19th-century travellers' inn and comes from a family tradition of exceptional cuisine, passed down and refined through the generations. Set in the restored family farmhouse, this Michelin-starred restaurant retains a rural spirit, but its gastronomic offering is bang up-to-date. The line-up of original creations—such as lamb served with porcini duxelles, thyme, anchovy, and glasswort, or turtle dove with oyster escabeche—represent a contemporary take on local specialties made using seasonal produce from the surrounding forests of La Vall de Bianya.

BETWEEN OLOT AND SANTA PAU

The following restaurants are listed in the order you'll encounter them when driving from Olot to Santa Pau.

Restaurant Hostal dels Ossos

Ctra. Santa Pau, 0, Sant Cristòfol de les Fonts; 97/226-6134; www.hostaldelsossos. com; €5.80-€16.50, weekday set menu €13.50, weekend set menu €28; cash only

For some hearty post-hike grub, tuck in to homemade country fare at Hostal dels Ossos, located on the road from Olot to Santa Pau. The very reasonably priced menu offers a multitude of traditional flavors, from the sauteed Santa Pau *fesols* (haricot beans) with *botifarra* (local sausage) and wild mushrooms to the pig's trotters with snails, grilled veal fillet, or duck and pear stew. Visit the nearby Fageda d'en Jordà forest beforehand to work up an appetite for the generous portions.

Can Xel

Ctra. Santa Pau, s/n, Santa Pau; 97/268-0211; www.canxel.com; Thurs.-Tues. 1pm-4:30pm, 8:30pm-10:30pm (closed Jan.); €25 average spend, €20 set menu

Traditional Catalan cuisine is the order of the day at Can Xel, a popular stopping point on or after the park's main hiking trails. Portions are generous and the set lunch menu is an excellent opportunity to sample the region's volcanic flavors at a reasonable price. Strategically located on the main road

from Olot to Santa Pau, in the midst of the natural park, there's room for groups of all sizes in the enormous dining room, and holiday apartments are available in the adjoining building.

✪ Restaurant Masnou

Passeig Mas Masnou, s/n, Santa Pau; 97/268-0061; Apr.-Nov. Wed.-Sun 1:30pm-4pm, Dec.-Mar. Fri.-Sun. 1:30pm-4pm; Sat.-Sun. dinner for groups (6-8 people minimum); tasting menu €44

A hidden treasure surrounded by farmland at the foot of Croscat, Restaurant Masnou is the perfect place to round off a hike among the volcanoes—especially if you've completed the full 10.5-kilometer (6.5-mile) loop. This family-run restaurant offers quality traditional fare made from local, farm-to-table produce, such as the *fesols de Santa Pau* (haricot beans) served with *botifarra* (local sausage) and crispy pancetta. The service is friendly, the atmosphere authentic, and the 12-course tasting menu a veritable feast.

ACCOMMODATIONS

OLOT

✪ Les Cols Pavellons

Mas Les Cols, Avinguda de les Cols, 2; 69/981-3817; www.lescolspavellons.com; €320 d

Designed by prize-winning architects RCR, Les Cols Pavellons is not a luxury hotel; it's an immersive, sensorial experience. Guests are invited to retreat into another dimension among these minimalist glass pavilions, where a delicate play of light and water induces a meditative state. The bathtub is particularly memorable. One night is enough to contemplate life in this disconnected hideaway, before the sparse amenities start to irritate the more practical-minded. Breakfast

amanida de fesols de Santa Pau (haricot bean salad)

This fertile land of volcanoes boasts a rich gastronomic tradition based on local, seasonal ingredients nourished by the mineral-rich soil. Chefs of La Garrotxa are incredibly proud of their heritage and are passionate about bringing the best of the region's produce straight from the farm to the table. Together they form a group known as **Cuina Volcànica** (www.cuinavolcanica.cat), literally meaning "volcanic cuisine." **Hostal dels Ossos** and **Can Xel,** located on the road between Olot and Santa Pau, are both members of the Cuina Volcànica group, and many more restaurants in the region draw their inspiration from the produce of the volcanic terrain.

The mainstay dishes of volcanic cuisine are typically hearty and wholesome, and reflect the earthy flavors of the landscape. *Fesols* (haricot beans) grown around the village of Santa Pau are among the most emblematic ingredients of the zone, together with buckwheat, potatoes, black turnips, onions, truffles, *escarlots* (a wild mushroom), chestnuts, snails, sheep's cheese, wild boar, and many kinds of sausage (*botifarra, piumoc, llonganissa,* and *fuet*). Through both traditional and innovative recipes, volcanic cuisine highlights these products and champions local farming. Keep an eye out for the following dishes on menus across the region:

- **Patates d'Olot:** roasted, meat-filled potatoes.

- **Botifarra amb fesols:** local sausage served with haricot beans.

- **Farinetes amb ratafia:** buckwheat pancakes flambéed in a sweet, local liqueur.

- **Amanida de peuada:** a boneless pig's-trotter salad.

- **Coca de llardons:** a flat savory cake made with pork crackling and pine nuts.

- **Iogurt de La Fageda:** a creamy local yogurt produced in the Fageda d'en Jordà beech forest.

- **Ratafia:** a local herbal liqueur made from cherries and almonds.

Besalú

in the orchard is pretty special, and a picnic from the two-Michelin-starred restaurant completes a surreal hiatus from reality.

SANTA PAU
Cal Sastre

Plaça dels Valls, 6-9; 97/268-0095; www.calsastre.com; €126 d

Deep inside the volcanic park of La Garrotxa, this boutique hotel lies at the medieval heart of Santa Pau. Eight stylish guest rooms adorned with antiques and lavish decor channel old-world charm, while the dynamic hosts, Eva and Jesus, ensure you have everything you need to enjoy this fairy-tale setting. After a day of hiking, gaze across the sleepy village from the hotel terrace before tucking in to refined local fare in the adjoining restaurant.

SOUTH OF OLOT
✪ La Rectoria de Sant Miquel de Pineda

Veïnat de Sant Miquel de Pineda, Sant Feliu de Pallerols; 69/135-3111; www.larectoriadesantmiquel.com; €100 d

Goretti and Roy treat their guests like family at this rural B&B in the southwest corner of La Garrotxa Volcanic Zone Natural Park. Housed in a 12th-century rectory that has been lovingly restored by the eco-conscious "Scotalan" couple, the seven beautifully appointed guest rooms are simply charming. Outside, a multitude of walking and biking trails await (it's on the Via Verde cycle route), as well as a leafy patio and saltwater swimming pool. Roy, a professional chef, designs and delivers the delicious dinner menu each day, served in an uplifting dining space with panoramic landscape views. Go half board and top it all off with a dram of whisky.

FESTIVALS

Fira de Fesol

Locals gather in Santa Pau to celebrate their favorite bean, the *fesol* (haricot bean), in mid-January, coinciding roughly with the feast of Sant Antoni (January 17). There's music on the eve of the festival, while on the day itself, stalls line the streets in the morning, followed by a mass in honor of Sant Antoni, the festival's patron. The highlight is the *fesolada*, a feast of dishes made from haricot beans, which takes place in Plaça Major.

Besalú

Built as a fortress between two rivers, the charming town of Besalú was once the thriving capital of a powerful and prosperous county. Although located outside of La Garrotxa's volcanic park, 21 kilometers (13 miles) east of Olot, the town makes a fine base from which to explore the area, and is a popular day-trip destination in itself.

The **tourist information center** in Besalú is located beside the Pont de Besalú, on the east bank of the Fluvià river (Carrer del Pont, 1; 97/259-1240; www.besalu.cat; 10am-2pm, 4pm-7pm daily). During summer, there are guided English tours of medieval Besalú (€4.50; 90 minutes) and the old Jewish quarter (€2.25; 30 minutes). Book in advance.

Pont de Besalú

Besalú

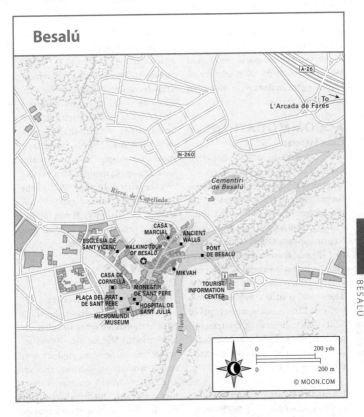

SIGHTS
⭐ WALKING TOUR OF BESALÚ

A small town with a long history, the following walking tour (allow one hour) takes in all the main sights of Besalú.

The magnificent, 11th-century **Pont de Besalú** (bridge), which spans the Riu Fluvià, is the grand gateway to a maze of cobbled lanes that make up one of the best-preserved medieval cores in the region. Considered one of the cradles of the Catalan nation, this was the stomping ground of legendary hero Wilfred the Hairy, a 9th-century count credited with unifying Catalonia.

After crossing the bridge, explore the old **Jewish Call**, once home to a vibrant community; don't miss the 12th-century **mikvah** (purification baths), one of only two examples found on the Iberian Peninsula (the other is in Girona). Meander the delightful, antiquated streets, pausing to contemplate the 12th-century **Església de Sant Vicenç**, the original facade of the **Hospital de Sant Julià**, the Romanesque **Casa de Cornellà**, and the 11th-century **Monestir de Sant Pere**, which presides over the vast town square, **Plaça del Prat de Sant Pere**. Also on the square, the **Micromundi** museum (Plaça del Prat de Sant Pere, 15; 97/259-1842; www.museuminiaturesbesalu.com; Mar.-Oct. 10am-8pm daily, Nov.-Feb. Tues.-Fri.

10-3pm, Sat. 10am-8pm, Sun. 10am-7pm; €4.90) houses a peculiar collection of microscopic dioramas from around the world. Finally, pace the perimeter on high along the ancient walls, and down low beside the river.

ACCOMMODATIONS

Casa Marcial

Carrer Comte Tallaferro, 15; 60/802-9427; www.casa-marcial.com; €97 d; adults only

Old meets new in Casa Marcial, tucked away in historic Besalú near the ancient bridge. Behind the 19th-century Neoclassical facade, a warm welcome awaits at this modern hotel. The 12 guest rooms are clean and simple, the buffet breakfast is delicious, and the honesty bar is open all hours. The remains of the medieval town walls and the Romanesque chapel of Santa Maria lie among the tranquil gardens, where lush landscape views can be enjoyed from the outdoor swimming pool.

L'Arcada de Fares

Can Figueres de Fares, Fares; 97/259-0855; www.arcadadefares.com; €102 d

There's something for all the family at this charming complex of holiday apartments. A restored 15th-century farmhouse located just a five-minute drive from Besalú, facilities here include an outdoor swimming pool, children's play area, barbecue, and an excellent restaurant. The one-, two-, and four-bedroomed apartments are simple but spacious and well equipped; many have a private terrace with uplifting views of the surrounding farmland and hilly horizon. The friendly staff run family-oriented activities and do their best to make you feel at home.

FESTIVALS

Medieval Besalú

During the first weekend of September, Besalú winds the clock back a thousand years to relive its heyday in the Middle Ages. Activities across town—including guided tours, music, workshops, jousting, theater, and fancy dress—transport visitors back to the medieval county of Besalú, once an important seat of power.

Information and Services

POLICE

For minor incidents, contact the Policia Municipal, the municipal police force in Olot (Plaça de Can Joanetes, 11; 97/227-9133). For major incidents, contact the regional police force, the Mossos d'Esquadra, also in Olot (Carrer de França, 36; 97/254-1700). Thefts can be reported at either station.

HOSPITALS AND PHARMACIES

For urgent medical needs, go to the Hospital d'Olot i Comarcal de la Garrotxa (Avinguda dels Països Catalans, 86, Olot; hospiolot.com; 97/226-1800), which operates a 24-hour emergency service. There are also primary care centers (Centre d'Atenció Primària or CAP) in both Besalú (Carrer de Prat de la Riba, 8;

97/259-0573; 8am-8pm daily) and Olot (Passeig de Barcelona, 42; 97/226-1916; Mon.-Fri. 8am-8pm).

Most small villages in La Garrotxa have one pharmacy, including Besalú (Farmàcia Gratacós; Carrer Ganganell, 44; 97/259-1273), Santa Pau (Farmàcia Soler; Avinguda dels Volcans, 15; 97/268-0159), and Castellfollit de la Roca (Farmàcia Tarrés Vila; Carretera d'Olot, 5; 97/229-4018). There are numerous pharmacies in Olot, and at least one of them is always on call. Check the notice posted on pharmacy doors or visit www.cofgi.org/farmacies/farmacies-de-guardia for details.

LUGGAGE STORAGE

There is no luggage storage service in La Garrotxa.

Transportation

GETTING THERE

The best way to reach La Garrotxa is by car. It is possible to get there by public transport, but driving will give you more flexibility to explore once there.

CAR

Driving time from Barcelona to Olot and Besalú are similar, though the routes are different.

Driving to Olot

Follow the C-33 heading north from Barcelona, then join the C-17. Exit the C-17 at junction 69, taking the C-37 towards Olot, and then the C-152 into the center. The 113-kilometer (70-mile) drive takes approximately 1 hour and 40 minutes and tolls come to €1.66 (only the C-33 is tolled). To go straight to the natural park, take the GI-524 towards Santa Pau before reaching Olot city center.

Driving to Besalú

Drive 100 kilometers (62 miles) northeast from Barcelona along the C-33 and AP-7 highway. Exit the AP-7 at junction 6, and follow the C-66 (direction Banyoles) for 25 kilometers (16 miles) to Besalú. The 133-kilometer (83-mile) drive takes approximately 1 hour 40 minutes, and tolls cost €10.

BUS

From Barcelona, Teisa (97/220-4868; www.teisa-bus.com) runs up to five daily bus services to Olot (2 hours 15 minutes; €18.85), passing through Besalú (1 hour 40 minutes; €15.70) and Castellfollit de la Roca (2 hours; €17.50). An additional three services travel to Olot via Amer (2 hours 10 minutes; €16.70). Teisa also operates an express bus to Olot via Vic (1 hour 45 minutes; €13.85), with four services on weekdays, one on Saturday, and two on Sunday.

Purchase tickets in advance from the Teisa office in Barcelona (Carrer de Pau Claris, 117; 93/215-3566; Mon.-Fri. 8:30am-3pm, 4:30pm-8:30pm, Sat. 9am-3pm). Buses leave from outside the office, at the junction of Carrer de Pau Claris with Carrer del Consell de Cent.

GETTING AROUND

The best way to get around La Garrotxa is by car, although it is possible to explore the area by public transport, cycling, and hiking.

PUBLIC TRANSIT

Buses run approximately every hour between Besalú and Olot, primarily coming from the surrounding areas and cities (Barcelona, Girona, Figueres, etc.). On weekdays, there is an additional local service, the Bus transversal de la Garrotxa (Les Planes d'Hostoles-Olot-Besalú), which operates hourly.

A local bus service (TPO) with four lines operates within the city of Olot, while the Bus del Volcans connects Olot with Santa Pau, stopping at the Can Serra (Fageda d'en Jordà) car park, Can Xel, and Santa Margarida car park en route (€1.75). All local buses are operated by Teisa (97/220-4868; www.teisa-bus.com).

CAR

Driving distances between towns in La Garrotxa are as follows: Olot-Besalú, 21 kilometers (13 miles); Olot-Santa Pau, 10 kilometers (6 miles); Olot-Castellfollit de la Roca, 8 kilometers (5 miles); Olot-Parc Natural Zona Volcànica de la Garrotxa (Can Serra information center), 4 kilometers (2.5 miles); Besalú-Castellfollit de la Roca, 14 kilometers (9 miles); Besalú-Parc Natural Zona Volcànica de la Garrotxa (Can Serra information center), 25 kilometers (16 miles); Besalú-Santa Pau, 30 kilometers (19 miles).

Parking in the medieval villages can be tricky. It is generally easier to park on the edge of the village and walk to the center.

TAXI

To order a taxi call Taxi Olot (97/226-1566), Taxitour Garrotxa (69/973-7301), or Taxi Besalú (65/992-2790).

LEAVING LA GARROTXA

The last bus back to Barcelona from Besalú leaves at 4:55pm (Sun. 6:55pm), while the last bus from Olot leaves at 6pm (Sat. 4:30pm, Sun. 8:30pm).

From La Garrotxa, visitors can travel on to the Costa Brava, Girona, and Figueres.

VALL DE BOÍ

A lush, narrow valley surrounded

by steep mountains, Vall de Boí is dotted with medieval villages and UNESCO-listed Romanesque churches, and leads to the breathtaking Aigüestortes i Estany de Sant Maurici National Park. It's the stuff fairy tales are made of, where bright blue skies contrast against snow-capped mountains and a whole spectrum of greens. Carve fresh tracks in the slopes of Boí Taüll, the highest ski resort in the Pyrenees, take a reviving dip in the hot springs of Caldes de Boí, or hike amid soaring peaks and glassy lakes in the national

HIGHLIGHTS

✪ **SANT CLIMENT DE TAÜLL:**
Witness a virtual recreation of a Romanesque masterpiece in this 12th-century church, known for its vibrant frescoes (page 343).

✪ **BOÍ TAÜLL SKI RESORT:**
Reach new heights on the slopes of the Boí Taüll, the highest ski resort in the Pyrenees (page 345).

✪ **HIKING IN AIGÜESTORTES I ESTANY DE SANT MAURICI NATIONAL PARK:**
Trek amid soaring summits, clear mountain streams, and glacial lakes in Catalonia's only national park (page 348).

Sant Climent de Taüll

park, where each twist and turn reveals another jaw-dropping panorama. This slice of heaven is one of Catalonia's best-kept secrets.

ORIENTATION

Situated in the central Pyrenees, Vall de Boí is about as far away from Barcelona (280 kilometers/174 miles) as one can travel while still remaining within Catalonia. The **Noguera de Tor river** runs through the sparsely populated valley, which lies southwest of the Aigüestortes i Estany de Sant Maurici National Park.

The valley begins just north of the town of **El Pont de Suert**, where the **L-500** (the main road through the valley) veers off the N-230, and stretches 23 kilometers (14 miles) northeast, culminating with the Cavallers reservoir. Nine **Lombard-Romanesque churches** are dotted across the valley, each one situated in an ancient stone village, and together form a UNESCO World Heritage Site, noted for their unified style and excellent state of preservation. The **Caldes de Boí** thermal baths are situated in the upper part of the valley, which is largely uninhabited and comes to an end at the Cavallers entrance to the national park.

PLANNING YOUR TIME

Vall de Boí is a 3.5-hour drive from Barcelona, and deserves at least a couple of days, or longer, to really connect with this natural kingdom.

Average temperatures in the valley vary greatly from winter to summer. August is the warmest time of year, when daily highs hit around 27°C (81°F), but even then, temperatures drop to around 15°C (59°F) at night, making for a dreamy escape from parched urban areas. January is the coldest month, with an average high of around 10°C (50°F), and lows of around freezing. In the Aigüestortes i Estany de Sant Maurici National Park, temperatures are notably lower than the Boí Valley, due to elevation (summer average of around 19°C/66°F, and lows of -4°C/25°F). Temperatures hover around freezing during winter, and snow lingers on the highest peaks for several months.

May or June is the ideal time to visit the area, when the snow has melted, the rivers are fast flowing, spring is in full bloom, and the summer heat hasn't yet hit. July and August are the busiest in terms of tourism, although there are things to do all year round in the valley. If traveling in low season (Sept.-Jun., except holidays and winter weekends), call ahead to confirm opening hours.

The Vall de Boí tourist information center is located on the main road through the valley (L500) in Barruera (Passeig Sant Feliu, 43; 97/369-4000; www.vallboi.cat; Sept. 12-Jun. 22 Mon.-Sat. 9am-2pm, 5pm-7pm, Sun. 10am-2pm, Jun. 23-Sept. 11 9am-2pm, 5pm-7pm daily). The tourist information center for the Aigüestortes i Estany de Sant Maurici National Park is in Boí (Casa del Parc Nacional a Boí; Ca de Simamet, Carrer de les Graieres, 2; 97/369-6189; parcsnaturals.gencat.cat; Mon.-Sat. 9am-2pm, 3:30pm-6pm, Sun. 9am-2pm).

Itinerary Ideas

Two days is enough to get a feel for the area's natural beauty, Romanesque heritage, and a healthy dose of mountain air, but to make the most of it, stay an extra night or two and arrive a day in advance. Before setting off on any hikes, ensure that you are prepared in terms of fitness, suitable equipment, food, and water. Take extreme care in the mountains, particularly in winter, and think about the way back.

VALL DE BOÍ ON DAY 1

1 Head for the hills first thing, taking a taxi from Boí to the Aigüestortes i Estany de Sant Maurici National Park.

2 Spend the morning hiking the classic trail from the plateau of Aigüestortes to Estany Llong.

3 Once back in the valley, refuel with a hearty, homemade meal at Restaurante La Granja in Erill la Vall.

4 Get up to speed on the valley's millennial history at the Centre del Romànic de la Vall de Boí.

5 Survey the surroundings from the six-story bell tower of Santa Eulalia d'Erill la Vall.

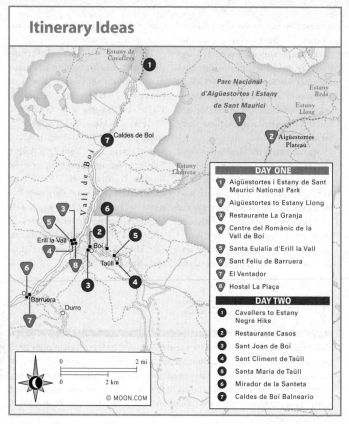

Itinerary Ideas

DAY ONE

1. Aigüestortes i Estany de Sant Maurici National Park
2. Aigüestortes to Estany Llong
3. Restaurante La Granja
4. Centre del Romànic de la Vall de Boí
5. Santa Eulàlia d'Erill la Vall
6. Sant Feliu de Barruera
7. El Ventador
8. Hostal La Plaça

DAY TWO

1. Cavallers to Estany Negre Hike
2. Restaurante Casos
3. Sant Joan de Boí
4. Sant Climent de Taüll
5. Santa Maria de Taüll
6. Mirador de la Santeta
7. Caldes de Boí Balneario

6 Drive 5 minutes south and delve further into the area's Romanesque heritage with a visit to the church of **Sant Feliu de Barruera.**

7 Dine at **El Ventador** in Barruera for a contemporary, creative twist on mountain fare.

8 Head back to Erill la Vall and rest up at **Hostal La Plaça.**

VALL DE BOÍ ON DAY 2

1 Drive to the Cavallers dam at the northern tip of the valley. Ramble around the rim of the glassy reservoir on the **Cavallers to Estany Negre hike,** surrounded by the wildest peaks of the national park.

2 Next, stop at Boí and tuck in to a well-deserved, post-hike pizza at **Restaurante Casos.**

3 Peep inside the church of Sant Joan de Boí, restored to reflect its original appearance.

4 Back in the car, drive 5 minutes uphill to the church of Sant Climent de Taüll, and witness the digital mapping of the emblematic Christ Pantocrator mural, a 12th-century masterpiece.

5 Round off the Romanesque reconnaissance at the church of Santa Maria de Taüll, in the village center.

6 From Taüll, make the 10-minute walk to the Mirador de la Santeta and take one last look over the verdant valley.

7 Finally, after two days of nonstop action, ease aching muscles at the Caldes de Boí Balneario.

Valley Villages

The Boí valley has cradled eight tiny, stone-built settlements in its clutch since time immemorial. Each village is home to a UNESCO-listed Romanesque church and a strong mountain community. For hundreds of years, this community lived in relative isolation, and to this day maintains rich local customs and traditions. Although the area's many highlights sometimes overshadow this beautiful backdrop, village hopping, by car or on foot, is, in itself, a wonderful way to experience the valley's unique medieval heritage.

The villages are no more than a 10-minute drive apart, and the easiest way to get around is by car. It is also possible to explore the area on foot, following hiking trails between the villages. The principal villages are: Barruera, the main urban center; Erill la Vall, at the heart of the valley; Boí, the gateway to the Aigüestortes i Estany de Sant Maurici National Park; and Taüll, which leads to the

highest ski resort in the Pyrenees, Boí Taüll.

BARRUERA

Barruera is the largest village in the valley. The L-500, the valley's main road, passes through the village, along which the area's main tourist information center can be found. The church of Sant Feliu de Barruera sits on the edge of the village, on the banks of the Noguera de Tor river, which is a lovely area for a stroll.

SIGHTS
Sant Feliu de Barruera
Carrer Església, 1;
10am-2pm daily; €2
A bull's head on the ancient door welcomes visitors to the church of Sant Feliu de Barruera. The church exemplifies architectural elements from both the 11th and 12th centuries, evident in the style variations between its two apses. Its haphazard layout feels distinctly less ordered than its

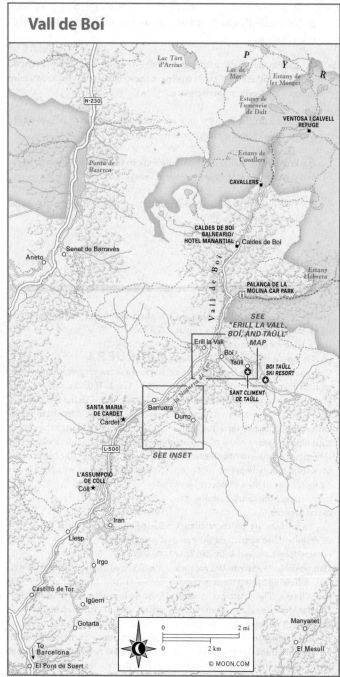

Vall de Boí

Lac Tòrt d'Arrius

Lac de Mar

PYR

Estany de les Monges

N-230

Estany de Tumeneia de Dalt

VENTOSA I CALVELL REFUGE

Estany de Cavallers

Pantà de Baserca

CAVALLERS

CALDES DE BOÍ BALNEARIO/ HOTEL MANANTIAL • Caldes de Boí

Aneto

Senet de Barravès

Estany Llobreta

PALANCA DE LA MOLINA CAR PARK

Vall de Boí

SEE "ERILL LA VALL, BOÍ, AND TAÜLL" MAP

Erill la Vall

Boí

Taüll

BOÍ TAÜLL SKI RESORT

la Noguera de Tor

SANT CLIMENT DE TAÜLL

SANTA MARIA DE CARDET
Cardet ★

Barruera

Durro

L-500

SEE INSET

L'ASSUMPCIÓ DE CÓLL
Cóll ★

Iran

Llesp

Irgo

Castilló de Tor

Igüerri

Gotarta

Manyanet

To Barcelona

El Pont de Suert

El Mesull

0   2 mi

0   2 km

© MOON.COM

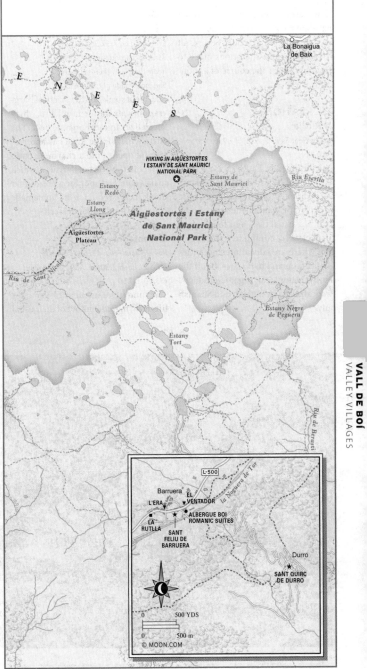

Romanesque contemporaries, which may date back to inconsistencies during construction, or could be a result of additions and alterations made to the church over the course of a thousand years.

RECREATION
La Rutlla
Passeig Sant Feliu, 2; 63/773-8996; 10am-8pm

One for the kids, La Rutlla is a leisure farm on the edge of Barruera. Visitors can go horse riding by the Noguera de Tor river, or wander the farm, home to all the usual two- and four-legged suspects. To complete the experience, there are educational activities for children and barbecues for all the family, using local, organic products. Programs are in Catalan and Spanish only.

FOOD
L'Era
Carrer Major, 7; 97/369-4192; www.restaurantlera.com; Mon.-Fri. noon-11pm, Sat. 11am-midnight, Sun. noon-midnight; €10-€15

Succulent steaks and a variety of burgers dominate the menu at L'Era, which specializes in local organic beef. The rustic-chic, alpine-style bar and restaurant opens onto a charming patio terrace in the heart of Barruera, which makes a perfect spot for a pre-dinner drink. Leave room for the homemade chocolate fondant for dessert.

El Ventador
Passeig Sant Feliu, 49; 66/186-3400; Fri.-Sun. noon-3:30pm, 7:30pm-midnight; €13.50-€17.50

The innovative menu at El Ventador lifts local ingredients out of their usual

Sant Feliu de Barruera

Erill la Vall, Boí, and Taüll

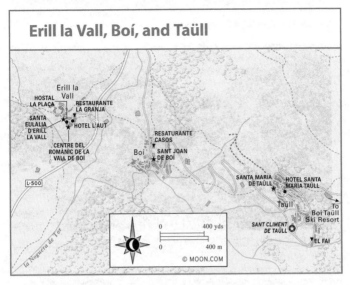

hearty mountain context, and gives them a creative twist and some international flavors. River trout sashimi, slow-cooked pork filet, and duck-confit spring rolls are among the delectable dishes served up in the simple, contemporary dining room, accompanied by a small but special selection of excellent wines.

ACCOMMODATIONS
Albergue Boi Romanic Suites
Passeig Sant Feliu-Barruera, 14; 61/902-5508; http://boiromanicsuites.es; €105 d

This basic but friendly guesthouse offers eight rooms and one apartment. Rooms vary considerably—five of them are located within the guesthouse, and three are in a building across the main road—so choose carefully. Suite five is the finest, with a private jacuzzi, terrace, and mountain views. Access to a shared kitchen, living, and dining space is included, and guests also receive a discount on activities with Guies de Taüll (see page 348).

ERILL LA VALL
Pretty Erill la Vall is situated at the heart of the valley, looking across at Boí. The Romanesque Visitor Center and the Romanesque church of Santa Eulalia d'Erill la Vall are the highlights here.

SIGHTS
Santa Eulalia d'Erill la Vall
Plaça de Baix-erill, 3; 10am-2pm, 4pm-7pm daily (Jul.-Aug. until 8pm); €2

The slender, six-story bell tower of this church presides over Erill la Vall, characterized by its square plan and decorative Lombard bands. Aligned with the bell towers of Sant Joan de Boí and Sant Climent de Taüll, it once served as a communications, watchtower, and meeting place at the heart of the medieval valley. Construction of the church began in the 11th century, while the bell tower and porch were completed in the 12th. Inside, there is a replica of the 12th-century "Descent from the Cross" wood carving, which depicts a scene composed of seven figures removing Christ from the cross (look for

The Sant Nicolau river meanders through grassy meadows and forests.

Throughout much of their history, the ancient settlements of the valley were only accessible on foot. A network of trails connected one village to the next, along which farmers led animals to market and villagers ran daily errands. These trails still exist, allowing visitors to follow in the footsteps of the valley's forebears and relive a part of its history.

Hiking the valley is a great way to discover the area and the landscape, and offers many easily accessible alternatives to the national park. There is a wide variety of trails to suit all levels, from family-friendly strolls to full-day hikes, categorized by degree of difficulty. The following trails are among the most popular; make sure you pick up a detailed map at the tourist information center.

THE WATER TRAIL
Distance: 27 kilometers (17 miles), one way

the thief on the right, sticking out his tongue). The original figures are now split between the MNAC in Barcelona and the Episcopal Museum in Vic.

Centre del Romànic de la Vall de Boí (Romanesque Visitor Center)

Carrer del Batalló, 5; 97/369-6715;
www.centreromanic.com; 9am-2pm,
5pm-7pm daily; €2

The Romanesque Visitor Center is a good starting point from which to explore the rich cultural heritage of the valley. This small interpretation space explains the historical and societal context within which the area's Romanesque churches were created, via a short multimedia exhibition and video. Although not especially informative, it's enough to give visitors a better understanding of the architecture, art, and iconography they will find throughout the area. The center is also responsible for managing all of the valley's Romanesque heritage sites and provides practical information, ticket sales, and guided tours (summer only).

FOOD
Restaurante La Granja

Carrer de Santa Eulàlia, 1; 97/369-6322;
Fri.-Sun. 1:30pm-3:30pm, 8pm-10:30pm;
€9-€24

At La Granja traditional mountain fare is served in a cozy, stone-walled dining

Duration: 8 hours

Effort Level: Moderate

The water trail is the backbone of the valley's network of traditional paths. It is 27 kilometers (17 miles) long, and connects El Pont de Suert with the Boí Valley, following the banks of the Noguera de Tor river. The trail starts at Escales dam, just south of El Pont de Suert, and finishes at the Caldes de Boí health resort. Along the length of the route, visitors get a taste of the area's natural and cultural heritage, from riverside meadows and oak and pine woods to valley views, a variety of birds, and the famous Romanesque architecture. The final stretch from Boí to Caldes de Boí is particularly nice.

The trail can be broken down into easier, shorter sections, as follows: Font de la Mena-Pont de Suert (2.5 kilometers/1.6 miles); Pont de Suert-Salencar de Llesp (6.5 kilometers/4 miles); Salencar de Llesp-Barruera (8 kilometers/5 miles); Barruera-Boí (3.5 kilometers/2.2 miles); Boí-Caldes de Boí (6.5 kilometers/4 miles).

ROMANESQUE TRAIL I

Distance: 16 kilometers (10 miles), circular

Duration: Variable, depends on departure point

Effort Level: Difficult

This route follows the traditional paths that connect the villages of Barruera, Erill la Vall, Boí, Taüll, and Durro. It can start at any one of them and can be broken down into shorter sections. The route takes in several of the UNESCO World Heritage-listed Romanesque churches, as well as the Romanesque visitor center in Erill la Vall. The stretch between Boí and Durro (3.4 kilometers/2.1 miles, 1.5 hours), known as the **Camí del Pago**, boasts superb views of the valley.

SALENCAR DE BARRUERA

Distance: 1.5 kilometers (1 mile), circular

Duration: 1 hour

Effort Level: Easy

This family-friendly, circular route starts and ends at the suspension bridge in Barruera. It covers a wetland area, the Salencar (or Cardet's Dam), on the east bank of the Noguera de Tor river, populated by a variety of willow species, ash, and poplar trees. Information panels, viewing points, and wooden walkways make for a flat and accessible route through a biodiverse landscape. Keep an eye out for migratory birds, mallards, sandpipers, gallinules, dippers, kingfishers, and marsh tits, as well as toads, otters, and roe deers.

room, or al fresco in the garden. The menu is short but the cuisine is exquisite, the service is exceptional, and the prices are very reasonable. Wild mushroom salad, mountain risotto, artichoke cannelloni, and succulent grilled meats are among the generous-sized dishes on offer, all made from local produce. Leave room for the homemade cheesecake or *crema catalana*. Reservations recommended.

ACCOMMODATIONS

Hostal La Plaça

Plaça de l'Església, 1; 97/369-6026;
www.hostal-laplaza.com; €85 d

Hostal La Plaça lies at the heart of Boí, facing the 12th-century church of Santa Eulalia d'Erill la Vall on one side and the snow-capped Pyrenees on the other. The simple but comfortable guest rooms include 12 doubles, 2 triples, and 4 duplex (4-5 person), all recently decorated. Dining at the reasonably priced hotel restaurant (1:30pm-3:30pm, 8:30pm-10pm daily) is a treat—homemade mountain fare served on the terrace against a lush Pyrenean backdrop.

Hotel L'Aüt

Carrer de Santa Eulàlia, 7; 97/369-6048;
www.laut.cat; €60 d

This charming stone building offers simple, alpine-style accommodation, close to all the highlights of the

Midsummer in the mountains is a special time. Across the Vall de Boí, and many other areas of the Pyrenees, a festival of fire, known as the **Falles**, coincides roughly with the summer solstice. It is the most important festival in the valley, traditionally linked to agricultural and solar cycles, and has been recognized by UNESCO as Intangible Cultural Heritage.

In Vall de Boí, each village takes its turn to celebrate between mid-June and mid-July, starting with **Durro** on the feast of Sant Quirc (June 16), followed by **Boí** on the eve of Sant Joan (June 23), then **Barruera, Erill la Vall,** and **Taüll.** The celebrations begin at nightfall, when villagers carry flaming torches (*falles*) down the mountains, lighting traditional beacons en route, in an ancient ritual to purify the land and its peoples. Upon arrival in the villages, the flares are greeted with music, dance, and merriment, and large bonfires are lit. It's a tradition deeply rooted in the community, kept alive from one generation to the next, and a special time for young and old.

Boí Valley. The medieval village lies on the doorstep, though with hearty local cuisine in the hotel restaurant, a cozy lounge, two terraces with quaint village views, and 19 cheerful rooms (catering to 2-4 people), guests have everything they need right here.

BOÍ

The valley was named after its most important medieval settlement, Boí, which was at one time protected by fortified walls and watchtowers. Today this is the gateway village to the **Aigüestortes i Estany de Sant Maurici National Park**—from here, hikers can take a taxi to the Aigüestortes plateau.

SIGHTS

Sant Joan de Boí

Ctra. de Taüll, 31; 10am-2pm, 4pm-7pm daily; €2

On the edge of the village, the church of Sant Joan de Boí has a basilica-style floor plan with three naves, separated by thick stone arches. The dimly lit interior has been restored to reflect its original appearance, featuring replica paintings of the frescoes now displayed in the Museu Nacional d'Art de Catalunya (MNAC) in Barcelona, among them "The Stoning of Saint Stephen," "The Minstrels," and "The Bestiary." It is the most representative example in the area of 12th-century church decoration. Outside, the bell tower construction reveals the building's chronological evolution, with large 11th-century ashlars at the base, followed by 12th-century Lombard bands and a more modern steeple. Spot the replica paintings on the exterior, framing the door on the north façade.

FOOD

Restaurante Casos

Ctra. de Taüll, 11; 97/369-6152; Thurs.-Tues. 1:30pm-4pm, 8:30pm-11pm; €7-€22

Situated on the edge of Boí, Restaurante Casos is perfect for post-hike refueling. Its cozy, stonewalled interiors embrace diners in a relaxed, family-friendly atmosphere, with a menu to suit all tastes. The homemade local fare—think snails, *ceps* (wild mushrooms) and grilled meat—is guaranteed to satiate weary walkers; or skip the mountain diet and go for a generously sized pizza, the *Casos*, topped with wild mushrooms, is particularly good.

TAÜLL AND VICINITY

Situated uphill from Boí, Taüll is home to two Romanesque churches, including Sant Climent, the most treasured of all, where vibrant frescoes are brought back to life via video mapping. The Mirador de la Santeta, a 10-minute walk from the village center, affords beautiful views of the valley. The road leading uphill from Taüll leads to the ski resort of Boí Taüll.

SIGHTS

✪ Sant Climent de Taüll

L-501, km.2, Taüll; 10am-2pm, 4pm-7pm daily (8pm Jul.-Aug.); €5

If you only visit one of the valley's Romanesque churches, make it Sant Climent de Taüll, consecrated in December 1123. Aside from its splendidly preserved architecture, Sant Climent is noted for its vibrant frescoes. The most prominent example is that of the central apse, which features the emblematic image of Christ in Majesty (*Pantocrator*), considered one of the masterpieces of Romanesque art.

To prevent it from being purchased by foreign collectors, the original fresco was removed from the church between 1919 and 1923, together with several more from the area, and moved to the Museu Nacional d'Art de Catalunya (MNAC) in Barcelona.

In 2013, an innovative video projection digitally recreated the fresco in situ, following a painstaking analytical process in collaboration with the MNAC. The mapping installation (pantocrator.cat) is screened every hour and lasts approximately 10 minutes, allowing visitors to visualize the 12th-century fresco in all its polychromatic glory, and understand the painting techniques used to create the original. Witnessing the video mapping is a satisfying, circle-closing moment for anyone who has seen the original fresco on display in the MNAC.

Sant Joan de Boí

the Pantocrator masterpiece recreated through video mapping

Vall de Boí's natural beauty is matched only by its outstanding cultural offerings. The soaring Pyrenees may grab the headlines, but the area's Romanesque heritage is just as alluring. Each pretty village dotted throughout the valley is home to a stone-built church dating from the 11th or 12th century, together recognized as a UNESCO World Heritage Site.

Built under the patronage of the Lords of Erill and the Roda de Isábena Diocese, the nine churches—**Sant Climent de Taüll, Santa Maria de Taüll, Sant Joan de Boí, Santa Eulalia d'Erill la Vall, Sant Feliu de Barruera, La Nativitat, Santa Maria de Cardet, Sant Quirc de Durro,** and **l'Assumpció de Cóll**—played a central role in the medieval mountain community and reflect a rural society structured around the feudal system. More than simply a place of worship, the church was a place to meet and seek refuge, and the bell towers were used to communicate with and protect all the villages in the area.

Architecturally, this cluster of buildings represents an exceptionally pure and unified example of the Lombard Romanesque style, which originated in northern Italy. Thick masonry walls, limited openings, and slender bell towers characterize the austere churches, with sparing exterior decoration—notice the "Lombard bands" of rounded arcading and pilaster strips—and colorful frescoes inside. The murals of Sant Climent, Santa Maria de Taüll, and Sant Joan de Boí (now displayed in the **Museu Nacional d'Art de Catalunya** in Barcelona) are of particular note, as well as the carvings in Santa Eulalia d'Erill la Vall.

To get a feel for the area's millennial Romanesque heritage, it is worth visiting at least a couple of churches. **Sant Climent de Taüll** is a must, where video mapping recreates the original frescoes, as is the **Centre del Romànic de la Vall de Boí,** which explains the historical context. Combined tickets are available for purchase in the center, churches, and online: 3 churches, €7; 3 churches + Centre del Romànic, €8; 5 churches + Centre del Romànic, €10; Vall de Boí + MNAC in Barcelona, €15 (www.centreromanic.com).

Santa Maria de Taüll

Plaça Santa Maria, 1, Taüll; 10am-7pm daily (8pm Jul.-Aug.)

Situated at the heart of Taüll, the church of Santa Maria was consecrated on December 11, 1123, just one day after Sant Climent, which gives some indication of its feudal patrons' formidable wealth. Like Sant Climent, most of its colorful murals were removed in the early 20th century and are now displayed in Barcelona's Museu

Nacional d'Art de Catalunya (MNAC). In their place, replica paintings depict scenes from the Epiphany in the central apse and along the southern wall, as well as the apostles and John the Baptist. From the church, follow signs toward the Mirador de la Santeta (a 10-minute walk) for beautiful valley views.

RECREATION
✪ Boí Taüll Ski Resort

Pla de l'Ermita; 97/369-6264; www.boitaullresort.com; 9am-5pm daily (Dec.-mid-Apr.); ski pass €39, €27 half-day (1pm-5pm)

With a maximum altitude of 2,751 meters (9,025 feet), Boí Taüll is the highest ski resort in the Pyrenees. Forty-three runs—9 black, 24 red, 8 blue, 6 green—cover its north-facing slopes, with a total skiable distance of 45 kilometers (28 miles). It's neither the biggest nor the busiest resort in the area, and therefore combines great snow with uncrowded pistes in a privileged natural environment. There is plenty of accommodation at the foot of the slopes, although the resort can be easily reached by car or by shuttle bus from anywhere in Vall de Boí. Parking, equipment rental, and lessons are available, and there is a snow park for small children.

FOOD
El Fai

Carrer dels Aiguals, 10; 97/369-6201; www.restaurantelfai.com; Thurs.-Tues. 1:30pm-3:45pm, 8:30pm-10:30pm; €7.80-€19.80, set menu €16

Dine with a view at El Fai, which overlooks the Romanesque church of Sant Climent de Taüll and the Boí Valley. Traditional Catalan cuisine is made using local products and served in an elegant dining room or outside on the terrace. The mushroom cannelloni,

Boí Taüll is the highest ski resort in the Pyrenees.

Caldes de Boí thermal and beauty center

organic grilled steaks, and homemade desserts are the highlights.

ACCOMMODATIONS
Hotel Santa Maria Taüll

Cap del Riu, 3; 97/369-6250; www.taull.com; €110 d

Relaxation is the raison d'être at this three-star, adults-only hotel. Overlooking the pretty mountain village of Taüll, Hotel Santa Maria is housed in a traditional stone building, recently renovated and oozing rustic charm. The seven spacious guest rooms include four doubles and three apartments, two of which enjoy a private terrace. Room five (double superior) is especially pleasant. The restaurant-bar opens onto a pretty patio, while a series of garden terraces step down the hillside—this is the spot for an early evening drink, as the golden light illuminates the Romanesque church of Sant Climent.

CALDES DE BOÍ SPA COMPLEX
SPA
Caldes de Boí Balneario

Caldes de Boí; 97/369-6210; www.caldesdeboi.com; 9am-1:30pm, 5pm-8pm daily; entry €29

Nestled in the upper end of the Boí Valley surrounded by pure air and Pyrenean peaks, it's hard to imagine a more idyllic setting for a thermal spa retreat. From Roman baths to sacred sanctuary, the natural springs of Boí have been venerated for 2,000 years, and today supply the Caldes de Boí thermal center with mineral-rich water, recognized for its medicinal and therapeutic properties. Spaces include thermal pools, saunas, jacuzzis, steam rooms, and various therapeutic showers and baths (entry from €29), as well as a wide range of treatments (€8-€475), from mud and massage to Ayurvedic medicine.

ACCOMMODATIONS
❂ Hotel Manantial

Caldes de Boí; 97/369-6210;
www.caldesdeboi.com; €120

Alpine chalet meets health resort at the four-star Hotel Manantial, one of two hotels in the Caldes de Boí spa complex. Immersed in the landscape at the upper end of the Boí Valley, this relaxing mountain hideaway has everything you need to disappear for a few days. The famous thermal baths are the highlight, though there are plenty more reasons to stay, including a gourmet restaurant (**Manantial Restaurant;** 1:30pm-3:30pm, 8:30pm-10:30pm; set menu €25) and four outdoor pools surrounded by lush hotel gardens. Though a little lacking in the spa-retreat glam factor, the 92 guest rooms are modern and spacious, the spa is supplied by natural springs, and the setting is unbeatable.

Aigüestortes i Estany de Sant Maurici National Park

97/369-6189; parcsnaturals.gencat.cat/en/ aiguestortes; entrance free

Deep in the Pyrenees and a long way from anywhere, the Aigüestortes i Estany de Sant Maurici National Park is almost too beautiful to believe. Soaring summits stretch to over 3,000 meters (around 10,000 feet), and nearly 200 lakes are dotted amid Catalonia's only national park. Water, in all its forms, sets this landscape apart. Clear mountain streams cascade over granite crags, while gushing rivers flow into glacial lakes, and fairy-tale forests cloak the snow-capped peaks.

Diverse ecosystems inhabit this magical high-mountain terrain. Agile chamois deer graze in alpine meadows, while stoats and asp vipers slink along the cool water's edge, and golden eagles glide overhead. Tiny miracles of nature bloom despite the inhospitable environment—orchids, alpenrose, Pyrenean lilies, and blueberries can all be found here—and tree species reflect the changing altitude across the park. Swathes of oak, ash, and beech blanket the valley floors, giving way to hardier firs and mountain pines as the rugged pinnacles reach for the sky.

ENTRANCES

There are two main entrances to the national park: **Boí** to the west (for Aigüestortes), and **Espot** to the east (a two-hour drive from Vall de Boí). At each entrance, there is a tourist information center and ample free parking. The park can be reached on foot from both entrances, or there is a 4x4 taxi service (€5.25 each way; regular departures 9am-6pm daily, Jul.-Aug. 8am-7pm), which transports visitors to and from the most popular areas; private vehicles are not permitted inside the park. From Vall de Boí, the park is best explored from the **Boí** entrance, or from the **Cavallers** entrance, at the northern limit of the valley.

Note: The park is a strictly protected area. Swimming, fishing, camping, fires, hunting, and loud noises are not permitted. Visitors must take trash home, keep dogs on a leash, and take

OUTDOORS GUIDES AND TOURS

Aigüestortes i Estany de Sant Maurici National Park offers activities for all seasons, from snowshoeing and ice-climbing to hiking and guided nature trails.

GUIES DE TAÜLL

67/622-5072; www.guiesmuntanyataull.com; from €25

Based in Barruera, this small group of professional guides offers a huge range of activities throughout the year, including tours of the valley and the Aigüestortes i Estany de Sant Maurici National Park on foot, snowshoes, mountain bike, or skis, as well as the *Carros de Foc* trek (4-6 days, €545). For those seeking bigger thrills, Guies de Taüll also organizes climbing, mountaineering, off-piste skiing, *via ferratas*, and canyoning expeditions that will get the adrenaline pumping. In summer, there is an office inside a sports shop (Esports Raspa Roia, Pla de l'Ermita), but normally they organize things online or via WhatsApp.

GUÍAS VALL DE BOÍ

69/938-3729; www.guiasvalldeboi.com; from €40

Guías Vall de Boí is a small but professional outfit founded by Sidarta Gallego Solis, a certified IFMGA mountain and canyoning guide. Born and bred in the area, Gallego is at home scaling the magnificent Pyrenean peaks and shares his passion for the mountains with confidence and ease. Activities run throughout the year and include rock climbing, canyoning, *via ferrata*, ice climbing, snowshoeing, cross-country skiing, and mountaineering among some of the area's highest summits.

---

care not to disturb the animals or pick flowers, fruit, or fungi.

✪ HIKING

A network of exceptional, yet accessible, trails invites visitors to explore this dramatic topography. For more serious hikers, the Carros de Foc (Chariots of Fire, www.carrosdefoc.com) 55-kilometer (34-mile) trek takes five to seven days, hopping from one mountain refuge to the next right across the park.

Aigüestortes to Estany Llong

Distance: 4.2 kilometers (2.6 miles), one-way

Duration: 1.5 hours

Effort Level: Easy/Moderate

This classic trail to the heart of the national park is suitable for all. The route starts on the Aigüestortes plateau (1,822 meters/5,978 feet) and runs along the banks of the Sant Nicolau river through woodland and grassy meadows, gradually climbing to a stunning natural lake known as Estany Llong. Before heading for the hills, visit the Mirador de Sant Esperit viewing point, just 50 meters (160 feet) from the Aigüestortes information center, for a magnificent preview of the countless breathtaking vistas to come. Visitors can reach the Aigüestortes plateau on foot or by taxi. A 4x4 taxi service (recommended) departs frequently throughout the year from Plaça del Treio, next to the church in Boí (8am-9pm summer, 9am-6pm rest of the year, weather permitting; €5.25 each way).

If desired, this hike can be extended in various directions. Option one is to start from the Palanca de La Molina car park outside the park's boundary, and follow the lower end of the Sant Nicolau valley on foot up to the Aigüestortes plateau, passing Estany Llobreta en route (allow approximately two hours extra each way). Alternately, this route can be undertaken as a separate hike. Option two is to extend the original hike up to Estany Redó, a small,

Estany Llong

round lake that sits just above Estany Llong (allow for an extra 30 minutes each way). Option three continues even further, climbing from Estany Redó up to Portarró d'Espot (2,427 meters/7,963 feet), a mountain pass that leads to the valley of Sant Maurici. The latter route takes approximately 5 hours 30 minutes round-trip from Aigüestortes (17.5 kilometers/11 miles).

Cavallers to Estany Negre

Distance: 4.4 kilometers (2.7 miles), one-way
Duration: 2.5 hours
Effort Level: Moderate
Known as the "Route of the Marmot,"

this hike starts at the Cavallers entrance to the park, at the northern tip of the Boí Valley. Surrounded by the towering peaks of the Besiberri massif, the route follows the edge of the Cavallers reservoir, climbing up to the Riumalo plateau. After crossing the plateau alongside a fast-flowing mountain stream, the path makes a steep, rocky ascent, known as the Llastres de la Morta (1,900 meters/6,233 feet), up to a deep glacial lake known as Estany Negre. Just above the lake, magnificent views of the wild natural scene can be enjoyed from the Ventosa i Calvell refuge (2,215 meters/7,267 feet).

Transportation

GETTING THERE

The best way to reach Vall de Boí is by car. It is possible to get there by public transport, but there is no direct route and driving will allow more flexibility to explore once there.

CAR

From Barcelona, head west on the A-2 highway toward Lleida (158 kilometers/98 miles). Exit at junction 462 onto the N-230 in the direction of Alfarràs and El Pont de Suert. Follow the N-230 for 118 kilometers (73 miles), then turn right onto the L-500 toward Vall de Boí. The journey takes approximately 3.5 hours.

BUS

Alsa (www.alsa.es; 90/242-2242) operates 5-6 daily bus services from Barcelona Estación Nord to El Pont de Suert. The journey takes between 4 and 6 hours, depending on the number of stops made en route (€33). From El Pont de Suert, connect with the local bus (see below) to reach Vall de Boí.

GETTING AROUND

The easiest way to explore the area is by car or on foot.

BUS

A local bus service (L0856) runs between the hamlet of Pla de l'Ermita near Taüll to El Pont de Suert on weekdays throughout the year, stopping at Taüll, Boí, Erill la Vall, and Barruera en route. The morning service departs Pla de l'Ermita at 8:20am, arriving at El Pont de Suert at 8:55am. The return leg leaves El Pont de Suert at 3:05pm and arrives at Pla de l'Ermita at 3:40pm.

Two additional services run according to season. During winter, the Bus de la Neu (snow bus) runs between Vilaller and the Boí Taüll ski station, stopping at El Pont de Suert, Barruera, Erill la Vall, Boí, Taüll, and Pla de l'Ermita en route (weekends throughout ski season; €1). The service departs from Vilaller at 8:05am and arrives at the slopes at 9:10am. The return leg departs from the resort at 3pm and arrives in Vilaller at 4:05pm.

In summer, the Bus del Parc runs between Pla de l'Ermita in Vall de Boí, and Espot, the eastern gateway to the Parc Nacional d'Aigüestortes i Estany de Sant Maurici, taking a wide, crescent-shaped route around the northern boundary of the national park. There are two round-trip services per day from each terminus (Jun. 21-Sept. 30; €1.70-€11.90, depending on journey length; 50 percent discount on round-trip tickets; one-day pass €8.50). The morning services depart simultaneously, at 9:45am, from Pla de l'Ermita and Espot, and arrive at their respective destinations at 12:25pm. Likewise in the evening, the return legs depart from the two termini at 5:45pm, arriving at their destinations at 8:30pm.

TAXI

The Associació de Taxis de la Vall de Boí serves the area (97/369-6314 during summer only, 62/920-5489 all year; taxisvalldeboi.com).

HISTORY

The region of northeast Spain nowadays
known as Catalonia has been inhabited since at least 4000 BC.

ROMANS IN BARCELONA

More than 2,000 years ago, the Romans established the settlement of Barcino in what was later to become the Barri Gòtic area of Barcelona. Remnants of its ancient walls and buildings can still be seen today. Their main urban center, however, was Tarraco—modern day Tarragona—to the southwest. The fertile hinterland and abundance of seafood provided a fine diet for these new settlers.

In the 4th century AD, when the Roman Empire fell into decline, Roman settlements—including Barcino—started to come under attack from invading bands of Franks and later Visigoths. By the time these invaders departed in the 6th century, the area had become largely lawless and ravaged by epidemics.

MOORISH INVASION AND FRANKISH RULE

In the early 8th century, the Muslim (Moorish) invasion from the south swept quickly through Spain and Catalonia, reaching the south of France. Barcelona fell under Muslim rule for a time, although their stronghold was south of the river Ebro, and by the end of the century the city was retaken by the Franks under Charlemagne.

The area to the north and northwest of Barcelona was by now inhabited by a people whose language was known as *Catalan*, similar to the Latin-based *langue d'oc* of southern France. Charlemagne incorporated the counties of modern-day Catalonia into his realm, which was known as the Spanish March and was ruled by a *Comte* (Count). It was, in effect, a buffer zone between the Frankish Empire and Muslim-controlled Spain. Frankish control was, however, only nominal and the Comtes de Barcelona soon became the de facto rulers of the area. Thus, Catalonia started to be recognized as a distinct entity.

THE RISE OF CATALONIA

By the 11th century, Barcelona was the area's most prominent settlement and had taken control of significant areas of southwestern France. In 1137, Catalonia and the Kingdom of Aragon became united through marriage under the joint rule of the Comtes of Barcelona and the Kings of Aragon. Although the new entity was known as the Crown of Aragon, Catalonia kept its own traditional rights and parliament. This union, however, may well have signaled the formal beginnings of Catalonia's turbulent relationship with the rest of Spain.

The new combined state of Aragon now had sufficient strength for an expansionist push. Although it did not carry its name, Catalonia became the dominant partner of the new state and controlled trade in the western Mediterranean during the 13th and 14th centuries. As a slew of cities and territories were conquered, from Valencia and the Balearics to Sicily and Athens, Barcelona became wealthy. This new wealth funded the building of many of the wonderful Gothic churches that adorn Barcelona to this day. The old city expanded with the erection of new outer walls to include the Raval area.

CATHOLIC MONARCHS AND CATALONIA'S DECLINE

By the early 15th century, the high cost of protecting their empire had caused Barcelona's commercial base to collapse. Disease and famine wiped out a large portion of the population. The line of succession of the Comtes of Barcelona came to an end due to the absence of an heir.

Their Aragonian partners saw this as an opportunity to reduce Catalonia's influence and proceeded to elect a Castilian prince to the throne. This led to resistance and ultimately an unsuccessful rebellion in Catalonia. Soon afterward, Ferdinand II of Aragon married Isabel I, Queen of Castile, and became known as the "Catholic Monarchs," thus uniting the crowns of Aragon and Castile. Catalonia, although retaining its autonomy and *Generalitat* (Assembly), had in effect been subsumed into a unified Castilian (Spanish) state, greatly diminishing its influence in the region.

The Spanish Inquisition and expulsion of the Jews in 1492 led to the fleeing of Barcelona's Jewish community, who controlled much of the city's remaining commerce. Ferdinand and Isabel's successors further tightened Madrid's control over Barcelona, ultimately giving rise to a series of Catalan separatist movements. The discovery of the Americas by Christopher Columbus in 1492, and the creation of Spain's overseas empire, only added to the decline of Catalonia, due to the transfer of much commercial activity to the Atlantic coastal areas.

WAR OF THE SPANISH SUCCESSION

In 1640 Catalonia revolted against Spain and declared its allegiance to Louis XIII of France. The revolt was suppressed, resulting in the widespread devastation of towns and villages in Catalonia. In 1702, after the Spanish monarchy was left without an heir, the War of the Spanish Succession broke out and France imposed a Bourbon, Felipe V, on the Spanish throne. Catalonia resisted the Bourbon accession and instead supported Archduke Charles of Austria but ended up on the losing side, and after an 18-month-long siege Barcelona was completely subjugated by Felipe V. Felipe V not only

abolished the constitution and autonomy of Catalonia in 1714, he also banned the Catalan language and seized the remainder of Catalonia's possessions. The region's national day, September 11, commemorates the day the city fell.

During the rest of the 18th century, the Bourbons allowed Barcelona enough latitude for a commercial recovery to take hold. In 1778, the Bourbon ban on Barcelona trading with the Spanish South American colonies was revoked, boosting Barcelona's industry and commerce. Following a brief interruption in the 19th century, when Catalonia was annexed by Napoleon, Barcelona continued to develop its industries of iron, textile, shipbuilding, wine, and cork, and railways were introduced. The working class, however, did not fare so well in this boom and continued to endure poor sanitation, substandard housing, and widespread disease. Occasional riots were put down swiftly and without mercy.

CATALAN REBIRTH

A movement to revive Catalan culture and language, known as the Renaixença (rebirth or renaissance), emerged around 1850, accompanied by a rise in Catalan nationalist and separatist sentiment. Buoyed by the relatively peaceful and prosperous environment, Catalan nationalism and cultural revival continued to strengthen during the second half of the 19th century. The Catalan Renaissance was particularly prominent in the world of art, where Barcelona became the home of Modernisme (Catalan Art Nouveau) and the leading avant-garde hub of Spain.

By 1869, with a burgeoning

population, a grand plan to expand Barcelona was tabled, known as l'Eixample (the extension). Consisting of an orderly grid layout of commercial and housing units, incorporating parks and gardens, it was a revolutionary concept, and still defines much of the city's urban fabric to this day. In this new development, wealthy middle-class families built extravagant homes, mainly in the impressive *Modernista* style.

RISING TENSIONS

By 1913, Catalonia had achieved some autonomy, as the four provinces of Catalonia were given limited joint self-government as the Commonwealth of Catalonia.

In the early 20th century, workers' unions came to the fore, the most significant of these being the anarchist CNT (National Workers' Confederation). Industrial unrest took hold, together with assassinations of union leaders by agents of employers. With Barcelona's working population growing fast through migration, the city had by now developed into a hotbed of political unrest. Anarchists were engaging in acts of violence, including bombings and shootings, particularly against the bourgeoisie. Rising tensions boiled over in July 1909, resulting in a week of violent confrontations between the Spanish army and the working classes, which became known as Tragic Week.

By 1913, Catalonia had achieved some autonomy, as the four provinces of Catalonia were given limited joint self-government as the Commonwealth of Catalonia. However, in the 1920s, the dictator General Miguel Primo de Rivera reversed Catalonia's autonomy and set about subduing all manifestations of Catalan nationalism. He banned the CNT and shut down Barcelona Football Club, which by then had become a powerful nationalist symbol. This suppression of nationalism united Catalonia's radical elements and led to the formation of a left-wing coalition party, the *Esquerra Republicana* (Republican Left of Catalonia), led by Francesc Macià and Lluís Companys.

In 1931, Spain became a republic and the Esquerra Republicana swept to victory, immediately proclaiming a Catalan Republic. An autonomous Catalan regional government, the *Generalitat*, was created within the Spanish state under Esquerra leadership, and in February 1936, Catalonia was granted full autonomy. This newfound status for Catalonia was to be brief, however. In July 1936 an insurrection of Spanish nationalist troops led by General Francisco Franco sparked the Spanish Civil War, which lasted nearly three years, and brought the country to its knees.

SPANISH CIVIL WAR AND FRANCO'S RULE

Barcelona fell to Franco in January 1939, resulting in the loss of autonomy for Catalonia, with Franco's new government adopting a particularly repressive policy toward Catalan nationalism. Barcelona was left defeated and destitute, Catalonia's *Generalitat* abolished, and the Catalan language and culture was repressed once more.

Throughout Franco's 40-year regime, systematic repression was legal and rife. In the years following the Civil War, those opposing Franco's regime were persecuted and imprisoned, and thousands were executed, including the former president, Lluís Companys. Several hundred thousand were sent to concentration camps in Spain, or fled the country, only to end up in refugee camps in the south of France—some of whom were later transferred to Nazi concentration camps during World War II. Many more fled into exile around the world. Nevertheless, Barcelona's industrialization marched on, attracting an influx of migrants from poorer parts of Spain, mainly Andalusia.

TRANSITION TO DEMOCRACY

After Franco's death in 1975, Spain entered a period of transition, during which its modern constitution was drawn up. Based on a system of 17 autonomous communities, Catalonia was granted full autonomy in 1979. Over the next 25 years, Catalonia pushed Madrid for more autonomy. A new cultural revolution took hold across Spain, particularly in Catalonia, where the Catalan language and culture once more flourished, reemerging as a symbol of the region's identity.

A major transformative milestone for Barcelona in this period was the staging of the 1992 Olympic Games. The games sparked a massive urban renewal of the city, with development and redevelopment of infrastructure, seafront and leisure facilities, and entire neighborhoods. This kick-started the rise of Barcelona's popularity as a tourist destination and paved the way for the modern, cosmopolitan metropolis that exists today.

MODERN INDEPENDENCE MOVEMENT

In 2006, the Catalan government negotiated a new autonomy statute with Prime Minister José Luis Rodríguez Zapatero's PSOE (Spanish Socialist Workers' Party) government in Madrid, giving Catalonia nation-type tax-raising powers similar to the Spanish state. Catalans approved the statute in 2006 via referendum, but it soon became clear that Madrid was going to be slow in implementing it. The right-wing Partido Popular (PP), which was not part of the Catalan coalition, launched an appeal in the Spanish Constitutional Court to repeal the statute, claiming it granted too much autonomy to Catalonia. In 2010, this led to parts of the statute being repealed.

This decision was criticized by the Catalan government, and around this time a series of informal votes on independence were held in towns and cities of Catalonia, including Barcelona. Since then, Catalonia has continued to push for fiscal independence from the central Spanish government, spurred on by the poor performance of the Spanish economy during the Eurozone debt crisis, and the reality that Catalonia—and particularly Barcelona—continues to punch above its weight financially in comparison with other regions of Spain. In 2012, 1.5 million people took part in the first of Catalonia's annual independence rallies in Barcelona, mainly to protest on this issue.

In 2013, then-Catalan President Artur Mas, of the pro-autonomy Convergence and Union (CiU) party, called for a nonbinding referendum on independence from Spain to be held in 2014. Although challenged by Spanish Prime Minister Mariano Rajoy, and declared unconstitutional by the court, Mas proceeded with the referendum, dubbing it an informal poll. The majority of voters backed independence, but the turnout was less than 40 percent.

2017 REFERENDUM AND AFTERMATH

Following regional parliamentary elections in September 2015, pro-independence parties just about managed to form a coalition and appointed Carles Puigdemont, former mayor of Girona and a staunch separatist, as president. Puigdemont affirmed his commitment to securing an independent Catalan state, and announced a binding referendum on independence for Catalonia to be held on October 1, 2017. As the date approached, tensions mounted, and the Spanish authorities moved to stop the vote, seizing ballot papers and arresting Catalan officials. Large street protests followed, and the Spanish interior ministry took steps to exert control over the Catalan police force.

Referendum day was marked by widespread violence, with riot police firing rubber bullets at crowds and physically preventing people from entering some polling stations. Hundreds of injuries were reported. Spanish national police and the Civil Guard members seized ballot boxes. Catalan officials stated that turnout was about 42 percent, with 90 percent of voters supporting independence, although accurate figures were difficult to establish because of the chaos surrounding the vote.

In the aftermath, each side blamed the other for the chaos; the EU stayed out of the dispute, regarding it officially as an internal Spanish matter. Then, on October 27, the Catalan parliament voted to declare independence from Spain. Rajoy responded by securing the approval of the Spanish Senate to invoke Article 155 of the Spanish constitution, empowering central government to take control of Catalonia. He dismissed the Catalan parliament and called for fresh elections to be held in December 2017.

The December 2017 elections were regarded by many Catalans as a re-run of the Independence Referendum, and turnout was high, at 83 percent. Although the pro-Spain Citizens' Party gained the highest single share of the vote, a collection of separatist parties, led by Puigdemont's *Junts per Catalunya* (Together for Catalonia), won 70 of the parliament's 135 seats, thus giving the pro-independence side an overall majority. Rajoy's PP was virtually wiped out.

When the Spanish government stated its intention to pursue criminal charges of sedition against the sacked Catalan leaders, Puigdemont and some of his closest advisors disappeared—turning up a short time later in Brussels, where he remains at the time of writing. He has called for talks to be held outside of Spain between the Catalonian leaders and the Spanish government. Meanwhile, 18 of his contemporaries were arrested in November 2017 and were put on trial in spring 2019, charged with rebellion, disobedience, and misuse of public funds. At the time of writing, no verdict had been reached. If found guilty, many of the accused face up to 24 years in prison.

ESSENTIALS

Getting There

Most international travelers arrive in Catalonia by air, landing at the region's main airport, Barcelona-El Prat. From the airport, there are many options to travel into the city and across Catalonia.

AIR

AIRPORTS

There are three international airports in Catalonia: Barcelona-El Prat, Girona-Costa Brava, and Reus.

Barcelona-El Prat (BCN, 90/240-4704, www.aena-aeropuertos.es) is the region's largest airport and the seventh busiest in Europe, with connections to 164 destinations worldwide, including direct flights to the US. Located 12 kilometers (7.5 miles) southwest of Barcelona, the airport has recently been connected to the city's metro system, although the commuter train (www.renfe.com) or airport bus (aerobus.com) are, as of 2019, the quickest ways to reach the center.

Girona-Costa Brava (GRO, information line 97/218-6600, customer helpline 97/218-6708; www.girona-airport.cat) is the region's second-biggest airport, situated 12.5 kilometers (7.8 miles) southwest of Girona and 92 kilometers (57 miles) north of Barcelona. It serves northern Catalonia and is convenient for those traveling to the Costa Brava, Girona, La Garrotxa, or the Pyrenees. There are connections to 10 destinations throughout the year, and many more during the summer months (Apr.-Oct.). **Barcelona Bus** (90/213-0014; www.sagales.com) runs direct transfers from Girona-Costa Brava Airport to Barcelona.

During the low-cost flight revolution of the early 2000s, Girona-Costa Brava Airport served as an alternative airport to Barcelona-El Prat, and was one of Ryanair's primary European hubs. When the new Terminal 1 opened at Barcelona-El Prat in 2009, Ryanair and other low-cost airlines moved into the old terminal (Terminal 2), cutting nearly all routes to and from Girona. Passenger numbers have

continued to fall since. There are tentative future plans to establish a satellite terminal of Barcelona-El Prat Airport at Girona-Costa Brava, and to connect the two by rail.

Reus Airport (REU, information line 90/240-4704, customer helpline 91/321-1000, www.aena-aeropuertos.es) is located 10 kilometers (6.2 miles) west of Tarragona and 106 kilometers (66 miles) southwest of Barcelona. It is convenient for southern Catalonia.

Girona-Costa Brava and Reus are small airports handling seasonal charter flights to European destinations, which operate primarily during summer. They can also serve as an alternative to Barcelona-El Prat; both airports have direct transfers to Barcelona city center. During low season (Nov.-Apr. approx.), flight frequency and routes are cut back considerably. This mainly affects the two regional airports, although certain routes from Barcelona-El Prat also run a reduced service. During holiday periods, such as Christmas, Valentine's Day, and Easter, more flights are scheduled.

AIRLINES

From the UK and Ireland

There are direct flights to Barcelona from several UK cities including London, Birmingham, Bristol, Dublin, Edinburgh, Glasgow, Liverpool, and Manchester. Barcelona-el Prat receives flights from the UK on airlines such as Ryanair, easyJet, Vueling, and Norwegian Air.

From the US and Canada

Barcelona-El Prat airport has direct routes from the US with Iberia (Boston, San Francisco), Norwegian Air (Los Angeles, Oakland, Newark), American Airlines (Miami, New York JFK), United Airlines (Newark), Delta

(New York JFK), and Air Canada (Toronto). Another option is to fly indirect via London, Amsterdam, or another European destination, which could end up being cheaper.

From Australia and New Zealand

There are indirect flights to Barcelona from Sydney, Melbourne, and Brisbane in Australia on a number of different airlines including Quantas, Emirates, and Singapore Airlines. (All flights make one stop en route, as is the norm with flights from Australia.)

From New Zealand, airlines including Etihad and Air New Zealand fly to Barcelona with an average of two connections en route.

For the cheapest flights, many passengers fly to London and then on to Spain on a budget airline such as easyJet or Ryanair.

From South Africa

There are no direct flights from South Africa to Barcelona. Flights fly indirect via other cities such as London or Frankfurt.

BUS

There are long-distance bus routes to Barcelona from all over Spain and Europe. International connections across mainland Europe are operated by Eurolines (90/240-5040; www.eurolines.es) and Flixbus (www.flixbus.com). There are no direct bus services from the UK, though connections via Paris do exist.

National services are operated by Alsa (90/242-2242; www.alsa.es) and include direct daily connections to Barcelona from all major Spanish cities, as well as a direct international service from Montpellier.

TRAIN

The AVE high-speed rail service, operated by Renfe (www.renfe.com), offers direct connections to Barcelona from Zaragoza and Madrid (2.5 hours, from €32). There are also direct daily international services to Barcelona and Girona from 15 cities across France, including Paris (6.5 hours), Lyon (5 hours), Marseille (4.5 hours), and Toulouse (3.5 hours), from €35. These services are a collaborative effort between the Spanish and French high-speed rail services, the AVE and the TGV (operated by SNCF). Cheap fares can be found if booked in advance.

It is also possible to travel to Barcelona from London by train. Take the Eurostar from London St Pancras to Paris Gare du Nord (2.5 hours), transfer to Gare du Lyon (there is a direct RER connection), then take the TGV service to Barcelona.

FERRY

Up to 18 daily ferry services connect the Balearic Islands, Italy, Morocco, and Algeria with Barcelona, operated by numerous ferry companies. Passengers can travel with or without a vehicle, and reserve a seat or cabin onboard; note that the cheapest tickets may be located outside on the deck. Sailing durations and frequency vary seasonally; check ferry company websites for current timetables.

There are three terminals for passenger ferries in Barcelona: Terminal Drassanes (Baleària), Terminal Ferry de Barcelona (Trasmediterránea), and Terminal Grimaldi (Grimaldi, Grandi Navi Veloci). All are easily accessed from the city.

From the Balearic Islands, Baleària (93/324-8980; www.balearia.com) runs seven weekly services from Palma de Mallorca to Barcelona

(7.5 hours; from €44), seven from Alcudia, Mallorca (6.5 hours; from €44), 14 from Ciutadella, Menorca (9 hours; from €44), and seven from Ibiza (8 hours 15 minutes; from €47). Trasmediterránea (93/295-9122; www.trasmediterranea.es) operates similar services, with 12 weekly sailings from Palma de Mallorca (7.5 hours; from €49), seven from Mahon, Menorca (9 hours; from €40), and six from Ibiza (8.5 hours; €41). For Formentera, change in Ibiza.

From Italy, services depart from Civitavecchia (Rome), Genoa, Savona, and Porto Torres (Sardinia) for Barcelona. Grimaldi (90/253-1333; www.grimaldi-lines.com) runs six weekly sailings from Civitavecchia (20 hours; from €36), four from Porto Torres (12.5 hours; from €36), and one from Savona (17 hours, from €36). Grandi Navi Veloci (93/443-7139; www.gnv.it) operates three weekly services from Genoa (18 hours; from €67).

From Morocco, Grandi Navi Veloci operates five weekly services from Tangier to Barcelona (26-31 hours; from €81), and one from Nador (24.5 hours; from €81). Grimaldi runs one weekly service from Tangier to Barcelona (28 hours; from €50).

From Algeria, Algerie Ferries (algerieferries.dz) operates one weekly sailing from Algiers to Barcelona (13 hours; from €90) and one from Oran (16 hours; from €150).

CAR

Spain is within the Schengen Area, where travel between EU countries is unrestricted. Therefore, there are no border checks when entering the country by car. If driving a rental car, ensure that the rental company allows and provides insurance for

international travel before entering or leaving the country.

If driving to Catalonia from the UK, make sure you have European breakdown coverage for your entire journey. All driving licenses from the European Union, Norway, Iceland, and Liechtenstein are valid in Spain. Drivers from outside the EU need to carry both a valid driver's license from their home country and an International Driving Permit (IDP), which can be purchased in your home country. IDPs are available at post offices in the UK, and at the American Automobile Association (AAA) and the American Automobile Touring Alliance (AATA) in the US.

HOLIDAY PACKAGES

Dozens of tour operators offer holiday packages to Catalonia, primarily for beach destinations during summer. Holiday packages traditionally comprise a charter flight, accommodation, and airport transfer, which normally works out to be cheaper than booking them separately, particularly during the shoulder season (7 nights from approx. £200pp from the UK). UK-based tour operators are strictly regulated, which means that customers are afforded financial and legal protection should problems arise before or during the holiday.

Research the location and accommodation before purchasing a package to ensure that it matches your expectations; many package holiday destinations have been heavily affected by mass tourism. The most popular package destinations along the Catalan coast include Lloret de Mar and Tossa de Mar on the Costa Brava.

The main tour operators offering holiday packages from the UK are TUI, Jet2holidays, Thomas Cook, Expedia,

On The Beach, British Airways Holidays, Travel Republic, and Virgin Holidays. From the US, tour operators offering Spanish destinations include Intrepid Travel, Trafalgar, Tauck, Butterfield & Robinson, Contiki, Road Scholar, G Adventures (Toronto-based), Topdeck, and Gate 1, among others. Besides mainstream holiday packages, specialist tour operators offer more tailored holidays according to age, interests, etc.

Getting Around Catalonia

Train is the quickest and easiest form of public transport to travel from Barcelona to other urban areas in Catalonia. To reach the Costa Brava and more rural areas, private transport is best, although there is usually a bus service that will get you there.

TRAIN

An extensive railway network links most major towns and cities throughout Spain, primarily operated by Renfe (www.renfe.com). Within Catalonia, the high-speed rail service (AVE) stops at Barcelona, Girona, Lleida, Tarragona, and Figueres, and is the fastest way to move between these cities. The Rodalies de Catalunya (www.rodalies.gencat. cat), also operated by Renfe, is the regional rail network and operates commuter and medium-distance services across Catalonia. Rail travel in Spain is generally efficient and tickets are reasonably priced. Tickets must be purchased before boarding the train; book in advance, either online or at the railway station itself, for cheaper fares. Booking online using the Renfe website with an American debit or credit card can pose problems; try www. thetrainline.com or buy your ticket directly at the train station.

BUS

Within Catalonia, a handful of bus companies operate the regional network. Traveling by bus can be the only way to reach some parts of the region by public transport. Unlike train and flight tickets, most bus routes have set prices and are, therefore, a good option if buying tickets at the last minute. All bus companies offer online booking, and some (Monbus, Teisa, Sagalés) have ticket offices, normally inside the local bus station, which are open during business hours. Monbus (90/229-2900, monbus.es) serves central and southern Catalonia, including Tarragona, Reus Airport, and Penedès; Sarfa (90/230-2025, moventis.es) covers the Costa Brava, including direct transfers from Barcelona-El Prat Airport; Teisa (93/215-3566, teisa-bus. com) covers the eastern Pyrenees and Girona; and Sagalés (90/213-0014, sagales.com) and Alsa (90/242-2242; www.alsa.es) operate throughout the region.

Barcelona's main bus station is Estació de Nord (Carrer d'Alí Bei, 80; barcelonanord.cat), situated in an old railway station dating from 1861. Most national bus connections depart from here. Buses also depart from outside the city's main railway station,

Barcelona Sants (Plaça dels Països Catalans, 1-7; 93/495-6020; www.adif.es), primarily international services. Some regional bus services depart from bus stops elsewhere in the city.

CAR

While accessing many parts of Catalonia via public transit is possible, renting a car is the best way to explore the region. Driving within the city of Barcelona is not advised and can add unnecessary stress to your visit, but outside of the city, driving in Catalonia is straightforward and comfortable. Car rental companies are based both in the city and at the airport. Ride sharing is also available through BlaBlaCar (blablacar.es) and Drivy (drivy.es).

RENTALS

Renting a car is relatively cheap in Spain, although prices fluctuate depending on the season. If booking a car in advance through a website or car rental search engine, make sure to check whether the car will be located at the airport terminal or if you are required to take a shuttle bus from the terminal to the rental company's office. Note whether you are required to fill the tank before returning (full-full or full-empty), and what is included in the insurance, as you may have to pay extra for full coverage. The main companies have an office at the airport and in the city, including Hertz (www.hertz.com), Avis (www.avis.com), Europcar (www.europcar.com), and Enterprise (www.enterprise.es). Smaller budget companies can sometimes offer great deals, but beware of hidden costs. Some options are Goldcar (www.goldcar.es), Sixt (www.sixt.es), and Centauro (www.centauro.net).

REGULATIONS

To drive in Spain you must be 18 years old or older, although to rent a vehicle the minimum age is often 21. Many rental companies require you to have had your driving license for at least one or two years, and it is likely that you will be asked to book with a credit card belonging to the driver.

In Spain, drivers are required by law to carry their driving license, insurance policy, high visibility vests or reflective jackets and a warning triangle (which are often present in rental cars), crash helmets (for motorcyclists), and a GB sticker or Euro plates.

Talking on a mobile phone is prohibited while driving except with a hands-free system; car radios and mobile phones must be switched off while refueling; and overtaking can only be done on the left. Established speed limits are 120 km/h (75 mph) on dual carriageways and motorways, 100 km/h (62 mph) on conventional roads, 90 km/h (56 mph) on all other roads, and 50 km/h (31 mph) in built-up areas. It is not unusual for the speed limit to change regularly and unexpectedly, and there are many speed cameras throughout the region. Hefty fines are issued for failing to comply, and Spanish authorities routinely deliver fines to foreign drivers, even after they have left the country. For many infractions, fines are reduced by 50 percent if paid within 20 days, and can be paid online at web.gencat.cat, by post or phone to the issuing agency, or in person at police or governmental offices.

Alcohol levels in the bloodstream must not exceed 0.5 g/l (0.25 mg/l in exhaled air) for drivers of vehicles and cyclists, although in special cases (vehicles with more than 8 passengers, drivers with less than 2 years' driving experience, vehicles used for school children, among others) the limit is 0.3 g/l. After a traffic accident, all drivers are breathalyzed. Drivers with a bloodstream alcohol level greater than 1.2 g/l (0.6 mg/l in exhaled air) may face prison. All passengers must wear seatbelts, and helmets must be worn on motorbikes, mopeds, and bicycles. Always check the current regulations before renting a car.

ROAD CONDITIONS AND TOLLS
Updated information about road conditions can be found via the Department of Transportation website (infocar.dgt.es/etraffic) or the Catalan government website (www.gencat.cat/transit), as well as by telephone (012 from Catalonia, 90/240-0012 from the rest of Spain). Toll roads in Catalonia include the AP-7, A-2, and sections of the C-16, C-31, C-32, and C-33.

PARKING
In most cities, parking is regulated and can be paid through meters via cash or credit card. Make sure to check signage for parking details, as operating hours and tariffs vary by street, day, and time of year. If you receive a parking ticket, you can make a "voluntary fine cancelation" by following instructions on the meter, which reduces the fine if paid immediately. Parking within the city of Barcelona can be difficult and expensive, and parking lots are often the best option.

Visas and Officialdom

PASSPORTS AND VISAS

EUROPEAN UNION/ SCHENGEN
Spain is part of the European Union and the Schengen Agreement, which allows border-free travel in much of Europe. Citizens of the EU, Switzerland, Norway, Iceland, and Lichtenstein need a valid passport or ID card, and minors traveling with an ID document must also have written permission from their parents.

UNITED STATES, CANADA, AUSTRALIA, AND NEW ZEALAND
Citizens of these countries do not need a visa to stay in Spain for less than 90 days. The only requirement is a passport that is valid for at least three months beyond the intended date of departure. By law, everyone in Spain is required to carry ID, including tourists. Police checks, however, are rare.

OTHER NATIONS
A visa is required for citizens of many other countries (including South Africa), who must submit documents justifying the object and conditions of their stay and displaying that they have sufficient economic resources. Visit the European Commission website (ec.europa.eu) for information regarding which nationalities require a Schengen visa and the details of required documents. Applications can be made online via the same website.

EMBASSIES AND CONSULATES

Consulates help with any problems concerning travel documents. A full list and information can be found online at www.maec.es (Embassies and Consulates Section). Embassies are located in Madrid, but most countries have a consulate in Barcelona.

US Consulate General Barcelona

93/280-2227; Passeig de la Reina Elisenda de Montcada, 23, 08034 Barcelona; Mon.-Fri. 9am-1pm

British Consulate General Barcelona

93/366-6200; Avinguda Diagonal 477-13, 08036 Barcelona; Mon.-Fri. 8:30am-1:30pm

Republic of Ireland Honorary Consulate General Barcelona

93/491-5021 (91/436-4093 out of hours); Gran Via Carlos III, 94, 08028 Barcelona; cons.irl@webcat.es; Mon.-Fri. 10am-1pm

Consulate of Canada Barcelona

93/270-3614; Plaça de Catalunya 9, 1º2ª, 08002 Barcelona; Mon.-Fri. 9am-12:30pm

Australian Honorary Consulate in Barcelona

93/362-3792; Avinguda Diagonal, 433 bis, 08036, Barcelona; Mon.-Fri. 10:30am-12:30pm

New Zealand Consulate Barcelona

93/207-5048; Travessera de Gràcia, 64, 08006, Barcelona; Mon.-Thurs. 9:30am-2pm, 4pm-6pm, Fri. 9:30am-2pm

South Africa

There is no South African consulate in Barcelona. The embassy is located in Madrid.

CUSTOMS

When entering the country, sums of money in excess of €9,999.99 must be declared. Over 18s are authorized to carry 200 cigarettes, or 100 mini-cigars, or 50 cigars, or 250 grams of rolling tobacco. The legal quantity of alcohol that visitors can bring into the country from outside the EU is one liter of drink with an alcohol content of over 22%, or two liters with a lower alcohol content. Meat, meat products, milk, and dairy products are generally prohibited from entering the EU. Exceptions may be granted for commercially packaged baby formula and foods required for medical reasons. Up to 1kg (a little over 2 pounds) of other foodstuffs may be brought into Spain.

While traveling within the EU, there are no limits on what you can buy and travel with, provided that it is for personal use. You can travel with up to 800 cigarettes, 400 mini-cigars, 200 cigars, 1 kg (2 pounds) of tobacco, 10 liters of spirits, 20 liters of fortified wine, 90 liters of wine, and 110 liters of beer, without proof that they are for personal use. For information on what you can bring from Spain back to your home country, check with your home authorities.

FESTA MAJORS

Catalan popular culture is never so present as it is during the *festa majors* (traditional festivals) that take place in every neighborhood, town, and city across the region. These festivals can last for up to a week and see a whole host of curious characters and customs fill the streets. The most popular and unique neighborhood festival in Barcelona is the **Festa Major de Gràcia** in Barcelona (page 138). From August 15 to 21, the streets are creatively transformed, each one representing a different theme. Music plays day and night, and all the "usual" traditional festivities also make an appearance: human castles (*castells*), papier-mâché giants (*gegants*), and a fire-breathing dragon parade (*correfoc*). Every week, somewhere in Catalonia, a similar festival is taking place.

Other popular festa majors take place in Sitges (in August; page 192) and Cadaqués (in September; page 275).

Festivals and Events

The Catalan calendar is packed with events throughout the year, celebrating music, culture, sports, food, and tradition.

Apart from the standard Spanish holidays around Christmas, the Epiphany (January 6), and Easter, some of the region's favorites include **Sant Jordi** (April 23), Catalonia's answer to Valentine's Day, when books and roses fill the streets, and **Sant Joan** (June 24), an all-night party across the region.

In recent years, the music and cultural scenes have reached new heights, particularly in Barcelona, with seemingly endless events taking place almost every weekend. Attracting the biggest crowds are music festivals **Primavera Sound** (late May/early June), **Sónar** (June), and **Cruïlla** (July). **Festa de La Mercè** (September 24), Barcelona's annual citywide festival, is also popular. For a more complete list of festivals in Barcelona, see page 136.

Beyond Barcelona, the **Sitges Carnival** (February) is one of the biggest in Spain, and the **International Fantastic Film Festival** (October), also in Sitges, attracts top Hollywood names. Girona celebrates a weeklong flower festival, **Temps de Flors** (May), and international music stars play at the **Cap Roig Music Festival** on the Costa Brava, as well as at the **Festival Castell de Peralada** (Jul/Aug). For more information on festivals outside Barcelona, see the relevant chapter.

REGION- AND COUNTRY-WIDE EVENTS

Epiphany

Jan. 6

On the eve of the Epiphany (January 5), there is the holy procession of the Three Kings. This holiday is celebrated country-wide, and in Barcelona the Three Kings or Wise Men arrive into the city by boat at Port Vell, and tour the streets amid a colorful, celebratory parade. On the morning of January 6, children awake to gifts left by the Kings.

CATALAN TRADITIONS

Weird and wonderful cultural traditions are ingrained in Spanish folklore. Every corner of the country celebrates its own peculiar festivities, and keeping them alive is a matter of regional pride and identity. From the beautiful, mind-boggling *castells* to the outright bizarre *caga tió*, Catalan traditions are alive and kicking, and you don't have to go too far to stumble upon some of the curious customs listed below.

CORREFOC

Literally meaning "fire-run," the clue here is in the name. Sparks fly as local groups dressed as devils, dragons, and fiery beasts parade through the streets to the sound of the drums, setting off fireworks as they go. The tradition is thought to have evolved from the *Ball de Diables* (devil's dance)—a medieval street duel of good versus evil—and it's a sight to behold, though perhaps not for the fainthearted.

Where/when to see it: The *correfoc* normally takes place at dusk during any local festival. In Barcelona's Festa de la Merce (September), the pyrotechnic procession runs the length of Via Laietana, one of the city center's main thoroughfares.

CASTELLS

Building castles in the sky is a Catalan specialty. In town squares across the region, 10-tier human towers (*castells*) climb into position, as bystanders hold their breath in anticipation. It's a temporary work of art, and an extraordinary balancing act of teamwork and strength.

Where/when to see it: Commonly practiced during local festivals (normally during the day), but also as a competitive sport in its own right, *castells* are most common in the Tarragona province.

GEGANTS

No Catalan festival would be complete without a giants' parade. Originally a religious tradition dating back to at least the 15th century, the parade sees towering papier-mâché figures dance down the street, accompanied by a local marching band.

Carnival

Feb./Mar.; carnaval.tarragona.cat

Cities across Spain join cities across the world in the Carnival celebrations, filling the streets for a week of color, music, debauchery, and float-filled parades. The event in Sitges is among the most extravagant.

Sant Jordi

Apr. 23

The feast day of Saint George, Catalonia's patron saint, is celebrated with a romantic twist across the region. Couples exchange roses and books, the streets are filled with book stalls, and the libraries and bookstores often have readings by authors.

Sant Joan

June 23-24

June 24 is the feast day of St. John the Baptist, and also marks the summer solstice. It is celebrated throughout Spain, with most of the festivities taking place the night before (June 23), known as the Verbena de Sant Joan, a long summer night of fiestas and fireworks.

La Diada

Sept. 11

Catalonia's national day is celebrated with the most typical cultural traditions—*sardana* dancing and *castells* (human castles).

All Saints' Day

Nov. 1

It is tradition to honor the dead on this day—many visit graves of the departed with flowers. The air is filled with the smell of roasted chestnuts, and the bakeries with *panellets* (traditional marzipan and pine-nut sweets).

Where/when to see it: Any local festival. *Gegants* can also be visited while they rest. In Barcelona, they reside in the Casa dels Entremesos (Plaça de les Beates, 2) near the Santa Catarina market.

SARDANA

The *sardana* is Catalonia's traditional folk dance. Participants join hands in a circle and move slowly round in two- and three-step movements. What it lacks in intricacy it makes up for with inclusiveness—the steps are easy to pick up and anyone is welcome to join in.

Where/when to see it: During festivals and on the weekend. On Sunday mornings, locals meet in Plaça Nova, outside the cathedral in Barcelona, to dance the *sardana* together.

TIÓ DE NADAL

The *Tió de Nadal*—also known as *Caga Tió* (poo log)—is Catalonia's answer to Santa Claus. This cheerful character is created from a wooden log wearing a traditional red hat (*barretina*). On December 24, children across Catalonia tap the log with a stick while singing a traditional song, and Tió obliges by expelling sweets and other goodies from his bottom. It brings a whole new meaning to the Yule log.

Where/when to see it: During December, *Caga Tió* can be spotted across the region. Go to the Fira de Santa Llúcia (Christmas market) outside Barcelona Cathedral and bring home a truly unique souvenir.

CAGANER

Christmas is a time for toilet humor in Catalonia. The *caganer*—a defecating figurine—is another favorite festive character, commonly placed amid the nativity scene in homes across the region. The meaning of this mischievous tradition has several interpretations, from fertilizing the earth to blasphemy.

Where/when to see it: Nativity scenes are commonly displayed in Catalan homes, churches, and public places throughout the Christmas season—keep an eye out for *caganer*.

Conduct and Customs

GREETINGS

Generally, Spanish people greet each other with a double kiss, right cheek before left. Often this is a kissing sound made in the air rather than a true lip-plant on the cheek. Close friends embrace more closely, while a handshake can suffice in a formal situation. Verbal greetings reflect the Spanish timetable. "Buenos días" (Spanish) or "bon dia" (Catalan) is used until lunchtime. "Buenas tardes" (Spanish), "bona tarda" (Catalan, for the afternoon), and "bon vespre" (Catalan, for the evening) are used after lunch and into the evening. "Hola" is always a safe bet, in both Spanish and Catalan, and a general informal "buenas" always works (in Spanish). To say goodnight and goodbye: "buenas noches" and "adiós" (Spanish) or "bona nit" and "adéu" (Catalan).

ORDERING COFFEE

Coffee in Spain is generally short and strong, made using espresso machines in most cafés and restaurants. You won't find filter coffee in many places, although third-wave coffee shops are springing up in hip areas, many of which offer pour-over coffee. The closest thing to "a regular drip coffee" is an Americano. Ask for it "para tomar aquí" (to drink in), or "para llevar" (to take away/to go).

- **Café solo:** espresso

- **Cortado:** espresso cut with steamed milk, 4oz

- **Café con leche:** a small latte, espresso with steamed milk in an 8oz cup

- **Americano:** espresso with hot water

- **Café con hielo:** café solo (espresso) with a cup of ice on the side

EATING (AND DRINKING) OUT

MEALS

Breakfast is normally light. Many locals eat very little before leaving the house, but it is common to see workers taking a break at around 11am for "breakfast," when they may have a coffee and pastry or sandwich; many cafés offer a breakfast deal to reflect this. Lunch is the largest meal of the day, and many restaurants offer a menú del día (menu of the day). This is a reasonably priced, set-course menu (€9-€15) consisting of a choice of drink (glass of wine, beer, or water), choice of first course (often salad or soup), choice of main course (often meat, fish, or grain dish), and choice of dessert or coffee. This option is generally only available at lunchtime from Monday to Friday, and it can offer a good opportunity to dine at a high-end restaurant for a reasonable price (menú del día rarely exceeds €20). Dinner is generally a lighter meal than lunch and is a good time for sharing a selection of tapas. Keep in mind that there is often a 5-10 percent surcharge when seated outdoors.

MEAL TIMES

Spain operates on its own timetable, which is especially important to note at mealtimes and when going out at night. Breakfast is served from 8am-11am, lunch is 1pm-4pm, and dinner is 8pm-11pm.

NIGHTLIFE

The Spanish know how to have a good time—it's something in the blood. Nights out start and end a couple of hours later than anywhere else. When you might normally be finishing your drinks back home, here the party's just getting started.

Typically, locals meet for dinner around 9-9:30pm, and bars get busy after dinner until closing. Some bars close around midnight, but many stay open until 2 or 3am, especially at the weekend. Clubs tend to open around midnight, but don't start filling up until about 2am, and keep going until 5 or 6am. You may need to adjust your body clock to party with the locals, but it's worth it to experience the city's nightlife at its best. Just don't plan anything for the morning after.

The minimum drinking age in Spain is 18; it is wise to carry identification although it is rarely checked.

Ordering Drinks

Typical Spanish beers include Estrella Damm (Barcelona), Moritz (Barcelona), Alhambra (Granada), Mahou (Madrid), and Estrella Galicia (Galicia).

- **Una caña:** a small draft beer, usually around 200 ml (7 oz), this is the most popular order, small and cheap and always extra cold. Larger glass sizes, *copa* (330ml) and *jarra* (500ml), are normally available too.
- **Una mediana:** a bottled beer, also known as *un tercio* (a third of a liter).
- **Un botellín:** or *un quinto* (a fifth of a liter) is a little bottle of beer.
- **Una cerveza sin:** a non-alcoholic beer.
- **Una clara:** beer mixed with soda or lemonade.
- **Un chupito:** a shot.
- **Vino tinto/blanco:** red/white wine. For the house wine, follow with "*de la casa.*"
- **Tinto de verano:** red wine mixed with soda or lemonade, a local favorite in place of sangria. More commonly consumed at home, but can be ordered in many bars.
- **Vermut:** sweet red vermouth, usually served on ice with an olive, a slice of orange, or both.

BUSINESS HOURS

SHOPS AND SUPERMARKETS

Although the siesta (afternoon nap) is not widely observed in large cities, many businesses close from 2-5pm. Nearly all shops, including supermarkets, are closed on Sundays, and many small shops remain closed on Monday morning. In the lead-up to Christmas and during winter and summer sales, some shops open on Sunday.

MUSEUMS

Normal opening times for museums and monuments are: Mon.-Sat., 10am-7pm in winter, 10am-8pm in summer; Sun. and public holidays, 10am-2pm.

ALCOHOL AND SMOKING

It is normal and accepted to drink beer or wine with every meal in Spain. The legal drinking age is 18. Only authorized establishments may sell alcohol after midnight, and supermarkets stop selling alcohol at 11pm. Although it is common to see the sale and consumption of alcohol in public spaces, this is forbidden by law. It is common to smoke in public spaces, on balconies, and in outdoor seating at restaurants. However, smoking is banned in all indoor areas including bars, restaurants, and other establishments, as well as playgrounds, schools, and hospitals.

ILLEGAL DRUGS

It is a criminal offense to develop, produce, or sell any of the substances included on the list of illegal drugs, such as cocaine, LSD, heroin, cannabis, ecstasy, etc., or engage in any activity designed to encourage their consumption. Although the consumption or possession of small quantities for personal use is not considered a crime, the consumption of drugs in public spaces or buildings is a criminal offense, and is subject to fines ranging from €300-€30,000.

Cannabis associations are legally constituted, but buyers must be members; they must wait 15 days from signing up until they are able to buy, and their personal consumption is limited. Twenty grams per month is allowed for those aged 18 to 21 years, and 60 grams per month for those over 21, increasing only for therapeutic reasons.

PUBLIC HOLIDAYS

In Spain, public holidays fall into three categories: national, regional, and local. The following public holidays apply across Catalonia and include national and regional holidays. Each local area has two more public holidays, which are allocated by the local council, and usually celebrate the feast day of a local patron saint. Public holidays are celebrated on the date that they fall, and are not moved to a Monday or Friday to create a long weekend, so it is common for holidays to be celebrated mid-week. If a public holiday falls on a Saturday or Sunday, there is no extra weekday holiday assigned to compensate. Business hours on public holidays are usually the same as Sunday business hours, though most shops and museums are closed on January 1 and 6, Easter Sunday, and December 25 and 26.

- New Year's Day (January 1)

- Epiphany (January 6)

- Good Friday (March/April)

- Easter Monday (March/April), only in Catalonia

- International Workers' Day (May 1)

- Sant Joan (June 24)

- Assumption (August 15)

- Catalan National Day (September 11), only in Catalonia

- Spanish National Holiday (October 12)

- All Saints' Day (November 1)

- Constitution Day (December 6)

- Immaculate Conception (December 8)

- Christmas (December 25)

- Boxing Day (December 26), only in Catalonia

TIPPING

Workers in the hospitality industry do not expect tips, and locals tip little or nothing at all. Customer service is not Spain's forte, although in restaurants an optional 10 percent is the norm, which usually buys you service with a smile.

CLOTHING

Modern Spain is liberal and almost anything goes, although most people dress relatively conservatively. When visiting Catholic churches, knees and shoulders should be covered. On the beach, going topless is accepted practice for both men and women.

RESPONSIBLE TOURISM

Thirty years ago, Barcelona received 1.73 million tourists per year. In 2016, that figure stood at 9.86 million, and does not include non-hotel accommodation, cruise ship passengers (2.68 million per year), or day-trippers.

How can a city with a population of just 1.7 million provide the infrastructure for this annual influx of temporary residents? The short answer is that it is struggling. In recent years, the city has become a victim of its own success, finding it difficult to balance popularity with physical limitations. Ultimately, this impacts on its citizens in a number of ways. For example, mass tourism is driving up rental prices in the city center, forcing residents to leave the area. Furthermore, with the rise in popularity of apartment rentals, areas of the city previously unexplored by tourists have seen an increase in visitors, which often causes disruption to residents living in quiet apartment blocks. The tension has led to some anti-tourism sentiment, which has hit the headlines globally.

Despite this sometimes-troublesome co-existence, most residents are helpful, welcoming, and incredibly proud of their city. The city council has developed a strategic plan to tackle overtourism and has become more vigilant about issuing fines to illegal tourist rentals. As a visitor, there are a few things to keep in mind that can help to ease these issues, and help the city to retain the character that made it so popular in the first place:

BEFORE YOU GO

- When booking a tourist apartment, make sure your accommodation is properly licensed (https://meet.barcelona.cat/habitatgesturistics/en). All the options in this online catalogue are properly licensed.

- Pack a refillable water bottle to reduce trash. You may want to bring one with a built-in filter, as the tap water in Barcelona is safe to drink but has a chlorine flavor.

- Sign up to volunteer with **Esperança** (www.facebook.com/groups/esperancabcn), which distributes food to homeless people in Barcelona every Saturday and Sunday evening.

AFTER YOU ARRIVE

- Respect residents by refraining from making excessive noise, especially at night.

- Treat your accommodation and public space with respect.

- Try to avoid public transport during rush hour (8-9am, 6-7pm).

- Choose restaurants, shops, and accommodations run by locals. Many locally run businesses are featured throughout this book.

- Try to speak the language—either Catalan or Spanish. Don't expect everyone to speak English.

- Recycle (there are large recycling containers across the city).

- Remember that the beachfront in Barcelona is not a holiday resort. The beachfront promenade is popular with families; dress and behave appropriately.

Health and Safety

EMERGENCY NUMBERS

- General emergency line: 112 (fire, police, ambulance)
- Medical emergencies: 061
- For general governmental information: 012, www.gencat.cat
- In case of emergencies or natural disasters, follow the instructions provided by the Fire and Rescue Services (Firefighters and Civil Defense) at www.bcn.cat/bombers, or issued by the authorities on official Twitter accounts:
- @VisitBCN_EN: Barcelona Official Visitor Information, in English
- @catalangov: Government of Catalonia information, in English
- The following Twitter accounts have been known to tweet in English in emergency situations:
- @bcn_ajuntament: Barcelona City Council
- @mossos: Mossos d'Esquadra (Police Force of Catalonia)
- @bomberscat: Bombers (Official Firefighters)
- @112: Emergency telephone number of Catalonia

CRIME AND THEFT

Catalonia is a safe place to travel, though Barcelona is known for its petty theft, mostly in the form of pickpocketing in crowded public places. Hotspots for this include La Rambla, El Raval, and public transport, but incidents rarely involve violence. As in every big city, visitors should be vigilant. Keep bags closed, wear them across the body, and keep hold of them in public spaces or restaurant terraces. Refrain from carrying large amounts of money or anything very valuable, and keep wallets and valuables in inner pockets, especially in tightly populated spaces such as busy streets, public transport, bars, and clubs. Try to blend in with the locals and, if you are lost, ask for help or pause to look at your map, so that your attention is not distracted. If somebody purposely tries to distract you with an obscure question, keep your guard up. Thefts can be reported to any Mossos d'Esquadra police station, or a report can be submitted online at www.gencat.cat (security section/internet police reports).

HOSPITALS

The quality of Spain's medical system is universally recognized. Always carry your passport or photo identification card, as you will need it if you require medical attention. The local health authority in Catalonia is called CatSalut (www.gencat.cat/catsalut).

There are also primary health-care centers in most neighborhoods of Barcelona (Centre d'Atenció Primària, or CAP). Larger CAPs provide emergency services, and may be the only option in small towns.

PHARMACIES

Pharmacies are numerous and are indicated by an illuminated green or red cross. Across Spain, nearly all medicines have to be purchased in a pharmacy; supermarkets do not sell any medications (not even acetaminophen, ibuprofen, aspirin, etc.). Pharmacists are generally helpful and friendly, and people often visit a pharmacy in lieu of the doctor, as pharmacists are authorized to sell many pharmaceuticals over the counter that would require a doctor's prescription in other countries. Sunscreen can be purchased in pharmacies or medium-large supermarkets.

Pharmacy opening hours are generally 9am-9pm, Monday to Saturday, closing for siesta sometime between 1:30pm and 5pm. There are also several pharmacies that operate 24 hours in Barcelona, while in smaller towns and cities across Catalonia, there is always a duty pharmacy on call after hours (*Farmacia de Guardia*). Check the local newspaper, pharmacy door, or web for the notice.

MEDICAL REQUIREMENTS

Unless you're traveling from an area known to be suffering from an epidemic (particularly cholera or yellow fever), inoculations or vaccinations are not required for entry into Spain.

HEALTH INSURANCE

If traveling on a European passport, be sure to acquire a European Health Insurance Card (EHIC) in your home country. This is free to obtain and entitles you to free or reduced-cost healthcare across Europe. UK residents can apply through the NHS, and other Europeans can find out how to apply through the European Commission's website. If you are not eligible for a European Health Insurance Card, purchase adequate health insurance before departure. Travelers from the US and other non-EU countries are advised to always travel with insurance. Anyone will be treated in case of an emergency.

DRINKING WATER AND AIR QUALITY

Water is safe to drink in Barcelona and across Catalonia, although most people prefer either bottled or filtered water for better taste. Bottled water is sold at all supermarkets and corner stores, many of which are open 24 hours. If opting for bottled water, a slightly more environmentally friendly choice is to buy a large bottle of mineral water (5-8 liters) to drink in your accommodation, and use a refillable bottle when out and about.

The air quality is good across Catalonia, although there are moderate levels of nitrogen dioxide in the Barcelona area, particularly during times of intense vehicular traffic. There are a number of initiatives underway in Barcelona to reduce vehicle use, including a very successful bike share system (for residents only), the creation of pedestrian zones in the Eixample neighborhood, and the prohibition of vehicles over 20 years old.

HEAT AND SUN

Temperatures can be extreme in summer. August is the hottest month, with temperatures typically ranging from 17-32°C (63-90°F) and humidity averaging 67-72 percent. The heat island effect can be particularly exhausting in Barcelona, day and night, but coastal and mountainous areas generally offer some relief from the heat in the evenings. Wear sunscreen (SPF 30+), especially in the summer and during the higher radiation hours between noon and 4pm, and drink plenty of water.

BEACH SAFETY

At the beach, try to bathe in areas that are supervised by lifeguards and take note of the **warning flags** used to indicate water safety.

- **Green:** Indicates that it is safe to swim.

- **Yellow:** Advises beachgoers to swim with caution, which may be due to large waves, rip currents, jellyfish or other harmful organisms, spills of foreign substances, or weather conditions that make surveillance difficult.

- **Red:** Indicates that no swimming is permitted due to dangerous conditions of the sea, including roughness, dangerous sea life, or pollution.

Jellyfish and **sea urchins** are not too dangerous or numerous, but can give a nasty sting. For jellyfish stings, wash with seawater.

Travel Tips

WHAT TO PACK

A **passport pouch or holder** that can be tucked under clothes. (You should carry some form of photo identification at all times, and it is important to have a safe place to keep your travel insurance and ID on your person.)

Lightweight scarf or shawl, which serves several purposes: It can cover exposed shoulders when entering a religious site, give protection from the midday sun, or keep off the sea breeze as evening draws in.

Comfortable shoes for navigating the sometimes-uneven cobblestone streets in Catalonia, and **hiking shoes** if you plan to hike.

Water bottle—especially a water bottle with a built-in filter to clear some of the mineral and chlorine flavor. (Tap water is safe to drink, and water fountains are numerous in city parks and plazas.) This reduces the consumption of plastic bottles, which is a small but important way to practice responsible tourism.

Power adapter for the European plug type, with two round pins; Spain operates on a 230V supply voltage and 50Hz. Although a simple plug adapter will be enough for many electronics, some will need one with a voltage converter, such as hair dryers that do not have dual voltage built-in. Many adapters also offer fuse or surge protection for extra safety.

Hats, sunglasses, and sunscreen if traveling in summer.

Recommended clothing varies by season. A general rule of thumb is to pack clothes that are easy to layer, particularly if traveling to different parts of the region. In the Pyrenees, for example, temperatures in summer vary significantly from day to night, so you will need to pack a light sweater and jacket for the evening.

WEATHER

Winter in Catalonia is December-February, with temperatures of approximately 7-15°C (44-59°F). Spring is March-May, with temperatures of 9-23°C (48-73°F). Summer is June-August, with temperatures of 18-30°C (64-86°F). Fall is

September-November, with temperatures of 11-27°C (52-81°F). July and August are the hottest and most humid months, and residents of Barcelona traditionally take summer vacations away from the city in August. There is more chance of rain in the spring and fall months.

LANGUAGE

Spanish and Catalan are both official languages of Catalonia. Despite this bilingual status, Catalan is the preferred language of the people in many areas, particularly in rural Catalonia. Signs and informational text at cultural sites, governmental offices, and official notices are usually bilingual. Street names and transit stations are written in Catalan, which has the potential for confusing those whose phones and computers auto-translate place names into Spanish.

Closely related to Spanish and other neighboring languages, Catalan is a romance language dating from the Middle Ages, of which the population is very proud. The extent to which Catalan is enforced (paperwork, schooling, public administration, signage) is, no doubt, a response to the historical oppression of the Catalan language and culture at the hands of General Francisco Franco and many who came before him. The regional government—the Generalitat de Catalunya—dedicates part of its annual budget to the promotion of Catalan. Language is deeply entrenched in Spain's cultural and political history and, to this day, is the topic of many an acrimonious debate between opposing parties and ideologies.

In Barcelona, however, you are just as likely to hear Spanish on the street as Catalan, partly because of the cosmopolitan makeup of the city's inhabitants (16.6 percent foreign-born), and partly because many locals are first- or second-generation Spanish, as a result of huge migration from other parts of Spain during the postwar period.

English is spoken by most people connected to the tourism industry across the region, although more English is spoken in Barcelona than elsewhere. Many locals also have a basic knowledge, particularly the younger generation. Speaking a few words of Spanish is definitely advantageous, and a little Catalan will go a long way with the locals. *¡Suerte!* or *Bona sort!* (Good luck!)

DISCOUNTS AND SIGHTSEEING PASSES

Discounted entry to sights usually applies to:
- Seniors (65+; the senior price is often extended to people with disabilities as well)
- Students (with a valid student card)
- Youth (usually indicating either under 25 or under 16)
- Children (usually 4-12 years old)

The best official sightseeing passes are the Hop On Hop Off bus (hoponhopoffbarcelona.org), which offers full access to the official tour bus of Barcelona, and the Barcelona Card (barcelonacard.org), which offers access to public transport, airport train, major museums, and discounts around the city. Both can be purchased at tourist offices in Barcelona or online. Multi-day passes (2-, 3-, 4-, or 5-day) on Barcelona's public transport system are available and can be purchased in metro stations. Depending on how much you plan to use the public transport system, it may work out better value to buy a T-10 (10-journey) travel card.

WHAT FLOOR AM I ON?

Floor numbers in Spain can be curious to visitors. The ground floor is usually designated as 0, B (*baja*), or PB (*planta baja*), and the first floor is above ground level. In many buildings, particularly those that date from the first half of the 20th century and earlier, the first floor can actually be located two or three stories up from ground level, as there is also a mezzanine level, designated by E (for *entresuelo*, meaning in-between floor), followed by another level known as *principal* (designated P). The latter was where the original patrons of the building normally lived, and tends to be more elaborate than the upper floors. Summarizing, the order is as follows (from bottom to top): ground floor (B or PB), *entresuelo* (E), *principal* (P), then 1st, 2nd, and so on (*primero, segundo, tercero, quarto, quinto . . .* or 1, 2, 3, 4, 5). The penthouse, or top floor, is often called *Ático*.

BOOKING A HOTEL

Catalonia has accommodation options for all tastes and budgets, from luxury beachfront hotels, renovated mansions, and backpacker hostels to eco-tourism, bed-and-breakfasts, and private apartment rentals.

When booking a room or apartment, you may notice the terms "interior" and "exterior" windows. Interior windows normally open into a lightwell or stairwell and have restricted daylight and ventilation, while exterior windows face the street or the inner courtyard of a city block (*patio de manzana*).

Addresses normally follow the following format: (Street Name), 123, 4º 1ª. The first number is the building number, the second is the floor number, and the third is the apartment number on that floor.

TRAVELERS WITH DISABILITIES

Catalonia is full of old, uneven cobbled streets, making smaller streets difficult or inaccessible to wheelchair users or those with reduced mobility. This is an issue mostly in the historic quarters of Barcelona, Girona, and medieval villages and towns. Main streets are generally more accessible, with ramps to the sidewalks.

The bus network in Barcelona is accessible to those with reduced mobility, with low-floor easy access, ramps, and reserved spaces. Buses have sound as well as visual warning systems outside the vehicles for the blind and visually impaired as well as Braille for bus identification. There are visual information screens for most bus and metro stations, as well as onboard most buses and trains. A Braille bus guide with removable pages is available on request (93/413-2775). The metro and many buses feature an audio passenger-information system that announces the stops. Nearly the entire Barcelona metro network is accessible for wheelchairs. The stations that are not adapted are identified on the metro map (15 out of a total of 159 stations). Taxis and transport for persons with reduced mobility include Taxi Amic (93/420-8088) and Cosmo Scooter (93/321-1124).

Mapp4all is a mobile application designed for travelers with reduced mobility, hearing, or visual impairment. This accessibility app describes unique buildings, museums, restaurants, banks, and other places according to the type of accessibility required.

TRAVELING WITH CHILDREN

Spain is very family friendly and there is a relaxed and tolerant attitude toward children. Restaurants and tapas bars extend a warm welcome to families with children at any time of the day, and you can generally relax and let children be children without feeling uncomfortable. Special menus are rare, but there are usually some child-friendly options. The Spanish timetable, however, can be challenging for children accustomed to earlier mealtimes, especially dinner time. Changing facilities and high chairs are not always available; it is advisable to bring a portable chair and changing mat if you require these facilities. There are often discounts for children on transport as well as sightseeing and cultural activities.

LGBTQ+ TRAVELERS

Spain is recognized as one of the most culturally liberal countries in the world, with one of the highest degrees of liberty for its LGBTQ+ citizens. Same-sex marriage, adoption rights, and the ability to donate blood became legal in 2005. Since 1995, employment discrimination based on sexual orientation has been banned nationwide, and sex reassignment surgery is not required in order to change one's legal gender. Public opinion on homosexuality polls overwhelmingly positively in Catalonia. Barcelona, with a thriving gay neighborhood known as "Gaixample," and Sitges, with its yearly gay-led Carnival and International Bears Week, are particularly welcoming. Pride festivals are lively celebrations in both cities.

FEMALE AND SOLO TRAVELERS

Catalonia is generally a safe place to travel. In Barcelona, the streets are lively until late, so walking is usually safe and comfortable. Nevertheless, it is sensible to stick to main roads, and avoid walking along the narrow streets of El Raval, which can be dark and a little intimidating late at night. Barcelona has a night bus service (*Nit Bus*; www.ambmobilitat.cat), which serves most of the city and runs from approximately 10:40-11:40pm until 5-6am, although buses are infrequent and it is best to look up the times in advance to avoid waiting.

Money and Communications

MONEY

CURRENCY

Spain joined the euro in 2002. Bills come in denominations of 5, 10, 20, 50, 100, as well as 200 and 500, although the latter two are rare and are not commonly accepted by most businesses. One euro is made up of 100 cents, and coins are available in denominations of 1, 2, 5, 10, 20, and 50 cents, as well as 1- and 2-euro coins.

CURRENCY EXCHANGE

Check www.xe.com for current exchange rates. The 2019 rate is 1 EUR = 1.13 USD and 1 EUR = 0.86 GBP. Currency can be exchanged at airports, banks, or moneychangers in tourist areas. Be sure to ask for the final exchange rate before making the transaction, as rates may differ depending on the amount of money you are exchanging. Beware of displayed exchange rates that only apply to large amounts.

ATMS AND BANKS

ATMs are located throughout the city. Most are on the exterior of buildings and are available 24 hours. The maximum amount that can be withdrawn per day is usually between €300 and €600, depending on the ATM and/or your bank. Banks are generally open on weekdays from 8:15am until 2pm and are closed on the weekend.

DEBIT AND CREDIT CARDS

Credit and debit cards are readily accepted across Spain in shops, restaurants, bars, taxis, and tourist sights. Smaller establishments may require a minimum spend (usually €5) and some don't accept cards at all. American Express and Diners Club cards are not accepted everywhere. Travelers' checks are not widely accepted and, although many banks will exchange them, the exchange rate and fees will give you a poor return. Remember to inform your bank and credit card companies of your travel plans before attempting to use your cards in Spain.

SALES TAX

For non-EU visitors, there are several ways to reclaim VAT (known as IVA in Spain, which is 21%) from your purchases in Spain. You can start the process in-store at many shops in Barcelona by asking for your tax-free check at the point of purchase. With that check, you can claim your VAT refund at a tourist information center or at Customs in Barcelona-El Prat airport.

COMMUNICATIONS

PHONE CALLS

The country code for Spain is +34. To call the United States or Canada from Spain, dial 001-area code-land phone number or 001-ten digit mobile number. To call the UK from Spain, dial 0044, followed by the UK number without its leading zero. For Ireland, dial 00353, followed by the landline or mobile number. Cellular phone numbers in Spain begin with a 6 or 7 followed by 8 numbers.

CELL PHONES

As a member state of the EU, there are no roaming charges incurred if you are traveling with a phone from another EU member state. Note that Andorra is not in the EU and roaming charges apply there. If you are traveling from outside of the EU, it's likely that you will be charged to use your phone in Spain, unless you have purchased a roaming package before traveling.

If your phone is unlocked and you do not have a roaming plan from your home country, it is very simple to purchase and set up a Spanish SIM card. The main network providers are Movistar, Vodafone, Orange, and Yoigo, and there are other smaller operators such as MásMóvil. You can set up your phone directly with these providers in-store, or visit cellular stores, such as the Phone House, that offer SIM cards from all major operators.

WIFI

Many cities and towns have public WiFi, but it is usually a little unreliable. Networks offered through cafés and restaurants are more reliable.

WEIGHTS AND MEASURES

Spain uses the metric system (1 inch = 2.54 centimeters; 1 pound = 454 grams; 1 mile = 1.6 kilometers). Celsius is used to measure temperature (21°C = room temperature). Spain is on Central European Time (with the exception of the Canary Islands); most written reference to time uses the 24-hour clock. Spanish uses commas where English uses decimal points, and vice versa. Note that dates are ordered by day, month, and year.

Resources

APPS

BARCELONA

- **TMB:** Information about the Barcelona metro and other public transportation.
- **Visit Barcelona:** Interactive tourist information.
- **Barcelona Restaurants:** Barcelona's official restaurant guide, published by *Turisme de Barcelona.*
- **Gaudí's Barcelona:** Official audio guide to the city's Gaudí sites.
- **BCN Visual:** An interactive map that shows how streets and buildings looked in the past.
- **Medieval Barcelona:** Official audio guide to the city's Romanesque and Gothic architecture.
- **Barcelona Metro Walks:** Audio guide that curates routes, combining transit and walking through the city and beyond its edges, to discover neighborhoods at your own pace.

BEYOND BARCELONA

- **GaleriesArt:** Information about the galleries that are part of the Association of Art Galleries of Catalonia.
- **Mapp4all:** Designed for people with reduced mobility, or those with hearing or visual impairment, this accessibility app describes unique buildings, museums, restaurants, banks, and other places.
- **iBeach:** Current information about temperature, waves, jellyfish, wind, and other weather indicators on various beaches across Spain.
- **Visitmuseum:** Information about the museums of Catalonia in four languages: Catalan, Spanish, English, and French.
- **Imageen:** An augmented reality app that brings Roman Tarraco back to life.
- **Tarragona Accessible:** Four themed routes around points of interest in the city. Specifically aimed at people with sight or hearing impairments, though useful for all.

WEBSITES

BARCELONA

- **barcelonaturisme.com:** Barcelona tourist guide.

BEYOND BARCELONA

- **gencat.cat:** Information, procedures, and services of the Government of Catalonia.
- **spain.info:** Spain's official tourism portal.
- **girona.cat:** Girona tourist guide.
- **tarragonaturisme.cat:** Tarragona tourist guide.

- **visitsitges.com:** Sitges tourist guide.
- **en.turismegarrotxa.com:** La Garrotxa tourist guide.
- **en.costabrava.org:** Costa Brava tourist guide.
- **vallboi.cat:** Vall de Boí tourist guide.

Phrasebook

Spanish and Catalan are both widely spoken in Catalonia. Both are Romance languages, derived from Latin, and there are many similarities between them, although Spanish is considered easier to learn. The phonetics of Spanish and Catalan differ, but much of the grammatical structure is shared. Catalan also has some similarities to Portuguese and French. In both languages, nouns are either masculine or feminine, and articles and adjectives must agree with the nouns they accompany. English speakers will recognize some vocabulary in Spanish and Catalan, as many words come from the same linguistic roots. Spanish has also borrowed many English words over the years, and vice versa.

PRONUNCIATION

Spanish is a phonetic language, meaning that letters are pronounced consistently, according to a few simple rules. Some syllables are stressed more than others. When a word ends in "n," "s," or a vowel, the stress falls on the penultimate syllable. Otherwise, the final syllable is stressed. If there is an acute accent (á) over a vowel, then that syllable should be stressed, cancelling out the standard rules. Those who are familiar with Latin American Spanish will probably notice that Spanish spoken in Spain sounds quite different. It may seem faster, and will have different pronunciation and some grammatical differences.

Catalan is not phonetic. Like English, Catalan spelling can be daunting, although English speakers have no trouble pronouncing consonant clusters. Catalan also uses linkage in a similar way to English, where two words merge smoothly together, sometimes creating a different sound, such as with *fins aviat* (see you soon), which creates a "z" sound between the words.

CONSONANTS

Both Spanish and Catalan have a silent double-L (**ll**), although the "ll" sound in Catalan is different from Spanish (more similar to Portuguese). However, the difference is difficult for the non-native ear to detect.

In Spanish, j is a harsh, guttural sound similar to a breathy "huh" in English. In Catalan, on the other hand, "j" sounds like the "s" in "pleasure." This is one of the easiest ways to tell the two languages apart, as the latter sound does not exist in Spanish.

The letter g is usually similar to an English "g" in both languages, except before an "e" or "i" in Spanish, when it sounds more like a Spanish "j."

In Spanish, the letter c is pronounced "th" when it comes before an "e" or "i" (e.g. "Barcelona"). In other cases it is hard (like "c" in cat). This lisp sound does not exist in Catalan.

SUGGESTED READING AND FILMS

SUGGESTED READING

- *Homage to Catalonia* by George Orwell, 1938. An account of Orwell's experiences of serving in the Spanish Civil War from 1936 to 1937 as a private for the POUM, the Workers' Party of Marxist Unification. A similar story is told by the Ken Loach film *Land and Freedom* (1995).

- *La Plaça del Diamant (The Time of the Doves/In Diamond Square)* by Mercé Rodoreda, 1962. Probably the most famous novel written in Catalan, it spans 25 years of Catalan life during and after the Spanish Civil War.

- *The South* by Colm Tóibín, 1990. A young Irish woman flees her home to start a new life in Barcelona.

- *Barcelona* by Robert Hughes, 1993. An informed and opinionated guide to Barcelona's history.

- *La sombra del viento (The Shadow of the Wind)* by Carlos Ruiz Zafón, 2001. This international bestseller is the first written in *The Cemetery of Forgotten Books* series. It follows the story of a young boy as he descends into the dark and secretive world of a writer in post-Civil War Barcelona.

- *Catedral del mar (Cathedral of the Sea)* by Ildefonso Falcones, 2006. An adventure novel about a man who moves to Barcelona in the 14th century, at the height of the Inquisition. The story has been adapted into a Spanish Netflix series.

SUGGESTED FILMS

- *Todo Sobre Mi Madre (All About My Mother),* d: Pedro Almodóvar, 1999. In this beautiful story of women, we view the world of theater and art in Barcelona, as Manuela (Cecilia Roth) reunites with an old friend, the transsexual prostitute Agrado (Antonia San Juan), while helping a naïve young nun (Penélope Cruz).

- *L'Auberge Espagnole (The Spanish Apartment),* d: Cédric Klapisch, 2002. This film follows a Parisian student on his year abroad in Barcelona, where he shares an apartment with six other international students.

- *En la Ciudad (In the City),* d: Cesc Gay, 2003. A glimpse into the interiors and secret lives of three middle-class thirtysomething couples in modern Barcelona.

- *El Taxista Ful (The Taxi Thief),* d: Jo Sol, 2005. A middle-aged cabdriver steals cars to drive as taxis around Barcelona.

- *Vicky Cristina Barcelona,* d: Woody Allen, 2008. The story of the relationships forged between two American tourists (Scarlett Johansson and Rebecca Hall) and two parted lovers in Barcelona (Javier Bardem and Penélope Cruz). Though this film may not be the Barcelona that most locals will recognize, it displays many of the city's important landmarks.

- *Biutiful,* d: Alejandro González Iñárritu, 2010. Uxbal (Javier Bardem) is a career criminal working in Barcelona's back alleys and underground sweatshops. Upon learning that he has only a few months to live, he attempts to get his affairs in order and do some good.

- *A Gun in Each Hand,* d: Cesc Gay, 2012. A tragicomedy following the lives of eight middle-aged men in Barcelona.

The letter h is silent in both languages.

In both languages, q is hard, like "k" in English.

Few words in Spanish include the letter x, but it is commonly used in Catalan and represents the "ch" sound.

Spanish has no z sound ("z" is pronounced "th" in Spanish). Catalan does have a "z" sound, pronounced like "z" in "zone."

Spanish usually has a vowel sound between consonants, while Catalan has many consonant clusters such as "ts," "ks," "gts," and "ls."

In both languages, v sounds more like "b," and the two sounds are easily confused.

Double "r" (rr) is rolled in both languages.

VOWELS

Spanish vowels are short and are always pronounced in the same way:

a (ah)	like "a" in cat
e (eh)	like "e" in bed
i (ee)	like "ee" in see
o (oh)	like "o" in pot
u (oo)	like "oo" in boot

Catalan, on the other hand, has up to eight different vowel sounds. Acute accents in Spanish indicate that the vowel is stressed, but in Catalan it also alters the vowel sounds: the grave accent (è and ò) implies an open sound, while the acute accent (é and ó) implies a closed sound.

ORTHOGRAPHY

Spanish has one more letter than the English alphabet: the ñ (the name of the letter is pronounced *eñe*, "en-yay"). This does not exist in Catalan, but almost the same sound is achieved with "ny."

While Spanish only employs the acute accent on vowels (á, é, í, ó, ú, ý),

Catalan uses the acute (é, ó, í, ú) and the grave (à, è, ò) accents.

Both languages use the dieresis (ï, ü), usually indicating the sound of an extra syllable, such as in the use of "ï" in "naïve" in English.

Catalan uses ç (*ce trencada*) to indicate a soft "c" (as in "cell") in front of an "a," "u," or "o," or as the last letter of a word to be voiced like a "z."

Catalan uses a *punt volat* or *middot* between a double "ll" (l·l, for example *Paral·lel*) to indicate a longer "l" sound than if there were only one (or if there were two, in which case it would be silent).

ESSENTIAL PHRASES

Phrases below are in Spanish, followed by Catalan.

Hello Hola/Hola

Good morning Buenos días/Bon dia

Good afternoon Buenas tardes/Bona tarda

Good evening Buenas tardes/Bon vespre

Good night Buenas noches/Bona nit

Goodbye Adiós/Adéu

Pleased to meet you Encantado/a/ Encantat

How are you? ¿Cómo estás?/Com estàs?

What's your name? ¿Cuál es tu nombre?/Com et dius?

My name is . . . Me llamo . . ./Em dic . . .

Where are you from? ¿De donde eres?/D'on ets?

I'm from . . . Soy de . . ./Sóc de . . .

Thank you Gracias/Gràcies

You're welcome De nada/De res

Please Por favor/ Si us plau

Do you speak English? ¿Hablas inglés?/Parles anglès?

I don't understand No entiendo/No ho entenc

Have a nice day ¡Que tengas un buen día!/Que tinguis un bon dia

Where is the restroom? ¿Dónde están los servicios?/On estan els serveis?

Yes Sí/Sí

No No/No

Maybe Quizás/Potser

TRANSPORTATION

Where is ... ? Dónde está ... ?/On es ... ?

How far is ... ? ¿A qué distancia está ... ? /Quina distància hi ha ... ?

Is there a bus to ... ? ¿Hay algún autobús para ... ?/Hi ha cap autobús per ... ?

Does this bus go to ... ? ¿Este autobús va a ... ?/Aquest autobús surt a ... ?

Where do I get off? ¿Dónde me bajo?/On he de baixar?

What time does the bus/train leave/ arrive? ¿A qué hora sale/ llega el autobús/tren?/A quina hora surt/arriba l'autobús/tren?

Where is the nearest subway station? ¿Dónde está la estación de metro más cercana?/On és l'estació de metro més propera?

Where can I buy a ticket? ¿Dónde puedo comprar un billete?/On puc comprar un bitllet?

A round-trip ticket/a single ticket to ... Un billete de ida y vuelta/ un billete sencillo para ... /Un bitllet d'anada i tornada/ un bitllet únic per ...

FOOD

A table for two/three/four Una mesa para dos/tres/cuatro/Una taula per a dos/tres/quatre

Do you have a menu in English? ¿Tiene un menú en Inglés?/ Té un menú en anglès?

What is the dish of the day? ¿Cuál es el plato del día?/Quin és el plat del dia?

We're ready to order. Estamos listos para pedir/Estem preparats per demanar.

I'm a vegetarian Soy vegetariano/Sóc vegetarià

May I have ... Podría pedir .../Puc demanar ...

The check please? ¿La cuenta por favor?/El compte, si us plau?

beer cerveza/cervesa

bread un pan/pa

breakfast desayuno/esmorzar

cash efectivo/efectiu

check comprobar/comprovar

coffee café/cafè

dinner cena/sopar

glass vaso/got

hors d'oeuvre entremeses/entremès

ice hielo/gel

ice cream helado/gelat

lunch comida/dinar

restaurant restaurante/restaurant

sandwich(es) bocadillo/entrepà

snack merienda/berenar

waiter camarero/cambrer

water agua/aigua

wine vino/vi

What is the local specialty? ¿Cuál es la especialidad local?/Quina és l'especialitat local?

Bon appetit Buen provecho/Bon profit!

Cheers! ¡Salud!/Salut!

SHOPPING

money dinero/diners

shop tienda/botiga

What time do the shops close? ¿A qué hora cierran las tiendas?/A quina hora tanquen les botigues?

How much is this? ¿Cuánto cuesta esto?/Quant costa això?

I'm just looking Solo estoy mirando/ Només estic mirant

HEALTH

drugstore farmacia/farmàcia

pain dolor/dolor

fever fiebre/febre

headache dolor de cabeza/mal de cap

stomachache dolor de estómago/mal de panxa

toothache dolor de muelas/mal de queixal

burn quemar/cremar

cramp calambre/rampa

nausea náusea/nàusees

vomiting vomitar/vòmits

medicine medicina/medicina

antibiotic antibiótico/antibiòtic

pill/tablet pastilla/píndola

aspirin aspirina/aspirina

I need to see a doctor Necesito ver un doctor/Necessito veure un doctor

I need to go to the hospital Necesito ir al hospital/He d'anar a l'hospital

I have a pain here ...
Me duele aquí .../Em fa mal aquí ...

She/he has been stung/bitten Le han picado/ mordido/Li han picat/ mossegat

I am diabetic/pregnant Soy diabético/Estoy embarazada/Sóc diabètic/Estic embarassada

I am allergic to penicillin/ cortisone Soy alérgico a la penicilina/ cortisona/Sóc al·lèrgic a la penicil·lina/ cortisona

My blood group is ... positive/ negative Mi grupo sanguíneo es ... positivo/negativo/El meu grup sanguini és ... positiu/negatiu

NUMBERS

0 cero/zero
1 uno/u/un (m) una (f)
2 dos/dos (m)/dues (f)
3 tres/tres
4 cuatro/quatre
5 cinco/cinc
6 seis/sis
7 siete/set
8 ocho/vuit
9 nueve/nou
10 diez/deu
11 once/onze
12 doce/dotze

13 trece/tretze
14 catorce/catorze
15 quince/quinze
16 dieciséis/setze
17 diecisiete/disset
18 dieciocho/divuit
19 diecinueve/dinou
20 veinte/vint
30 treinta/trenta
40 cuarenta/quaranta
50 cincuenta/cinquanta
60 sesenta/seixanta
70 setenta/setanta
80 ochenta/vuitanta
90 noventa/noranta
100 cien/cent
101 ciento uno/cent un
200 doscientos/dos-cents
500 quinientos/cinc-cents
1,000 mil/mil
10,000 diez mil/deu mil
100,000 cien mil/cent mil
1,000,000 un millón/un milió

TIME

What time is it? ¿Qué hora es?/Quina hora es?

It's one/three o'clock Son las tres en punto/Són les tres en punt

midday mediodía/migdia

midnight medianoche/mitjanit

morning Mañana/matí

afternoon tarde/tarda

evening noche/vespre

night noche/nit

yesterday ayer/ahir

today hoy/avui

tomorrow mañana/demà

DAYS AND MONTHS

week semana/setmana

month mes/mes

Monday lunes/Dilluns

Tuesday martes/Dimarts

Wednesday miércoles/Dimecres

Thursday jueves/Dijous

Friday viernes/Divendres

Saturday sábado/Dissabte
Sunday domingo/Diumenge
January enero/Gener
February febrero/Febrer
March marzo/Març
April abril/Abril
May Mayo/Maig
June junio/Juny
July julio/Juliol
August agosto/Agost
September septiembre/Setembre
October octubre/Octubre
November noviembre/Novembre
December diciembre/Desembre

VERBS

to have tener/tenir
to be ser/ser
to go ir/anar
to come venir/venir
to want querer/voler
to eat comer/menjar
to drink beber/beure
to buy comprar/comprar
to need necesitar/necessitar
to read leer/llegir
to write escribir/escriure
to stop parar/detener/parar
to get off bajarse/baixar-se
to arrive llegar/arribar
to return regresar/tornar
to stay quedarse/per quedar-se
to leave dejar/deixar
to look at mirar/mirar
to look for buscar/buscar
to give dar/donar
to take tomar/agafar

Index

List of Maps

Photo Credits

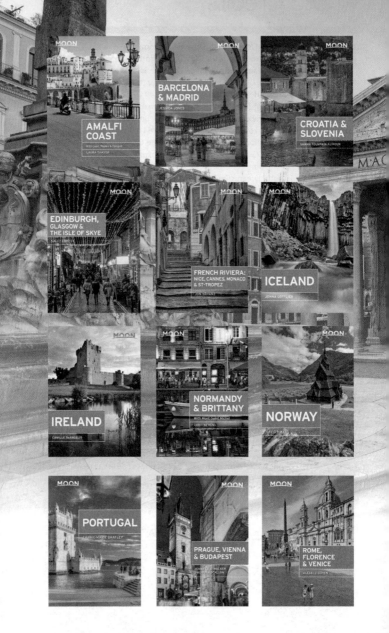

GO BIG AND GO BEYOND!

OR TAKE THINGS ONE STEP AT A TIME

MOON ROAD TRIP GUIDES

PACIFIC COAST HIGHWAY
Road Trip

CALIFORNIA,
OREGON & WASHINGTON

IAN ANDERSON

Drive & Hike
APPALACHIAN TRAIL

THE BEST TRAIL TOWNS, DAY HIKES,
AND ROAD TRIPS IN BETWEEN

TIMOTHY MALCOLM

BLUE RIDGE PARKWAY
Road Trip

INCLUDING SHENANDOAH & GREAT SMOKY
MOUNTAINS NATIONAL PARKS

JASON FRYE

CALIFORNIA
Road Trip

SAN FRANCISCO, YOSEMITE, LAS VEGAS,
GRAND CANYON, LOS ANGELES,
& THE PACIFIC COAST HIGHWAY

STUART THORNTON

NASHVILLE TO NEW ORLEANS
Road Trip

NATCHEZ TRACE PARKWAY · MEMPHIS ·
TUPELO · MISSISSIPPI BLUES TRAIL

MARGARET LITTMAN

NEW ENGLAND
Road Trip

BOSTON, ACADIA NATIONAL PARK, WHITE
MOUNTAINS, BERKSHIRES, NEWPORT, AND CAPE COD

JEN ROSE SMITH

NORTHERN CALIFORNIA
Road Trip

DRIVES ALONG THE COAST, REDWOODS, AND MOUNTAINS
WITH THE BEST STOPS ALONG THE WAY

STUART THORNTON & KAYLA ANDERSON

Advice on where to
sleep, eat, and explore

Detailed driving
directions including
mileage and
drive times

Itineraries for a
range of timelines

MOON
PACIFIC NORTHWEST
Road Trip

SEATTLE, VANCOUVER, VICTORIA,
THE OLYMPIC PENINSULA, PORTLAND,
THE OREGON COAST & MOUNT RAINIER

ALLISON WILLIAMS

MOON
ROUTE 66
Road Trip

JESSICA DUNHAM

MOON
SOUTH FLORIDA & THE KEYS
Road Trip

WITH MIAMI, WALT DISNEY WORLD, TAMPA &
THE EVERGLADES

JASON FERGUSON

MOON
SOUTHWEST
Road Trip

LAS VEGAS, ZION & BRYCE, MONUMENT VALLEY,
SANTA FE & TAOS, AND THE GRAND CANYON

TIM HULL

MOON
VANCOUVER & CANADIAN ROCKIES
Road Trip

VICTORIA, BANFF, JASPER, CALGARY,
THE OKANAGAN, WHISTLER &
THE SEA-TO-SKY HIGHWAY

CAROLYN B. HELLER

MOON
YELLOWSTONE TO GLACIER NATIONAL PARK
Road Trip

JACKSON HOLE, CODY, THE GRAND TETONS
& THE ROCKY MOUNTAIN FRONT

CARTER G. WALKER

Gear up for a bucket list vacation

MAP SYMBOLS

■	Sights	◉	National Capital	▲	Mountain	═══	Major Hwy
■	Restaurants	◉	State Capital	✚	Natural Feature	───	Road/Hwy
■	Nightlife	○	City/Town	⚑	Waterfall	───	Pedestrian Friendly
■	Arts and Culture	★	Point of Interest	⚑	Park	------	Trail
■	Sports and Activities	•	Accommodation	▲	Archaeological Site	⌷⌷⌷⌷	Stairs
■	Shops	▼	Restaurant/Bar	❶	Trailhead	·········	Ferry
■	Hotels	■	Other Location	❷	Parking Area	~~~~~	Railroad

CONVERSION TABLES

$$°C = (°F - 32) / 1.8$$
$$°F = (°C \times 1.8) + 32$$

1 inch = 2.54 centimeters (cm)
1 foot = 0.304 meters (m)
1 yard = 0.914 meters
1 mile = 1.6093 kilometers (km)
1 km = 0.6214 miles
1 fathom = 1.8288 m
1 chain = 20.1168 m
1 furlong = 201.168 m
1 acre = 0.4047 hectares
1 sq km = 100 hectares
1 sq mile = 2.59 square km
1 ounce = 28.35 grams
1 pound = 0.4536 kilograms
1 short ton = 0.90718 metric ton
1 short ton = 2,000 pounds
1 long ton = 1.016 metric tons
1 long ton = 2,240 pounds
1 metric ton = 1,000 kilograms
1 quart = 0.94635 liters
1 US gallon = 3.7854 liters
1 Imperial gallon = 4.5459 liters
1 nautical mile = 1.852 km

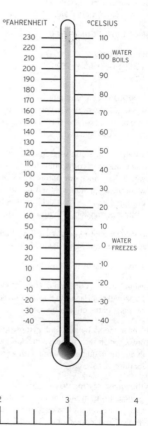

MOON BARCELONA & BEYOND

Avalon Travel
Hachette Book Group
1700 Fourth Street
Berkeley, CA 94710, USA
www.moon.com

Editor: Nikki Ioakimedes
Copy Editor: Chris Dumas
Graphics Coordinator: Scott Kimball
Production Coordinator: Scott Kimball
Cover Design: Faceout Studio, Derek Thornton
Interior Design: Megan Jones Design
Moon Logo: Tim McGrath
Map Editor: Albert Angulo
Cartographer: John Culp
Proofreader: Matthew Hoover
Indexer: Sam Arnold-Boyd

ISBN-13: 978-1-64049-084-0

Printing History
1st Edition — January 2020
5 4 3 2 1

Front cover photo: Lucas Vallecillos / Alamy Stock Photo
Back cover photo: Achim Baqué / Dreamstime.com

Printed in China by RR Donnelley

All recommendations, including those for sights, activities, hotels, restaurants, and shops, are based on each author's individual judgment. We do not accept payment for inclusion in our travel guides, and our authors don't accept free goods or services in exchange for positive coverage.

Although every effort was made to ensure that the information was correct at the time of going to press, the author and publisher do not assume and hereby disclaim any liability to any party for any loss or damage caused by errors, omissions, or any potential travel disruption due to labor or financial difficulty, whether such errors or omissions result from negligence, accident, or any other cause.

The publisher is not responsible for websites (or their content) that are not owned by the publisher.